Christmas 1993
To Daddy With
        Bernadette x

C000215366

Marsigli's Europe

Marsigli's Europe

1680–1730

*The Life and Times of
Luigi Ferdinando Marsigli,
Soldier and Virtuoso*

John Stoye

Yale University Press
New Haven & London 1994

Copyright © 1994 by John Stoye

All rights reserved. This book may not be reproduced in whole or in part, in any form (beyond that copying permitted by Sections 107 and 108 of the U.S. Copyright Law and except by reviewers for the public press), without written permission from the publishers.

Set in Ehrhardt by Best-set Typesetter Ltd., Hong Kong
Printed and bound in Great Britain by St Edmundsbury Press

The right of John Stoye to be identified, as author of this work has been asserted by him in accordance with the Copyright, Designs and Patents Act, 1988.

Library of Congress Cataloguing-in-Publication Data

Stoye, John, 1917–
    Marsigli's Europe, 1680–1730 : the life and times of Luigi
Ferdinando Marsigli, soldier and virtuoso / John Stoye.
        p.   cm.
    Includes bibliographical references and index.
    ISBN 0–300–05542–0
      1. Marsili, Luigi Ferdinando, 1658–1730.   2. Generals—Europe—
Biography.   3. Scientists—Europe—Biography.   4. Europe—
History—1648–1789.   5. Bologna (Italy)—Intellectual life.
I. Title.
D274.M37S88   1993
940.2'52—dc20   93–24053
                                                                              CIP

A catalogue record for this book is available from the British Library.

Contents

List of Illustrations

Illustrations

Maps

Sources

1: J. Blaeu, *Civitates Status Ecclesiatici*, 1663; 2: F. di Gnudi, *Disegno dell'alma Città di Bologna*, 1702; 3: [G. D. Cassini,] *La meridiana del tempio di S. Petronio*, 1695; 4: MS Marsigli 50, c.33; 5,6: *Osservationi intorno al Bosforo Tracio*, 1681; 7: *Stato militare dell'Imperio Ottomanno*, 1732; 8: J. C. Muller, *Mappa Hungariae*, 1709; 9,10: Kartensammlung, Haus-, Hof- und Staatsarchiv, Vienna; 10: MS Marsigli 50, c.49; 12: *Danubius*, i.tab.16; 13: Haus-, Hof- und Staatsarchiv, Turcica 159; 14: Turcica 160; 15–20: *Danubius*, i.87, vi.29, iii.73, ii.tab.6, iv.tab.7, v.tab. 53; 21: *Danubialis operis Prodromus*, 1700; 22: MS Marsigli 47, c.4; 23: MS Marsigli 60, c.321; 24: Museo Civico Medievale, Bologna; 25: *Elenchus librorum*, 1702; 26: MS Marsigli 145; 27: *Informazione*, 1705; 28: *Histoire physique de la mer*, 1725; 29: Glyptothek, Munich; 30: Gemeentearchief, Amsterdam, Not. Arch. no. 5830; 31: print by L. Basoli, 1824.

Acknowledgements and thanks for permission to reproduce the illustrations are due to the British Library Board (nos. 2, 5, 6, 8); Bodleian Libary (nos. 3 [Montara 1275], 7 [Douce M. Subt. 50], 12 [18876 a. 1–3], 15–20 [18876 a. 1–3], 21 [Savile B. 1], 25 [Caps 5. 16], 26 [Vet. B4.e. 7]); Biblioteca Universitaria, Bologna (nos. 4, 11, 22, 23, 26); Österreichische Staatsarchiv (nos. 9, 10, 13, 14); Deutscher Kunstverlag, Munich (no. 29); Gemeentelijke Archiefdienst, Amsterdam (no. 30).

Preface and Acknowledgements

This is by no means a formal history but an account of someone who lived through the age of Louis XIV. Count Marsigli was a witness to several aspects of the scene in several parts of Europe, and it seemed worthwhile combining a biography with some notice of the intricacies knotting together the course of events in eastern and western Europe, in this way trying to do justice to the amazingly broad span of Marsigli's interests. For he thought of himself as a soldier on the move in Hungary and the Balkans while continuing his study of the sciences, and as a devotee both of Roman antiquities and natural history. In later life he viewed with equal pride his record as a benefactor, spending energy and riches on behalf of Bologna his native city, and his never ceasing activity as geologist and hydrographer. A lot of the story is doubtless missing. A lot more could be discovered in further enquiries. A lot may be found here.

I once wrote a description of the great Turkish siege of Vienna in the year 1683 and Marsigli became known to me as a witness of that event. He set down afterwards the record of his experience while a prisoner in the Otto-man camp, where he was employed digging and brewing coffee for the besiegers. This took me to his autobiography, printed in 1930. When exactly he wrote or dictated it, through whose hands the copy passed, are alike uncertain. It deals mainly with his youth, with his life in the Turkish wars, and his sudden downfall as a Habsburg general by court martial in 1704. I wondered how much of his story could be true, how much could be checked by other documents, and so was led for several enjoyable years to the manuscript collections in Vienna and Bologna. Little by little I turned to other aspects of Marsigli's long life. There were discoveries to make in London, Amsterdam and Zurich; the record of his contacts with Rome, Nuremberg and Montpellier to explore; the interviews with commanding figures to fit into place, with Emperor Leopold I and Popes Innocent XI and Clement XI, with Louis XIV and Sir Isaac Newton and Herman Boerhaave, each of them immensely significant in his own estimate of his career. Gradually the study of a single person embraced a notion of something more broadly based, and a possibly novel conjunction of interests for those who care to study this phase of the European past.

The eminent founder of an Academy of Sciences, Marsigli would perhaps have preferred a committee of experts to compose his biography. A military historian, a historian of science, an authority on the history of south-east Europe, a historian of the European book trade and a chronicler or analyst of Italian social history would all be needed. Nonetheless, for the time being let me use two old-fashioned phrases and invite the gentle reader to begin with my account of his life and times.

Anyone who has ever climbed the stairs of a building for the first time, on the way to look through the ancient records it is said to hold, will know the thrill of untying the bundles or boxes, the smell of dust with the paper, the despair over items illegible or missing, and then the singular pleasure in finding what was hoped for or proves to be unsuspected treasure. This sense of encounter, with letter writers and their correspondents long ago, explains my gratitude to all those who look after the documents I searched through on the trail of Marsigli, or Marsili, or Marsilly – every spelling is possible – and pre-eminently in the Haus-, Hof- and Staatsarchiv and the Kriegsarchiv in Vienna; in the University Library and the Archiginnasio of Bologna; in the library of the Royal Society, the library of the School of Oriental and African Studies, the Public Record Office and the British Library in London; and the Stadtbibliothek of Zurich. In several cases these were also the great libraries preserving the printed books consulted, but I owe as well enormous debts to the Bodleian Library, the Taylorian Library, the Codrington Library of All Souls College, the libraries of Magdalen College and of the Botany Department, all in Oxford; to the London Library, the Nationalbibliothek of Vienna and the Bibliothèque Nationale, where it would likewise have been impossible for me to find my way without innumerable hints from their staff, from chance acquaintances met in such places, and from many old and recent friends and colleagues and pupils. I owe particular thanks to the Leverhulme Trust for giving me an Emeritus Fellowship in order to work on Marsigli, and to the Yale University Press, as also to Mauro Ambrosoli, Sonia Anderson, Leopold Auer, Robert Baldock, Peter Barber, Lajos Bartha, Jeremy Black, Peter Broucek, Bojan Bujic, Lionel Clowes, Robert Evans, László Gróf, Erich Hillbrand, Anita McConnell, Angus Macintyre, Carlo Poni, Dusan Radojicic, Ian Robertson and Oliver Taplin. I dedicate this enquiry to the memory of John Bromley, who not long ago taught and teased so many of us to look both backwards and forwards.

John Stoye,
Magdalen College, Oxford,
December 31st, 1992.

Chronology

	Marsigli	Europe
1658	His birth in Bologna	Leopold I elected Emperor
		War between Venice and the Sultan (1645–69)
1660–1		The Royal Society founded in London
		Louis XIV takes over the government of France
1663–4		War in Hungary between Emperor and Sultan
1672–8	His excursions in Italy	War in western Europe, in Poland and the Ukraine
		Innocent XI elected Pope
		Kara Mustafa the new Grand Vezir in Istanbul
1679	His journey to Istanbul	Peace in western Europe
1681	His first publication: *The Bosphorus*	Peace in the Ukraine, war imminent in Hungary
		Louis XIV occupies Strasbourg and Casale
1682	His journey to Vienna	Halley's comet
1683	His captivity	The siege of Vienna
1684	His liberation, and return to fight in Hungary	The League of Austria, Venice and Poland, the 'Truce' in Germany and the first siege of Buda

1685–6	His second publication: *Coffee*	The second siege and capture of Buda
1688	In Rome and Belgrade	Louis XIV v. Innocent XI
1689–97	Colonel Marsigli, F.R.S. in Hungary and the Balkans	War in western Europe
1697–9	His third publication: *Stones of Bologna*	Peace treaties in western and eastern Europe
1699–1701	General Marsigli as Imperial boundary commissioner	
	His fourth publication: the prospectus for an account of the *Danube*	General war in the west recommences
1701–2	In Vienna, and founds a new scientific 'studio' in Bologna	Clement XI elected Pope
1702	He goes with his regiment to Germany	The siege of Landau
	His command in the fortress of Breisach	
1703	In Breisach; his study of mushrooms	The surrender of Breisach Civil War in Hungary
1704	The court martial: his dismissal, and final visit to Vienna	The battle of Blenheim
1705	In Switzerland	Death of Emperor Leopold
1706–8	In Paris, Montpellier and Provence. His marine researches	The Royal Academy of Sciences founded in Montpellier The French withdraw from Italy
1708–9	Returns to Italy as the Pope's general	War between Emperor Joseph I and Pope Clement

1709	Returns to Bologna: his lively patronage of the arts and sciences	Peace in Italy
1711	Journeys to Provence and Rome	
1712–4	His benefactions to Bologna for the Academy of Arts and the Institute of Sciences	Treaties of peace in western Europe
1716–7	He advises on a defence of the Adriatic against the Turks	War between Venice and the Sultan, and Emperor Charles VI's intervention
1718–9	He buys a printing press	Peace in eastern Europe
1721	He sails from Livorno for England and Holland	Bubonic plague in France Death of Clement XI
1722–3	In London he meets Newton and Halley, in Leyden Boerhaave, and the Dutch accept his works for publication	
1724–6	His residence by Lake Garda The *Danube* and the *Sea* appear in print. His return to Bologna	
1728	Departure for Provence and swift return	
1730	Marsigli's death	

CHAPTER ONE

Bologna and Istanbul

I

The city and university of Bologna perhaps enjoyed greater fame in Europe during the twelfth century than at any other time. Then also the families of Asinelli and Garisenda built those wonderful brick towers, the first so tall and the second so crooked, still standing so close to each other: the emblem of Bologna for all who ever visited the city. Since then its two communities, municipal and academic, have passed through nine hundred years with varying fortune, but like the towers they seem indestructible; and it was midway through this long period that the Popes established an ascendancy, merging the city into the Papal states of central Italy. Legates or vice-legates from Rome took a responsibility for government in Bologna which lasted continuously from 1506 until 1796, and critics have held that the Roman overlordship ushered in a phase of decadence, diminishing the political and intellectual vitality of the place. The theory is a possible one, but certainly could never by itself explain why our hero Count Luigi Ferdinando Marsigli preferred to make his career abroad whenever he could. So unusual, so eccentric a man was almost bound to attempt escape from the narrowly enclosed society into which he had been born. The mould was there in Bologna; the metal escaped.

At the point where a great Roman highway, the Via Emilia, in a long straight line down the eastern edge of the Appenines crossed the rivers Reno and Saverna – in the small area between their perpetually shifting channels – the town had grown out of its Etruscan past. It came to control a sizeable plain which merged into marshes flattening out towards the Po delta, together with some of the hilly country west of the Via Emilia. Its population grew, and twice during the medieval period a new surrounding wall had been built further out from the original centre where the main piazza, municipal offices, and a number of churches clustered on the site of a Roman amphitheatre, which stood formerly on one side of the great road. On the other were the cathedral of S. Pietro, and the bishop's residence. Large open spaces long remained within the latest of the perimeter walls, incidentally allowing the friars of various orders – Dominican, Franciscan,

Servite, Augustinian – and also the Jesuits and Barnabites to settle and develop their own communities. Then expansion stopped. Between 1500 and 1800 the total population of Bologna rose and fell around an average of 60,000. Immediately after the shattering epidemic of 1630 it would fall to 47,000.[1]

As to the mode of government, a great reforming legate of the eighteenth century divided the people of the city and its dependent countryside into '60 or 70 tyrants and 200,000 slaves'.[2] Certainly a small group of ascendant families had taken a firm grip on the assets of the community between 1400 and 1500, and kept them for another three centuries. They held most of the urban and rural property, and controlled a goodly part of the municipal finances. When the Bentivoglio family's bid for dominance was defeated by Pope Julius II in 1506, its principal supporters and clients had little difficulty in coming to terms with the new order, in which government was divided between the two interests, Roman and Bolognese. Neither wanted, thereafter, further changes of any substance. A part of the new order was a body named the Senate, of 40 and later 50 members, but it simply conferred a formal title on the hereditary patriciate already emerging.[3] During the following centuries, when the direct male succession of a family failed, and in failing extinguished a senatorial title, it was for the Pope to transfer this to someone else but in practice the senators themselves co-opted the newcomer. The constitution remained static generation after generation, and in this era neither the barbarians from Asia, nor Germans from the Empire, nor French revolutionaries arrived over the Po to disturb it.[4] Not even the sovereign Popes wished to remodel the government on a more absolute pattern: it was a significant negative feature of Roman rule after the Council of Trent, their failure to extend the greater practical authority they claimed in church government into the temporal administration of the Papal states. There resulted a fusion of interests which to some degree limited Bolognese dominance in governing the city, and to some degree left the Papal legate with less control over affairs than a plenipotentiary would have wished. It was a condition of holy deadlock, one might say. There was equilibrium. The sovereign across the Appenines never taxed directly the property of the Bolognese patriciate, although increasing bit by bit the amounts of papal debt funded on Bolognese tolls and tariffs; then he raised the level of this indirect taxation to increase the debt still further.[5] Even so a strong consortium of citizens including such names as Gozzadini, Fantuzzi, Monti, Marsigli and Caprara, great senatorial families of the future, had already in 1440 won control of part of the municipal revenues, and still functioned as a powerfully entrenched interest of tax farmers in 1700. It resisted and resented Roman inroads, and nobody visualised any serious change in the local balance of power.

On the grand central square of the city stand the Palace of the People and the Palace of the Podestà. Both have had many names, and the first was described as the 'People's' palace, the 'Legate's', the 'Palace of the

Government', or simply 'the Government'.[6] In the seventeenth century it visibly displayed this mixture and intermingling of powers. The legate or vice-legate resided here with his officers and guards; but the Senate and senatorial committees, the justiciar or Confaloniere di Justizia, the Anziani or 'seniors', and the tribunes or deputies of the guilds, all in different ways representing the city and state of Bologna, held meetings or audiences, granted interviews and reached decisions in the same notable cluster of courts and buildings. These also accommodated the Senate's library, the legate's chapel, a botanical garden and a prison. In the smaller neighbouring palace, the Podestà – that ancient officer of the municipality – and his lawyer colleagues adjudicated in open session on Mondays, Wednesdays and Fridays. Opposite, across the square, stood the church of S. Petronio who was bishop, saint and presumed founder of the city, a building which was the largest and boldest enterprise of the Bologna government. Taking over more ground piece by piece it had risen slowly through decades of intermittent work, to completion of the Gothic nave (but without any transepts) by the mid-seventeenth century. A notable feature was the siting of S. Petronio, on an axis running almost due north and south, at the municipality's request in 1388, which wanted the front of the church to stand 'on the piazza of our city'.[7] With that orientation the rulers of the day secured the incomparable focus of civic life which their successors have enjoyed for centuries. It was a broad and open space, with the buildings housing the civil government west and north, on the south S. Petronio and the notaries' office, while along the eastern side ran the frontage of S. Maria della Morte, the hospital.

In the quarter behind S. Petronio, on either side of the street running south to the city gate of S. Mamolo, the medieval civil and canon lawyers were for a long period accustomed to teach, and their students to find lodging. Close by, the Dominicans had their church and friary. Instruction in the liberal arts (including medicine) seems at first to have been given in the neighbourhood of the Franciscans half a mile west, but in due course teachers and scholars in all disciplines were scattered more widely through the town. In consequence vice-legate Cesi's decision in the mid-sixteenth century to have a new building put up on the space between S. Petronio and S. Maria della Morte, where all the public business of the university could in future be carried on, was an innovation.[8] In the era of European religious reform and counter-reform he certainly wanted, not only an imposing academic forum, but a closer regulation of lecturers and students in a central building. This new 'archiginnasio', as it was soon called, also owed something to the architectural revival in Bologna between 1560 and 1580. A number of the wealthier familes altered or rebuilt their houses. Bishop Paleotti began remodelling his cathedral of S. Pietro (though preserving the older tower), and nearby the municipality put up a stately new tax-office. Adjoining the main piazza, between the palaces of Government and Podestà, a space was likewise cleared for the fountain commissioned

1   Bologna in the seventeenth century.

from a fashionable Flemish artist. Today, standing by the coolness of Giambologna's Neptune an onlooker gazes with pleasure at the front of S. Petronio, but what he cannot see from that angle is the university building of 1563, just behind and parallel with the gigantic nave. At one end of a long frontage were grouped lecture rooms and a 'great hall' for the lawyers. At the other, the 'artists' had their own great hall and other rooms. Around the elegant central court was the accommodation where an anatomy theatre would in due course be built. Architect and vice-legate had between them modified an earlier, informal element in the university's proceedings, and it became a more tightly knit structure. Now and for many decades ahead, from the campanile of S. Petronio across the narrow street the 'scholar's bell' rang the hours of the lectures. Every April the legate or vice-legate paid a visit to the two halls to preside over the election of counsellors in the law and arts faculties for the coming year. In certain respects the formalities of university life in the centre of the city had been tightened up,

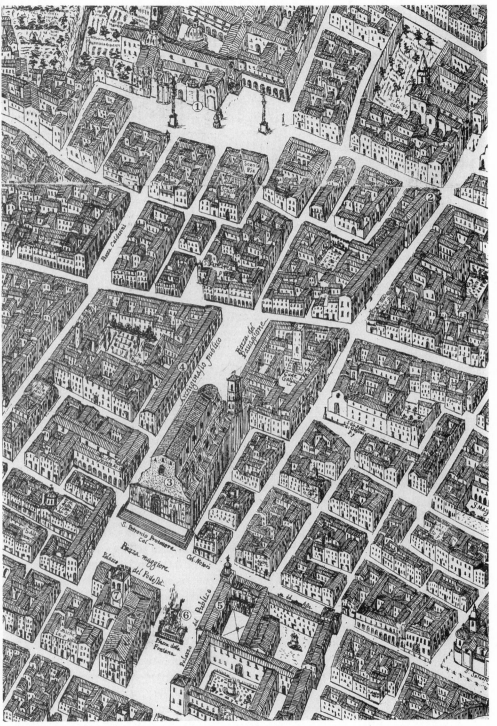

2   Bologna: the centre of the city, showing ① The Dominican church; ② the palace of the Marsigli family; ③ S. Petronio; ④ the University building; ⑤ the Government; ⑥ Neptune's fountain; ⑦ Court and Offices of the Podestà.

and matched the routine already accepted in the seat of civil government across the piazza.

A rapid rotation of offices and an emphasis on ceremony were elements in the partial eclipse of the city's sovereign freedom. They filled up the time of day for persons compelled to be leisurely, and denied the fuller exercise of their authority. While most legates and vice-legates remained four or five years in Bologna, the Confaloniere and the eight Anziani were changed six times a year; and to judge from the complacent Bolognese historians of the sixteenth, seventeenth and eighteenth centuries, the life of many individuals was eternally involved in the procedure of rotation.[9] Three days before the end of every February, April, June, August, October and December a procession of officers, trumpeters and Swiss guards marched off to the friary of the Dominicans, who were the keepers of the ballot box. They brought it back to the Palace, and in the legate's presence the Confaloniere and Anziani in office 'extracted' from the box the names of those who were to succeed them. The procession duly re-formed and returned to the Dominicans with the precious bauble. At midnight and during the next two days there followed a series of meetings, in which compliments were exchanged between the retiring and incoming dignitaries. Then on the first day of the month the bells rang out, escorts processed again to the Palace, and the legate presided over the ceremonies inducting the new men – who in many cases had served in these offices before. There were appropriate clothes to be worn, appropriate protocol, appropriate menus, and a pervasive tendency to make things more elaborate as time went by and never to simplify them. In 1485, we are told, the Switzers were sent for the first time to escort the new Confaloniere from his home on the day of his inauguration. In 1540, for the first time the retiring Confaloniere gave the subsequently anticipated banquet in honour of his colleagues, the retiring Anziani.[10] Nor did the principle of rotation cease to apply at this point. There were many other officials and committees and tribunals elected for two, four or six months at a time, and others were chosen annually. The administration could rely on a body of humbler permanent officials, but this is less remarkable than the extent the more privileged elements in society were satisfied, or had to be satisfied, by a dignified nominal role for a ludicrously short time. After an interval of a year or so they could expect to repeat the familiar gestures in a second or third term of office. It is an example of the more trivial elements of republican life in seventeenth-century Italy. It matched similar elements in the protocol of princely and vice-regal governments at the same period.

Or consider the official ceremonies on the occasion, fairly frequent, of a new legate's arrival in Bologna.[11] Reports of his progress from Rome through the Appenines would be relayed to the city at intervals, while individual senators were authorised to meet him, and their carriages and gear prepared. With a choice company they then set out along the Via Emilia to the old frontier of the state at Castel S. Pietro. The night was passed here, and the inaugural banquet prepared. Early next morning the whole party, with as many escorts as possible, moved up the road as far as the point where it crossed into the neighbouring territory of Imola. His Eminence appears, gets out of his carriage, is welcomed, and gets into a different carriage to be taken to the banquet at Castel S. Pietro. There are still more arrivals of senators, functionaries, churchmen, before they all move on again. It was a satisfyingly lengthy procession that entered Bologna by the great gate of Santa Maria Maggiore, passed onward towards a notable cluster of medieval brick towers (including those of the Asinelli and Garisenda), bore right to the cathedral, and then finally reached the Palace in the piazza. The keys of the city were handed over to the legate. The senators reported to the Confaloniere, who was waiting in his apartment, that their mission had been completed. They could then go home after a hard day's work. There is little doubt that an emphasis on formal procedure of this kind – and on the whole art of entertainment – pervaded the political life and absorbed the energy of a majority of the Bolognese patriciate.

In matters of religion they sometimes showed more thrust. Taught to insist on the value and duty of endowing the church, by providing the means which enabled the clergy to celebrate the divine offices, and putting up the buildings where this could take place in the appropriate setting, they did so. Notions of economy or frugality were balanced against, often counterbalanced by, the ideal of costly magnificence in modern styles of church decoration. The practice of religion embraced much new building, so that an immense volume of savings was expended on the architects, masons, decorators of every kind and their materials, for work commissioned by and for the clergy of the city and its outskirts. The derelict nave of the cathedral had to be replaced. Or the Barnabites wanted a new foundation on a large scale. Or the parish church of S. Salvatore was remodelled in partial imitation of a classical temple, and the rich patrician family of the Caprara – with its palace in the parish – paid part of the costs. In the next generation another nobleman, senator Gian Giacomo Monti, was himself an active painter and architect. He helped to redecorate and modernise the church of Corpus Domini to the greater glory of Caterina de' Vigri, a favourite Bolognese patroness and miracle worker; while one of Monti's brothers administered its property and one of his sisters was a nun there.[12] Meanwhile the foremost of the city's miracle-working ladies remained the Madonna of S. Luca, whose image was annually brought down from her sanctuary high on a nearby spur of the Appenines to rest for a few weeks in a number of churches within the walls. Her popularity and influence must account for the most remarkable enterprise of an entire generation in seventeenth-century Bologna: the project of continuing the arcading of the city streets out from the Saragozza gate and up the steep slope to the sanctuary of S. Luca.[13] Seriously considered in 1655, it was promoted by a committee of clergy and nobility from 1666 onwards. The first stone of the first stretch was laid in 1674. Funding depended on the liberality of donors, who would get a tithe of their satisfaction from the placing of their armorial bearings in an arcade for which they had found the money. Thirty years later, by 1707, this costly and beautiful covered pathway was almost complete. The rebuilding of the sanctuary church, which forms the present matchless silhouette on the height above the city, was delayed some while longer. Many hands, and a particular point of view urging them how time and human energy should best be spent, had contributed to the result.

II

Among the ruling patriciate of Bologna was the Marsigli or Marsili family, divided in the seventeenth century into various branches and connected with many other noble families in and outside the territory of Bologna. A little way south of S. Petronio and close to the Dominican church stood the house where Luigi Ferdinando Marsigli was born on 20 July 1658.[14] His parents were Carlo Marsigli and Margarita Ercolani. Of his two elder brothers the second died in early manhood, leaving Antonio Felice, born in 1649. There was a younger brother Filippo. Two sisters both became nuns.

When Marsigli looked back on his early days, on starting an autobiography, what he could recall most clearly were journeys and teachers.[15] First of all he remembered going with his father to Venice and Padua. Thanks to the hospitality of an elderly cousin[16] they were able to enjoy fully the great Venetian summer festival. At Padua the famous physic garden certainly impressed him; and returning home he started to study botany with Lelio Trionfetti, one of the cathedral canons. He also became a private pupil of the celebrated Malpighi, university reader in anatomy, while his enthusiasm for mathematics brought him to the notice of Geminiano Montanari, a highly distinguished experimentalist. Unlike his elder brother he never enrolled in the university, but took fullest advantage of the unofficial instruction and advice offered by several university teachers. In 1677 his mother died, and at the age of nineteen he went on his travels again, going first to Rome to see his uncle Alfonso Ercolani. Joining a group of tourists and others he visited Naples, and on the way home stayed at Florence and took a trip to Livorno and Lucca. Significant events in his life even at that time seem to have been meetings and conversations with men of letters who were scientists, and he was able to profit from one of the greatest civilising merits of seventeenth-century Italy, which indeed counteracted the political particularism of city states and small principalities. This was the open character of intellectual society. Educated strangers quickly gained admission to 'academic' meetings wherever they went. Scholar gentlemen and scholar clerics in one town customarily gave their friends recommendations to present to other scholar gentlemen and clergy elsewhere.[17] Young Marsigli on his journey was able to meet Magliabechi, librarian in Florence and correspondent-in-chief of European booklovers, Cornelio the noted medical philosopher in Naples, and in Rome Borelli, one of the greatest scientists of his day. There must be some hindsight in his retrospective account but these early acquaintances proved of lifelong importance to Marsigli.

Returning to Bologna he soon did his conventional duty as a citizen of noble birth, accepting election as one of the Anziani for the two-monthly spell of January and February 1678.[18] He played a prominent role in the official pomposities for the carnival season of that year; and we catch a glimpse of him showing English tourists round the city and introducing them to Malpighi, who was (as they knew) a Fellow of 'our' Royal Society.[19] The beginnings of a romance with the countess Eleanora Zambeccari ended quickly enough, and he went off on a second visit to Padua. This time he accompanied his teacher Montanari, who was transferring to a new post. Marsigli enrolled as a student. Mathematics and anatomy continued to hold his attention, and early in 1679 he was able to send Malpighi a surprisingly full and technical account of the anatomy-lecture demonstrations he was attending.[20] But he returned home again, apparently to his father's displeasure. He was restless, purposeless at the time, but with a will of his own. One of the pastimes that evidently took his fancy was walking or riding in the neighbouring hills where there were diggings for gypsum and clay.[21] Samples of marchesite and other stones could be found, and men of science had already recognised that the most exciting of these was the so-called Bononian or Bologna stone, discovered earlier in the century: a substance which, suitably calcined and exposed to the light, became phosphorescent. Marsigli was impressed by such topics, and began making some effort to sort out and classify different types of gypsum or stone in terms of shape, colour and friability. But this was for the moment a diversion while he must have wondered what sort of career he should try to follow.

One possibility was the service of the city state. In Bologna many noblemen, as we saw, spent a lifetime weaving their way through the rotation of offices in a fairly static community. There were few risks, some dignity and colour, and a certain dullness. Marsigli never says a word to suggest that this ever attracted him; he must have felt himself too stirring a fish for that little pond. The prospect was the less inviting because his branch of the Marsigli family was junior in precedence in this period, offering its sons no chance of reaching senatorial rank in the municipality, while the number of his brothers and sisters diminished the considerable hereditary wealth available for each. Countess Zambeccari, he confesses, was entitled to look for a better placed suitor. A more serious and promising challenge was offered by the service of the church state. It had attracted many of the ablest, most ambitious Bologna citizens in the sixteenth and seventeenth centuries. Careers were open to talents of every kind in Rome, capital both of a principate and of the entire Catholic world. One of the civic chroniclers of Bologna had no difficulty, when he reached the year 1700, in listing an imposing array of the citizens who had become cardinals or held senior ecclesiastical posts in the previous hundred years.[22] Or a churchman could simply remain in Bologna and follow his bent. Count Carlo Cesare Malvasia, in Marsigli's day, had been first a lawyer in Rome, then a priest, and returned to his native city to take up a canonry and a lectureship. For thirty more years he went on in a leisurely but industrious way with his literary work, a patriotic piece of art history. Modelled on Vasari, his massive and admirable *Felsina Pittrice** was first printed in 1678.[23]

Much closer to our Marsigli was another churchman, his own eldest brother. Antonio Felice Marsigli accepted the framework of local institutions and of the church state. Appointed archdeacon of Bologna in 1686 and bishop of Perugia in 1702 he had private riches enough for his needs while pursuing his intellectual interests.[24] He belonged, as a young man, to the group which revived a famous academy of the previous century in Bologna, the Gelati. Earlier Gelati had been literary folk who produced verses but the members of Marsigli's generation looked further afield.[25] In their proceedings, printed in 1671, Montanari's contribution exhibits genuine mathematical and astronomical argument. Marsigli's own paper describes a number of 'philosophical' schools or sects in cloudy enough language, but suggests that the Royal Society of London had not accomplished less than the Ancients by encouraging Harvey, Wallis and Boyle. He also thought that the truths of scientific knowledge grew from age to age while states or principalities merely rose and fell. It seems that some of the Gelati were associated earlier with the astronomer Gian Domenico Cassini's use of the nave of S. Petronio as an observatory. An old device there, of aligning a 'great gnomon' of metal along the floor of the church, and piercing a hole in the vault above to let the sunlight fall on the meridian below, had been renovated; more accurate solar observations than before became possible, thanks partly to the unusual height of the building.[26] It provoked great interest in Bologna before Cassini departed in 1669, to begin soon afterwards his long reign as director of Louis XIV's new Observatory on the height of Montmartre. The intelligentsia of Bologna, like the Marsiglis, found other remarkable teachers in Montanari and Malpighi. Antonio Felice himself started two new study groups: the one scientific and experimental, the other committed to a series of discussions on the history, dogma and discipline of the church. Emphasis on a fresh historical treatment of Christian religion, no less than the search for truly experimental sciences, was just then much in vogue in Catholic as in Protestant Europe. Nor did the elder Marsigli stand alone in thinking that the same people should and could tackle both tasks.

---

* Felsina as Painter. Felsina was the name given to the Etruscan city which preceded Roman Bononia and medieval Bologna on the same ground.

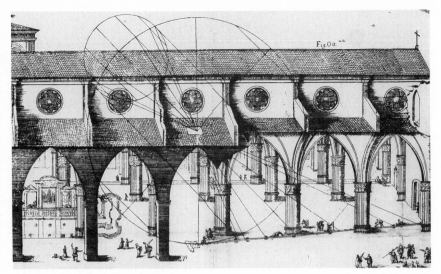

3 The observatory in S. Petronio.

It did not prove a dull career for him, or without controversy. It was one thing to follow respectfully in the wake of the great Malpighi, dedicating to him a little work in 1683 which paid tribute to the master's research in embryology, by adding a mite to it from the examination of certain snails' eggs found in Marsigli's own garden.[27] It was another to find that his friendship, for different considerations, with academics who opposed Malpighi's entire approach to medicine involved fearful hostilities. The greatest scientist in Bologna had joined the die-hards resisting a plan for university reform sponsored by archdeacon Marsigli between 1689 and 1694.[28] Marsigli – *ex officio* the university's chancellor – deplored the falling number of its students, the inflated number of lecturers with few or nominal qualifications, and the insufficient university revenue supplied by the city's taxes. His proposals for altering these things by the enforcement of much severer standards, and the appointment of fewer but better paid teachers, were fought over obstinately by senators and academics alike. The conservatives finally won the support of Pope Innocent XII; the reforming senators and the archdeacon-chancellor gave up the struggle.

The younger Marsigli in 1679 had no inkling of such storms ahead, nor of his own part in the cause of academic reform. In addition nothing suggests that he ever thought of becoming a churchman like his elder brother. There were other careers open, as he knew. For example count Alberto Caprara had been appointed a university lecturer in moral philosophy a decade earlier, and duly gave his lectures in Bologna during the academic year 1678 –9;[29] but duties of a different kind usually detained him elsewhere. Having become the secretary and envoy of cardinal Rinaldo d'Este in Rome, Caprara acted for the Este family for almost twenty years at various foreign courts. Then he appears as a Habsburg envoy from time to time, accredited by Emperor Leopold. It was one possible career for a bright young man to consider, while other members of the same family had moved along a different path again. The four sons of Niccolò Caprara, who died in 1634, all served in the armies of the Habsburg emperors; their uncle was general Piccolomini, their cousin general Montecuccoli, both wonderfully placed in Vienna to help them. When the eldest son at last retired and came home, he was duly elected Confaloniere. The second died in the course of warfare. The third finally transferred from Habsburg to Medici service. And the fourth was Aeneo Caprara, whose long military career epitomised a whole series of campaigns in different parts of Europe between 1658 and 1697.[30] He rose to become one of Leopold's senior commanders, in earlier years returning to Bologna occasionally to play his part as one of the Anziani. Thereafter his fellow citizens had to rest content with local news sheets celebrating the great man's actions in the field. His was a marvellous illustration, already notable by the 1670s, of what could be done abroad with competence and luck, an example to all those young patricians who wanted to get about the world, even if they returned later to the palace of their families in the grand old city. Ultimately Luigi Ferdinando Marsigli followed the Caprara example with some variations all his own. For several preliminary years he still looked around, and while doing so developed the preferences which would mark him wherever he was, and whatever he did.

III

He belonged indeed to the second generation of 'Post-Galileans' and shared in their heritage.[31] In seventeenth-century Italy nothing had been more remarkable than the resilience with which Galileo and his followers responded to Rome's emphatic and hostile pronouncement in 1632. They and then their own successors adopted various tactics. Where the damage was ostensibly greatest, in astronomy, they 'saved appearances' and went back to hypothetical Copernicanism. They continued to use their telescopes but laid more stress on mathematical studies, as Cavalieri showed in Bologna and Castelli in Rome, where a group of outstanding younger men came forward. They also investigated physical properties by using new instruments and techniques, some of which they had helped to devise. This became the first age of the thermometer, barometer and microscope in Italy. Amateurs like the Marsigli brothers or professionals like Malpighi, Borelli and Redi looked with new eyes at minute living structures in man, plants, insects, fish, birds and animals. They collected and examined minerals, rocks and fossils. They tabulated daily temperatures and varying air pressures. Moreover, belonging as a matter of course to literary societies and social academies, they sometimes persuaded them to accept their work on these topics; such learning was after all literature as well, and 'natural' history was a part of history. They even formed societies of a more specialised kind. The 'Investiganti' of Naples, the academy 'del Cimento' of Florence and 'della Traccia' of Bologna reveal by their titles the members' trust in the value (or pleasure) of experimental investigation.* With this went their eagerness to become associated with any similar work going on elsewhere, in Protestant countries or in France, thus diminishing the threat of intellectual isolation posed by the Index and Inquisition operating in Italy. The correspondence of the Medici princes with Huygens, and of Malpighi over a much longer period with the secretaries of the Royal Society, radiated much valuable information to other Italian scientists. It encouraged a point of view which accepted the philosophical claims of the Roman church, but kept them at a working distance from this kind of subject. When Montanari felt angry, as he did one day in March 1677, he complained bitterly that he was playing the roles of both Martha and Mary in Bologna, giving his official lectures while at the same time trying to introduce the new mathematical and experimental physics to pupils in his house. When he felt confident and happy he wrote instead: 'my experience in Germany has taught me to believe more firmly in the Catholic faith, but controversy between Catholics gives my poor little head a *noli me tangere*, and I run to my more innocent astronomical or physico-mathematical speculations, leaving the Thomists and Scotists to fight it out . . .'[32]

The bolder spirits avoided trouble most of the time. Their cautious friends and critics, embracing the new learning and using new apparatus, were even more determined not to err in the sight of the church, and the reception in Italy of ideas associated with the names of Descartes and Gassendi was accordingly warm but wary. Gassendi himself, the worthy canon of Digne cathedral, had brought the atomism of the ancient world into a fairly safe anchorage within orthodoxy. Malebranche would do like-wise for the Cartesians. In Italy it proved equally possible for most thinking men to rely on a working compromise between old and new schools of thought in both philosophy and science, although the boundary edged backward and forward from time to time. The Bolognese publisher Manolessi got a great many of Galileo's works past the censor and reprinted them in 1656. The Medici Grand Duke Ferdinand II and his brother Leopold paid for and patronised for many years the experimental activities which at length brought their Florentine academy 'del Cimento' into formal existence; its proceedings were printed in 1667. The 'Investigators' started up in Naples with an overriding concern for medical studies, under the guidance of Tommaso Cornelio. When Marsigli was in Rome for the first time, staying with his uncle, he met the 'abati' Francesco Nazzari and Antonio Oliva, as well as the more celebrated Borelli. But for ten years

---

* The 'cimento', or cementation, referred originally to the process of refining by which a goldsmith produced the highest quality metal; the 'traccia' was the 'trace' or track of the evidence guiding an enquirer towards the correct conclusion.

Nazzari, a teacher of philosophy at the university of the Sapienza, had been editing the *Giornale de' Letterati*.[33] This periodical was started in 1668 with the intention of giving excerpts to Italian readers from the Parisian *Journal des Sçavans*, subsequently also from the papers of the Royal Society of London, at the same time giving publicity to current Italian literary work. By 1677 there were two versions of the *Giornale* printed in Rome, one still edited by Nazzari and the other by G. G. Ciampini, who used a different team of assistants. It has been claimed that Ciampini was less 'Galilean' in outlook than Nazzari. His journal did less reviewing and used more space in giving up-to-date lists of Italian and foreign books actually on sale in Rome. But he was the moving spirit behind a 'physico-mathematical' academy founded in this same year, 1677, meeting at his house on the Piazza Navona. As for Oliva, also mentioned by Marsigli, he had been an intellectual radical in the Neapolitan tradition of Campanella, and was earlier described as a 'bizarre' person but later became Pope Clement X's physician.[34] Such people were at least innovative by temperament.

Against them the more rigidly orthodox occasionally banged the drum, and canvassed the statesmen. In Bologna the great Jesuit astronomer Riccioli broadcast the text of Galileo's abjuration, and refuted his views (although adopting some of them). The Medici had offered posts in Tuscany to Torricelli and Viviani, Borelli and Oliva, but conservative academic influences regained dominance in their university at Pisa by 1670. By that time prince Leopold was a cardinal usually in Rome, his Florentine academy was dispersed; and the remarkable Danish physiologist and geologist Niels Stensen (or Steno), whom the Medici had supported for a number of years, announced his conversion and took orders, giving up all scientific work. The Investiganti in Naples were meeting no longer, after a hint from the Spanish viceroy. In Rome Nazzari and Ciampini halted their journalism. The 'physico-mathematical' academy, although intending to keep a record of its proceedings for publication, failed to do so after 1681. It continued to meet at intervals for another ten years, but any experimental work in Rome gradually fades from view during the pontificates of Innocent XI's successors.[35] Oliva's fate would be the worst of all. He was a victim of the Inquisition after 1688, when a more active campaign began against those denounced as 'atheists', and other so-called 'sects' in the Papal states and the kingdom of Naples.

In some respects the most practical spokesmen of compromise were the Jesuits, who harboured among themselves very diverse views. If Riccioli and many like him appear generally hostile to novel concepts, others teaching mathematics or philosophy in their numerous colleges did not. This was the more important because the Society acquired part of its singular influence by offering the public an orthodox educational programme, which offered a little of nearly everything currently attractive to the upper ranks of society. It was the Jesuits, for example, who had played a part in depleting

– by competing with – the ancient university of Bologna.[36] In effect they challenged the old order of academic studies in the town. First they opened a novitiate in 1627, aiming to attract serious young students who would join them. Ten years later they proposed moving their popular classes in law and arts from Parma to Bologna. The Senate, alarmed, persuaded Pope Urban VIII to pronounce against this in 1641. The veto was evaded, the classes were maintained in Bologna, and prospered. It was part of a struggle over education going on in many parts of Catholic Europe. Jesuit colleges, often reserved for the sons of noblemen, where boys were lodged, taught academic subjects in organised classes, and instructed in fashionable exercises like dancing, fencing and theatricals, outmoded the more haphazardly organised system of public lecture halls and private lodgings. In certain cases the Jesuits themselves took control of the universities. In central Italy their colleges of Parma, Bologna and Siena simply outshone the older, and in certain aspects decrepit, academic institutions of Bologna's university. They offered the sons of Italian and foreign families, noble or citizen, an education judged more up to date. The Jesuit colleges at their best were both flexible and highly organised. It was possible to enter them at any age between ten and seventeen, to break off a formal education early or to continue it late. While the elder Marsigli, as archdeacon and chancellor, deplored the decline of the venerable 'studio' of his native city, Jesuit institutions on the spot had developed to rival it. There was certainly adaptation as well as decay in this world of teachers and pupils. There were also, fortunately, other ways of learning and growing up.

IV

That the countess Zambeccari had married someone else, and others teased him for it, troubled the young man. He tells how he fell back on a promise given him by his father a year earlier, to let him join the official embassy going from Venice to the court of the Sultan. Yet no more than a hint survives of the first thought that made such a venture attractive. In the account of his journey in 1677 from Rome to Naples he recalls meeting an Englishman of long experience in the Levant, and asking many questions about the Turks.[37] How he secured entry to the household and joined the staff of the new Venetian envoy, Pietro Civran, is also uncertain. The real stroke of fortune was that for personal reasons Civran had delayed his departure,[38] which gave Marsigli a chance to get to Venice in time.

Ever since the great struggle over Crete between the Republic and the Sultan's government had ended in 1669, Venetian ambassadors had been trying to re-establish their old position in Istanbul. They wanted to recover the old mansion on the height of Pera which had served their predecessors as a residence,[39] and to revive trade between the two empires, including the profitable sale of Venetian luxuries to the Sultan's household. Such aims meant keeping on reasonable terms with the statesmen who ruled on behalf of Sultan Mehmed IV, but the rise to supremacy of grand vezir Kara Mustafa, after the death of the great Fazil Ahmed Köprülü in 1676, gravely complicated their task. The new Ottoman management appeared to repudiate the whole notion of diplomatic privilege, normally claimed by and granted to foreign envoys. It also treated the Venetian envoy – or *bailo* – worse than anyone else. The mission of Civran, who was succeeding the much harassed Giorgio Morosini, would live up to the most pessimistic expectations. But for a lesser mortal like young Marsigli there was greater promise of enjoyment or profit, and less risk. His association with an official mission made easier the otherwise difficult journey to the East. Lodging and introductions became simple matters. Celebrated buildings, panoramas, festivals, and the local colour of Turkish sports and customs could be viewed at leisure. A returned traveller's tales were always popular at home; and more seriously, the Ottoman empire offered a significant field of observation in politics, religion and history, setting up standards for comparison with western ideas and western practice. In the course of three centuries this great military power had posed an intractable problem for its neighbour states. It was still doing so, and also on that account deserved scrutiny at close quarters.

Civran, in choosing his staff, can hardly have taken more trouble than Giambattista Donà who followed him as envoy two years later. Donà took general advice from men with previous experience, from Cornelio Magni, who had published an account of local conditions in Turkey, and Giovanni Agop, an Armenian Catholic from Istanbul, author of books on the Armenian and Turkish languages.[40] The envoy needed a dragoman or interpreter, a doctor, an accountant, a secretary, together with young men willing to serve him while studying oriental languages. As dragoman Donà wanted Rinaldo Carlì, a scholarly person who later translated the Turkish historian Mustafa Haǧǧi Chalifa.[41] Carlì was not available, so two members of the Tarsia family (formerly from Istria but domiciled in Istanbul) were chosen: Giorgio as interpreter during the journey out, and Tommaso as senior Venetian dragoman at the Ottoman court. Donà engaged Michael Andriola as his physician, a prolific medical author whose published work appeared afterwards in Italy, France and Austria. One of the language students was Antonio Benetti, a full and scrupulous diarist on his travels. He died young, but an enterprising Venetian publisher acquired his journals and produced an account of the whole mission.[42] The dedication to Donà contains the interesting statement that the editor had seen 'in his Excellency's own room' many papers, including a list of the Islamic sects which deviated from orthodoxy, observations on Turkish literature, an account of Turkish military institutions, and a history of the war of 1683. None were printed, it seems, except for Donà's own essay on Turkish literature, with its admirable thesis that the Ottoman world was not merely a particular form of military organisation but enjoyed standards of cultural excellence and a literature deserving respect. Such details suggest that the intellectual level of the Venetian *bailo*'s own household, which in Donà's case became an incipient school of Turkish studies, could be very high. These men equalled or surpassed the best elements in the French and English embassies at Istanbul in the same period.

Marsigli set out with Civran's party which left Venice on 22 July 1679 in two galleys, transferring to another pair of 'splendid' warships at Corfu. The course followed took them first to Istria and down the Dalmatian coast, but at Split our young man had time for an excursion a few miles inland to the fortress of Klis, a point very close to Turkish Bosnia.[43] The voyage continued south, skirting past mainland and islands as far as Corfu, then via Zante and Cerigo, across the Aegean to Smyrna, and from Smyrna northwards. Marsigli already believed that nearly everything he did or saw on a journey was memorable: he kept a diary and made notes of the most varied kind. He also had with him a thermometer and a simple kind of hydrostatic balance for weighing samples of water, occasionally recording temperatures and densities, and he mentions using a microscope. Almost everywhere he landed he looked at and collected plants or seeds. In Corfu he was first of all impressed by the new defence works being built, but then realised that the excavation this entailed allowed him to study the nature of the ground, and particularly the local deposits of gypsum which could be compared with what he had seen at home. The novelty of Zante was a bituminous well, which he sketched; of Chios, it was the turpentine plant. Nor did he neglect the miscellanies of his experience on the journey: at sea the sighting of possible corsairs – who fled; at Smyrna, the good living evidently enjoyed by the Europeans; or the superstitions of the Greek rite, as he observed it; and his first and friendly contacts with Turkish officials and soldiers. So Marsigli, in this new phase of his life, waited eagerly for the attractions he reckoned to find at each successive landfall and was already what he would remain, a very busy traveller. As it turned out the expedition struck bad weather in the Aegean and zigzagged between Smyrna, Mount Athos, Lemnos and Tenedos before entering the Dardanelles. Marsigli refers briefly to his arrival at Istanbul, after dark and with the lamps lit in the towers of the mosques. It was the fast of Ramadan. The voyagers then made their way to the ambassadorial house on Pera, which by day commanded so thrilling a view (as Benetti the diarist observed) of the landscape and seascape where Europe and Asia meet, the site of an imperial city since Emperor Constantine's inauguration.

Soon after the new Venetian envoy's arrival the Ottoman government accused him of having uncustomed goods smuggled ashore, and permitting his ships to be used as a refuge for runaway slaves. One result of this rumpus was a ban pronounced on the entry of Venetian warships into Ottoman harbours, which would remain in force until the Republic itself expired in 1797. At the time the possible fate of Civran at the hands of the grand vezir, and of Morosini whom he had come to replace, dominated the talk of diplomats in Pera. Marsigli, as a Bolognese and not a Venetian subject, seems to have been less perturbed and indeed enjoyed brushing with irate Ottoman officials, as he played his role of messenger between the two Venetian envoys. When the dust settled he used his leisure and followed his bent. He employed a Jewish interpreter named Abraham Gabai, and took his first steps in learning a little Turkish. He became acquainted with Turkish scribes and scholars, and started to collect copies of documents and maps. Meeting a friendly Venetian described as the Sultan's chiropodist, he secured access to some of the less public quarters of the imperial palace. On another occasion he was given a seat in the admiral's galley for a ceremonial review of Ottoman warships in the Sea of Marmara, saying long afterwards that he compared adversely the management of these with what he had seen earlier of the galleys of Venice.[44] He took up the case of a Bolognese galley slave, and began corresponding with a charity at home to raise the funds needed to redeem him.[45] He also went on an excursion to Bursa, which led him to conclude that the Sultans' power was hardly significant before they had won a foothold in Europe. He picked up another notion, more relevant to his own day: any settlement of the Turco-Muscovite quarrel then being fought out in the Ukraine might well lead quickly to renewed Turkish action in Hungary. The possible pendulum swing of warfare from one side of the Carpathians to the other obviously deserved attention from a student of politics in Istanbul. Yet none of this stopped him for long from attending to the pre-eminent physical feature of the place, the channel linking the Sea of Marmara with the Black Sea. What did earlier writers say about the Bosphorus? And had they understood correctly the action of the tides and currents? Here surely was the perfect problem to examine on his travels for a modern virtuoso, Montanari's pupil. While he considered this, and still flitted from topic to topic – including the pleasure of acquaintance with the French ambassador's beguiling daughter – fresh news arrived from Venice. The government of the Republic had determined on another move in its dispute with the Sultan, or rather with his grand vezir, and was recalling Civran at once. Marsigli, realising that he too would have to return to Italy, then made the enterprising decision that he would see as much as possible on the way by following a long route overland. Even Hungary and Austria might be included in an itinerary back to Venice and Bologna. His travelling companions were a friend named Gaetano Foresti, and the interpreter de Tarsia. They left Istanbul on 22 August 1680.

There were, there always had been, several routes through the Balkans by which the Christian states could be reached. Most of these led to the Adriatic ports where the traveller found shipping for Brindisi, Ancona or Venice. Others led through Wallachia and Moldavia to southern Poland. Above all there was the grand old route which linked Istanbul, Adrianople

(Edirne),* Philippopolis (Plovdiv), Sofia, Niš and Belgrade.[46] It had been the principal highway of the Ottoman forces bound for Hungary before the start of every campaign against the Habsburg emperors. During Marsigli's childhood, war in Transylvania and Hungary in 1660–4 reasserted this function of the itinerary from Istanbul to Belgrade and Buda. Later, from 1688 until the great war ended with the peace treaties of Carlowitz in 1699, it was used year after year, and few men had a more detailed knowledge of many stretches of it than the Habsburg officer count Marsigli. In 1680 there was still peace, and he was still a young tourist inquisitively on the move. He found Balkan towns generally dismal, jumbles of suburbs without a centre or focus, but at Philippopolis it seemed worth his while enquiring for an Orthodox priest known formerly as the patriarch Dionysus IV before his deposition by the Turks, and a noted bibliophile.[47] In Sofia he went to a church served by a Franciscan, while noting that the Catholic bishop resided in greater security at Ciprovets, a remote place in the hills northward. Also in Sofia, a certain spring of water seemed worth a visit: its odour was sulphurous, Marsigli decided, its taste acidic. On the way through Bulgaria he copied out some fragmentary Roman and Greek inscriptions which were pointed out to him.[48] Others he missed, as at Niš, but his little party now moved fairly fast into Serbia, crossing the river Morava by a 'splendid' bridge at Jagodina (Svetozarevo) and so north to Belgrade. The frightening news that infection of the worst kind, bubonic plague, was spreading fast stopped further sightseeing. Marsigli learnt that the deaths in Buda, according to report, were even more numerous than in Belgrade; mortality certainly reached horrifying levels at many points in central Europe during 1679 and 1680, one of the worst epidemics of the century. A journey through Hungary to Vienna would have been rash, if not impossible. Having reached the Danube they had to alter their plans and a route across Serbia and Bosnia to the Dalmatian coast was preferred.

The little party first rode about 40 miles along the north bank of the Sava, one of the Danube's larger tributaries, as far as the site of the old Roman capital of Sirmium at Mitrovica. Crossing over near this point they began to move up the valley of the Drina, an ancient boundary between the medieval principalities of Serbia and Bosnia. After four days they reached Zvornik and from there went over the hills to Sarajevo, where Marsigli handed over a letter of introduction from Civran to a merchant named Bernaković and secured extra money. A larger number of travellers now grouped together for safety's sake. The riskiest stretch of the whole journey to the coast lay ahead. Moving westwards, up and down wild country, they approached the higher ground of the main Dinaric Alps. They camped out, crossing

---

* Placenames in Hungary and south-east Europe, in the text, are those usually found in a modern English atlas. In certain instances, alternatives have been added when a name occurs for the first time.

ridges and *poljes* – upland basins characteristic of the karst limestone and descended to where the water courses start to flow quickly to the neighbouring sea. Marsigli finally caught sight of the Venetian fortress of Klis, which he had visited on his excursion from Split during the voyage out to Turkey. They were indeed nearer home, with Bosnia behind them.

V

This first journey outside Italy brings all the closer some areas and problems which shaped Marsigli's later career. For example the Bosnian and Dalmatian stage of the itinerary had an extraordinary sequel. In 1683 a massive force of Ottoman and Tartar troops passed through Hungary and attempted their famous unsuccessful siege of Vienna. On the way, and close to the Austrian border, certain Tartars captured a young Italian who prudently described himself as 'Federico', servant of a Flemish merchant in Venice and formerly in the service of the *bailo* at Istanbul.[49] This 'Federico' was Marsigli, now a volunteer officer in the Habsburg army, who survived several days of extreme disorder and cruelty before being sold by one set of masters to another, and employed as a labourer in the Turkish siege works. He also worked at an extemporised coffee shop near the western end of the besiegers' encampment. He roasted, ground and boiled the coffee. Trying but failing to escape, he was next sold to two Bosnian horsemen and undertook to purchase his freedom by paying a ransom through the agency of the merchant Bernaković of Sarajevo, a name familiar to his new masters. After two months the siege of Vienna failed, the invaders retreated, and the Bosnians took Marsigli with them to Buda. They were able to make their way southwards along the Danube before getting across the Drava (another right-bank Danube tributary) and then the Sava. Safely arrived at Sarajevo, a note was taken from Marsigli to Bernaković reminding him that he had earlier paid out a sum of money, on the security of a letter from the Venetian *bailo* Civran. Alas, Bernaković utterly declined to recollect this earlier transaction. Marsigli's hopes of freedom, the Bosnians' for cash, were equally disappointed. 'Omer' and 'Gellilo' tried without success to find a new buyer and finally took their captive with them and went home. Home meant a crowded timber house, an old mother, brothers, wives, many children, and a small corner or stall for Marsigli where he was tied at nights to a pole. Home also meant a village by a stream called Rama, reached from Sarajevo by going down the valley of the Neretva in its course to the Adriatic. The Rama is a tributary, and the entire area of this river system was still nominally the Sultan's, but Venetian harbours and garrisons were not far off to the north and west.[50] In Marsigli's more hopeful moods, early in 1684, he considered that the Blessed Virgin had providentially brought him near the sea again, within reach of his friends. At other times he despaired.

Learning that there was a Franciscan house in the neighbourhood he

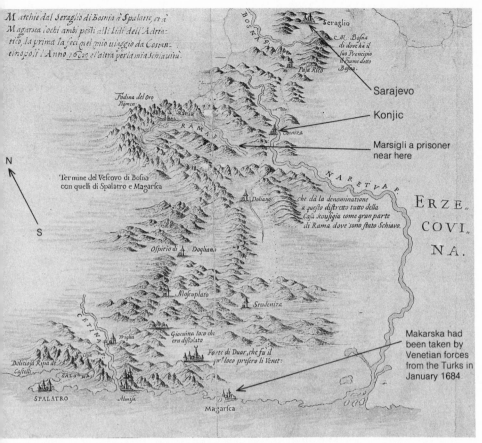

Within the map image:

Marchie dal Seraglio di Bosnia à Spalatro, et à Magarsea, lochi ambi posti alli Lidi dell'Adriatico, la prima la feci nel mio uiaggio da Costantinopoli l'Anno 1680 e l'altra perla mia Schiauitù.

BOSNA

Seraglio

M. Bosna di doue ha il suo Prencipio il Fiume detto Bosna.

Pasa Rico

— Sarajevo

— Konjic

Fodina del Oro Pigmen

Rama

Coniza

Marsigli a prisoner near here

RAMA

Termine del Vescovo di Bosna con quelli di Spalatro e Magarsca

N A R E T V A F

Doliano

che dà la denominatione a questo distretto tutto della Casa Kousigia come gran parte di Rama doue sono stato Schiavo.

ERZE "

COVI "

N A.

N

S

Ospitio di Doghana

Moscuplato

Studeniza

Cetina

Trigla

Giacuina loco che era distolato

Forte di Duar, che fu il pr.° loco presero li Venet.

Makarska had been taken by Venetian forces from the Turks in January 1684

Delitiosa Ripa de Castelli

SALONA

SPALATRO

Almisa

Magarsca

From Sarajevo to the Adriatic: an example of Marsigli's early map-making, with his later annotations. Routes from Sarajevo in Bosnia to Split and to Makarska . . . I followed them for the first time on my journey from Constantinople in the year 1680, and again in my captivity'.

asked to see a priest. A Franciscan arrived. Marsigli made his confession and revealed his identity. It proved possible to bargain afresh with his masters. Messages were sent over the hills to Split and to Makarska which had recently been taken by the Venetians;[51] here was the chief Franciscan house on this part of the coast. The good news that Marsigli was alive reached Venice, then Bologna. Civran himself – who had long since returned from Istanbul – sent an agent with all the funds needed. There were still many hazards to face in mid-March 1684, mainly because it proved difficult to find a go-between who could be trusted with the money. At length intermediaries were found to manage the rescue. For Marsigli the final episode was a painful traverse over high and rugged ground, warily bypassing a hostile outpost. So, happily, two poor brothers in the Rama valley got their money, and their captive his freedom. Marsigli found clean linen in Makarska, hot water and a soft bed.

This biographical fragment fits into a long historical perspective.

Spreading the authority of Rome into the Balkans had been a persistent
missionary endeavour for centuries, though in 1684 there was precious little
to show for it. Catholic churches and populations under Venetian and
Ragusan sovereignty dominated the narrow littoral, with a much thinner
sprinkling in the Ottoman hinterland. Small colonies of Catholic traders
existed in some Serbian and Bulgarian towns. In Bosnia and Hercegovina,
however, Rome had earlier fought seriously for mastery. Hungarian kings
in their period of rule south of the Sava, and the native rulers seeking to
defend themselves against Magyar or Turk, looked to the Popes for support; while a great prosyletising effort of Franciscan inspiration radiated
inland from the Adriatic. When Sultan Mehmed the Conqueror finally
overran Bosnia his charter of 1465 assented to the Franciscans' claim to
practise their religion. In the following centuries restraints on Catholic
freedom proved cramping enough. Orthodoxy was dominant, Islam attracted support, but the Catholics did not vanish. We hear for example of a
rich man from the Bosnian lead-mining town of Olovo, about the year 1440,
who helped to pay for rebuilding that Franciscan house at Makarska.[52]
Catholic refugees from inland added to the island population between
Zadar and Dubrovnik while Bosnian friars went back from such places to
labour in their own country; and the family of Bernaković, Marsigli's
Sarajevo merchant, played a part. In 1651 Rome made the head of the
Bosnian Franciscans the bishop of Belgrade. His modest church had been
burnt down, and the Catholic community paid for its rebuilding in 1675.[53]
At this point, we are told, two influential brothers named Philip and James
Bernaković pushed strongly for the nomination of their Franciscan brother
Patrick as the next bishop of Belgrade. Rome approved, and the choice was
confirmed in 1679. It is impossible to show whether he arrived in the city
before or after Marsigli's visit, and indeed this Bernaković disappears from
our view; but the persistent, if subdued presence of the Franciscans in these
regions had contributed to Marsigli's rescue.

Orthodoxy and Islam had long before secured the whole region south of
the Sava against Rome. Catholic missionaries depended on migrants and
immigrants thinly distributed. Then in Marsigli's lifetime it seemed possible that the whole situation might be changed. After the Ottoman retreat
from Vienna in 1683 the Emperor and Venice and Poland joined in attack-
ing the common enemy. In 1686 Buda fell. In 1687 Athens fell. In 1688
Belgrade fell and a deeper penetration of the Balkans seemed imminent. Yet
the assault failed, as we shall find, and the only transfers of territorial
sovereignty were along its outer rim. In the west the Turks lost ground in
Dalmatia – as at Makarska – to Venice, while certain segments of Croatia
formerly in their hands fell to the Habsburgs. Marsigli played a part in
determining the new boundary when peace was made in 1699 and, as
Emperor Leopold's commissioner, was in Croatia and Dalmatia surveying
the territory in question. One day he recognised the landscape. Not far from
the valley of the Rama[54] he enquired for two inhabitants, 'Omer' and

'Gelillo', and not long afterwards these Bosnians like poor and broken ghosts appeared before him, and he tried to be generous. His old masters were indeed his benefactors, because they had by chance and mischance contributed to his exceptional knowledge of scarcely known country. A reputation for that sort of expertise helped him throughout his political and military career.

VI

On his first journey overland from Istanbul in 1680, Marsigli naturally brought with him the notes and drafts he had been making since he left Venice, together with purchases which included copies of documents and maps. He resumed his diary and his style of travel began to prefigure what it became later. By then he would be writing to ministers at Vienna or other officers in the field, while keeping the drafts or copies; and what he received, he also kept. But in 1680 it was enough to be preoccupied by two literary projects, for which he had the materials with him.

One concerned his observations on Ottoman rule and Turkish society. They were Marsigli's early steps in a study which fifty years later took the form of an important volume on the 'Rise and Fall of Ottoman Military Institutions',[55] appearing in print after his death. The lengthy interval between the idea of 1680 and publication in 1732 is tantalising enough at this early point in our acquaintance, but as a young man he had settled briskly to work. In Istanbul he began with notes on the usual miscellany of exotic facts which intrigued the western traveller about Turkish food, dress, coins, games etc., collecting as well the 'maxims' of the Sultan's extraordinary mode of government. He looked for material on Turkish office holders, Turkish troops, and Turkish taxes. Accompanied by his Jewish interpreter or the dragomans of the Venetian embassy, willing if not apt to learn Turkish himself, infectiously eager, young Marsigli managed to become friendly with a handful of well-informed men who moved fairly close to the ruling circles of the Ottoman court. They were doctors, astronomers, geographers, historians. Some were, or accounted themselves, universal experts. Muneğğim-basi, astrologer and herbalist, gave Marsigli the horoscopes of Sultan Mehmed IV and his son Mustafa, and discussed with him the question of calculating Istanbul's latitude; the two differed in their estimates. Hezarfenn, an encyclopaedic author to whom he pays affectionate tribute, generously showed him his own 'compendium' of official texts listing the forces of the Ottoman army and navy, with figures for the revenues supporting them. Marsigli was able to have this copied or at least summarised in an Italian translation. Another piece by Hezarfenn, who had travelled to Mecca and the Yemen as a young man, discoursed on the coffee plant, coffee-making and the medical virtues of coffee. This too was transcribed for Marsigli.

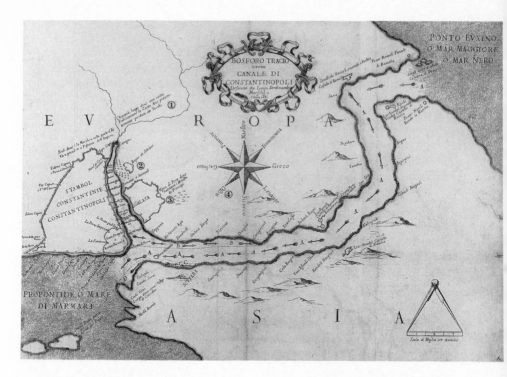

5 Marsigli at work in Istanbul: ① he learns that paper was formerly manufactured here, by 1680 a lost art in Ottoman countries; ② he identifies the naval docks, with the compound of the galley-slaves adjoining; ③ in Pera he visits the households of the foreign ambassadors; ④ accompanying his text, the wind compass – *tramontana* pointing north – illustrates the direction of the currents in the Bosphorus.

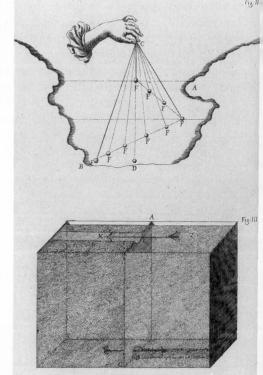

6 Marsigli shows the deflection of the leadline by the currents at differing depths, and the water of higher and lower densities moving between two chambers.

Not least among his acquaintances was Ebu-Bekr from Damascus. Ebu-Bekr had been officially commissioned to deal with a matter which from time to time preoccupied members of the Ottoman court. In 1668 the Dutch Resident had offered the Sultan a fine copy of Blaeu's great Atlas of the world in eleven volumes, recently printed at Amsterdam. There was debate whether this might be worth scrutiny in case anything novel or important could be learnt from it about central Europe and other regions bordering the Ottoman empire. After some delay Ebu-Bekr was ordered in 1675 to commence work on a full translation. As it happened, therefore, a young Italian sought him out at a time when he was completing his own studies of the Atlas, who asked (and probably paid) for instruction in the geography of the Ottoman empire.[56] With some pleasure the oriental scholar emphasised to Marsigli that he found misinformation in addition to fact in Blaeu about the Sultan's lands. Marsigli drew the conclusion that he himself would be singularly well placed to correct errors current in western Europe on the cartography of Asia Minor, just as he could use Hezarfenn's work to give an improved account of Ottoman resources or the defects of Ottoman government. These attractive ideas were then unfortunately modified, to judge from his papers, and he adopted the more commonplace plan of writing discursively informative sketches about the Ottoman world in general. The boundaries of that despotic empire, and the multiplicity of its peoples, the state of the Christian churches under Moslem rule, the secrets of the Sultan's harem, the qualities of the air in Istanbul: such topics would all have to find a place in his work. There were soon first drafts of this or that section, and second drafts. When he left Istanbul late in 1679, possibly with his interpreter Tarsia's help as they journeyed through the Balkans, fair copies were made. At the end of one of the versions discussing the Sultan's palace occurs the phrase: 'the rest will be finished in Bologna'.[57] The year after his return to Italy Marsigli declared (in August 1681) that his work on the Turks was ready for the press.[58] It did not appear in print.

Difficulties of which nothing is now known may account for this. Or, as happened so often later, Marsigli abruptly lost interest in one piece of work to turn to something different. He in fact finished and published much more quickly a different memorial of his stay in Istanbul. First during the voyage out, and then later, he thought of communicating his observations for the 'study of nature' in the form of letters addressed to teachers or patrons. He would submit his record of daily temperatures to senator Girolamo Corraro of Venice, and an account of the various vines he identified in Cephalonia to the botanist Guglielmo Bonfigl|uoli. A great deal more on other plants and points of geological interest was reserved for Malpighi, while his conclusions on the currents of the Bosphorus were appropriately intended for that master of hydrology, Montanari.[59] He certainly wrote to Malpighi before leaving Istanbul, and may have written to the others, but on returning to Italy he brought much of his materials together in a single letter addressed to Queen Christina of Sweden. Marsigli's 'Observations on the Thracian Bosphorus',[60] an essay of 108 pages, a map and several diagrams, was published in Rome in 1681.

This piece, in a small compass, discusses many aspects of its subject: the geographical setting, the currents of the strait and their speeds, barometric readings at various places, the prevailing wind system, the salinity of the water, the fish of the Bosphorus and their habits. One smiles all the more to find tacked on his description of the bituminous springs in the island of Zante his notes of an experiment on salt water made in Venice and some references to other work (already commenced, he claims) examining the 'Bononian stone'. Yet on some of these matters he has a claim to be heard; his work is a tribute to the influence of Montanari and considers the Bosphorus from his teacher's point of view. Discussing a topic previously dominated by authors in the humanist tradition, Marsigli observed the criteria more recently set by seventeenth-century scientific academies. Returning to Italy, he would use an apparatus of tank and taps, and samples of water, to demonstrate to audiences of virtuosi in Venice and Rome what he had seen at Istanbul.[61] In doing so, he was a stage ahead of the English observers reporting to the Royal Society at this period on certain similar, puzzling conditions in the Straits of Gibraltar.[62]

He gave most attention to that famous phenomenon, the currents of the Bosphorus. Describing and distinguishing four different currents near the surface of the narrow channel, A, which flows from the Black Sea to the Sea of Marmara, then B, C, and D running the other way, he marked them out on the map he was making. Using the testimony of fishermen – he would be quick to appeal to fishermen all through his life, here and on the Danube and Lake Garda, in Provence or along the Adriatic – he also checked what they said for himself. Next he experimented with weights at varying depths of water in order to study what seemed mysterious and important, the current beneath A which ran in the opposite direction, out of the Sea of Marmara and towards the Black Sea. He tried hard to understand why this occurred by using his apparatus and emphasised the role of the fresh water of the Danube and other large rivers entering the Black Sea, by contrast with the relative salinity of the heavier sea water of the Aegean and, in the depths, of the Bosphorus. He was unaware of the importance, in this context, of the great amount of evaporation occurring in the whole Mediterranean area,[63] but paid attention to the salinity and colour (denoting other ingredients) of water, using his balance to weigh its specific gravity at intervals along the Bosphorus, and comparing the results with his earlier findings at Split and Smyrna. He was also deeply interested in the tides. From a viewpoint in Galata he timed the tides daily between 21 February and 25 April. On 2 and 3 March he stood on the shore after dark, something normally forbidden, to satisfy himself about reports he had of the uneven periodicity at night of the rising and falling tides.

It was Montanari, he repeats, who taught him to investigate such problems, but his debt was not only to his teacher. It had origins in the longstanding preoccupation of his countrymen with hydraulic matters. The control of rivers and torrents and the techniques of irrigation were always important in the landscape familiar to Marsigli.[64] The route running north from Bologna to Ferrara is so flat, or was so taken for granted after centuries of use, that it could appear featureless to the long-distance travellers bound for transalpine countries or returning from them. People like Montanari and Marsigli knew better. They understood that the plain stretching to-wards the Adriatic, with the Appenine ridges receding on the westward side, was deeply deceptive. Flooding constantly imposed on the population an ordeal which overpowered resources in the small states of this part of Italy. Hardship, as well as fertility, derived from floods. Safety depended on embankments and water levels. The Venetians wanted to hold back from their lagoon the accumulating silt brought downstream by the Piave and Adige and the several channels of the Po, and in 1594 managed to divert one of the channels further south. But this affected to Po di Ferrara which the men of Ferrara wanted to keep navigable. They blamed the Venetians and at the same time Bologna blamed Ferrara: their river Reno, instead of draining into the Po di Ferrara as previously, meandered increasingly on a separate course eastwards to the sea, ruining more and more once valuable land. But the politicians had long since called in the academics. Engineer architects and clergy mathematicians joined forces on advisory committees in Bologna, Modena, Ferrara, Parma and Venice, and consequently a firm intellectual tradition in this part of Italy emphasised the importance of hydraulic study. Montanari, for example, notes at the beginning of his work on 'The Adriatic Sea and its Currents' that his entry into the service of the Venetian republic immediately induced him to examine the subject, which was so important to the interests of the state.[65] Domenico Guglielmini, who remained as professor in Bologna, responded to Montanari's encourage-ment by researches which culminated later in some very notable published work. In Ferrara a contemporary historian tells us that a new 'public lecturer' was appointed in 1675, father Lana, S. J., with an obligation to expound the problems of hydraulics. In 1679, 1681 and 1682 he refers also to the terrible floods of the Po, and to another plan to cut a new channel for the river Reno.[66] It was therefore no accident that Marsigli, in 1682 after his return from Istanbul, drew a sketch map to display a scheme which he had devised for saving the town of Cremona from flooding by the Po.[67] The whole environment in fact offers a clue to his development as a virtuoso. His first published work studied the Bosphorus. Later enquiries concerned the Danube. His most influential book – which he entitled the *Natural History of the Sea* – made him a respected forerunner in the modern science of oceanography. It was an important, if only a single facet of his career.

CHAPTER TWO

The Link with Vienna

I

Marsigli returned to Venice in the summer of 1681, after that first and easy journey through the Balkans. Coming from plague spots in a plague year he was detained in the lazaretto but his father meanwhile travelled from Bologna to meet him. Sadly, it was he who caught a fever and died in Venice. Marsigli took the body home for burial in November, shared in the settlement of family affairs, and his life began anew.

What should he do with it? What should the other members of the family do with theirs? The answers to be given, in due course, were not entirely conventional. It was the eldest son who entered the church. It was the youngest, Filippo, who married and continued the line of the family to which Carlo Francesco's children belonged. Our Marsigli by contrast never indicated after 1680 that he wished to or felt obliged to marry and set up a household. Instead Luigi Ferdinando Marsigli, now enjoying the assurance of an inherited income sufficient to maintain himself, and a share in the family apartments at home in Bologna to which he could always return, was a free man. He was free to pursue his preferences, limited only by the degree of his ability to decide what these were, by his luck, and by various restraints of the social and political situation in which he found himself.

Later he gave as a reason for his interest in mathematics at the age of nineteen, in 1677, his idea of becoming a soldier. He says that in 1681 Pope Innocent XI accepted his choice of profession, and that in the same year he told the Queen of Sweden that he was 'girding himself' for a military career.[1] Fantuzzi, his eighteenth-century biographer, concluded that after his father's death Marsigli made up his mind in favour of the calling to which he had always been attracted. It may be so; just possibly the beginning of his long period of military service should be viewed in this way. It assumes that the two years spent in Italy beforehand were something of a spree, enjoyed in the belief that there was no hurry before starting on serious business. In any case he would wait because there was peace in Europe at the time, if a precarious, armed peace. Yet it is more likely that he had no firm ideas when he left Bologna after Carlo Francesco's death except to multiply contacts, look for opportunities, and remain open to offers. He had a wonderful buoyancy, depending partly on an image of himself as someone with a gift for dealing with urgent matters in high places. It would be a never-fading dream for thirty years, but at this early stage he was simply aware that negotiations between Italian courts or governments were usually in the hands of a small circle of well-placed persons surrounding a still smaller circle of patrons. To that first group he was confident that he belonged by birth and education. The network of Italian principalities and republics of the time may have looked a feeble affair, of relatively slight account in the European state system after the peace treaties of the Pyrenees in 1659, but the relations between them still needed continuous mainten- ance or adjustment. For this purpose envoys and agents were needed; it was a possible field of activity for Marsigli. Across the Alps there were of course similar opportunities. Cardinal Mazarin, of Sicilian and Roman origins, was the glittering genius among Italian men of affairs who rose highest in the politics of seventeenth-century Europe, but the more mod- estly placed count Alberto Caprara (whom we have met) had been and would be an active diplomat in the Habsburg service, and there were other examples to follow. Marsigli in 1681, while perhaps contemplating a mili- tary future, was equally a would-be courtier or diplomat. Unfortunately, as a Venetian ambassador later commented, someone aiming in this direction learnt in his youth to be *umile, gentile, sofferente, lentissimo e dissimulante*,[2] and Marsigli never came near to possessing such qualities. He struck most people throughout his life as vehement, impatient and unsubtle. On the other hand it turned out that his ever-increasing knowledge, gained by travel and experience in eastern Europe, persuaded one or two great persons that here was a man who could be useful in their diplo- macy. They were mistaken; he was better as a soldier and commander, rising to respectable heights before his military career appeared to end in a crushing failure.

From Bologna he first of all paid several visits to nearby Modena where the reigning Duke Francesco II* – with whom his sister in England, the new duchess of York, corresponded affectionately – contemplated mar- riage. How would the republic of Venice regard this ruler's suggested marriage treaty with the Grand Duke of Tuscany's daughter? Marsigli offered his services as go-between, claiming excellent contacts in Venice. And in Venice he pushed and talked but the whole matter was soon dropped. He went on to Rome 'to revisit my cousins and friends', and would recall spending a part of every evening in cardinal Chigi's assembly.

---

* The Italian sovereign dukes of Mantua, Modena, Parma, Piedmont and Tuscany appear in these pages from time to time. So do the Imperial Electors of Bavaria, Brandenburg, Cologne, Mainz, the Palatinate and Trier, who had elected the hereditary ruler of Austria, Bohemia and Hungary as Emperor Leopold 1 in 1658.

Flavio Chigi, formerly the omnipotent nephew of Pope Alexander VII, remained an important politician in Rome. He had met Marsigli in Venice, and for many years continued to be his good friend. Two other influential mentors were Giambattista de Luca, a distinguished jurist who had become Innocent XI's datary and almoner, and Michelangelo Ricci, counsellor of the Inquisition.[3] Both were made cardinals in September 1681 when Innocent, after five years' rule, at last took steps to satisfy a mounting demand for promotions, and nominated to some of the vacancies in the college of cardinals.[4] Ricci was one of the ablest 'post-Galileans', a mathematician by training who was the valued correspondent of Borelli, Montanari and prince Leopold of Tuscany.[5] Marsigli had every reason to admire him, and they were brought together in assemblies sponsored by Christina.[6] In 1674 she had inaugurated a 'royal academy' in her splendidly furnished palace by the Tiber, not very far distant from the apartment in the Vatican where Pope Innocent (from 1676) led his utterly simple, unadorned existence. It seems that in 1677 Ciampini began introducing to her the members of his own gathering of virtuosi, who in 1680 and 1681 were busy observing the first of two famous comets in this decade. Their results appeared in the *Giornale de' Letterati* of which Ricci had been one of the original sponsors.[7] Marsigli says that he called on Christina at least twice a week at this period, interesting her in his chosen topics such as the Ottoman empire and the currents of the Bosphorus. His little treatise on the latter was addressed to the queen, and at the same time rather elegantly printed for Tinassi, who published several scientific works written in Rome in these years. He was also received by the Pope, and they discussed the prospect for Christian missions in Ottoman territory and the flaws of Ottoman government. Unfortunately Marsigli's continuing search for preferment did not prove successful. He had rivals or enemies. Otherwise a mysterious phrase of his, that 'cardinal Chigi advised me to go' in view of the 'emulation' in Rome, is hard to understand. He had a further audience with Innocent, who instructed his secretary of state cardinal Cibo to write to the nuncio Buonvisi at the Emperor's court, asking him to find something for the young man in Vienna.[8] This was one ploy. Then another attracted his attention.

For the second time a chance occurred of acting as a confidential agent. Cardinal de Luca, at this stage the secretary in charge of papal correspondence, was following a line of policy not favoured by cardinal Cibo, and sent Marsigli to negotiate in Venice. It seems a small matter, but associated with de Luca's instructions was a fresh general crisis in Europe. In the east, a long war in the Ukraine between the Ottoman and Muscovite powers had just ended. Istanbul seemed likely to deploy its forces elsewhere, in Hungary or Poland or Dalmatia. Emperor Leopold wanted above all to keep the peace in Hungary. But meanwhile in the west Louis XIV occupied Strasbourg and also Casale, the duke of Mantua's famous citadel in north Italy. Alarm in the courts of Germany was echoed in Milan by the Spanish governor. At Milan, surprisingly, resided the papal nuncio for Venice: he had left his post when the Venetians withdrew their own ambassador from Rome in 1679 in a quarrel with the Pope;[9] while the Pope was bitterly confronting Louis XIV over similar issues, refusing to accept nominations to church offices made by the state in either Venice or France. To a remarkable degree this and the other problems interacted. Renewed Ottoman pressure in central Europe encouraged the French government to make moves in Germany intended to weaken the Emperor. Leopold resisted, but also needed more foot and horse, fresh volunteers and recruits, to oppose the Turks. The governor of Milan feared a further French advance along the line of the Po, on which Casale stood; he tried anxiously to strengthen his own fortresses. French offers to Venice were therefore anticipated, in order to increase the pressure on Spanish Lombardy; and this was the reason why de Luca in Rome, more nervous than his colleagues, thought that the Pope's quarrel with Venice should be settled as rapidly as possible. Papal territory, after all, reached as far as the Po.

Marsigli was unlucky and perhaps unskilful in Venice.[10] His acquaintance with the former *bailo* Morosini paved the way for him at first, and he had serious discussions with Venetian spokesmen on the points at issue. Before long it became clear that the offers he made needed confirmation from Rome, but Cibo reproached de Luca for acting without authority and de Luca asserted that Marsigli was exceeding his instructions. Marsigli protested but his mission in Venice ended, and his reputation in Rome suffered. It really was time to look elsewhere.

To repair the damage, at least in part, he visited Milan and conferred with the nuncio there. He secured an introduction to the governor, count Melgar, to whom he aired his views on a different topic, the science of fortification.[11] One would guess that his readiness in sketching, plus a little mathematical competence, helped him to persuade Melgar of his understanding in such matters. With some audacity Marsigli offered to survey and report on defence matters. Accordingly he went first to Casale, where the new French garrison occupied the defences, and reported back to Milan.[12] Then he inspected the Spanish fortresses in the area, returning shortly afterwards with his proposals for improving them. What he earned from this work was a letter of recommendation to Borgomanero, the Spanish ambassador in Vienna. As the Habsburg interest everywhere was month by month increasingly under threat, with war imminent, he focused his hopes on the Emperor's service. He took the plunge as he saw his opportunity, whirling round north Italy during the autumn of 1682 to say goodbye to friends in Bologna, Padua, Venice and Milan – with a quick look at the flooding of the Po round Cremona, in order to offer his thoughts for dealing with it to the authorities – and went on his way via Domodossola and the St Gotthard pass.

This familiar route over the wall of the Alps hardly leads from Milan direct to Vienna. But Marsigli, as his future career would show, always travelled with an eye for pleasure and instruction. Intellectual stimulus had to go in parallel with business. On this occasion he admired Lake Como and took a short trip across Lake Lugano, like a modern tourist carrying with him a printed map of the Ticino region. Then he proceeded to draw for himself another map, showing the landscape which leads up to the St Gotthard and on the way looked for rock crystals.[13] This sketching of routes linked with a concern for geology would one day prove a normal feature of his style of travel. In 1682 he followed in the footsteps of Nicholas Steno, the Duke of Tuscany's scientific and medical adviser, who had visited the same district in 1671 and inaugurated the modern science of stratigraphy.[14] Marsigli was satisfied by a first peep at the subject and in due course reached Basle. From here he went through Alsace to Strasbourg and then faced east, going down the Danube from near Ulm as far as Vienna.

He gives his own account of the winter. He held several cards for the next round of his game, and played them one by one. The first was a note from cardinal Accioulli in Rome to the Capucin friar Emmerich Sinelli, bishop of Vienna, arguably Leopold I's closest adviser at the time. Accioulli, in Rome the official cardinal protector of the Capucins, had helped in persuading Pope Innocent to authorise the friar's elevation as bishop. Marsigli's second card was his letter from the governor in Milan to the Spanish ambassador, another influential figure at the court.[15] Sinelli and Borgomanero were generally in agreement on the main political problem of the hour, pressing Leopold to conciliate the Magyars and Turks while resisting Louis XIV with maximum firmness. Marsigli's third card was cardinal Cibo's letter from Rome to the nuncio, Buonvisi; but after the fiasco of his secret Venetian mission, begun without authority from Cibo himself, he apparently met with a chilly reception. Nonetheless the more friendly contacts were sufficient, and the bishop presented the young Bolognese noble to Emperor Leopold I. Ordinarily taciturn to petitioners and envoys, Leopold always took pleasure in speaking Italian, and this may have given Marsigli his chance. He referred to his wish to serve the Habsburg interest in the profession of arms, and played his final card. Just as he recommended himself in Milan by reporting on the defences of Lombardy, so the little tour through Alsace had given him a sight of the new French fortifications at Hünigen, Breisach and Strasbourg. He had composed a memorandum about them, adding a sketch map, and these he duly presented to the Emperor, 'the first things of mine he saw'. It was a fair beginning.[16]

Then, against his expectation, the course of events turned Marsigli abruptly round to face east again, a commitment from which he never wished to escape for twenty years.

II

The Ottoman army mobilised during the early months of 1683 and its various components assembled at Adrianople and Belgrade. At the same time many fortified places constituting the Habsburg defence, scattered across Hungary and Croatia, came under hasty review at the Habsburg court. Improvements were planned and it was realised that even Vienna itself might be vulnerable. In this context Marsigli appealed to his new friends, the bishop and the ambassador. They introduced him to Hermann, margrave of Baden, who presided over the main Habsburg military agency, the War Council. Baden welcomed volunteers as a matter of course, and sent him to the commanders responsible for defending the areas north and south of the Danube below Vienna. One senior officer was Aeneo Caprara, the Bolognese nobleman, who greeted his countryman 'politely enough, but not very warmly'. Another officer, Rüdiger Starhemberg, was cool (a statement possibly influenced by later feuds). But the Neapolitan Antonio Carafa encouraged him. He was also introduced to Lewis of Baden,* the young nephew of Hermann, and to count Rudolf Rabatta, who were both volunteers like himself, although Lewis enjoyed much higher standing at court than his brother officers. Soon the troops assembled at Caprara's quarters moved away eastwards, to cover different sections of a landscape merging into the no man's land which, still further off, merged into Ottoman held territory. At Györ (Raab), on one channel of the Danube, the river Rába flowed in from the south. Further down, at Komárom, the main channels of the Danube met again and were joined by the river Váh from the north. Györ, Komárom and these tributaries were the points and lines which Leopold's forces had to defend if the Turks chose to aim their main thrust up the Danube.

At this stage it seems that Caprara passed Marsigli back to Baden. The president of the War Council's deputy commanded at Györ, and here a place in the colonel's company was found for the newcomer. He learnt his drill as a musketeer, and in the course of a few months went up through the ranks, became a corporal, a sergeant, and began looking for a captaincy. An official in Vienna commented that 'for weighty reasons count Marsigli deserves help',[17] which suggests that he was continuing to develop his technique for recommending himself. He had examined the defence works at Györ, proposed improvements and sketched out a plan of the place which he sent to Caprara, who forwarded it to Baden.[18] Baden responded favourably by directing him to survey a much larger area south of Györ for which the Hungarian Palatine, Paul Esterházy, was responsible. Such journeys of inspection were hard going, the evidence about them is meagre, but Marsigli rapidly explored the ground in relation to the vast surrounding stretches of water and marsh. West of the Rába, what we know as the Neusiedler See covered a much larger area than nowadays. The tributary Rabnitz gradually soaked its way from the lake to the Rába. The terra firma between Rába and Rabnitz was virtually an island. Marsigli was ready by the time that Baden himself came out to Györ: he produced his maps and

* Lewis of Baden, Marlborough's colleague at the battle of Blenheim in 1704, properly Ludwig Wilhelm, remains Lewis here to distinguish him from Louis XIV.

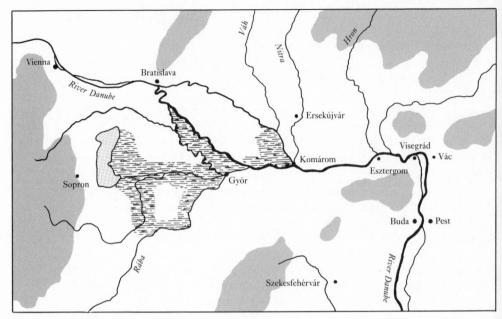

1 From Vienna to Buda, 1683–86

took part in discussions on the plan of defence. He considered that he knew accurately enough where impassable marsh aligned with the vulnerable strips of traversable ground. He held optimistically to the view that a defence was viable at this point, and his canvassing of Baden was tireless. A speedy journey back to Vienna won him a new assignment; he was to inspect the defences along the Rába as far upstream as the Styrian border. This followed on a proposal made by the leading local lord Nicholas Draskovich for strengthening the line of the river after a thorough survey had been carried out by a qualified person.[19] Marsigli did his best, preparing more reports and sketches, but returned in time to attend Emperor Leopold's review of his field army on 16 May 1683. The forces paraded on the plain by the Danube, opposite Bratislava, and for the occasion one extra volunteer was attached to Caprara's foot regiment. Shortly afterwards he was interviewed by the recently appointed commander in chief, Duke Charles of Lorraine. It ended with a rather cool dismissal, Marsigli thought, but almost immediately the terrifying emergency approached its first climax with reports of immense enemy forces moving fast through Hungary towards them, and Lorraine himself instructed Marsigli to go back to the Rába defences and collaborate with the Magyar leaders on the spot. He placed surprising trust in this stranger who was also a novice, but Marsigli had the advantage of not being German at a moment when the Magyars' dislike of German-speaking officers was manifest – after fifteen years of dispute between the Hungarian Estates and the court of Vienna – and deeply disturbing. He might win the Magyars' support. He might at least manage not to push them into outright defection.

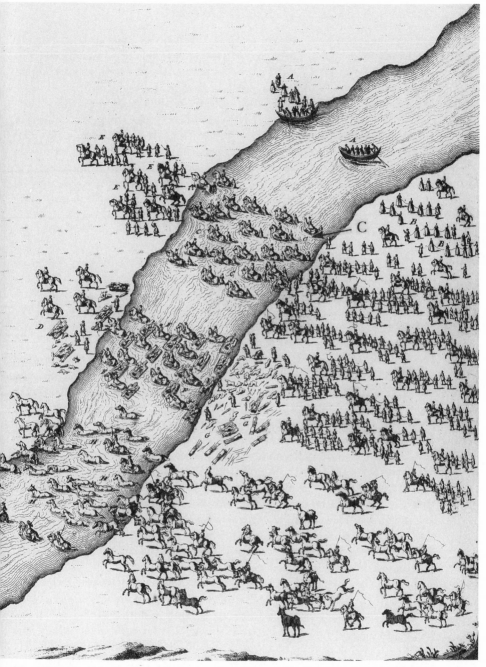

Marsigli captured by the Tartars: an engraving of Marsigli's sketch, to show the Tartars crossing a channel near the Neusiedler See with their supplies and booty, with weapons kept dry, and their men and women prisoners. He says that he was one of group C, with feet bound, and forced across the water by clutching the horses' tails.

Lorraine was mistaken in thinking that Draskovich and the neighbouring Batthyány lords would not go over to the enemy. Marsigli was mistaken in his belief that the Turks and Tartars could be stopped. He was soon trapped in a world of woods and water, his escort of dragoons dwindled to one or two, and the Tartars appeared to multiply by hundreds every day. Captured, he was lucky to escape with his life. As we know, he became a prisoner outside the walls of besieged Vienna. It must have been small consolation to realise that he had managed, in a surprisingly short time, to gain a footing in the Habsburg court and camp before Tartar horsemen cut him off from Christian Europe. The question was whether he would ever be able to repeat this promising experiment.

III

After the raising of the Turkish siege of Vienna, some believed that the expulsion of the Turks from Hungary would be as easy as it was desirable. Yet the campaign of 1684 proved a dismal affair almost from the start. Lorraine first moved down the right bank of the Danube, then withdrew and advanced along the other shore. He was nervous of enemy forces coming up from the south to support their garrison holding Buda, still the seat of Ottoman government in Hungary. At this point a successful engagement at Vác (Waitzen), where the river begins its great bend to the south, brought Lorraine close to the village of Pest opposite Buda. It was therefore necessary to decide for, or against, an assault on Buda itself. Starhemberg, the defender of Vienna, was opposed. Lewis of Baden, margrave Hermann's increasingly influential nephew, wanted to attack. Lorraine decided in favour of the bolder course.[20] Marsigli arrived on the scene after this decision had been taken but was certainly one of those who asserted that Buda would fall very quickly; one man said in five days, another six, and he said ten. In spite of the fortress on the hill and the walls of the lower town, Buda's defence works were reckoned poor and obsolete, without a ditch, ravelins or properly designed bastions.

So Marsigli was back! The wonderful escape from Bosnia, a spell of sickness in Venice, a speedy pilgrimage to Loreto to give thanks to Our Lady, and a journey as far as Florence, simply preluded his return to the Habsburg service.[21] Indeed letters had been sent as early as possible from Venice to Vienna to announce Marsigli's safe arrival.[22] They mentioned his broken health, his zeal for duty and gave some details of the defences of Buda, which he had gleaned there during his flight with the Bosnians from Hungary. Friends and relatives, he wrote later, could not keep him at home, so that by the end of June 1684 he had ridden over the Brenner to Innsbruck and then to Linz. Here he saluted Emperor Leopold and other members of the Imperial family, discoursing at length on his captivity and escape. In

Vienna he saw the president of the War Council, who hastened him on to Lorraine's quarters in Hungary.

Buda in 1684 successfully withstood a longer siege than Vienna in 1683. The army of Leopold and his allies at this stage lacked the numbers, expertise and organisation needed to take a large town on a site favouring the defence. Failure by artillery and miners to crack these defences sufficiently for an attempt by storm, was accentuated after a month by the rapid spread of sickness. Medical services were pitiably slight. Disagreement between Lorraine and Starhemberg, who commanded the infantry, made things worse. As for Marsigli, he was wrong about the siege but erred in good company. He acted as a technical adviser on the site, writing a number of detailed reports for the president of the War Council who remained in Vienna.[23] He relates, for example, how Lorraine sent him at an early stage to inspect the mines which were being laid under the Turkish defences on the north side of the town. Marsigli criticised the location of one of them: in his opinion it needed extending further under the defending wall, but stated confidently that he detected no sign or sound of countermining by the enemy. He used his phrases of Turkish to question Turkish prisoners. He pressed for action along the riverside, recalling that during his enforced stay in Buda ten months earlier he had become aware of the townsmen's and the garrison's dependence on water carried up from the Danube. Unfortunately neither the efforts of the engineers, nor a belated Habsburg move along the river front, nor the arrival of a large Bavarian force under Elector Max Emmanuel in September, altered the situation. More Ottoman troops approached and the besiegers withdrew. The Turkish commanders, in spite of substantial losses elsewhere in Hungary during the year, had scored a major success by repelling Lorraine from Buda.

While great men gave Marsigli a hearing, he wanted also status and emoluments.[24] A captaincy in the Dieppenthal regiment, promised at one stage in 1683, had been given to somebody else after his disappearance. The Emperor's recent offer of compensation for his ransom did not provide for the future. He now pressed Baden for further help, and wrote disarmingly that the command of a citadel like Esztergom (Gran), would suit him best. He offered to improve its defences, collaborate in similar work in the neighbouring strongholds, and maintain himself without cost to the court by relying on local supplies: he was aware, he said, 'of the methods which are used to raise contributions from the surrounding villages', a phrase which only hints at the harshness keeping the allied forces intact at the cost of the population of Hungary during the next fifteen years. Marsigli did not get Esztergom. There would be no such instant reward for the offer of faithful service.

Very primitive standards in 1684 and 1685, in certain parts of the Habsburg army, must explain why Marsigli so easily won a hearing from Lorraine and Baden. The troops in the field lacked the auxiliary resources in transports, munitions, tools, guns and personnel to undertake the siege of

Turkish forts, except by starving them out. The campaign of 1684 and the siege of Buda were a shambles; the soldiers and statesmen would learn very slowly what was needed in Hungary. Marsigli, having observed the Turkish military apparatus during the siege of Vienna, at least had the boldness to offer advice on engineering matters to princely commanders. It was they who too often thought of engineers and sappers as '*dise Canallia*', a phrase of Starhemberg's, the hero of 1683.[25] There is likewise little evidence that the government tried to transfer to the Hungarian front anybody with experience of siege warfare in the wars of the 1670s in Germany or the Low Countries. These things took their course slowly, and standards improved gradually. Marsigli refers to the Spaniard Antonio González who came, or was invited, to Vienna during the winter of 1684–5 and demonstrated the technique for manufacturing the improved mortars which Louis XIV's fleet had recently used with devastating effect against the Genoese.[26] González would be a much prized and highly successful gunner in Hungary during the following campaigns. More important, it seems clear that Marsigli's colleague Rabatta, appointed commissary-general in the spring of 1685, was one of the true architects of Habsburg expansion in the next few years. The increased powers of the commissary-general's office was itself a significant administrative reform, and Rabatta's death in 1688 was a misfortune for the Vienna government. He had been as efficient as possible in seeking to wring out essential supplies from the Habsburg lands for the use of the army.[27] Earlier, during the winter of 1684–5, it was Marsigli who appeared with González at the Arsenal in Vienna, where both were encouraged by Baden and Rabatta in bringing together a group of properly trained craftsmen in the business of gunnery.

He had returned after the siege of Buda feeling very enfeebled, and consulted Leopold's Bolognese physician, Pio Garelli, another of the Italian voices at the Viennese court. A long letter to Malpighi gave details of all the ills – his weeping eye, his injured right arm, his terrible stomach – for which Garelli treated Marsigli.[28] We hear also of his frenzied activity. He became all the more interested in gunnery after attending the Arsenal, and accordingly tried to study the elements of ballistics by carrying on a correspondence with the Duke of Tuscany's scientific advisers in Florence. He used his rudiments of geology and mineralogy to examine the metals required for casting the new ordnance, and collected samples taken from the Slovakian copper and iron mines. He even considered writing a study of 'masters of the art of fortification'. It soon disappears from view but he had learnt enough to improve his claim to be an expert on siegeworks. On this foundation his promotion in the years immediately ahead would be steady, if not spectacular. In 1685 he reported to Baden on the fortifications of Esztergom, Komárom and Visegrád, receiving payment for current – and some past – expenses. In 1686 he was for the first time described as an inspector, writing reports on the quality and defects of other engineers in the Emperor's service. By 1687 it was possible to draw up a list of 27 'engineer' officers in Leopold's dominions. A few were stationed in places like Vienna, Prague and Constance, but 20 were on the front in Hungary. Marsigli was no. 18 in this list, and the highest paid; no one else had such big allowances for additional staff and horses. He was described as an inspector of fortifications with the pay of a lieutenant-colonel.[29]

In January 1685 Marsigli argued, in writing to Malpighi, that 'study' and 'ordered reflection' were by no means alien to his profession as a soldier. They were necessary, hence his work on gunnery and fortification; but this winter of convalescence and addiction to military science has a surprise for us. Marsigli used some of his leisure to complete a literary trifle pleasantly remote from the needs of war. Having brought from Bologna to Vienna one of the manuscripts obtained in Istanbul from his friend Hezarfenn five years earlier, he now prepared for publication the original Turkish text and an Italian translation. Meninski, the great orientalist in Vienna, advised him. Accordingly, during the year the Habsburg court printer produced a pretty little volume containing both versions, with an exuberant title: *A Tipple from Asia drunk to the health of his Excellency Buonvisi, Apostolic Nuncio*.[30] This, Marsigli's second printed work, contained a discourse on coffee and its medical virtues, with an introduction describing his time as a prisoner during the great siege of Vienna when he spent critical days brewing coffee for all comers in a smoky tent. It is great fun, a miniature opus suggesting that the Roman nuncio's former disapproval of the author had now been mollified. From this date Buonvisi seems to have been in constant touch with Marsigli, of whom he reported approvingly in his despatches. It was a fortunate change of view because every new friend in high places mattered to Marsigli, in his role as a volunteer making his way in the Emperor's service. To keep a footing between Hermann of Baden and Lorraine, or between Baden and Buonvisi (who thought Baden useless), was difficult but essential. Rabatta, Caprara and Carafa, Italians already higher up the ladder, could help if they wished but even they had to reckon with one formidably hostile shadow across their path. General Rüdiger Starhemberg, as continually ill as he was truculent, was the dogged Austrian who considered Baden an ambitious fool and Lorraine a weakling. He disliked outsiders, and saw no grounds for respecting the judgment of Italians. When he opposed the plan for besieging Buda, a young Italian informed him that he had recently been inside Buda, and predicted its swift surrender if besieged. Marsigli was wrong, and Starhemberg was right. On many future occasions the first would advise in favour of aggressive warfare, while the other remained cautious or unenterprising. In due course Starhemberg succeeded Baden as president of the War Council, the permanent chief of the Emperor's military staff. Marsigli always regarded him as hostile, and this partly reflected the fact that he himself had found other patrons.

In 1685 Leopold's ministers and forces, and the personal fortunes of count Marsigli, prospered together. A new political framework in the 'holy alliance' with Poland and Venice, and the 'twenty years' truce' momentarily stabilising Germany, gave the Habsburg interest a firmer basis for its second campaign in Hungary. There was a spasm of nervousness over Louis XIV's intentions when the Elector Palatine died in May but a calmer appraisal of the position, and the arrival of French volunteers eager to fight the Turk, reassured Vienna. More troops reached the Danube from north Germany while the marriage of Leopold's only daughter to the Elector of Bavaria purchased the renewed service of his troops in Hungary for the coming campaign.[31] Pope Innocent sanctioned heavy ecclesiastical taxation, and with Rabatta as commissary-general the Habsburg regiments seem to have been better supplied than in 1683–4. Another problem was solved more by luck than wisdom. To Lorraine's great irritation, Leopold had agreed to the Elector of Bavaria's demand for a fully independent command over his own forces on the campaign. But Max Emmanuel, after his marriage, arrived late on the scene and left early. Starhemberg declined to serve. Lorraine had therefore a better grip on the entire force of the allies in Hungary than earlier or later. He was notably successful.

At first the court talked of a second attempt on Buda, while admitting that a sizeable Ottoman garrison was still intact at a point called Ersekújvár (Neuhäusel/Nové Zámky) a long way further west. However the allied forces moved out of their winter quarters in Moravia, Austria, Bohemia and Germany more slowly than expected, and during the delay the argument for turning a blocade of this Turkish strong point – lying north of the Danube, not far from Komárom – into an all-out siege and assault gradually prevailed. First things first: Ersekújvár before Buda. It was reckoned that once the siege was begun, the Ottoman field forces would probably try to relieve the place, either by moving from Pest directly towards it, or by marching past Buda to threaten Visegrád and Esztergom, the recently acquired Habsburg outposts south of the river. So Marsigli first received orders to try and strengthen the decayed defence works at these two points.[32] Lorraine arrived to see for himself, approved Marsigli's work,[33] and then crossed the water to take a sweep eastwards. He concluded that he could safely turn back and lay siege to Ersekújvár.

This hexagonal fortification was described by an English volunteer:

> The true ancient name of this place is Oyvar, though the Germans call it Neuheusel; it is a large Fort, and situated upon a firm foundation, though the Plain about is full of Moras, and Fenny Grounds, which makes the Town almost inaccessible, as its strength is invincible, having six Bastions lined with very good Stone work, without which is a vast Ditch of about ten foot deep, and twenty broad. The river Neutra is on the East side, not above a Pistol shot from it: on the South it has the Danube, at about two furlongs distance . . .[34]

Between 4 and 9 July Ersekújvár was surrounded with Habsburg forces taking over the western sector, troops from the Empire the northern, and the Bavarians what remained on the south and east. The approaches to the moat were dug with much more attention to professional detail than a year earlier at Buda. The batteries were heavier and the works constructed to protect the besiegers were more solid. Marsigli, delayed for a while at Esztergom, must have reached the scene shortly after this first stage of the action. Under cover of the batteries, the approaches being dug were coming close to the great 'impediment' of the moat. Marsigli commented:

> I was commissioned to discover whether it would be possible to get the water out of the moat, at least along some sections of it if not everywhere. Thanks to good guides and colleagues, and to the low water level in the river Nitra, I managed to produce a plan – which was carried out, though with heavy losses – for a 'cut' diverting water from the moat to the channel of the river.[35]

Contemporary accounts agree that the Nitra was low in July, in spite of the profuse spring rainfall. One pamphlet refers to the besiegers 'cleaning out' a channel linking the river to the moat, which suggests that the Ottoman garrison was accustomed to filling it as high as possible during the thaw, and then blocking the outfall. The besiegers tried to reverse the procedure, which proved difficult in the face of enemy fire and enemy sorties, but they did not actually have to make a new 'cut' to unstopper the moat. In either case Marsigli, with his hydraulic and hydrographic interest in the Po and Bosphorus, was certainly a man for the job at Ersekújvár, and there seems no reason for disbelieving his assertion that the commanders put him in charge of a venture which he understood better than anyone else.[36] The English narrative explains that Lorraine ordered the Hanoverian troops to cut the channel, so that on 19 July 1000 men were at work; the water went down as much as five feet. Later it was no more than knee deep in places. Accordingly, near two of the bastions the besiegers began building dams and traverses to help them to get across to the main wall and its outworks. They were well supported by the artillery. Then, near the end of July, what some had feared duly occurred. The Ottoman forces approached Esztergom 60 miles away across the Danube. Lorraine and his generals had to decide whether to sit tight or divide their own force between Ersekújvár and a second front. Would a relieving army, as at Vienna and Buda earlier, defeat or harass the besiegers to the extent that they could only retreat?

Lorraine divided. He moved with almost 40,000 men, including cavalry, towards his pontoon bridges across the Danube above Esztergom. Caprara with 15,000 continued to bombard Ersekújvár. At both points Lorraine scored a success. Esztergom held out and the Ottoman commander was beaten off. Ersekújvár fell. In the final assault Marsigli played an active role until he was hit by a flying stone, so that he fell from the top of a breach and into the moat.[37] His convalescence was spent in Vienna while the reports of victory elsewhere flowed in. Habsburg consolidation along the Danube below Vienna was complemented by successes in Upper Hungary, and by expansion into Slavonia from Croatia. A year of distinct personal achievement for Marsigli reflected the advantages secured in the campaign for the empire he served. Moreover if the often meagre surviving evidence allows us little relief from his role in this warfare, which he took with the utmost seriousness, little by little Marsigli's scholarly dreams and instincts will be found breaking a way through his strenuous military life.

IV

His winter quarters were in or near Sopron, that ancient town south of the Neusiedler See, and he spent part of the time carrying out an order from his friend the commissary-general.[38] This concerned the inspection of a certain captain Lamboyne's company of miners and siege workers, which Rabatta believed to be scandalously incompetent. He relied on Marsigli's expertise, he wrote, and asked him to help in making recommendations after a thorough enquiry. Every member of the company was to answer a questionnaire; some questions dealt with an individual's personal record, others with the terminology and usages of siege warfare. Marsigli's report roundly condemned the men as an ignorant lot, formerly tailors, tinkers, wigmakers and plasterers, although the officers replied with what sounds like a reasonable show of knowledge. The result was an order cashiering the captain and a majority of his men. In practice this meant that they were enlisted into other units, doubtless taking with them no great love for Marsigli. At the same time he himself satisfied the efficient Rabatta, also Lorraine. A little later Marsigli was promoted as a general inspector of siegeworks. He belonged to Lorraine's staff and depended on him, but his responsibilities were greater than before, with an entitlement to higher pay. He was now closer to the generals' councils of war in the field, and the risks of giving offence in high quarters were greater too.

He had also been sent out on another survey. Not far from Buda and still in Turkish hands, the town of Székesvehérvár (Stuhlweissenburg) enjoyed high symbolic importance for the Magyars as the burial place of their kings in pre-Ottoman days. The Turkish commanders valued it as a redoubt from which they could threaten any besieging force at Buda, and accordingly the question was raised in Vienna whether an assault on Székesvehérvár ought to precede a second siege of Buda. To judge from Marsigli's remarks, someone suggested that a winter attack on the smaller stronghold would be feasible and he was sent to look at the approaches. Nothing came of the idea, but it merged into the customary annual wrangle at court – as the winter drew to a close – on the strategy to follow in the coming campaign,[39] taking into account the Elector of Bavaria's insistence that he should enjoy an independent command. The two sovereign princes, Lorraine and Bavaria, were respectively the Emperor's brother-in-law and son-in-law. One had been thrust out of his territory by Louis XIV but was the senior Habsburg commander. The other ruled unchallenged, raising troops which were indispensable to Leopold, and his supporters now proposed that the Elector should be given his chance to besiege Székesvehérvár while Lorraine kept the Ottoman field army at a safe distance. Others argued for a siege of Buda in the campaign ahead, with Lorraine in command of all the forces that the Emperor could muster. An interest formed by Hermann of Baden (now generally opposed to Lorraine), Lewis of Baden and Max Emmanuel appeared to be winning the struggle, and on 18 May Leopold indicated that he wished the Elector to advance on Székesvehérvár while his brother-in-law covered the operation.

Nonetheless talks continued.[40] Whatever the Elector's pretensions, he was inexperienced. He looked a risk. Whatever the nuisance value of Székesvehérvár in Turkish hands an attempt on Buda promised much more, and the forces available were stronger than in 1684. Stratmann, the Austrian chancellor, evidently took this view and Hermann of Baden at length gave way. A fresh decision by the Emperor was taken to military headquarters by Stratmann himself, and further plans were laid. The objective was now Buda, but the Elector was given his independent command: one army under Lorraine moved along the right bank of the Danube, while the Elector and Lewis of Baden took another down the left bank as far as Pest, and crossed the river there. Only later was an agreement reached that Max Emmanuel should direct his attack against the southern sector of Buda's defences while Lorraine laid siege from the north. Honour was saved by this division of responsibility between the sovereign commanders. By then Marsigli was Lorraine's man. He no longer considered Hermann his own supporter and patron, having taken sides against him in the party struggle. A champion of the siege, involved with the leading troops, he would play an unexpected role in the aftermath of that remarkable allied triumph.

The English engineer Jacob Richards describes how forces under Lorraine began digging on 21 June 1686, at a distance of 500 yards from the not very substantial walls of the lower town.[41] Using what remained of the old siege works, of two years before, they started at a bath house close to the Danube with a trench parallel with the wall, and then began a number of angled approaches leading towards it. A battery was mounted and started firing, and made a sizeable breach. On the 24th, says Richards, 'a party of grenadiers were commanded to discover the Breach, if it were accessible, who reported it was', so that during the following night Lorraine's principal officers in this sector, Souches and the prince of Neuburg, organised attacks at two points. One of them was this breach, through which the besiegers entered the lower town. It was a necessary first step, a heartening early success. Other accounts refer to the digging of approaches towards the breach, and to an attack starting at ten o'clock in the evening.[42] Marsigli relates that he worked throughout the preceding night and day, on Neuburg's instructions, in order to bring the trench as close as possible to the foot of the wall. He was then struck by another flying fragment of stone and rather seriously hurt: his phase of active service in the siege of Buda had ended early.[43] After about ten days he was well enough to become an alert spectator from Lorraine's quarters, which had been moved inland from the Danube to higher ground further west. He watched the progress of the siege during the next five weeks[44] while Habsburg, Swabian, Brandenburg and Hanoverian troops tried to batter their way through the defences dividing the lower from the upper town, defences which were an integral part of the Ottoman stronghold. He knew only by report of the progress of Max Emmanuel's advance on the southern, steeper side where the citadel stood.

A desperate Turkish resistance continued to block successive assaults. Unlike the siege of 1684 the allied force gradually grew stronger. Fresh troops arrived from other parts of Hungary and from Transylvania; they were no longer pinned down by the continued tenacity of the enemy elsewhere. The grand vezir's relieving army, on the other hand, was not strong enough to break through the allied defences – the 'circumvallation' which on this occasion Lorraine and Max Emmanuel had taken care to construct in a wide semi-circle round Buda, in order to protect the besiegers. This gradual tilting of the military balance against the Ottoman interest did not yet look obvious; the eye of faith, rather than insight, was needed to see it. After the failure of a combined attack on 25 August at every possible point of entry, arguments for breaking off the siege seemed all the stronger, and it was decided to shift responsibilty back to the Emperor by asking for his decision. When he received the request in Vienna, Leopold – as in 1684 he had sent Hermann of Baden – instructed his chancellor Stratmann to visit the camp outside Buda and resolve the issue.[45] Stratmann arrived on 1 September to find that another council of war had been held the day before; after much anxious debate there was a decision in favour of attempting a general storm. The arguments were repeated in Stratmann's presence, and he was able to give an assurance of the Emperor's willingness to accept the commanders' view on this crucial military problem. Interestingly enough, after the discussion a colonel Vecchi wrote to Baden, giving his opinion that the allies would have done better to satisfy themselves with a siege of Székesvehérvár, not Buda.[46] It is also interesting to hear Marsigli: he was summoned to general Rabatta's quarters where Stratmann had his lodging, and 'I gave my advice on the question whether it would be better to attack at once or to wait'. As usual he urged immediate action. Lorraine then asked Marsigli to discuss the issue with the officers actually engaged in the fighting. Some, colonel Vecchi among them, evidently thought it pointless and dangerous to continue the siege. Marsigli describes how Lorraine listened to the debate and, according to his custom, said very little while he 'stroked his nose between finger and thumb',[47] while he himself appears as an expert witness whose opinions were certainly considered worth hearing. His introduction to Stratmann proved important. It was the first time (so far as we know) that the two men met. The Austrian chancellor found a useful servant. The Italian won a new patron high in government, prepared to support him against Baden, whose backing he had lost, and against Starhemberg, who would never be his friend.

The grand assault on 2 September ended the Turkish resistance in Buda. It was over by 5 o'clock in the afternoon. The buildings and people of this battered city were given up to plunder by the victorious troops. Their search for booty, and for prisoners worth a ransom, became a matter of individual initiative. Discipline was suspended, and only after an interval did a settled military government take charge of the place again. During the phase of maximum disorder Marsigli reacted with singular originality, and it was indeed one of his most felicitous moments. For him the prizes in the lottery would not be cash or captives, but manuscripts.

His various narratives of what occurred during the sack of Buda differ on points of detail, but probably he thought first of adding to the small collection of oriental texts which he had assembled at Istanbul in 1679–80 and carried home to Bologna.[48] Finding his way to the principal mosque of the upper town, formerly the Christian church of St Stephen, he hurriedly explored. He looked into one apartment, where soldiers had already left the decapitated body of a Moslem teacher, but in another he discovered a number of Islamic writings. These were later found, naturally enough, to be theological and legal in subject matter, but the interest or value of such pickings could hardly be established on the spot. Marsigli was no doubt satisfying his collector's itch, and elsewhere he took what proved to be Turkish administrative records. Like many fortune hunters in Buda that day, he thought next of the Jewish quarter.[49] Jews, better treated in the Ottoman empire than in most Habsburg towns, had valuables. Jews, the besiegers claimed, had played a part in the Ottoman defence of Buda. Now they were a quarry for the Christian troops who killed some, selected others for future ransoming, and seized their goods. Marsigli likewise entered Jewish houses and synagogues and carried off Hebrew codices to be added to his haul.

Next he moved up the hill to the medieval castle buildings, most of them battered and ruinous. He had another mission here, inspired by misinformation.[50] At this period many people like Marsigli, if they enjoyed any tincture of learning, credited the old Christian kingdom of Hungary with a matchless treasure once preserved in Buda, the famous library of king Matthew Corvinus. The fate of his manuscripts, written and illuminated by the best Italian masters some years before the Turks overran the country, lost from view during an apparently permanent Ottoman conquest, remained uncertain. Common opinion in western Europe, earlier in the seventeenth century, held that many of these masterpieces had not been despoiled by the Turks or taken away: they were still in Buda. The Turkish authorities meanwhile barred the collection to those who begged to see it. Neither point was true. The manuscripts had long been dispersed, and around 1670 one or two travellers were admitted to those quarters in the old Buda palace where they hoped to find this vanished treasure, only to be disappointed. Marsigli, unaware that even Emperor Leopold's librarian had made one such useless tour of inspection, still hoped to find lost master-pieces of Italian origin as he wandered through the ruins so recently in Turkish occupation. According to one of his narratives he came to a 'second courtyard', and saw on the right a room with shreds of old colour still visible on the vault above, while on the floor were heaps of shovels, hoes, axes and other mining tools, interspersed with old books and rolls. In the neighbour-ing room he saw also ten wooden chests, leather-covered and broken, containing more books. From all these he took a few written in Latin for himself, but with the help of some soldiers – on the prowl as he was – he collected the rest together, and informed general Rabatta. Some time later the commissariat took steps to have them listed, packed and sent off to Vienna. In due course a catalogue appeared of about 600 items brought from Buda.[51] It was a fairly undistinguished antiquarian remnant, not con-sidered of great interest by Marsigli's contemporaries. What he had unearthed came from a library belonging to the medieval royal chapel in Buda. It had nothing to do with the splendid humanist collection housed by the kings of Hungary in the same set of buildings. He would reach the mistaken, depressing conclusion that the 'Corvina' had been much overrated.

From a different point of view that day's work appears as a weighty gesture in his life. His acquisitive love of books and manuscripts of all sorts in all circumstances, even in the smoking aftermath of a siege, was accentuated. His education as a bibliophile moved a stage further. A great public library in Bologna was the ultimate beneficiary of this growing enthusiasm.

V

By 1687, after the taking of Buda, the Habsburg empire in Hungary was at last expanding, and the Ottoman empire shrank. Most of the hill country immediately north of Buda, and the whole region between Lake Balaton and Buda (Székesvehérvár excepted) changed hands. So had Szeged and Pécs, south-east and south-west, while Habsburg commanders made their first entry into Transylvania. The Sultan's field forces, sent from the Bal-kans to recover lost territory and strongholds or rescue places under threat, were since 1685 pinned down further south. On the Danube's right bank they could not expect to move unopposed beyond the Drava. They still held Osijek (Eszek), from which Sultan Suleyman the Lawgiver's famous old timber bridge crossed the river and surrounding marsh (on the Drava's northern shore), giving access to the usual route to Buda. Parts of the bridge were unusable in 1687. Between the left bank of the Danube in this latitude

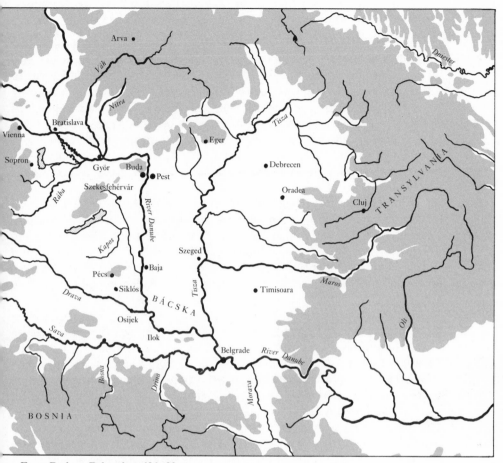

2   From Buda to Belgrade, 1686–88

and the southward meandering of that other great tributary the Tisza, lay a
no man's land, the 'Bácska'. Turkish forces, if they crossed over the Danube
at Belgrade, had just a chance of lunging through this waste to rescue their
isolated garrisons much further north in distant Oradea (Nagyvárad/
Grosswardein) and Eger (Erlau).

It was for a new grand vezir Suleyman (sometimes called in old sources
'the Sly'), after those blamed for the loss of Buda had been removed, to
decide what the Turks should do. By masking his intentions until as late as
possible he could choose on which side of the Danube to make his main
thrust, either directing the Sultan's army to the bridge at Osijek, or crossing
the Danube nearer Belgrade to penetrate the Bácska. For their part, with
increasing confidence in his superior resources, Leopold's advisers felt able
to adapt their plans as the campaign developed, engaging the Turkish forces
as these tried to penetrate one area or another.[52] Indeed they had to wait.
Beforehand, as all concerned well understood, their invincibly civilian

Emperor would be required to offer the usual inducements to his commanders before they willingly began serious work. A strong dose of ritual bargaining was essential. So Leopold offered the Elector an independent command on the left bank of the Danube, while Lorraine remained as the Emperor's 'general-lieutenant' on the right bank. It was hoped that if the two were sufficiently amenable they could decide later whether Lorraine needed more, or less, support. It was known that Max Emmanuel's second-in-command, Lewis of Baden, highly ambitious and highly influential, wanted to keep the Bavarian forces as far apart from Lorraine as possible.

The political struggles at court can be viewed at a humbler level. Marsigli described in a memorandum (of 27 March) some of the less happy aspects of his new promotion as inspector general of fortifications.[53] He owed this to Rabatta's and Lorraine's support, and Hermann of Baden treated him accordingly as a client of his rivals. He was not permitted to see the War Council's list of its engineer personnel while Baden appointed another inspector, La Vigne, with the same rank and responsibilities. La Vigne and a brother of his dominated the miners and engineers. They befriended Lamboyne, whom Marsigli had cashiered at Sopron. They declined to assist him in his preparation of plans for the re-fortification of Buda. Then matters took a more sinister turn. Marsigli claimed that Lamboyne had forged a letter to incriminate him, and threatened violence. He asked for his arrest, and claimed that Baden was deflecting the course of justice by protecting Lamboyne. So he appealed to the Emperor. Leopold graciously appointed a committee to which Marsigli submitted his memorandum. This contained more than a whiff of overloaded vehemence but sheds a little extra light on the elements of patronage at court and in the army, by linking together different levels of the factional struggle. Marsigli was using his own grievances to join the battle to discredit Baden, while bidding for support from the politicians appointed to hear his case against Lamboyne. They included Stratmann and the newly appointed Bohemian chancellor, Ulrich Kinsky. Upholding his appeal,[54] these two were ready thereafter to agree with Leopold in regarding Marsigli as a valued, confidential servant. With such a triumvirate behind him, he would have nothing more to fear from Lamboyne, Hermann of Baden or the War Council's secretariat. In 1687 that relative security was not yet confirmed, and during the summer Baden declined to authorise his pay or give him instructions. Marsigli retorted with another appeal to the ruler, this time for honourable dismissal to be transmitted 'through some other chancery than that of the Council of War'. The Emperor duly received the highly wrought Italian letter. Its author was paid his arrears through Rabatta, and assigned to Lorraine's staff for the campaign ahead.

Marsigli, like the generals, at once exchanged the acrimonies of the court for those of the camp. He also entered what was for him a new world extending beyond the walls of Buda to the south and, during the next ten years, would be studying it more carefully than any of his contemporaries. Those river landscapes, the water and marsh of the Danube and the plains on either side, became an adopted country.

When he presented himself to Lorraine in Hungary at the end of June the original plan of a divided allied command had been modified. For reasons which are not entirely clear, although a shortage of supplies east of the Danube was one of them, Max Emmanuel accepted an appeal from Lorraine to join him.[55] The grand vezir and the Ottoman forces were reported to be on their way from Belgrade to Osijek. Lorraine wished to confront them as soon as possible with his maximum strength, and Max Emmanuel agreed to collaborate in spite of Lewis of Baden's dissatisfaction. The Bavarian and other troops under the Elector, instead of continuing their march south, were brought westwards to the left bank of the Danube in the neighbourhood of Baja, in order to cross it. At the same time Lorraine, on his side of the river, had summoned Marsigli and ordered him to go ahead immediately towards the Drava, and advise whether the troops could move directly on Osijek.[56] It was understood that sections of the causeway over the marshes remained intact, and that the Turks had been repairing the damaged bridge. The river Drava itself – as wide as the Seine at Paris, the French officer Villars remarked a little later – might be crossed by using the boats already ordered downstream from the upper Drava in Styria. Such were the considerations for Marsigli to bear in mind. But, quickly exploring the terrain and the causeway until he came within range of Turkish gunfire, he reported back that a crossing of the river at this point was inconceivable in the face of any serious opposition. It is possible, as Marsigli hints, that Lorraine intended to bamboozle the enemy by his show of activity opposite Osijek. More probably he wanted, and hoped, to get over the Drava as quickly as possible before the grand vezir arrived. He soon began moving most of his troops westwards. A few detachments were left beind, in order to deter the Turks from crossing by the bridge. Max Emmanuel's army, having made its way over the Danube, was some distance from Lorraine's, but catching up fast.

The Elector and the duke of Lorraine met on 13 July at Siklós, a small stronghold not many miles distant from a favourable approach to the Drava, and during the night of the 18th many troops of both commanders got over the river using the boats and rafts brought down from Styria. Resistance was slight. Marsigli played some part in designing defences for a new bridgehead at this point. A general advance was organised, and a few days later the allied army emerged from a difficult tract of watery ground and scrub to approach Osijek. Unfortunately the main Ottoman force had arrived in time and was awaiting them. When observers such as Marsigli scouted ahead to examine the enemy's defence through their glasses, they could only report that the grand vezir's advisers clearly appreciated the lessons of last year's struggle for Buda: the entrenchments, the 'circum-vallation' protecting the Ottoman troops, which in turn protected Osijek,

8 The battleground of 1687: from the large map of Hungary published in Vienna in 1709. It shows clea[r]
the marshes on the left bank of the Drava and along the Danube, and was the work of J. C. Muller, w[ho]
would become Marsigli's principal assistant in Hungary.

were well contrived and probably solid enough to resist an attack. A day's skirmishing confirmed this view, and Lorraine then made his famous decision to withdraw the army back to the bridgehead, and return over the Drava to the very region from which he had started moving three weeks earlier. It was an extraordinary setback. The retreat was well managed but the evidence suggests that Lorraine himself had little idea what to do next. Afterwards it was somewhat easier for friendly observers to conclude that he lay cannily waiting for his opponents to blunder. The wonderful Christian victory of Nagyharsány (Berg Harsan, 'the second battle of

Mohács'), a struggle on the grand scale, had by then set everything to rights.

Marsigli describes his own share in the complication of manoeuvres during the first week of August. The allied troops (now north of the Drava again) were withdrawing eastward towards the Danube while the Turkish command – having used the patched traverse over the water from Osijek – were likewise filling up the triangular space between Drava and Danube, using swarms of light horsemen to harass the enemy but without allowing a formal engagement to develop. They stripped the country of its meagre supplies. A large Ottoman camp was at the same time placed on a secure site protected by swamp, and for almost a week the grand vezir wisely refused to be tempted out of his lair. Food and stores for the allies were running short. Lorraine, Max Emmanuel, Lewis of Baden and other senior officers met to discuss their problem.[57] It was necessary to stop the Turks recovering such places nearby as Siklós and, more important, Pécs. It was necessary to obtain fresh supplies, or to shift as many men as possible to better stocked country. Above all, it was necessary to win an engagement somehow, somewhere, in order to revive morale and recover reputation. Lorraine accordingly looked at a scheme for a new fortified point on the Danube near Mohács, with bridges laid across the principal channels which were here separated by a large island. On this 'Mohács island', one of the largest below Buda, he wanted additional defences dug and built. The bridgehead, held by a comparatively small force, would pin the enemy down in the Drava region while most of the allied army withdrew, either north towards Székesvehérvár – still in Ottoman hands and well worth taking – and Buda, or over the Danube to besiege one of the surviving Turkish strongholds further east. It was Marsigli who found himself instructed to work on the details of such a plan for strengthening Mohacs and making a viable route across the great river. It was the first occasion that he confronted on this scale the problems of Danubian topography, the labyrinthine windings of different channels, the network of islands large and small, the marsh, the fluctuating water level – and with no usable maps. A tour of inspection quickly demonstrated that it would be easy to protect Mohács; but a traverse across the island and pontoons over the many waterways was out of the question. Dense woodland and deep marsh appeared as barriers too difficult to surmount in the short run. A safe, swift crossing for both foot and horse from Mohacs to the other shore did not exist, and could not be improvised.

The prelude to the battle of Nagyharsány remains a mysterious affair.[58] Undoubtedly on 9 August Lorraine, Max Emmanuel and others conferred and decided that the army should move to the left bank of the Danube. It was also thought necessary to demolish the fortification at Siklós and Pécs, before the Turks reoccupied them. Yet on the next day, 10 August, Lorraine began moving more and more of his main body of troops westward towards Siklós; the Bavarians and others under Max Emmanuel started to follow them; and they did so although a few picked detachments would have been enough to level the defences at Siklós and Pécs. There had been a change of plan, and either Marsigli's findings or some other twist in subsequent discussion led the generals to drop the idea of getting across the Danube.

Tempted by the signs of this withdrawal the grand vezir finally decided, or was forced by colleagues to decide, that he ought to risk an engagement en masse. Early on 12 August the Turks came out of their well-protected camp to assail the troops nearest them, those under Max Emmanuel's command. They were checked with some difficulty. Lorraine continued for several hours to move his own men still further west, away from the higher ground separating him from Max Emmanuel, but at length he summoned them back. Even his vanguard, which included Marsigli, was recalled to the fringe of the great battle. Max Emmanuel and Lewis of Baden had refused to disengage, even when they appeared to have a fair chance of doing so, and thereafter the combined allied forces first gained the upper hand and then a complete superiority. Their unexpected triumph, totally reversing the gloom felt at the retreat from Osijek, and the tremendous losses they inflicted, disturbed profoundly the morale of both military forces and civil population on the Ottoman side. This Christian victory,[59] this Ottoman defeat, soon fired the starting pistol for a revolution which spread from Ottoman army headquarters (by then near Belgrade) to Istanbul.

For Marsigli the sequel was equally interesting. Statesmen in Vienna and commanders in the field now began to think of exploiting their new military advantage at widely separated points. Lorraine sent a sizeable expeditionary force over the Drava into Slavonia but determined for his own part to move east. He had his eye on the whole terrain beyond the Danube, from Ottoman strongholds holding out in the plains to a broad tract of Transylvania beyond the Tisza. The Habsburg command and commissariat viewed this principality as a land relatively rich in food, accommodation and timber, inviting occupation for acceptable winter quarters; but it was first necessary to cross the Danube.[60] So once again Marsigli was usefully employed, setting up a new traverse over the river about 25 miles north of Mohács to reach Baja on the left bank. A crossing was feasible here, at the other end of the elongated Mohács island, and he acted as Lorraine's chosen agent in supervising the work needed to bring the troops, especially cavalry, across the several channels. It was discovered at Baja that essential supplies from Buda had not yet arrived, and Lorraine made the best of an unwelcome delay by a diversion south along the most easterly arm of the river. Halting at a spot opposite the confluence of Drava and Danube,* he sent Marsigli forward again to examine whether troops could possibly get through the marsh and thicket to the main channel. But any notion of ferrying the forces

---

* He reached Szonta (Zunta) which is shown on the map, p. 50 above.

across the river again was set aside by Marsigli's emphatic, negative report. Lorraine returned to Baja, the stores arrived, and his men were soon moved east across the plain to Szeged on the Tisza. His tireless scout, our Marsigli, again went ahead to discover what he could about routes and landmarks, and inhabited or habitable places. He found few of any of these, but it was useful experience in fresh country.

The rest of the year 1687 brought other landscapes to his notice.[61] Like all Habsburg generals before him, Lorraine entered Transylvania from the north-west, so that Marsigli left the plain beyond Debrecen to move into areas where a rather different medley of races and languages confronted him; if he had known it, his decade of intermittent dialogue with 'Dacia', and with the Szeklers, Saxons and Romanians was beginning. At the first point held by a Transylvanian garrison Lorraine sent Marsigli forward with a small detachment to look around and parley. The opposing commander proved to be a Genoese, putting on a bold front in the presence of his men but happily speaking Italian *sotto voce* to Marsigli. The fort was handed over immediately after a token attack began. The much more important town of Cluj (Kolozsvár/Klausenburg) likewise accepted a Habsburg garrison as soon as Lorraine threatened to use his not very formidable field artillery. An easy, speedy advance ended when Prince Michael Apafy and the Estates of Transylvania agreed to Lorraine's demand for winter quarters and supplies. A permanent Habsburg presence in their country seemed assured. By the beginning of December the Emperor's troops were moving to their new billets, while most of the generals and staff went west and homeward. Marsigli was delayed by another special mission. Eger, with an Ottoman garrison, still held out in northern Hungary, and it had been suggested that a person 'speaking some Turkish' would be useful in bringing the commanding officer to see reason. Marsigli duly crossed the lines to brief him on Turkish losses at Nagyharsány and the Ottoman army's subsequent demoralisation and rebellion. The Sultan's prudent servant thereupon left Eger with his wife, retinue and personal goods while Habsburg units entered the place. Marsigli accompanied a messenger bearing the good news to Bratislava. But even then, he scarcely paused for breath.

VI

The close of a wonderful year of conquest had brought the Emperor on one of his rare visits to Hungary. He was in Bratislava to preside over a fundamental constitutional event: the coronation of his elder son Joseph as king of Hungary was intended by the Habsburg ministers, although not by the Magyar nobility, to reflect in its formulae the recent momentous transfer of power in central Hungary from the Sultan to the Habsburg ruler. The legislation they wanted was complete on 25 January 1688, but in the background Leopold, Lorraine and the nuncio Buonvisi were already deep in discussion of other matters. Greeting Marsigli on his arrival in the town, they sent him immediately on a mission to Rome.

Leopold wanted urgently to persuade Innocent XI of the need to maintain and indeed increase the church's financial contribution to the Turkish war. Any sum to be taken from the famous reserve fund in Rome, which was earmarked for crusades against the infidel, depended absolutely on the Pope. Clerical taxation in Italy, Spain, or the Austrian Habsburg lands for the same purpose depended, in varying degrees, on his agreement. For business of such significance the Habsburg court relied on a number of spokesmen. They included the 'Austrian' group of cardinals led by cardinal Pio, and the nuncio writing from Vienna (or Bratislava). Marsigli, as Leopold's personal 'orator', was intended as another voice in the chorus to urge the case.[62] Not everyone considered him a good choice; the setback in Rome in 1682 was not forgotten. The Emperor evidently thought otherwise, while according to Marsigli's account the Pope treated him with great cordiality in three separate audiences. At the first of these Innocent forgave the young man immediately for any past indiscretions, and Marsigli described the recent campaign in Hungary and prospects for the one ahead. Probably he helped in winning for Vienna the handsome papal subsidy of 1688. He also carried out a more formal commission by expressing Lorraine's gratitude for ecclesiastical revenues assigned by Innocent to his son Charles. As a sort of echo to this another matter was raised, but not in Innocent's presence. The Pope's nephew Livio Odescalchi, immensely wealthy but denied any political influence by his uncle's rigorous principles, approached Marsigli. He offered him money and the authority to negotiate on his behalf in Vienna. His objective, perhaps given extra definition by Marsigli in conversation, was the gift or sale to him of a principality in newly conquered Hungary. This young but ageing Roman grandee did not intend to be forgotten.[63]

The Emperor was satisfied when the traveller returned to Vienna and reported. The two evidently had a long discussion, with questions and answers about the Pope's health and the tenor of his views on the questions of the day. Marsigli then prepared to join Lorraine's staff for the coming campaign – after an excursion to Slovakia* – but Lorraine fell ill.[64] He was helpless for many weeks, so that the politicians visualised Max Emmanuel taking sole charge of the forces in Hungary, to his own satisfaction and the disgust of others. He would restore unity to the command, but at a heavy price for those who enjoyed Lorraine's patronage. Before the problem could be resolved, for Marsigli and for everyone else, deeper concern was felt in Vienna over another great personage stricken with illness. Plainly Max

---

* He went to Arva, in the Tatra mountains, a patrimony confiscated from Imre Thököli, the Magyars rebel and patriot then fighting with the Turks. The possible sale of Arva to Odescalchi had been mooted, and Marsigli carried out a survey.

Emmanuel's elderly uncle, Max Henry, the archbishop-Elector of Cologne, was at last on the point of death. His succession, recognised by all as a crux in the political struggle for ascendancy in western Europe, was now open. On one side stood Louis XIV's candidate as the ruler of Cologne, cardinal Fürstenberg, already nominated as coadjutor with a presumptive right to succeed Max Henry. On the other was the Wittelsbach family interest with its own candidate, Max Emmanuel's brother Joseph Clement, joined with the interest of every power opposed to France. One of the Emperor's measures, when he heard of the old man's grave illness, was to send Marsigli post-haste back to Rome.

Again he had formal or what he called 'public' business. It concerned another piece of useful preferment to be begged from Innocent for Lorraine's son. Again there was more important 'secret' business, the attempt to commit Innocent to oppose Fürstenberg's candidature at Cologne in the most positive manner possible. Cardinal Pio, the official 'protector of Germany' in Rome, had so far failed to get the Pope to pronounce on this point with anything like the forthrightness he usually displayed in his differences with Louis XIV. Innocent had not used his influence to block the appointment of Fürstenberg as coadjutor; there seemed a chance that he would continue to stand aside, and do nothing to influence the Cologne chapter's proceedings when Max Henry died. It was hoped in Vienna that Marsigli, the confidential agent, might have better luck than Pio in bending the Pope to favour a policy on which the Emperor and the Elector were agreed. Certainly, his recent audiences in Rome had been fruitful and friendly.

This second visit in 1688 proved to be his last essay in Italian diplomacy. His own account of it, written many years later, has a certain nostalgic splendour as if he were looking back with tinges of regret at the next long phase of his life spent outside Italy. The Pope received him in audience, and began by responding to the news of Max Henry's death: he did so with sorrow, adding criticism of the dead man for disregarding certain papal instructions. Marsigli's studied oration against Fürstenberg was then followed by another response, solemn in tone but inconclusive, as if Innocent sought to wrestle with the problem of equating his decision in the matter (which might lead to a great war between Christian powers) with the will of God. He declined to consider Leopold's proposal, explained by Marsigli, for a defensive league of Italian states against Louis XIV. He refused even to discuss another request from Lorraine for extra preferments for his son. The audience ended, Pope Innocent reserving his judgment on each one of the more serious topics raised.[65] Afterwards Marsigli continued to urge the Emperor's case with the Roman statesmen, while Innocent's instructions to his nuncio in Cologne veered more sharply against Fürstenberg. He pronounced the Wittelsbach prince, Joseph Clement, a suitable candidate for election in spite of his youth, without giving any equivalent encouragement to Fürstenberg's supporters. Marsigli was justifiably pleased by what he could discern of the general bias of papal policy. At a further private

audience the talk turned from western Europe to the Turkish war, and both
men encouraged one another in their common desire to see Ottoman Belgrade besieged and taken as soon as possible. Marsigli described at length
the territories still under Ottoman rule, building for all he was worth on
memories of his Balkan journey eight years earlier. Innocent repeated his
plea that these lands should be freed from the tyranny of Islam, but parried
yet another petition for extra funds.

While attending to the work of his mission Marsigli enjoyed himself. He
visited Odescalchi, gave him a demonstration of the methods used in firing
off modern types of mortar and cannon, and discussed once more the
purchase of a title and territory in Hungary. He went sometimes to pay a
compliment to Queen Christina who on one occasion said that, valuing his
high qualities as she did, she wished to offer Marsigli a very honourable
employment. He answered that he could not leave the Emperor's service,
and the queen seemed tactfully to turn to a different subject. Walking up
and down, he wrote, past big tables laden with open atlases, she asked me
questions about Turkey, Hungary, and the navigation of the Greek
islands . . . and next day he learnt that the commission in her mind concerned a fantastic and impossible plan for naval warfare against the Turks.
Then he took leave of the Pope in a final audience, and was offered a career
in Rome if ever he chose to return to Italy. Marsigli reasserted his preference for a place in Leopold's army, and departed with the customary
blessing. On the way back to Vienna at the end of July he spent two days in
Bologna; it appears that he took away with him some of his early geological
notes.[66] It proved to be a last visit home for twenty years. He had made
his choice.

By the time he reached Vienna Max Emmanuel had left to take command
of the army, with which it was intended to besiege Belgrade.[67] Lorraine,
although apparently over the worst of his illness, still lacked the strength to
participate. Yet for both men the prestigious character of this enterprise was
overpowering. Neither could bear the thought of the other's interference,
let alone of his triumph by conquering the place. Lorraine in Vienna
suffered in spirit as in body while on 28 July Max Emmanuel buoyantly
took control of the forces at Petrovaradin on the Danube, only 50 miles
from Belgrade, a rendezvous much further south than had been possible for
Habsburg commanders in any previous year.[68] Marsigli meanwhile reported
to Stratmann on his recent mission; and to Lorraine, who complained of
Innocent's coldness towards his son's petition while the Wittelsbachs received full papal support in the business of Cologne. But Marsigli could not
bear to sit still as the season for military operations came nearer. He asked
for and received instructions to join the army. Riding away like mad, 'in
four days and four nights I went from Vienna to the outskirts of Belgrade,
to the amazement of the whole army'. He had the best of reasons for
hurrying: to reach the defences of Belgrade the besiegers would have to
cross the Sava, and Marsigli believed that this sort of move, which involved

deciding precisely where and how to move the troops over the river, securing the pontoons and protecting the bridgehead, was a part of his expertise.
It would give him an opportunity to shine and do good work. Besides, he
now had leverage with Max Emmanuel to whom he could report on his
handling of the Cologne affair in Rome. Unfortunately he was too late. The
forces were across the Sava when he reached it and digging their approaches
to the main defence works (8–12 August).[69] The Turks, after trying to burn
down a goodly number of buildings and removing by boat anything of use
or value, had left a relatively small garrison in the citadel. Soon it became
clear that the siege would have every chance of success, on one condition:
heavy artillery was needed to breach the walls. A decisive attack was delayed
until the siege train, still coming slowly down the Danube, arrived from
Buda. After twelve tense days of idleness the big guns arrived on 24 August,
and 150 more boats were floated into position to construct an extra
bridge for the attackers. By this time, further down the river, Smederevo
(Semendria) and Orsova were in Habsburg hands. A strong expeditionary
force led by Lewis of Baden was outside Brod, a long way up the Sava and
poised for a raid deep into Bosnia.

   None of this directly affected Marsigli who was soon given work of a
significant and delicate nature. Everything had so far gone well for the
Elector when news arrived, like clouds on the horizon, that Lorraine, in
spite of continued ill-health, was on his way to Belgrade by boat from Buda.
Leopold had weakly agreed to this.[70] Max Emmanuel expressed anger to the
council of officers who feared the gravest embarrassment. If we can believe
count Öttingen-Baldern, colonel of a Swabian foot regiment, the army
welcomed the report of Lorraine's journey, which made matters worse.[71] A
compromise was essential and the new Habsburg commissary-general,
Antonio Carafa, undertook to mediate. Summoning Marsigli he entrusted
him with a mission to Lorraine, to suggest that the duke should leave the
neighbourhood of Belgrade immediately after paying a formal visit to the
allied camp and siege works, and then take command of the cavalry (with
any available foot) at a convenient distance, in order to guard against enemy
attempts to relieve the Ottoman garrison in the citadel. Such an arrangement simply echoed what had been suggested to the two commanders
before the Elector left Vienna, but the difficulty remained of persuading
each of them that the other would abide by it. A boat and crew were put at
Marsigli's disposal, and he was taken up the Danube to intercept Lorraine.

   At sunset on the third day of his journey, somewhere between
Petrovaradin and Ilok, he encountered Lorraine, who lay in bed as his craft
moved down the stream. A salvo of gunfire, salutations between the two
men, and a halt by the shore followed. A sad discrepancy between the great
personage's wishes and his feebleness of body becomes plain enough from
Marsigli's sympathetic account of their discussion. The offer of a subordinate role at a distance from Belgrade, while the assault was being launched,
seemed an unbearable affront to Lorraine. His independent command of

the cavalry, not merely to protect the besiegers but also to sweep further south into the Serbian hinterland – a notion examined earlier in Vienna[72] – was more honourable but looked at the time an unlikely project. Marsigli talked on, doing his best to state in conciliatory language the case for Carafa's plan. Lorraine protested again, but finally paused: then, 'violently twisting himself in bed, he took hold of the rope which hung from the frame above, to help him getting up', and expressed agreement with what was proposed in order (he said) to show the greatest possible devotion to the Emperor's service.[73] Marsigli returned down the river to confer with Carafa, who came to meet Lorraine at Petrovaradin. Peace between the princes seemed assured, thanks to deft mediation.

Below Petrovaradin is Slankamen, also on the right bank, facing the region where the Tisza enters the Danube. It is a world part sky, part water, part the flattish plain stretching from Slankamen towards the Sava which flows in from the west. Across the Sava was higher ground on which the citadel of Belgrade stood. Lorraine, as he approached Slankamen, apparently talked to Marsigli of getting fortifications built to guard the mouth of the Tisza, and then again of a plan for the general advance of his troops into the Balkans after the fall of Belgrade; but such feverish determination took him only a few miles further. His visit of inspection to the siege works, the cursory interview with Max Emmanuel, the speedy departure to a separate encampment well removed from the scene of action, all passed off serenely.[74] Three days afterwards, the artillery having done its work, the assault took place, and the siege ended on 6 September after a Turkish defence which had been far less sustained than at Buda in 1686. Max Emmanuel, enjoying his personal triumph to the full, returned homeward at once. Far too ill to take up an active command in the field, Lorraine also left.[75] Marsigli, for his part, had attended him until the day of the final storming at Belgrade. Given leave to be present he viewed the attack as a mere spectator, but then stayed behind for several weeks to work on plans for refortifying the city and citadel. A touch of fever ended the campaign for him, and he too went back to Vienna. It was time for a pause and recuperation.

VII

The years from 1680 to 1688 offered Marsigli a series of fresh starts. We have watched him to the age of thirty, looking out for a path to eminence either as a soldier of fortune or the envoy of princes. There were setbacks and mishaps but one element in his activity remained constant after entering the Habsburg service. This was the search for effective patrons in the hierarchy of the court and government at Vienna. By great good fortune he early found favour with Emperor Leopold, a usually passive and hesitant man who was also an autocrat by inheritance. Leopold happily employed him on personal business, and acted as a benevolent protector when Marsigli's enemies pressed him too hard, even if he never took the initiative in promoting him. At the next level our careerist had to play a risky game, and it was not at first easy to be sure that a transfer from Hermann of Baden's patronage to Lorraine's would turn out to be the right tactic. The doubts about Lorraine's health soon posed a worrying problem and Marsigli looked for as much extra support as possible from Stratmann and Kinsky, the two Habsburg chancellors; in this context he never refers to Königsegg, the Imperial vice-chancellor of this period. His relations with Max Emmanuel and Lewis of Baden, the two German princes, were cordial but distant; while neither Caprara his countryman, nor Carafa the Neapolitan commissary-general ever offered him real assistance. If Marsigli survived with credit this phase of the great war, and its attendant stresses at court, he was evidently judged useful as a roving engineer and staff officer, or a confidential envoy speaking Italian plus a smattering of Turkish. A respectable future in the Emperor's service seemed assured. He clearly enjoyed one priceless advantage. Without dependants, he could pay for himself with funds from Bologna if an official salary or allowances were slow in coming or were withheld. That point, his personal finance, never worried him to the extent that it worried many others.

Historically, one thread in the disordered fabric of events in which Marsigli found himself involved is of great interest. When Buda fell in 1686 the chances of a permanent Habsburg domination further south visibly increased. As scout, engineer and transport officer who took part in the campaigning to master this region, Marsigli undoubtedly looked with professional attention at the main physical feature before his eyes, the Danube with its several channels flowing south, the highway for manpower and for supplies and a barrier too often deflecting the manoeuvres of rival armies. Gradually, by close observation in the course of his duties, a sequence of working models or pictures was formed in his mind. In 1687 he had become familiar with the river above and below the mouth of the Drava, from Baja as far down as Ilok. In 1688 his mission from Carafa to Lorraine took him from Slankamen to near Ilok and back, and he examined attentively the site of Belgrade in order to produce plans for rebuilding the defences. His drawings of the place, which demonstrated what could be done simply and cheaply, or what would be more costly and elaborate but more secure, were duly offered for inspection to Leopold during the winter.[76] In addition, while Marsigli remained with Lorraine in the cavalry encampment below Belgrade, the idea of an autumn campaign in Serbia had been discussed. Such a scheme accorded with the high hopes already expressed in Rome and Vienna for a final reckoning with the Ottoman empire of Islam. Marsigli consequently began to interest himself in the topography of a new area, in which the course of the Danube below Belgrade became the baseline. He drew a map showing the Morava basin to the south, and the river

Drina (which flows into the Sava) far to the west. He later described this as his 'first ideas for a map of Servia . . . to guide the duke of Lorraine's suggested march to join prince Lewis, but his illness put a stop to it'.[77] Indeed, he deplored what actually occurred: the allied commanders, instead of moving into Serbia after the seizure of Belgrade, were returning limply home laden with spoil. He wanted them to plunge ahead to take advantage of the Turkish disarray, and was no doubt reckless by comparison with such a prudent commander as Lewis of Baden, who emphatically turned down a suggestion from Vienna of the same date, that he should extend his raid over the Sava by moving his men deeper into Bosnia or even Dalmatia, considering that it would lead to the 'total ruin' of his army.[78] Marsigli, for his part, never resisted the lure of more distant landscapes, in Danubia or the Balkans.

CHAPTER THREE

The World of Danubia
1688–90

I

An overwhelming victory against the Ottoman forces in south Hungary, the occupation of Transylvania and the capture of Belgrade, in 1687 and 1688, looked at the time like startling events. For a hundred and fifty years the Ottoman government had been dominant in the whole region. Now it was gone. In the opinion of many observers the stage was cleared for a new act to begin, with as yet unfamiliar scenery to be set in position by the victorious power. The coronation of Joseph symbolised the change. Every advance into Transylvania, Slavonia, Serbia and Croatia further extended the effective range of Habsburg authority but its theoretical claims, as kings of Hungary, stretched beyond those areas. For optimists even Constantinople now beckoned, the city of the Christian emperors. On 15 January 1688 Sultan Mehmed IV was deposed by his own troops in the aftermath of their Hungarian defeat. The new Sultan, his brother Suleyman II, authorised the departure of an embassy to the Emperor with instructions to announce his accession, and these envoys after many delays reached the neighbourhood of Belgrade when the city fell. It was a convenient assumption in Vienna that they came to offer negotiations for peace,[1] and they were escorted slowly forward into Austria.

Yet future events in the east obviously depended, if to a degree hard to estimate at the time, on the diversionary impact of a new war in western Europe. Leopold was just then being forced to break with a line of policy which had worked well enough in the past five years. The peace or 'truce' maintained in Germany since 1684 allowed the forces of the Holy Alliance, of the Emperor, the Poles and the Venetians – with much assistance from the German princes – to advance confidently into the frontier lands of the Ottoman empire. In the second half of 1688 French pretensions in the Rhineland at length became intolerable, further endangering many interests strongly represented in Leopold's court, such as the rulers of Baden, the Palatinate, Cologne and Lorraine. His consequent decision, to make a new alliance with William of Orange to resist the French, was reached when there were reasonable hopes in Vienna that a victorious peace with the

Turks could be signed.[2] None of the Habsburg politicians, apparently, argued that a pacification of the eastern front was a condition to be satisfied before engaging in war with France, although Carafa and Kinsky maintained that military needs along the Danube deserved priority. The view that renewed western warfare made peace with the Turks essential was at first loudly canvassed, but was not in the end accepted by Leopold.[3] It seems that he could not have refused to join the opposition to Louis XIV without unthinkable losses of prestige and influence in Germany. Yet the negotiations in 1689 with the envoys Sulfikar and Mavrocordato, in which Ottoman conditions for peace looked totally unrealistic, proved sterile. Leopold and his statesmen were unwilling to end a sequence of stunning victories in Hungary with an inglorious compromise, by which they would hand back a large part of what had been won by conquest.[4] Those most anxious for a treaty failed to allow sufficiently for the encouragement which the outbreak of war between Leopold and Louis XIV gave the Turks, who expected easier terms than would have been possible earlier. Even so, it is a remarkable point that the Vienna government now committed itself to campaigning in areas so distant from each other and from Austria itself. The Emperor's generals would soon be reporting back to his ministers from the Rhine, north Italy, the Iron Gates of the Danube, and Macedonia.

There was intense discussion in eastern Europe at the end of 1688 on the possible effects of the Ottoman recession. For example, in Transylvania both rich and poor were under the thumb of Habsburg troops for a second winter in succession. The soldiers squeezed out supplies in order to live at the expense of an economically decaying region, accustomed during the last twenty years to fairly remote Turkish control. Prince Michael Apafi was too weak and his son and heir too young to play an active role. A Transylvanian delegation had been in Vienna since 1686, but always offered concessions too late to the Habsburg demand for sovereignty; as the military presence in their country grew stronger, more concessions were demanded. The commander at Sibiu, the ubiquitous Carafa, made it clear that he favoured a fully autocratic government in which the old Estates would lose their political and ecclesiastical privileges. This was not an attractive case-study of the effects of Leopold's triumph, and it cast a warning light eastwards. News travelled readily from the ancient Saxon towns in the Carpathian valleys to Bucharest. Here, prince Serban Cantacuzene of Wallachia had died on 9 November 1688. He too had recently sent a mission to Vienna in order to discuss the relationship of the two courts, and it was a sign of the times that the boyars of the country proceeded to choose a new prince without referring first to the Sultan. Rather surprisingly they chose, not the son of Cantacuzene, but Constantine Brancoveanu, his nephew; the struggle of the factions had been feverish, and the defeated leaders fled for shelter to Transylvania. At Vienna the Wallachian deputation found itself representing a new ruler who avoided committing himself to the Habsburg interest, preferring to remain in touch with the Sultan's court and wait a while.

Prince Constantine was a politician to his fingertips. He was intent on resisting Habsburg pressure if Leopold's theoretical and historical claim on Wallachia threatened in practice to limit his own power, or if Habsburg commanders on his border made fiscal demands no less harsh than the old Ottoman extortions, or indeed if they encouraged his opponents in Bucharest itself. He had also to reckon with church problems, then giving rise to anxiety almost everywhere in south-east Europe. Whose church, it might be asked, and what church? As the Turks retreat or weaken, men realised, not only the Emperor but the Pope advances. Soldiers of one and clergy of the other were entering Slavonia with their predominantly Orthodox populations. They were entering eastern Hungary and Transylvania with their Protestant ascendancies together with Orthodox and Catholic minorities. They were approaching other Orthodox peoples in Wallachia, Bulgaria, Serbia, and Bosnia. For the population of this entire area it was important, and very difficult, to guess what the defeat of Islam and subjection to Catholic rulers temporal and spiritual might mean, whether it was good news or bad. One response would be for the diverse Christian interests to try to group together, in a common design to destroy a long-resented Ottoman and Islamic supremacy. Another was for Orthodoxy to stand on guard, mistrustful of the old Catholic enemy who would gain most by the defeat of Islam, and to appeal for help from Orthodox Muscovy. Messengers and envoys (travelling great distances) peddling these two points of view were active during the winter of 1688–9. A third tactic, intuitive for the masses, was to do nothing while doggedly waiting for old preferences to come to terms with a novel political framework appearing after years of warfare.

In 1689 a Catholic bishop was appointed to the ancient diocese of Dakovo. It covered the recently conquered land of Syrmia (or Srem), the eastern tip of Slavonia situated between the Sava and Danube. He had, as suffragan or assistant, someone named Longin Raić who came from the Orthodox monastery of Hopovo in the Fruška Gora hills of the same region, a warm supporter of the Habsburg cause. A brother, Job Raić, was another Orthodox monk willing to adopt the Uniate compromise between Orthodoxy and Rome, keeping the old rites and the liturgical practice of the Greeks while recognising the Pope's supreme authority. In November Job undertook to persuade a large number of Orthodox churches on both sides of the Danube to follow his lead. Meanwhile, in the nearby town of Pécs, north of the Drava, the Jesuits had begun work as the effective champions of a strongly Catholic interest. While some Serbs became Uniate, a powerful and uncompromising Roman missionary impulse was also strong. Both groups confronted a population generally mistrustful of the new Habsburg regime, which was identified with a church stained by the darkest reputation in Orthodox notions of past history.[5]

The Raić brothers were influential in their own region. Another pair of brothers, with a much wider potential sphere of activity, bore the celebrated name of Branković, rulers of medieval Serbia. George Branković and his brother Sava were members of a family possessing a good deal of wealth and influence in the seventeenth century in south-east Hungary.[6] In 1656 Sava moved from his bishopric at Jenö (Ineu) to another at the more important centre of Sibiu in Transylvania. Here he did his duty as a good churchman by resisting the dominant Calvinist party of local lords and pastors, and by seeking to protect a Romanian, Wallachian element in Transylvanian Orthodoxy, which the court and clergy of Bucharest patronised from a safe distance. George Branković meanwhile worked for the prince of Transylvania as an agent in Istanbul. He visited Moscow. He visited the Serbian patriarch at Peć (a town deep in the Ottoman territory of south Serbia), from whom he obtained a cautiously worded attestation of his descent from the old native rulers of his country. He appeared also in Vienna in 1683 and again in 1686. Leopold conferred on him the respectable title of 'Imperial Count', indicating that by the time of his second visit the war was bringing Branković closer to serious politics. A leader with a name to rally the Serbs, who peopled both sides of the Danube in its middle reaches, could be useful to the Austrian command. He could also be dangerous if he pushed his claim as a legitimate prince. Aware of this ambivalence the pretender and the Habsburg authorities stood cautiously on their guard, waiting for the next campaign against the Ottoman to begin. Branković looked for help to the new ruler of Wallachia. From a refuge in Constantine's domain, he began to organise a following which would recognise 'George Branković II, by the grace of God and lawful succession hereditary despot of all Illyria, great Lord of Upper and Lower Moesia, prince of Hercegovina, duke of Syrmia, etc.'

The Serbian patriarch of Peć, Arsenius III, was playing a different but related role.[7] The Sultans had endorsed the claim of his predecessors to act as father and chief of the whole Serbian people, and he tried to extend it by tactics both agile and cautious. At Peć, in 1688, he was in a situation of the greatest difficulty. The Ottoman provincial government had broken down after the recent revolution, and he found himself plundered and fined by the Turks. From over the hills the Venetian authority on the Adriatic littoral offered a prospect of liberation, at a price which looked likely to involve more power for the Roman clergy, with whom the patriarch normally kept up a guarded but suspicious friendship. One of them was Peter Bogdan, Catholic archbishop of Skopje who – like George Branković – boasted of his ancestors, asserting that they had once been princes of Macedonia. Another was Raspassan, a Franciscan described as Bogdan's vicar, who enjoyed considerable popular influence: he, 'Father Thomas', wanted above all the liberation of his countrymen from the Turk, and appears to have overlooked or played down ecclesiastical distinctions between Orthodox, Uniate and Catholic which others emphasised.[8] They were not overlooked by, and mattered profoundly to Arsenius, who had already joined with the prince of Wallachia and the Greek patriarch at Istanbul in sending an envoy – the archimandrite Isaiah – to Orthodox Moscow to plead urgently for assistance.[9] In the early months of 1689 they waited for an answer and meanwhile it was impossible to foresee whether the Turks, in the campaign ahead, would lose control completely or on the contrary tighten it again in the Balkans. However, in August an Ottoman officer arrived in Peć, with orders to take the patriarch as a hostage to Istanbul.[10] Arsenius escaped, and from a refuge in Montenegro negotiated with the Venetian governor-general in Dalmatia. His acceptance of Venetian protection 'under the ensign of St Mark', as the governor-general expressed it, seemed possible.[11] As some observers realised, his change of front would cause instant alarm in the neighbouring republic of Dubrovnik, where the senators feared the imperialism of Venice, collaborated with the Habsburg agent in the town, and still remained discreetly in touch with the Ottoman court.

Like the archimandrite, another churchman on the move at this time was Antonio Stefanov, a Bulgarian Franciscan and a bishop.[12] He championed the small Catholic community in Bulgaria (with a focus at Ciprovets) which had risen against the Turks and suffered defeat earlier in 1688. From a refuge in Wallachia, Stefanov would be making the journey to Vienna on three occasions in two years, in order to ask for help.

At scattered points on the Balkan map, therefore, secondary figures manoeuvred for position and tried to exert some leverage on the greater powers. There are few signs of either Habsburg or Ottoman statesmen accepting the possibility that the subject peoples' interests could affect the combat between their two empires. The political system of the Sultan's government never envisaged a notion of tactical concessions, calculated to induce stronger support from subject princes or peoples in defending its empire. Vienna was a little less rigid, but viewed the issue primarily as a transfer of territory and sovereignty from the defeated Sultan to the victorious Emperor. That transfer, once made good by conquest, was confirmed by the claim that the kings of Hungary had reigned and ruled in the Balkan principalities. Leopold's due right, by inheritance and conquest, overshadowed a whole cluster of negotiations at this date with princes and pretenders, who tried to claim their own authority over subject populations in south-east Europe. On the other hand it was agreed that statesmen need information about unfamiliar or unknown tracts of country: why not, someone suggested in Vienna, why not ask count Marsigli?

II

Early in 1689 he was sent on a special mission, and told to report on two problems: the features of the country known as 'Syrmia', and its alignment with 'Bosnia'. The specific terms of a possible peace treaty with the Turks, still to be negotiated with the Turkish envoys now in Vienna, naturally depended on answers to this sort of enquiry. On 6 February Marsigli was writing from a tiny settlement on the Danube 60 miles above Belgrade, between Ilok upstream and Petrovaradin further down.[13] He had survived a terrible journey, he said, all snow and with horses hard to find anywhere. He had also completed his reconnaissance, which took him across the wooded heights of the Fruška Gora and over the plain as far south as the Sava: it brought him to the firm conclusion that the Emperor must insist on holding Bosnia as the price of peace with the Sultan. His argument asserted that the security of Slavonia – between Sava and Drava, one of the largest new territories recently won for Leopold – depended on the occupation of Bosnia south of it, just as the security of northern Hungary depended on the permanent control of Transylvania. If raiders could cross the Sava from Ottoman strongholds on its southern shore, the defence would have to rely on an unruly population of irregulars, 'heyducks' and 'hussars', who were in any case likely to hinder any commerce by river between Belgrade and Styria. Yet such a trade route offered many advantages by comparison with the alternative itinerary, which passed through Zvornik and then across difficult upland country before reaching the Adriatic. Another section of Marsigli's screed discusses areas of which he then knew very little: 'Russia' or Rascia, a country west of the river Morava; 'Bulgaria' which Leopold was entitled to claim as king of Hungary; and Thessaly which belonged to Bulgaria. He judged all these worthy of a place in the brave new Habsburg empire, and imagined its boundary extending as far as the Aegean coast.[14] He reserved his view of other possible frontiers on this occasion, subordinating wider and wilder considerations to his main plea: to take and keep Bosnia. He mentions another topic, one likely to impress Leopold. Marsigli believes that he had seen the uncorrupted body of John of Capestrano, the heroic and saintly Franciscan who died at Ilok in October 1456 after inspiring a successful defence of Belgrade against Sultan Mehmed the Conqueror. The miracles associated with John, the legends and controversies about the fate of his tomb and its contents after the Turks sacked Ilok early in the sixteenth century, and the seventeenth-century agitation to have him canonised, help to explain why Marsigli was delighted by such a discovery.[15] It symbolised perfectly Leopold's achievement in turning back the terrible tide of Islamic conquest after more than two centuries of Catholic failure. At the same time he advised due caution in dealing with this marvellous relic. If it were too brusquely carried off from its Orthodox guardians he warned that depopulation would occur in what was in any case a far too thinly peopled area. He criticised the Catholic clergy on the spot who failed to do their duty in admittedly difficult conditions, and by contrast he welcomed the idea of a well-organised mission led by the Jesuits. Syrmia needed a Catholic reformation, but religion appears in his account as the most sensitive and least tractable local issue.

He wrote two more reports on Syrmia, addressing them to Livio Odescalchi in Rome.[16] Negotiating the sale of a fief or principality in Leopold's expanding dominion to the Pope's nephew still looked an attractive

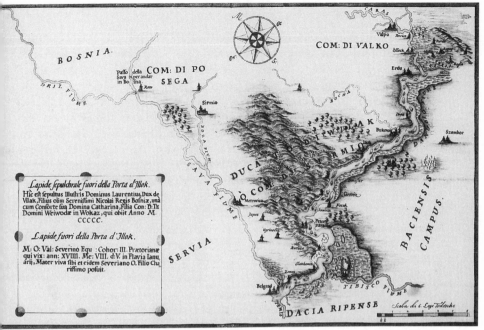

Within the map:

BOSNIA.

Paſſo della
Saua ſperandar
in Boſina

COM: DI PO
SEGA

COM: DI VALKO

Lapide ſepulchrale fuori della Porta d'Jllok.

Hìc eſt ſepultus Illuſtris Dominus Laurentius,Dux de
Vllak,Filius olim Sereniſſimi Nicolai Regis Boſniæ,unà
cum Conſorte ſua Domina Catharina,Filia Con: D:Tẽ
Domini Weiwodæ in Wokaz,qui obiit Anno M.
CCCCC.

Lapide fuori della Porta d'Jllok.

M: O: Val: Severino Equ : Cohor: III. Prætorianæ
qui vix: ann: XVIIII. Me: VIII. d:V. in Flavia Ianu,
arij ,Mater viva ſibi et eidem Severiano O. Filio Cha
riſſimo poſuit.

SERVIA

DUCA

BACIENSIS CAMPUS

DACIA RIPENSE

Scala di 6 Legi Todeſche

Marsigli's view of Syrmia: he submitted copies of his drawing both to Odescalchi and the Emperor, no
doubt expecting them to take pleasure in the Latin inscriptions he had copied at Ilok, one medieval and the
other Roman. His siting of places along the Danube is generally correct. His notions of the river Sava and
its tributaries are by contrast guesswork.

Marsigli's view of the western Balkans: a second drawing offered to Leopold (May 1690).

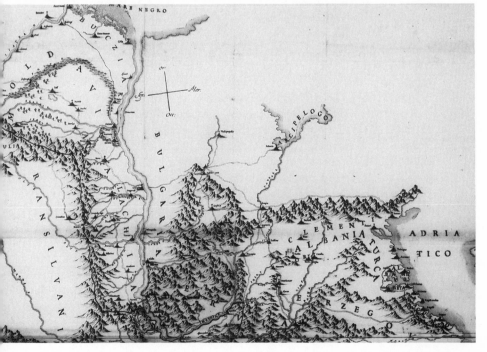

scheme and Marsigli had received encouragement from cardinal Kollonich, president of the Hungarian treasury, and from father Ederi, S. J., one of the clergy round Leopold. He now reported glowingly to Odescalchi on the historic past and future economic promise of the 'duchy' of Syrmia. Adding a sketch map[17] he explained his ideas in some detail. He hoped that the new duchy would extend from the Danube westwards, as far as a boundary drawn north and south between the Drava and Sava, with the important centre of Dakovo inside the Odescalchi domain. He named ten different townships, each with its cluster of villages, and methodically tried to list the Serbian or 'Illyrian' placenames with their Latin and Magyar equivalents.[18] Admitting that the amount of livestock in Syrmia was too small because of the recent fighting, he hoped that during the coming spring the villagers would return to work and begin reviving the economy. What excited him more, as he had already informed the Emperor, was the possibility of a thriving commerce. Trade would pass from Belgrade through Syrmia to Styria and the Adriatic. And Rome itself was not too far distant: in that context he laid stress on the classical remains of the country, which was therefore not too alien from the Rome of Odescalchi. This point, although he made it sound far-fetched, certainly impressed Marsigli. He discovered how thickly the country was strewn with the vestiges of Roman roads and settlements. He had seen, adjoining the village of Mitrovica, the site of a city which was once a great provincial capital. The Roman presence in a distant region first struck him in Syrmia and the study of antiquity, at least of its archaeological remains, would become one more segment of his intellectual activity.

Continuing his journey he crossed over the Sava to Belgrade, where he encountered the Habsburg troops under Guido Starhemberg's command.[19] They were quartered in the former Turkish citadel, then badly in need of repair after the siege, and in other encampments along the Serbian shore below the city. Under their protection in this recently occupied country Marsigli went as far as the Morava, the great right bank tributary of the Danube flowing from the south, and crossed it to the settlement of Požarevac. Returning to Belgrade he next visited the Habsburg posts along the Sava. With orders to look for a viable frontier, he was surveying the ground; and having advertised himself as one who could put the lie of the land on paper, the commission was much to his taste. But first he groped for even a minimum of information. Adding new impressions to memories of his Balkan journey in 1680, he tried to devise a more reliable image of the landscapes which stretched away east, west and south from Belgrade.[20] His thought took visible shape in sketches, bird's-eye views and maps. Some of these he kept, some he copied and recopied, others were sent to ministers and even to the Emperor. It was an exercise he practised constantly at this period. He never became a reliable draughtsman, or a surveyor with instruments, but what he drew had primitive liveliness and expressed his passionate concern for topographical knowledge.

At Požarevac or Belgrade in 1689 he was able to form a rough idea of the course of the Morava. He knew that the route he followed in 1680 from Adrianople and Niš crossed this river higher upstream, before it entered the thickly wooded country of central Serbia which lies south of Belgrade. He knew also that the waters of the Morava flowed partly from the mountains further east in modern Bulgaria, partly from the south and west, the 'Serbian' Morava. The junction of the two occurred near Niš. On little real evidence he also assumed that the main ridge of the Balkan mountains, which he called 'Mount Haemus', began somewhere along the eastern limit of the Morava basin and then curved gradually south, south-west, and west, until it reached the Adriatic coast. This misleadingly simple notion of Mount Haemus as a ridge of high ground, dividing Balkan Europe neatly between outer and inner semi-circles (from a centre at Belgrade), was axiomatic with old mapmakers and geographers. It still had important strategic implications for politicians and commanders in 1689. Marsigli, as one of them, visualised the two semi-circles as a framework to describe alternative propositions for a frontier between Ottoman and Habsburg. One possible frontier followed the course of the Serbian Morava. Starting at Požarevac it continued upstream a long way south and then west until the confines of 'Hercegovina', an enormous tract, were reached. Further round still, it followed the river Bosna north until the Bosna reached the Sava. There were great gaps, and much evident guesswork by Marsigli, but significantly this project for the boundary did not differ greatly from the existing no man's land between areas firmly held by the Habsburg or Ottoman forces at the end of 1688. A map signed by one of Marsigli's engineering colleagues, dated 27 March 1689, shows most of northern Serbia under Habsburg control; but this extended only as far west as the river Drina, on which Zvornik stands, not to the Bosna.[21]

Marsigli next drew out his larger semi-circle. This possible boundary started well east of the Morava, where Mount Haemus was thought to rise above the plain, somewhere near the Iron Gates of the Danube. It followed the mountain line south to the passes between Niš and Sofia, and then swung gradually south-west and west to the Adriatic. This greater arc therefore included such regions or places as 'Bulgaria', Niš, Skopje, Peć and large parts of 'Albania'. Here, among both Moslems and Orthodox he located a Catholic population called the 'Clementi', the natural and proper allies for any Catholic invader.[22] Hercegovina, Bosnia and Ottoman Croatia all fell within this imposing, new, hypothetical Habsburg domain. The views of Venetian statesmen, Leopold's allies, with their own plans for pressing inland from the Adriatic littoral, were not for the moment our traveller's concern. Nor did he here refer to Transylvania.

The line of the Morava, or the line of Mount Haemus; a frontier embracing Albania, or one omitting Albania but still including Hercegovina and Bosnia: these were alternatives for the court of Vienna to consider. Marsigli's reports and maps became an element of the discussion through

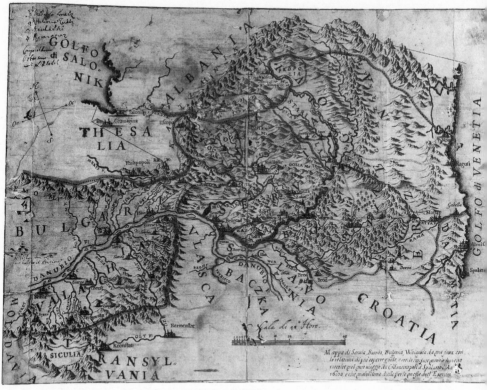

11 Marsigli's notion of the Balkans in 1689 and 1690.

which the Habsburg court tried to formulate a policy for the Emperor,
between September 1688 and the summer of 1689. A modern phrase like
'the definition of war aims' almost describes what Leopold and his politicians groped for in the course of this long debate. But economic potential
and geographical features in the areas recently conquered, or judged to be
still worth fighting for, were by no means uppermost in their minds.[23]
Instead they appear to have been obsessively preoccupied by matters of
protocol, by the problem of deciding how to organise their contact with the
Ottoman envoys now in Austria. Once this was settled the fundamental
tactic was to exploit the military collapse of the Ottoman empire, by insisting on Habsburg historical claims to sovereign authority in Hungary and its
medieval dependencies in the Balkans, whether these were at the time
occupied by Habsburg forces or not. Knowledge of old diplomas and charters rather than maps was deemed appropriate for an assessment of the
Emperor's interest. But coming nearer the issue of power, and the balance
of power between states, it was admitted that the likely strain on Habsburg
resources – if they were stretched by fighting on both fronts, east and west,
in the coming year – posed a terrible dilemma: it could be resolved, some
Habsburg statesmen argued, because there was a chance of ending the
Turkish war on highly favourable terms. Accordingly Kinsky, Stratmann,

Carafa, and Starhemberg, the relevant committee of ministers, had advised Leopold on 30 October to agree to a negotiation with the two Ottoman envoys, Sulfikar and Mavrocordato, the Turk and the Greek respectively.[24] The ministers also pointed out, and Leopold agreed, that while they could put forward broad claims to territory and sovereignty, a new boundary or frontier was needed to complete a settlement between the two empires. A good frontier had to be easy to recognise, and to defend. The available maps were admittedly unhelpful, and it was therefore suggested early in the new year that the commanding officers in Croatia, Slavonia and Transylvania should send in memoranda and recommendations.[25] Carafa summarised the views of these officers a few weeks later. In addition there was Marsigli's advice on the same topic.

The notion of a peace treaty with the Sultan, or even of a truce, soon wilted and gradually died away in the conferences held at the Vienna Landhaus of the Lower Austrian Estates. There were meetings at intervals in February, March and April 1689 and it transpired that the envoys from Adrianople had no authority to give up any part of the Sultan's old empire except in the area between Esztergom, Buda and the river Drava.[26] They emphatically declined to discuss a surrender of his right to Belgrade or Transylvania. They were obeying instructions given them many months earlier, but they had reason to be encouraged by what they knew of the outbreak of a fresh round of war in western Europe, and of Louis XIV's early successes in Germany. Cut off from correspondence with their own government, they knew well enough that no Ottoman minister dreamt of a humiliating treaty which would antagonise the principal cadres of the empire, the soldiers, teachers, lawyers, and officials, by the cession of territory which had been gathered for centuries into the 'sacred domain' of Islam. On their side of the conference chamber, the Habsburg ministers remained insistent on the demand for very wide transfers of Ottoman territory to Leopold, in Bosnia and Serbia as well as Hungary and Transylvania. At one moment (in the conference of 17 March) their response to the Ottoman 'offer' implied demands which would have satisfied even Marsigli's wildest hopes for entry into both Bulgaria and the land of the 'Clementi'. These they toned down later, but at the time Leopold's servants never felt able to claim less in the Balkans than an exceedingly wide tract extending between the Morava and southern Bosnia. They had to take sufficient account of popular and clerical sentiment in Vienna, Rome, Cracow and everywhere else in Christian Europe, whose voice was the voice of charismatic father Marco d'Aviano pleading with Leopold to continue the Turkish war, to destroy the ancient enemy of the Church, and to remember always that this duty transcended the secular struggles of the western states. The terms for peace with the Sultan had therefore to be stiff enough to maintain the Emperor's good name and to satisfy his allies in the Holy League. Moreover, with Belgrade already occupied and Christian troops wintering south of the Drava and Danube, it was extraordinarily difficult to contemplate giving up such a forward position because larger military commitments in the Rhineland were anticipated. Instead, the largest possible defensive terrain or glacis was needed to protect what had recently been gained; and for this reason the Habsburg politicians in the Landhaus dialogues never abated their demand for Serbia and Bosnia. They were echoing the teaching of Marsigli's maps and reports. He was indeed an articulate spokesman for that point of view which the Habsburg government endorsed.

While the debate with Sulfikar and Mavrocordato continued instructions were prepared for a new commander of the field army in Hungary.[27] Prince Lewis of Baden, with a wonderful record of success in the recent Hungarian campaigns, replaced Lorraine and Max Emmanuel who were both intent on a leading role in Germany during the coming months; Lorraine was, or imagined himself to be, in better health. Much depended on the manner in which Lewis chose to understand these instructions, drafted by Starhemberg and signed by Leopold (6 April, 10 May). A long sequence of clauses was filled to bursting with ifs and buts. Each positive request was balanced by a corresponding caution, but the leading ideas were that he should defend the line of the Morava south of the Danube, while north of it Ottoman Timisoara – and the Banat of Timisoara, the surrounding territory – should be taken. Bosnia and Hercegovina were desirable objectives. In more general terms a further advance was recommended into those lands still held by the Turk. It was a recipe for expansion. Lewis studied the text of his masters, raised certain questions and received answers to some of them. Among his queries was one: could he have a positive order about count Marsigli, to settle his status and responsibility during the coming campaign? An uncertainty is implied here, as if he had lost a patron in Lorraine, without as yet finding another in Lewis. On the other hand, it was understood that he would be required.

On 15 May 1689 Marsigli wrote to Malpighi. On the point of his departure for the army, he says, he has collected together and sent off to Bologna certain samples of copper acquired during a recent trip to Slovakia. He would like the members of his brother's group of virtuosi to examine them.[28] He had found enough time to pay a second brief visit to Arva on Odescalchi's behalf,[29] visiting one or more of the Slovakian mines on the way. These minerals offered another field of enquiry, not to be forgotten in spite of the warfare.

III

On 11 June 1689 the new commander in chief reached Belgrade, and on the 17th June Palanka, about halfway between Belgrade and Jagodina.[30] Jagodina is close to the spot where the Morava was usually crossed on the journey – for soldiers, diplomats or traders – from Belgrade to Niš, Sofia

The Campaigns of 1689–90

and Istanbul, and here a few Habsburg troops under colonel Hofkirchen
had been stationed for some time to observe enemy movements farther
afield. It was hoped that Lewis of Baden and his army would make their
rendezvous at this point; such a force could then consolidate the Habsburg
position south of the Danube, while testing the strength of the Turks and
tracing out a viable borderland in that region. But Lewis stopped at Palanka,
and indeed called Hofkirchen back.[31] There were several reasons for caution but most important was a long, vexatious delay in the arrival of troops
from their winter quarters. Bad weather with heavy flooding along the
Danube and Tisza explain this. General Veterani, bringing his men from

Transylvania, had to make an enormous circuit to reach Serbia. The march of other regiments from more distant quarters in Slovakia and Moravia also took longer than expected while stores, and artillery, and the materials needed for bridge building, advanced at a snail's pace. In one letter Lewis indignantly complained that nothing had reached him except half the field chancery and a solitary chaplain. What he did have was news, though unconfirmed, that the Turks had brought together an army which was approaching Belgrade from the south. Other reports spoke of the Khan of the Tartars and the leader of the rebel Magyars, Thököli (long since cut off from his inheritance), who were said to be in Bulgaria preparing either to move along the southern shore of the Danube to Belgrade, or to cross the river and join the Ottoman force still holding Timisoara. Nor was Lewis more confident that his detachments to the west were safe if the Moslem Bosnians decided to attack them. While politicians in Vienna assumed that the Habsburg military presence around Belgrade was strong enough to be extended further south in reasonable security, their commander in the field considered himself exposed and even isolated. His despatches nervously reviewed the position. Certain points were clear, the rest appeared very uncertain. To repell Thököli or the Tartars he needed better protection along the Danube from Belgrade downstream, at least as far as the confluence with the Morava. To guard this base-line he needed better communications, including a sufficient number of boats or rafts for bridging, and other shipping for transport. And he needed supplies on the spot, not at Buda or Szeged far away in Hungary. He wrote copiously, badgering, complaining, petitioning. Among other items a letter of 2 July referred to Marsigli, whom he had sent out on reconnaissance, while another of 8 July mentions his safe return.[32] It was thanks to Marsigli's mission that Lewis developed the startling tactical surprise which transformed the Serbian campaign of 1689 into a successful enterprise.

Marsigli's first assignment was to inspect the military defences along the Danube.[33] He went back to Smederevo (about 60 miles below Belgrade), where the lofty medieval towers and walls still offered shelter in an emergency. He made a survey and sketch, wrote a report, and started to have the ground cleared in front of the defences. By then, further instructions ordered him to go south to the Morava, and find out where and how to get an army across it. With sufficient troops at last beginning to arrive from Hungary Lewis wanted to take the field, but considered that a force of approximately 16,000 should not run the risks of a direct advance from Palanka to Jagodina. The Turks in front of him, he feared, were numerous enough to make a crossing of the river in that area very difficult. Equally dangerous, if he moved too far forward, would be the Tartars venturing out of Bulgaria and advancing west at their usual breakneck speed on one side or the other of the Danube. What he wanted to find, therefore, was a line of march enabling him to hold off the Tartars or Thököli, while also offering a chance of catching the Turks at a disadvantage. One possibility was for his own forces to cross the Morava much lower down than Jagodina, and nearer the Danube, in order to confront the swift horsemen of the Khan or of Thököli if they appeared. If they did not, or were driven back, a subsequent move upstream along the Morava's east bank might outflank or surprise the Sultan's own forces.

After a search Marsigli found what Lewis was looking for, in the triangular space between the Danube and the west bank of its tributary: a feasible approach route through woodland and marsh, and an easy crossing just above the point where the Morava divided into several channels before entering the Danube. After fifteen days of intensive preparation the way overland was ready, and enough boats had come from Smederevo via the Danube. The troops arrived at the water's edge and were ferried safely across the Morava. Some defences were built around an encampment on the further shore but after a few days' halt, with still no sign of the Tartar host or of Thököli, Lewis took the decision to advance south (not far from a route once used by the Romans but discarded by later Christian and Ottoman commanders) as fast as possible. He wrote confidently to Leopold, expressing particular satisfaction on one point:[34] he was taking with him 60 small boats on carts for a pontoon, with which he would be able to recross the river if any chance occurred of making a surprise attack. Marsigli later described this in slightly different terms.[35] On reconnaissance he found that a large number of tributary streams flowed into the Morava from the east, which would have to be crossed, and he drew attention to the problem. Then, he adds, Lewis approved of a search for the little craft used locally, the *gianaki*, mere tree trunks hollowed out, and when it was objected that these were far too flimsy Marsigli himself showed what could be done. His men constructed a pontoon using them, the doubters were convinced, and Lewis was satisfied.

Events soon came to a climax. We learn of a second bridge built some days later, and of most of the Habsburg infantry beginning to cross again to the west bank. Ottoman forces which had already crossed higher up attacked them, and were defeated in battle near a settlement called Batočina; but on the day before this, the Tartars had approached and they too were beaten off by the Habsburg cavalry, which then likewise crossed the river to play its part in the bigger battle. Lewis, at last confident that he had made sure of his position in central Serbia, advanced to the bridge at Jagodina and crossed it. He was on 'the main road' once more.[36] After a successful engagement with the reinforced Ottoman army outside Niš, he entered the town on 25 September. Niš was celebrated as the Emperor Constantine's birthplace; but no Christian army had gone so far on the road to Constantinople since 1442.

Yet this triumphal progress, when looked at in greater detail, began with a near disaster which Marsigli played his part in averting. Lewis had begun the long march along the further side of the Morava without considering that the heavy summer rains might continue into the third week of August.

They did so, and his route became all but impossible for laden carts and animals. Not only were his stores left far behind; his commissariat never set out with sufficient supplies. The army, in some danger of being surrounded or cut off, also ran the risk of starving. Its commander wrote an almost despairing report on 26 August, and during the next two days retreated in order to rejoin the transports pulling slowly across the hills and through the streams. (Rivers had become lakes, Lewis lamented.) At or near a place called Grabovac a report was considered that the Morava could best be crossed in that neighbourhood. Lewis summoned Marsigli. With the help of cash provided by the commander, he found local guides who pointed out the best site for a crossing. A battery was set up on a height by the shore to give protection to the workers whom Marsigli directed, and they hastily constructed pontoons with his precious stock of boats. The infantry began crossing the Morava, and the Turkish command then spotted what looked like a golden opportunity to attack the divided Habsburg force. The Tartars, and others, were sent to harass Lewis and his cavalry near Grabovac, while an assault began on the Habsburg foot already over the river. On this occasion Lewis was the better or luckier general, and his men were stronger than the enemy. They won the engagements on both sides of the Morava.[37] The cavalry led by Lewis, having beaten the Tartars, in their turn used Marsigli's bridge to join in the victory of Batočina. After that, in spite of the stores and booty found in the Turks' deserted camp, a pause was needed to wait for supplies from Belgrade and Smederevo before the advance to Niš began.

Lewis, rarely generous in praising his subordinates, warmly commended Marsigli.[38] In a despatch drafted after the battle he stated that his forces crossed the Morava thanks to the bridge-building 'and also to the outstanding energy and industry of count Marsigli, who was the responsible officer', words which were soon in print in Germany and no doubt soon forgotten.[39] Of greater interest, Marsigli's knowledge grew as he moved through the landscape. At Smederevo, inspecting the medieval walls he realised that they encased much older fragments. And further down the Danube, he could locate some of the islands in his sketches while judging whether they could be used for crossing the enormous stream, with the help of pontoons to link the patches of solid ground.[40] He also surveyed in some detail the lower reaches of the Morava and Jesava, two parallel tributaries reaching the Danube in this area: if Lewis of Baden chose one route to Niš, others had been discarded in the light of Marsigli's reconnaissance. He was rapidly becoming as useful in his own sphere as the other senior officers serving with him: Veterani, Piccolomini, Croy, Guido Starhemberg, or Hofkirchen. Each, including Marsigli and the men under them, contributed to this successful campaign of 1689 when the Habsburg forces were certainly more effective than their opponents. Ottoman defeat and revolution in the two preceding years had taken a heavy toll of the Sultan's best manpower; the Ottoman government was manifestly disorganised at the centre and in the provinces. It was less easy at the time to see that Lewis of Baden, with his excellent assistants, was merely able to take advantage of this Ottoman setback to carry out a long-distance raid into the Balkans. It was equivalent to the devastating sweeps of the Tartars through parts of eastern and central Europe earlier in the seventeenth century. Unfortunately for Emperor Leopold, to convert such a raid into the permanent annexation of another segment of the old Ottoman empire, even further removed from Vienna than Transylvania or Slavonia, proved insuperably difficult.

IV

During the ten days Lewis stayed at Niš, some of his troops were spread across the surrounding country to hold it firmly, and to gather provisions following the harvest. He pondered his ideas meanwhile and during the first week in October wrote at length, responding to Leopold's and the Council of War's instructions in the light of his recent experience.[41] After a long advance towards the heart of the enemy empire, he had decided against moving his outposts any further ahead than the main watershed between Niš and Sofia. Instead he wanted to occupy the territory further to the west, in south Serbia, and also further north – from Belgrade down the Danube. For this reason he proposed dividing his army, to give Aeneo Piccolomini command of about half the total force and instructing him to lead it westwards, and take control of an extensive region where Turkish rule was said to be crumbling fast. Of the topography or population in this part of the Balkans Lewis certainly knew little. Hoping that Piccolomini would find well-stocked winter quarters, he advised him to advance 'in the direction of the sea, on this side of Haemus and the Albanian mountains',[42] that is, not to cross the hills to the Aegean but to ride on westwards towards the Adriatic. This agreed with Leopold's earlier instructions, later confirmed, that Lewis should try to surround or isolate Bosnia in order to detach it from other Ottoman territory in the Balkans. A few weeks later it was known that Piccolomini had been highly successful, having moved with ease and speed over the plateau of Kosovo, south as far as Skopje and north-west to Peć (the Serbian patriarch's residence). He had also found grain for his men and their mounts.

The second part of the plan employed the remainder of the army, under Lewis of Baden's own command. It concerned a region of similar size, also imperfectly known, and responded to several calculations. From the day he left Belgrade, aiming for Palanka and Niš, Lewis had been alarmed by the frailty of his defences along the Danube. His wretched communications with Buda, of which he complained incessantly, were continually at risk from the Turks still in Timisoara, from the forces under Thököli who in

August and September were variously reported to be occupying points on the Danube or to have crossed into Transylvania, as well as from Tartar bands irrupting into the same area. But if Lewis brought his victorious host northward again, then Thököli and the Tartars could be crushed or at least driven out, while the Turks of Timisoara were kept hemmed in and isolated. There would be a chance of finding quarters for the winter along the Danube, and if necessary the Wallachians might be made to provide food and remounts from their more fertile country. If all, or at least most, of this programme was carried out during the autumn and winter the commander offered those at court in Vienna the bright future of a fresh advance 'to the heart of the Turkish provinces in Europe, through Bulgaria to Nicopolis and the Black Sea', or 'to the right hand' towards Sofia.[43] Therefore, as a first step, he intended to withdraw immediately with his force of 8000 from Niš to the Danube, not to Belgrade but to Vidin 200 miles downstream. It was still in Ottoman hands, but had the advantage of being closer to Niš and within reach of the Habsburg garrisons across the river in Transylvania, and the flocks and herds of the rich Wallachian lords.

Connected with this general plan were two proposals, to which he drew the Emperor's attention. He wanted to build a road – what he called a 'Hauptstrasse' – from Vidin to Smederevo, linking together a number of fortified points on the right bank of the Danube.[44] He hoped in addition for the construction of a bridge across the river, adjoining the road and permitting easier contact between Habsburg forces in Serbia and Transylvania.[45] Better communications offered the Emperor a stronger defence in Danubia and, in the future, greater offensive power further afield.

Lewis had profited by some guidance from Marsigli. A 'map drawn on the instructions of His Highness of Baden . . . 1689' shows a stretch of country extending from the Iron Gates of the Danube as far as south Serbia.[46] Various lines traced across it suggest alternative courses of action. Marsigli's own opinion was at the same time rejected. He tells us that at Niš he spoke up in favour of the boldest possible step, an immediate advance to Sofia. Conceding that the watershed beyond Niš was the line of Mount Haemus, a frontier line corresponding with Vienna's fervent hopes earlier in the year, he argued that prospects for the future were now brighter than before thanks to the recent victory. The whole region as far as Istanbul lay open, he thought. It was inhabited by Christian Bulgars, Christian Rascians and Greeks who realised that the old Ottoman government could not survive. 'I was the only person present who knew that part of the world,' he reports of a council of officers; and after asserting his superior knowledge he offered to guide them in six days to Sofia.[47] It was a large and open city, with quarters and supplies enough for the whole army. Marsigli believed that the victory of Niš in 1689 was equivalent, for the Habsburg empire, to the victory of Mohács for the Sultan in 1526. It opened wide the door to a more extended conquest. Quite clearly he spoke with vehemence. He notes also that he was ill with a fever. His argument must have seemed visionary and mistaken to Lewis of Baden.

The march over the hills to Vidin was a success.[48] Marsigli claims that he was responsible for the route chosen, which took them first across high ground before descending to the upper valley of the Timok, a river flowing north to the Danube. One of Marsigli's colleagues remembered later the forests they crossed and the ravines they had to follow. Another found it a waste and empty land. Leaving the Timok, the army passed through an opening in the final ridge eastwards and descended to the plain where Vidin, town and fortress, stood close to the Danube. Lewis attacked at once and took the town, but the strongly built fort with a large garrison threatened difficulties. The defence rather surprisingly collapsed after five days, and agreed to surrender on easy terms. The Turks, the men and their families, were shipped down the Danube while Habsburg officers waited for their own boats, stores and cannon to arrive from higher up the river. Nothing came. The troops were hungry. They were increasingly hard to control. Any notion that the country between Vidin and Sofia had enough food and fodder to help them proved mistaken, and this dearth compelled Lewis and his staff to look across the water as a matter of urgency. It persuaded him that he must at once beg, borrow, or simply take what was wanted from the richer land of Wallachia. Whether or not Vienna preferred to coax, rather than coerce prince Constantine into accepting Leopold as suzerain, subsistence for the army was the paramount need.[49] But at Vidin the waters of the Danube were broad, and the routes on the other shore looked too exposed to be safe. Instead, leaving a garrison in Vidin and some Serbian contingents in the neighbouring hills, the invaders followed the exceptionally winding course of the Danube upstream until they reached Kladovo (Fetislan or Feth-Islam), on the long reach which lies below the Iron Gates.[50] This is (or rather, was) the famous barrier of rock in the river bed where the Danube, having forced its way through the Carpathians, finally emerges into the plain. Here, Marsigli says, he carried out the construction of a bridge of boats, and a despatch of 10 November confirms that materials for the pontoons had at last arrived:[51] Lewis took his army across the river and entered Wallachia. Soon afterwards general Heisler joined him from Transylvania bringing additional forces, and together the two commanders compelled the prince of Wallachia to come to terms. His deputies signed an agreement conceding quarters to the desperate, marauding Habsburg soldiers. Finally, having drafted fresh instructions for all the divisions of his command, from southern Serbia to Wallachia,[52] Lewis left officers and men behind, retiring speedily through the Transylvanian hills to the creature comforts of Germany.

In the European social rhythms of this period the departure in early winter of a few grandees from the zones of warfare, for consultation and refreshment at court or at home, was a common feature. They came from

Flanders, the Rhineland, Lombardy and Hungary; they arrived at Versailles, Paris, the Hague, London, Vienna and Augsburg. On this occasion, in the early months of 1690 Lewis of Baden took the opportunity to find a rich bride in Bohemia, and to share in the proceedings of the Imperial Diet.[53] Most of the Emperor's troops in the south-east had also withdrawn from the Serbian frontier, to be scattered in quarters very far from home, living on the backs of a resentful, alien population in Slovakia, Transylvania and Wallachia.

V

These four weeks of the troops' advance from Vidin to Wallachia, and the winter months following, were memorable in Marsigli's long life. Here the ancient Romans made their grand entry into his imagination, after the original flush of interest a year earlier in Syrmia, and they drove him to work. But first he had to construct the bridge required by Lewis.

The Habsburg camp was placed at Kladovo on the south bank, in order to take advantage of the firm and level shore there, and the absence of marsh or cliffs. Marsigli's staff made what preparations they could, while waiting for a sufficient number of boats or rafts and additional timber to enable them to begin putting pontoons across the channel. With a few days' leisure he found himself staring at the modest remains of one of the classical age's more remarkable achievements: Emperor Trajan's stone bridge across the Danube. Erected here nearly sixteen centuries earlier, in AD 103–4, its builders had likewise taken advantage of what they considered the first favourable site below the Iron Gates.[54] Two pillars still rose above the water level, and something survived of the original work at both ends. There were, clearly, many other ancient ruins and relics in the neighbourhood; Marsigli had seen for himself vestiges of old towers or walls along the river during his ride from Vidin. With the help of soldiers and labourers under his direction he examined everything they found which he believed to be Roman. They began putting together their new timber bridge, but he also measured the total width of the river where Trajan's bridge crossed it, and the span between Roman piles visible below the water level.[55]

There are, naturally, scattered references to classical antiquity in Marsigli's notes of his earlier travels.[56] As an educated man from Bologna-Felsina who had entered polite society in Rome, he could hardly know nothing of such matters; but scientific enquiries, and an interest in the Ottoman rather than the Roman empire, absorbed more of his enthusiasm. On the other hand it is possible that he had come across a notable book about Trajan's column in Rome, by L.F. Fabrizi, issued by his own publisher in 1683.[57] This contained illustrations of the frieze round the column, showing views of the Emperor's Danube bridge and the passage of his troops into the land of Dacia lying north of the river. What cannot be doubted is that Marsigli's experiences on campaign during the winter of 1689–90 matured his enthusiasm. Trajan's bridge, and the conjunction which required Marsigli to build another bridge at nearly the same spot, for the passage of another emperor's army into Dacia/Wallachia/Transylvania, made him a student of the Roman empire.

He soon had to give up the plan for placing his pontoons immediately alongside Trajan's ruin.[58] On that site the wind blew too strongly and put at risk his precious, irreplaceable boats. Everything was accordingly moved further upstream to where a group of small islands, on which he noted further Roman remains, made the work of engineers and boatmen a little less daunting and a little more secure. They were a short distance below the Iron Gates and afforded better shelter. Even so, the channel was rocky and the current strong, and it was by using large wicker containers filled with heavy stones that Marsigli at length anchored his pontoons, which allowed men, horses and wheeled traffic to get across.[59] Lewis of Baden's forcible entry into Wallachia began. It led to the treaty with prince Constantine; and then Lewis drew up his plans for the winter. In these, Marsigli was by no means forgotten. 'A good, reliable roadway,' wrote the commander in chief, 'will be dug and completed as soon as possible, from Ram to Kladovo. For this purpose a commission will be given to count Marsigli for the survey, and the work will be carried out by engineer Morandi . . . with the assistance of the Imperial commissary in Belgrade . . . officers employing peasant labour will do whatever is necessary'.[60] For the first time in these Turkish wars, therefore, Marsigli would not be permitted to spend an easy winter in Vienna. Having built a bridge, he must now build a road. Not far from his, was Trajan's bridge, and soon he would find the trace of a road along the Danube which took the Roman legions to it.

After the brief foray into Wallachia and a speedy journey with Lewis (on his way homeward) as far as Braşov (Kronstadt) in Transylvania, Marsigli returned to the Danube. He studied with growing familiarity the landscapes which he had seen only in passing two months previously.[61] Then he went upstream and encountered first of all the calmer water above the Iron Gates, and the settlement of Orsova on the left bank. Nearby a tributary flowed in from the north, a prominent island lay in midstream, and another settlement stood on the opposite shore. He does not say so but this configuration helps to explain why a very ancient route north and south had crossed the Danube here. Continuing the inspection, he soon passed up through the 'Kasan', grandest of all the Danube gorges, where a channel of great depth was compressed to a width of 200 yards, with rocky heights on either side. Beyond this point he ascended for 50 miles south-west and then west. Thereafter a fairly level shore for a few miles gave easier access to the hinterland on his left, but the Danube then turned north-west, where a new world of rapids and defiles began. At this point, the 'Greben', which is just before a steep wall of cliff descends almost sheer to the water, Marsigli picked out three islands close to the Serbian or southern shore, 'separated from each other by such narrow channels that they almost seemed like one',[62] and decided to make them his working quarters during the winter.

It was primarily a base from which to carry out his survey in the Emperor's service. His superiors wanted to tighten the encirclement of the Ottoman garrisons still in Timisoara, and further north in Oradea. They wanted, more urgently, a watch kept on the lower Danube, an area from which the Turks or Tartars or Thököli could still attack the Habsburg outposts in Serbia. Lewis and Leopold therefore concurred in wanting an efficiently speedy route for troops and stores along this unfamiliar section of the great river, which would bypass the defiles and cataracts, Accordingly, count Marsigli and engineer Morandi set to work as instructed. Marsigli examined the lie of the land, the existing tracks and pathways, the ruined towers and bits of old wall, which were useful quarries of stone for any new works to be put in hand.[63] He inspected the sites of possible military significance on both banks, and their approaches. He located and mapped the islands in the stream which would make easier the construction of pontoon bridges. We find him measuring the varying depths of the water, and the varying speed of the current at different points along the river; and he could claim that these were relevant to his duties as he gave an order for digging, measuring or taking soundings. Yet this quickly spilled over into observations of a different kind. Not only was the Danube a second Bosphorus, with the currents to be measured as a scientific phenomenon, with unusual fish – 'so plentiful between the cataracts' – to examine. There were also the astounding traces of antiquity to admire, inducements to delight which had little enough to do with seventeenth-century emperors or sultans, but much with the lure of the past. This was even more so if it is true, as he claimed later,[64] that he secured a copy of Dion Cassius on Roman History in the course of the winter, giving the outlines of a story which confirmed what was just visible at select points in the landscape between Belgrade and Vidin. It showed Marsigli in 1690 that he was residing on the frontier, the *limes*, of Roman Moesia. The Danube, *his* Danube, was flowing past the ruined walls or camps guarding what had been Roman provinces, first Pannonia and then Moesia. The legions evidently occupied forts on the right bank, and then moved over the river to conquer the land of Dacia. For the moment that insight was enough to alert his zest for archaeological observation as he travelled through the country. These remains impressed him more than any reading of Dio Cassius, but the two together helped to inspire the idea of a work, an 'opus' on the Danubian world in which the remains of antiquity, measured and depicted, would have their place. They enabled Marsigli to make his own mark on the history of imperial Rome.

That history presented a contrast with the seventeenth century. Advancing into Ottoman Hungary and Serbia the Habsburg army entered regions fairly well insulated from western and central Europe. Ultimate authority over them, however fitful its incidence, was imposed from Istanbul up till

1683. Trade from and to the Adriatic ports was maintained at a modest level, having declined since the sixteenth century. Internal migrations within the area were incessant, but there were no pilgrimage journeys to monasteries in distant countries, or diplomatic missions to foreign courts, to bring the population of Serbia and south Hungary into direct contact with more than a very few Italians, Germans or northern Slavs. A handful of Catholic missionaries and Dubrovnik traders inconspicuously represented an exotic culture, whereas Marsigli, looking backward to the Roman phase in Danubia, glimpsed something markedly different. Control from Italy had been imposed on a large Danubian and Balkan empire. Its precise extent may have altered from one phase to another, as he soon understood, but it left an indelible mark on the ground for an attentive observer. If he enjoyed no more than a tiny segment of the wonderfully elaborated modern view of classical antiquity, his instinct that he was 'on to something', by the accident of his presence among the ancient fragments which he identified, was correct.

From the period when the Romans conquered Macedonia in the mid-second century BC until the reign of Augustus, who died in AD 14, Roman dominance south of the Danube increased, contracted, and increased again in a cycle several times repeated.[65] Imperial conquests were counter-balanced by popular risings and insurgent local rulers. At last, under Augustus, the commanders were better able to combine the forces which made their leverage on the whole region irresistible. They could strike at the middle Danube from several directions: from the Adriatic and down the river Sava, from Macedonia and down the Morava, from both the upper Danube and their strongly held bases in the delta by the Black Sea. As a result Roman influence stretched over the river, and penetrated what were called in Marsigli's day the Banat of Timisoara and the principality of Wallachia. The Carpathian region separating these two – Dacia/Transylvania – remained longer in the hands of the local princes, who could choose to resist or submit to the greater power of Rome. Meanwhile that remarkable revolution of the west of AD 6–9, a protest movement spreading from the lower Rhine to the Danube and Illyria, was finally curbed. Augustus and his successors took the steps designed to promote a durable peace in the Danube lands. Roads and river transport were completed to link Aquilea and Salona with Siscium/Sisak on the Sava, and with Sirmium/Mitrovica further downstream. Two important routes from Macedonia and Thrace met at Naïssus/Niš: one continued down the Morava valley and the other was taken through the hills further east to reach the Danube not far from Vidin. As for the Danube, it seems that in quiet times the Romans were content to provide no more than a protective shield for the commerce going upstream and down. In war, or if war threatened, the river became a military frontier adjoining a communication system for the forces, with defence works strung along the shore to accommodate them.

What did Marsigli see of all this in the winter of 1689–90? Travelling by water, or overland, to determine the course of his own route for the Habsburg troops on the Serbian side, he was well placed to detect the vestiges of a Roman road there. Its main function (he did not know this) had been to assist the haulage of shipping upstream. It was a tow path. For preference, a level, accessible foreshore would be used for this purpose, but where this existed very little construction or repair work was needed – and the Romans left behind few traces. In the defiles it was different. The cliffs fell sharply to the water. There were no easy foreshores, and so the Romans had the rock hewed out in order to construct a flat surface, or drilled boreholes for the timbers they used to hold in position a projecting cause-way. To find evidence of their work Marsigli no doubt owed a great deal to the reports of local people, fishermen, herdsmen, and others. What they could not do, what delighted him, was to put down on paper their findings.[66] He added the Roman road to his trace of the prospective modern road. He combined historical information with the many geographical sketches which he drew of the river, setting down his notion of its course from several viewpoints, and adding the situation of the various ancient sites. The idea of a continuous sequence of maps showing the course of the Danube, like his study of Roman antiquities, became part of his notion of an 'opus Danubiale'.[67]

It seems that in the defile of the Greben, Marsigli's base, the Romans built a road in AD 33–4. Their labour was commemorated by an inscription (possibly by two others) in honour of the Emperor Tiberius. Six other inscriptions named later rulers, Vespasian, Domitian, and Titus. The road, therefore, was extended or repaired at intervals during the first century AD. Marsigli has the credit for recording three of the inscriptions, including one depending on his sole testimony because it later ceased to be legible.[68] His 'tres lapidae . . . supra Tataliae' were a short distance above his quarters. In the next defile downstream, the Kasan, he marked the Roman road on his map; but the signs of ancient construction were by this time limited to holes in the rock which he could only have observed from the water. The last and shortest defile, above Orsova, preserved more fragments of the roadway and also Trajan's celebrated inscription which records the labours of his troops in AD 100. The words have been much eroded and defaced in the passage of centuries, puzzling Marsigli and all his learned successors down to the present day. They may refer to a new stretch of road leading to the new bridge, as preparations began for an attack on the strongholds of Dacia. They may simply indicate that Trajan intended to repair or widen the old road of Tiberius's time. We cannot be certain.

Sixteen centuries later Marsigli and Morandi directed the soldiers of their own Emperor, or hired local labour to dig for them. From Belgrade down to Vidin, ran the order, they were to plan and make a route along the southern shore of the river. Marsigli, viewing the ruins while engaged on his survey, usually saw Roman construction surmounted by later building or Roman pieces inserted into later walls. Digging unearthed more. 'A

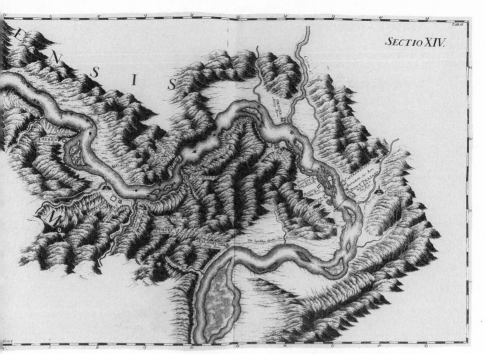

2 The Romans, the Iron Gates and the Danube. This is Marsigli's map as finally published in 1726.

marble base found when Fetislan was fortified', 'a burial inscription discovered when excavating the moat at Belgrade', would be two later comments on what he saw in 1690. During the winter he examined as many sites as possible, measuring what he believed to be Roman remains, drawing plans and elevations. As a pioneer, he naturally missed a good deal. In the three great defiles six Roman forts or round watch towers were identified by Marsigli; later authorities have found traces of an almost continuous line of forts and towers along the Serbian shore. He surveyed the banks opposite at one or two points only, but it was understandable that he should have been more successful on the sites placed close to the tributaries entering the Danube from the south. These had attracted the soldiers, traders and routemakers of every period, Roman, Byzantine or Ottoman. He was most likely to find something precisely where he had been ordered to examine the terrain. He did so, with good fortune as an antiquary, but it did not save him from charges of negligence when the next campaign began.

The Romans claimed his fancy at the time, while as a younger man he had studied the physical geography of the Bosphorus more attentively than the antiquities of Istanbul. In 1690 the Romans seem to have come first as a favourite study, then the physical properties of the river Danube, followed by one other topic: fish, their anatomy and habits. Wherever he had to secure a pontoon he considered the force of the current, and the shape of the river bed. But on the island of 'New Orsova' (Adeh Kaleh) above the Iron Gates, he tells us that he spent part of his time watching the fishermen catch and gut their sturgeon.[69] Consequently, while absorbed in a Roman frontier world to which his career as an Imperial officer had so unexpectedly brought him, it was still an amalgam of interests which claimed his attention. In this state of mind Marsigli continued for a number of years, and it led him on one occasion (which cannot be dated) to scribble a revealing page, with apparently random entries: 'the river Danube. Bed, banks, marshes, sands . . . show them with separate illustrations. Width at the fishermen's island [New Orsova]. Width at Trajan's bridge. Roman remains on the banks of the Danube. Vestiges of forts, bridges, roads, inscriptions.' The top line on the page was crossed out but under the erasure are the words: 'book for fishes'. It was a memorandum of diverse topics, which had still to be put together; but as he wrote later, referring to the last weeks of the winter spent by the river in 1690: 'there I reached a firm conclusion to develop my idea for a work on the Danube'.[70]

VI

An escape to the past could not be sustained for long. As Marsigli would have wished, important events near and far soon swept him out of his seclusion.

Before Lewis had left Transylvania he received news of Piccolomini's death on 9 November 1689 at Prizren, a town deep in Serbia, 100 miles from Niš and 250 miles from Lewis himself. He decided at once to send the highly experienced Veterani to take command in the south.[71] The differing views of Veterani and Lewis were to have a profound effect on the next campaign, differences which involved Marsigli at every stage.

Quickly setting out for Niš from his quarters in Wallachia, Veterani has left an account of conditions along the Danube at the end of December.[72] His fear was that he would be dangerously exposed to Tartar raiders, who were reported on the move, if he crossed the river too far downstream. With a small staff and escort he went first overland to Orsova, where the Habsburg commander put four or five boats at his disposal, and 60 local men. The wind was often high – sails were split, boats were lost – but Veterani was taken up the river through the Kasan defile, and past Golubac to Ram. From here, through the snow, he joined the route taken by Lewis and the army a few months earlier. Marsigli's Danubian landscapes in winter were cold and comfortless, and the latest news was bad news.

Piccolomini and his troops had experienced first triumph, and then a dismaying defeat.[73] The Turks, having stripped their provincial government of its forces in the effort to find men for the field army, almost vanished from the region. There were few left to resist the incursion of the Habsburg leader with some 8000 horse and foot, Germans and Serbs. By taking Prokuplje, south-east of Niš, and then Priština, on the edge of the well-stocked plateaux of Kosovo and Metoya, they were entering more populous country than anything seen at the same time by Lewis or Marsigli on their journey from Niš to Vidin. Piccolomini, assuring himself of supplies, felt strong enough to send smaller detachments in several directions. In one district the local leader submitted to the Emperor. In another the pervading excitement shook people into summoning the patriarch Arsenius, who hastened back through the hills from Montenegro to safeguard his position as head and spokesman of the Orthodox.[74] Piccolomini himself went south as far as Skopje where he burnt down parts of the town, and as far west as Prizren, where he was rapturously received by the Christian populations and welcomed by the patriarch and other dignitaries Orthodox and Catholic; and it was there that he died suddenly of fever. He had just begun, it seems, the difficult task of putting together an alliance between the Habsburg sovereign and the local peoples, that fatal amalgam of Christians and Moslems, Serbs and Albanians, clansmen and unattached migrants. The senior officer on the spot to survive him was duke Christian of Holstein, competent but harsh and unwinning, who had to pay the price for Piccolomini's blend of rashness with success. His troops were spread with dangerous thinness over a large area; those to spare for any rescue operations were very few. The Turks, from beyond Skopje and beyond Prizren, with auxiliary Tartars also appearing, began to rally. Their fresh forces won a clear victory over colonel Strasser, commanding just 300 dragoons, 400 musketeers and 1500 Serbs, on 2 January.[75] A week later Veterani arrived in Niš.

He did his best to hold firm but withdrew the troops still in the Kosovo region. He continued to have the passes guarded which led from there to Niš, and from Niš to Sofia. Bridges were repaired and some rudimentary forts built. In this context he summoned Marsigli from his quarters on the Danube to advise on the defences to be put in hand round Niš itself. Veterani, like Piccolomini, fully realised that his army of occupation ought to rally, rather than merely use, the local population. Volunteer fighters led by a captain Zvorić and father Raspassan (p. 64 above), having withdrawn from Prizren, were employed to carry out raiding further afield. One sweep, at the end of January 1690, was in the direction of Sofia; another in March took them back towards Prizren and Peć. Their effectiveness encouraged Veterani, who wanted to hold his ground by relying on this tactic of co-operation with the Serbs, in order to compensate for the small number of his own more disciplined troops. Raspassan, who had learnt Italian as a student in Loreto, and Marsigli, who learnt what he knew of south Serbia from Raspassan, were present in Niš to urge this on Veterani. Raspassan also sent a paper to Lewis of Baden in which the Emperor was urged to appeal to the Serbian and Albanian population, promising freedom of worship. In particular, he should ask for the patriarch's collaboration in the war against Islam.[76] Unfortunately the men in Niš did not foresee the extraordinary resurgence of Ottoman power in 1690 under a new, effective grand vezir of the Köprülü family, nor did they appreciate all the checks and balances inhibiting the Habsburg court's direction of policy and conduct of war. One sign of this ambivalence, with they had disregarded, was the fate of George Branković.

In 1688 it was understood in Vienna that Leopold's patronage of Branković could help to rally the Serbs against the Turks. Auxiliary troops from the local population became ever more important as the Habsburg army advanced to the Danube and the Sava, and then further. It was believed that Branković had useful contacts in Bosnia and Hercegovina whose support would be valuable. But already early in 1689 Marsigli, then in Vienna, states that the Austrian chancellor Stratmann asked him to test opinion among the Serbs and Greeks in the town.[77] There was some suspicion that if the Habsburg forces advanced any further the Tsar of Muscovy would intervene, seeking through local leaders such as Branković or Arsenius to attract support from the Orthodox population. It sounds like another rumour, but among those to whom Marsigli talked was Stefanov, the roving Bulgarian Franciscan who evidently feared and hated Branković. His appeal to the people to rise against the Turks endangered the Catholic interest, asserted the Franciscan; his claim by inheritance was a fraud. Lewis of Baden, having reached Belgrade and Palanka at the start of his campaign, began to receive intelligence equally unfavourable to Branković. The 'despot', the so-called hereditary lord of Serbia, Bosnia, Thrace and Syrmia, was said to be conspiring with the prince of Wallachia. His agents were canvassing support on both sides of the Danube. A request to Vienna for guidance brought a response from Leopold, dated 5 August 1689, and it authorised – if it was thought advisable – the arrest of Branković. In November, while waiting to cross the Danube at Kladovo, Lewis invited this suspect and unsuspecting ally to a meeting, and arrested him.[78] Branković, adventurer and martyr, spent the rest of his long life as a prisoner in Austria and Bohemia without ever being brought to trial.[79] It was an episode in Habsburg history strongly Ottomanic in flavour: the Sultan's political prisoners thrust into the fortress of the Seven Towers at Istanbul were one element in the popular western view of Turkish history. It was also the Habsburg government's error. An unwillingness to use Branković suggests that at this period Vienna could not seriously conceive of a political programme designed to support its military presence in Serbia.

During the winter this spirit of caution gained the upper hand. Lewis of Baden, writing from Augsburg, submitted a strongly argued paper in which he held that the defence of Leopold's eastern empire depended on standing fast along the Danube.[80] Without an army much larger than the forces under his command in 1689, he says to the Emperor, you cannot hold the Serbian conquests made during the campaign. This year the Turks will be too numerous and powerful. Neither the Transylvanians nor the Magyars are sympathetic. Foreign powers encourage the 'malcontents' among them. Reviewing the setback in the south since Piccolomini's death, he advised bringing the troops in advanced positions back to Belgrade, stripping and wasting the right bank of the Danube, and even the destruction of defence works at Vidin, Kladovo and Ram. He suggested that Marsigli, whom he believed to be on the spot, should now concentrate on the fortification of Orsova on the north bank; he hoped for the presence of an effective naval force to counter any Ottoman offensive using shipping brought from lower down the river. Lewis still accepted in principle the alternative of employing a more powerful army than before to fight offensively in the Balkans, but his new preference was really for a prudent Habsburg withdrawal in this part of Europe. His earlier concept of the Danube and its Serbian shore as a military corridor, employable as a base for further penetration into the Ottoman empire, was set aside. The strain of the Emperor's war against the French monarchy certainly weighed with Lewis and other observers, while in Vienna Veterani's early reports from Niš could hardly have made gloomier reading. In consequence, as Marsigli stated, soon after he reached Niš instructions had arrived requiring the withdrawal of the forces to Belgrade.[81]

Veterani demurred. In his opinion, and his fellow officers agreed, they should stand their ground. He decided to offer a submission to the Emperor which put the case for holding on at Niš and elsewhere. He chose the obvious messenger and spokesman, Marsigli, and hurried him north.

Evidence for the discussion at court is patchy, but Marsigli later recorded an intensive debate in which he claims to have played a prominent part. He explained why the officers on the spot wanted to stay in Niš; but if there had to be a retreat, he advised standing on the Morava, provided that some extra troops could be sent from Hungary. A map of Marsigli's was submitted. His explanations were considered. It was then agreed to support Veterani, to send him funds, and to continue building better defences at Niš. But Marsigli had also brought with him to Vienna the proposals of Raspassan and his friends. To their grief they realised that in the southern regions, liberated by Piccolomini in the previous October and November, the population was now vulnerable to Turkish reprisals. It was highly important to stop them tamely submitting to the restored Ottoman regime. For this reason their leaders argued that the Emperor must not merely redeploy his forces. He should stiffen the popular resistance. He should win people over by making fair offers. What they wanted from the Catholic Emperor was an undertaking to favour the Orthodox church and maintain ancient liberties in lands recovered from Turkish oppression.

The proposal was described in a paper written (or at least copied) by Marsigli, dated 1 April 1690. It has the title 'Memorandum for Albania',[82] by which he denoted those lands traversed by Piccolomini, a region somewhere between Bosnia, Thrace and the Adriatic coast. It was divided into various regions, with an Orthodox population except for the 'Climenti', who were Roman Catholic. The difficult terrain and the character of the people had prevented the Turks from ruling them 'despotically', the paper continues, and government remained in the hands of local chiefs who were sometimes nominated by popular choice. Consequently the Emperor could not hope to win control in that part of the world by the force of his arms alone, and the memorandum suggested that he should issue a patent or manifesto which made known the old claim of the Hungarian crown everywhere beyond the Danube as far as Thrace. In view of these rights, now vested in the Habsburg kings of Hungary, Leopold should confirm the ancient privileges of his new subjects. They included the free election of *voyvodes* or governors, the free exercise of religion, the security of property, and freedom from taxes except for taxation formerly enjoyed by the old Christian rulers. In return, it would be proclaimed that every subject had a duty to take up arms against the Turks, obey the orders of 'the German General', and find supplies for those fighting. Particular emphasis was laid on the influence of the patriarch of the Serbs. Marsigli knew that Arsenius had fled from Peć and was by then a refugee in Belgrade. The Emperor was advised to write to him there, and ask for his support. Extra copies of the appeal to the peoples were to be prepared for Veterani and his officers to distribute at their discretion. 'None of this will cost much and it may be useful', was the modest conclusion of the memorandum. It nonetheless strengthened Veterani's case for maintaining the Habsburg presence around Niš during the coming summer. It went a step further than the bleakly negative attitude which had eliminated George Branković from the scene.

Emperor Leopold already, in December 1688, offered the inhabitants of Bosnia and Hercegovina a guarantee of their ancient privileges if they chose to repudiate Ottoman rule.[83] His general Patent of 6 April 1690 followed Marsigli's recommendation very closely. Addressed to the peoples of Albania, Servia, Moesia, Bulgaria, Illyria, Macedonia and other provinces, it appealed to them to rise in arms, seizing the chance to free themselves from oppression.[84] Their old privileges, together with the free exercise of their religion and the abolition of Turkish taxes, were promised. Lands taken from Turkish owners could be kept. Here was indeed an insurrectionary call, but remarkably few traces have been recovered of any attempt to proclaim or publish it, or of much popular resistance to the powerful Ottoman counterattack in the summer. A patent was also addressed to Arsenius, but before he could receive it the ministers had sent Marsigli off on a new mission, inspired this time by more cautious war aims.[85] For Leopolds's allies in western Europe were again pressing him to make his peace with the Turks. They knew that the Ottoman envoys, still detained in Austria, were available for another round of negotiation. Marsigli's business was accordingly to go to Croatia, in order to advise where a viable boundary might be set between Ottoman territory and the recent Habsburg conquests in that region.

On 5 May he was already south of Zagreb. In country under Ottoman control from early in the sixteenth century until 1688, he penned his first report.[86] He had surveyed the river Una, which in its upper course flows north and then, bending around the stronghold of Bihać, flows east to the Sava. He had crossed the mountains to reach the distant plateaux of Lika and Crbava (Corbavia). He had halted at a point not more than ten hours' riding from Zadar, the Venetian city in Dalmatia. Slowed down by the 'diabolical' travelling, troubled by a touch of fever, he was working hard on plans for a new boundary between the Ottoman, Habsburg and Venetian empires. By 24 May he had returned to Vienna, to complete his sketch maps and draft a fuller report for Leopold.[87] This emphasised how his journey helped him to a clearer understanding of the problem: the course of the river Una would not provide a suitable frontier between unfriendly powers. He explained in detail that it was too narrow a stream, with too many fords; it was dominated by Ottoman forces from higher ground on the further side. Moreover Habsburg control only reached as far as the river in its upper and lower stretches, leaving in between a large Turkish salient surrounding the stronghold of Bihać. Marsigli considered the place almost impregnable, and indeed it remained in Turkish hands until 1878. So he proposed that the Habsburgs should accept the Ottoman salient in Croatia. He also studied the defence of the Una further down, and the novel question (for Leopold's ministers) of an acceptable frontier with the Venetians in Dalmatia. He considered the routes for trade, which he thought Vienna ought to control. Some passes through the hills should be closed, others protected; traffic from the Bosnian hinterland was worth funnelling towards the harbour of Karlobag, now in Austrian hands. He had noticed the marks of ancient wheel-tracks in flagstones at points where he met only horsemen or travellers on foot, and insisted on the need to repair ruined roadways. The recent immigration of Bosnians into the plateaux of Lika and Crbava, owing to dearth in their own country, equally won his approving comment.[88] His instinctive mercantilism was aroused.

With the survey completed, he drew a map of Croatia showing his recommendations for the possible frontier between Ottoman and Habsburg.[89] The old Turkish wedge – often a no man's land reaching the northern Adriatic littoral – was eliminated, and replaced by a boundary between Venetian Dalmatia and Leopold's new stretch of coast. The Ottoman salient across the Una was recognised but thereafter the projected frontier followed the line of both Una and Sava in the direction of Belgrade. Marsigli placed Belgrade itself well inside Habsburg territory by drawing a second, larger salient round it as far as the Morava. This provided, he must have believed, a sufficiently large glacis in Serbia for the defence of the city and citadel. From the Morava his frontier followed the Danube down to the Iron Gates, from where it continued along the Carpathians, a line separating Transylvania from Wallachia and Moldavia. Such a plan, whatever its merits or faults as a blueprint for peacemaking, seems in contrast with the ideas of Veterani and of Marsigli himself, expressed in Niš and Vienna only a few weeks earlier. They leave the Sultan with a vast territory to the south, master of the 'oppressed' peoples to whom the recent manifesto was addressed. But possibly Marsigli never considered the point. He saw himself as working out, in response to instructions, the practical version of a ministerial plan to negotiate a peace or truce with the Turks. If the ministers then decided to let another campaign run its course before a treaty was concluded, and if the Habsburg troops still held Niš at the end of it, which he personally anticipated, a new peace offer could leave intact the suggested boundary in Croatia while assigning the Emperor much more ground in the Morava region, extending towards Sofia or Skopje, or both. From this standpoint Marsigli was simply the expert witness, the scout and surveyor, expected to comment knowledgeably on certain outline proposals. From another, he had his own conviction that a further expansion of the Habsburg empire was still possible.

The memorandum and the map were not yet complete when a message arrived from Veterani urging his speedy return to Niš. In the next few days he scribbled several hectic notes to say that everything would be ready shortly.[90] One regrets that he cannot oblige chancellor Stratmann at the moment. Another asserts that he is about to present his report to Leopold at Laxenburg; after a farewell audience he will hurry away to Serbia, leaving the ministers to make their decisions on the basis of his work. He offered to take with him the patent for Arsenius. After all, he was passing through Belgrade en route for the most exposed section of Leopold's new dominion, which he hoped to defend. The Croatian interlude was over.

VII

Emperor Leopold has often been criticised for his excessive loyalty to his servants. He kept them in office, it is said, however incompetent they were in other people's eyes. The case of Lewis of Baden in 1690 is a different one, but illustrates Leopold's style of management. Lewis was once again appointed commander in chief in Hungary and Serbia, after a fine record of success in earlier years, but on this occasion he was required to follow instructions which he believed misguided. Returning to Vienna in May 1690, he still held the opinion given earlier advising a Habsburg withdrawal from south Serbia. Yet in discussion with politicians and councillors about the strategy of the coming campaign, he found that they generally accepted Veterani's optimistic judgments. Leopold concurred, but at the same time would not permit Lewis to decline the command. Instead, it was settled that the rendezvous of the field army and its commanders would take place at Jagodina. When Lewis reached it he should then decide what to do in order to defend Habsburg conquests.[91] In some respects this was a compromise. After a final protest he left Vienna and set out for Serbia. His views were unchanged, as he speedily showed.

Meanwhile Veterani and Marsigli, in June and July, maintained their confidence. They knew of a great Ottoman mobilisation in Thrace slowly gathering impetus under a new grand vezir, and of Thököli and the Tartars almost ready to break out of Bulgaria, but away in the west their own raiders were penetrating Hercegovina and Albania again; captain Zvorić and father Raspassan were very active. Marsigli, on returning from Vienna, approved of the new defences nearly ready at Niš. Then he went to Pirot, a Habsburg outpost almost 50 miles along the road to Sofia.[92] Again he wrote confidently, asserting that the reason for keeping this exposed point was to protect the surrounding country where a numerous population expected what looked like a wonderful harvest. When it had been gathered – partly for the benefit of the Habsburg forces – they would carry off their grain and goods and retire to the hills. He repeated one of Veterani's arguments in favour of such outposts, which encouraged local men to raid Ottoman-held territory on their own account, committing them to the struggle against their old oppressors, correspondingly strengthening the Austrians' position. This popular support was important. To avoid misunderstanding with such people, Marsigli considered, it would be an error to abandon any place or area except in cases of evident necessity.

At the same time Veterani wanted to link Niš as effectively as possible with Belgrade, the Danube and the depots in Hungary. He longed to receive additional supplies, and to hear of fresh disciplined troops on the way. So Marsigli was kept hard at work to improve the communications running through Serbia. Between Niš and Jagodina he surveyed the main route, and at one point cut a new stretch through the forest. Then he went back to the scene of his winter activity along the Danube, to Orsova and Vidin, before moving upstream again to report to Lewis of Baden who had finally reached Belgrade. Lewis listened, and at last understood what Marsigli had failed to make clear to the authorities in Vienna.[93] He and the engineer Morandi were ordered earlier, as we know, to construct a military route along the Serbian shore of the river; in July Marsigli still airily referred to the 'new road'. Yet very little had been done, and the commander in chief could now appreciate that in fact it amounted to no more than a series of old tracks artificially tidied up as a project on a sketch map. Marsigli had never pointed out unambiguously in reporting earlier that the original order asked for the impossible, given the few men and materials at his disposal. 'Cliffs and rocks' prevented the making of a new route along the Danube.[94] As an alternative he and Morandi decided to improve the existing itineraries which wound through the hills many hours distant from the river, with paths branching down some of the tributary streams to places by the shore. The first part of the route eastward from Požarevac was in fair condition by July. Beyond this 'strada battuta' there was one track suitable for horsemen for a few more miles, and another for carts, but Marsigli admitted that further repairs would still be needed.[95] Worst of all, there was no link between the barely visible 'new road' and the new bridge now in position at Orsova, or with the Habsburg garrison in Vidin, a point most in need of speedy help if the enemy advanced from Bulgaria.

Marsigli at first confidently asserted that all would be well if, for ten days, he could employ a thousand labourers over whom he was given exceptional disciplinary powers.[96] Elsewhere he said that the work was already in hand. The draft of a letter to Veterani refers in purple prose to the commanders 'of our modern Caesar' who would soon be following the ancient Romans along a road which he, Marsigli, is busy restoring;[97] but one is forced to doubt whether more than a very few labourers were found to make good the ancient itinerary which went from Trajan's bridge, and through the hills south of Orsova and the Kasan gorge, to reach the Danube again near the Greben rock, from which it could be connected with the route coming from the direction of Belgrade. It was an ingenious project for a 'new' road, but too circuitous, on too small a scale, and nothing was done until too late. One of the officers on the spot, in a message to Vienna, expressed horror at the abrupt request of Marsigli and Morandi for labourers. It was to ask for the impossible.[98]

Marsigli could be more positive about the defence of the crossing to Orsova, on the other side of the river.[99] The boats and pontoons were safely in position, with fairly simple defences constructed at each end. His earlier plans for building a fortress, 'Forte Carlo', on the large island below Orsova had not been carried out, but the redoubt on a neighbouring smaller island satisfied him. To use his own phrase, below Orsova the Danube could be 'effectively closed', provided that the defenders kept control of the towing space on either shore. Visiting Vidin next, he was equally confident. The citadel was in good order, and it should not be difficult to check any attack across the water from Wallachia. But Marsigli's despatch to Leopold suddenly changes theme here and switches to a tirade of despair, a feature which recurs in his correspondence with the court for many years to come. At Vidin, he says, where the river protected one side and the marsh another, the enemy appears less hostile than those in Vienna who intrigue against him. Emperor Leopold, the 'Padrone', never had a more faithful, willing servant than he who now wished to end the labours which brought him only misery, ill-health and poverty: the pay and rewards promised were never forthcoming. Several paragraphs of this kind followed before he switched back to the main theme of his report, the defence of the Danube. Such an insertion deserves notice for illustrating a prominent element in the style of his approach to the sovereign. He was theatrical in expressing both loyalty and disappointment, which he counterbalanced by an unvarying confidence in the effectiveness of his work. On this occasion, nonetheless, one point is clear: Marsigli much underestimated the scale of the forthcoming Ottoman thrusts in the whole area he was surveying.[100] He satisfied himself too easily with what he had done for the defence, even if Habsburg military administration did not set high standards of competence, or give him proper support. In 1690 Lewis of Baden's fears and doubts were all justified.

During the fourth week of August Lewis, Marsigli and many other officers and men of the Habsburg forces – although they were decidedly less numerous than in 1689 – advanced through the thick woods towards Jagodina. Veterani, leaving behind a garrison in Niš under Guido Starhemberg, was ordered to come and meet them, and hoped to impel the army still further forward to defend the more exposed positions. Lewis, on the contrary, wished to withdraw as many troops as possible for the defence of Belgrade and the line of the Danube. On 27 August a council of war was held at Jagodina.[101] On this and the following day, in the course of a long discussion, one side gave reasons for not attempting to relieve Niš where forces under the grand vezir had already reached the neighbourhood, and the other disagreed. Then terrible news arrived. Thököli, having broken into Transylvania with Wallachian, Tartar and Turkish support, had completely defeated general Heisler. Heisler, with many colleagues, was a prisoner. Thököli might well seize the whole of Transylvania. From there his advance into Upper Hungary and Austria or Moravia, Lewis pronounced, was only a step. Accordingly he wanted to move back at once, to try and rescue the endangered Habsburg strongholds and resources still intact. In the face of this greater emergency north of the Danube, Niš and the Serbian territory would have to be sacrificed. Amid a flurry of altered plans Marsigli received fresh instructions. He had expected to be spying out the Ottoman encampments near Niš. Instead he was sent to accelerate the army's move towards Transylvania, by dismantling the bridges across the Danube at Ram – which seemed more exposed to a sudden attack – and moving the equipment 50 miles upstream to Smederevo.[102] Lewis brought most of his force safely across the river. A few days earlier Vidin fell. A few days later Starhemberg had to withdraw from Niš. Lewis and Veterani hastened towards (and into) Transylvania in order to hunt for Thököli, while the Ottoman host moved from Niš to Smederevo and from there to the outskirts of Belgrade. Serbia, but not the fortress of Belgrade, was lost to the Emperor. Or so it appeared for the shortest possible period; because even at Belgrade the Habsburg defences crumbled. After a siege lasting one week – explosions in the powder magazine, the duke of Croy as a faint-hearted commander, and treachery by a French engineer have all been blamed for this brief defence – Belgrade too became Ottoman once more (8 October). Ottoman control extended down the Danube all the way to Vidin. Indeed Turks and Tartars started to cross the river.[103] Once on the further shore the Turks made for their surviving garrisons of Timisoara and Oradea, which had been wedged for the past two years between Habsburg conquests east and west. Were they now to become part of an Ottoman platform, from which to aim further assaults at Transylvania or Hungary?

These events were the very gravest setback for the government Marsigli served. In their outcome they also dealt him personally a blow of peculiar force. He was unaware of it at the time, but the 'Opus Danubiale' of his dreams was now condemned to be no more than a fragment. The opportunity for studying an immense tract of the river between the Iron Gates and the delta, for studying again the Roman past in Serbia, for turning sketches into measured maps, for collecting samples, or for using his microscope and other instruments in that region, had vanished. In September 1690 he saw no need to anticipate the finality of recent events. Always an optimist in warfare he hoped to return to territories soon to be recovered for the Habsburg Emperor. There was no such reconquest in the campaigns of the next eight years, and no other virtuoso or historian from western Europe could follow him into the Balkan regions for a much longer period. It was a signal misfortune, though Marsigli's surviving letters and papers show few traces of his own regret for what had occurred. Perhaps a more single-minded pioneer, as historian or geographer or natural scientist, would have felt the grievance more acutely of such a deprivation. In practice he contented himself, as a student of the Danube lands, with what came within reach inside Habsburg territory, all the while continuing his search for reward or promotion in the Emperor's service.

He could hardly have done more than he did, under Lewis of Baden's command in the latter months of 1690. Entering Transylvania at its south-west corner, Lewis sent Marsigli through the hills to Orsova again. There he directed the transfer of more men, guns and stores to the islands surveyed a few months earlier. He hoped to bar the way to Turkish craft coming upstream, but Ottoman control of the opposite bank quickly made this a hopeless prospect.[104] Marsigli returned to Lewis, whose small but relatively disciplined force had the task of subduing Thököli, already acknowledged as the new 'Prince' of Transylvania by certain local leaders; while the Habsburg garrisons were isolated. Thököli dodged and turned. At one moment he withdrew eastwards, taking shelter on the Carpathian ridges which bordered Moldavia.[105] Lewis advanced in pursuit and Marsigli played his familiar role as scoutmaster-cum-geographer. With his guides and beaters ranging widely, he first went to close a route by which Thököli could double back to the west along the Maros valley.[106] The fall of Belgrade momentarily increased the risk of a total Habsburg collapse, and if Thököli held his ground or went westward the greater the chance of more Turks or Tartars advancing across the Danube to cut the Austrians off. It was helter-skelter for Marsigli, who next moved with a picked group of men aiming to rescue the garrison at Braşov.[107] Then Lewis gained the upper hand. Thököli was not defeated in battle; but by the end of October was driven from Transylvania, to take shelter in Wallachia. As the confusion cleared Marsigli found himself entrusted with a commission to survey and block the Carpathian passes, in order to stop enemy raiders trying to use them.[108] This would be his work for the winter. Snow had started to fall.

A hard struggle to salvage the new Habsburg eastern empire offered him, therefore, some compensation for his greater loss in Serbia. He was again entering unfamiliar country which he tried to explore segment by segment. He had made a start the year before, when Lewis first crossed the Danube to look for winter quarters in the Wallachian lands. Marsigli would recall in dismayed language that desolate tract of 'Oltenia', the marshland and plain (west of the river Olt) where the rain poured down, the peasants fled, the troops found nothing, and there were no bridges.[109] The rudiments of Wallachian political strife had emerged when he was told to impound the treasure (kept in an Orthodox monastery of the Carpathian foothills) belonging to members of the Cantacuzene family who were rivals of the reigning prince, Constantine Brancoveanu. And it will be recalled that he accompanied Lewis, returning homeward, as far as Braşov, which was a highly important trading centre for Wallachians and Transylvanians alike. Now, a year later, Marsigli's mission to inspect and barricade the Carpathian passes gave him by degrees a more accurate notion of the regions and races of Transylvania within the surrounding ring of mountains, together with Wallachia, Moldavia and Bukovina outside it. He collected his materials on the spot. He made sketches of mountain ridges and passes, historical notes, and lists of placenames in different languages.[110] During part of this winter of 1690–1, he tells us, he was able to write a general account of the whole country. Meanwhile the government in Vienna tried to soothe the Transylvanian Estates with its 'Leopoldine Diploma', which appeared to offer them constitutional guarantees under Habsburg sovereignty. Veterani, as the commander in chief's deputy, attempted some tactful diplomacy in Bucharest; and this helped to push Thököli to the other side of the Danube. The Tartars meanwhile failed to re-enter the country, and Marsigli considered that his defensive measures in the passes were proving their value. He could spend at least part of the winter at Ghiurgiu, an ancient castle of the Transylvanian princes, contentedly assembling his papers.

By the end of February in the new year 1691, he was on his way back to Vienna. He travelled at a leisurely pace through Upper Hungary, in order to observe 'the line of the mountains' which divided Hungary from Poland. At the towns of Košice (Kassa) and Prešov (Eperjes) he halted to draft one of his longer reports, as usual adding the sketch map to which it referred. This was a paper on Moldavia addressed to chancellor Kinsky, and gave a useful account of the political and military pressures bearing on a large area.[111] In that principality, he wrote, the Poles have occupied the hilly ground where they have put garrisons in the principal monasteries. On the other hand, across the plains the Turks keep up communication with their great fortress in Podolia, Kamenets. Their frequent passage across the country has left it utterly waste. Beyond the plain, further east, were the delta lands of the Dobrudja occupied by the Tartars. It was their forward base – with the Tartars of the Crimea many days' ride behind them – which made it easy for the Ottoman government to summon auxiliary raiders at short notice to break into the neighbouring principalities, into Transylvania, Poland or Hungary. Then followed Marsigli's recommendation: the Habsburg government should encourage the Poles to keep what they had in Moldavia, in order to create a new barrier protecting Habsburg territory from Tartar raids. It should also try to annex for itself the region of Moldavia which lies between the river Seretz and the Danube. The plains could be consigned to 'total desolation', as a protective no man's land. Unfortunately the map, with an area marked in red assigned to the Turks and certain points marked for Habsburg occupation, does not survive. The general argument may not have impressed Kinsky at the time; but it interestingly anticipated by a century the Habsburg acquisition in 1775 of Bukovina, a region not very different from the extension of Leopold's empire proposed here.

In Vienna he found the politicians awaiting his arrival. There was always more work for count Marsigli.

VIII

On his circular retreat from Serbia to Transylvania, from there to north Hungary and back to Vienna, Marsigli had distanced himself from areas which engaged his full attention only a year earlier, Slavonia, Croatia, Bosnia and Albania: they too were deeply involved in the Ottoman recovery of 1690, and the Habsburg reverses.

Shortly before the Ottoman forces returned to Belgrade, an assembly of Orthodox clergy had met in the same city.[112] Those present duly ratified an agreement between Emperor Leopold I and the Serbian patriarch. The former recognised the latter's rights over Orthodox peoples of the Serbian language, not only in Serbia, Greece, Bulgaria, and Bosnia, but also in Croatia and Hungary. Correspondingly there was an undertaking given that these peoples would all serve the Emperor with due loyalty. Such vague assurances mutually given were understood in a context which everybody knew to be obscure and changeable. No one could predict where the border between Moslem and Christian empires would ultimately be placed, but the patriarch was now acknowledging his commitment to and reliance upon Habsburg support in the face of an Ottoman revival. For this reason the fall of Belgrade in September 1690 gave extra impetus to the long-standing migration northwards – tradition speaks of 36,000 families in this phase – of Orthodox people across the Danube and Sava into what had recently become Habsburg territory. The patriarch himself, as an exile from south Serbia, placed his see at Sremski Karlovci (Carlowitz)* in Syrmia. It was at the time only a few miles from Ottoman Belgrade, but would become an important Orthodox ecclesiastical and political centre from the last years of Leopold I until the reign of Franz Josef. The transfer of the patriarchate from Peć to Karlovci nevertheless underlined the failure and end of a great crusading design cherished in certain Catholic quarters, in Rome as in

---

* Sremski Karlovci, or Karlovci on modern maps. 'Carlowitz' is the usual English rendering for the treaties of peace concluded there in 1699.

Vienna. It also strengthened substantially the Orthodox and Slav presence in the Habsburg empire.

One who now declared himself opposed to the entire venture of a forward policy was Marsigli's acquaintance and superior, Antonio Carafa the commissary-general. In a memorandum probably written during the same winter of 1690–1 he gave his version of recent history.[113] From the beginning of his administration of the commissariat, he wrote, he disapproved of the decision to besiege Belgrade; if he was wrong, given the wonderful triumph of 1688, his was a just estimate of the resources available. He also disliked, and had argued against, the despatch of troops to fight in Germany before a peace treaty with the Turks was negotiated. The Ottoman power remained too strong an opponent – *non è un nemico d'esser mai disprezzato* – to make this sensible. He was against the extension of winter quarters into Bulgaria and Wallachia in 1689, Carafa continued, because it was open country vulnerable to enemy attacks. In the event we lost the flower of our army amd 'millions' of florins, putting both Transylvania and Hungary at risk. He objected equally to Veterani's proposals for the refortification of Niš. It was much too far away, a waste of money and effort, and the result was a disaster. In general, warfare on several fronts at the same time with Habsburg troops spread too thinly over a vast area east and west, and excessively long lines of communication stretching south from Hungary filled him with foreboding. What he preferred was the defence of a more compact region; and here in Hungary, he concluded, the efficient organisation of government should be Vienna's principal aim.

This summary must have tidied up, and possibly remodelled Carafa's varied pronouncements over a fairly long period, but there is no reason to doubt that he reckoned the conquest of Hungary and Transylvania between 1684 and 1688 a sufficient achievement. He had come to believe that these should be defended along their own boundaries, without further lunges into the Balkans. Their future depended on efficient, rigorous government. He was touching a sensitive nerve here – the controversy over administrative reform in Hungary in which he was deeply involved. A commission set up in 1687 to report on the topic met on 80 occasions in the course of 1688, received memoranda and considered recommendations. These in turn prompted a tremendous row between the leading reformer cardinal Kollonich, and Carafa as director of the military commissariat. Kollonich persuaded the Estates to join with him in blaming the army commissariat for chaotic and oppressive misgovernment in Hungary, and Carafa was edged out of his office. Gradually the Hofkammer or Treasury in Vienna increased its share of Hungarian revenues, but the military interest remained as oppressive as ever. The Estates' resentment at Viennese domination persisted. There were consequently few reforms of any kind.

Another shadow weighed on Leopold in 1690. His most fervent supporter in the Turkish war had been Pope Innocent who died in August 1689, and he was anxious to secure the election of a new pope who would accept Innocent's view of the great political questions of the day. Vienna looked for support from Innocent's nephew Livio Odescalchi, but erred in thinking that he had the will or the weight to influence sufficiently the votes of the cardinals' conclave. Leopold's letter of condolence, of 25 August, informed Livio of his elevation to the dignity of a 'Prince of the Holy Roman Empire'.[114] The Emperor could make this gesture with a stroke of his pen; the project associated with Marsigli, the elevation of Livio Odescalchi as prince or duke of Syrmia, was also revived but ran a more leisurely course.[115] Such a sweetener did little good. Innocent XI's successor adopted new policies. Pope Alexander VIII was friendlier than Innocent to the French king, he declined to find money for the Turkish war, and affronted Leopold by declining to adopt a single Habsburg nomination in either his first or second 'honours' list of new cardinals. He even announced a new proposal for the canonisation of John of Capestrano – the saviour of Belgrade in 1456 – in a manner considered insulting by Leopold's ambassador at Rome.[116] Rome in fact no longer moved in step with Vienna; from this point of view, if from no other, it became easier for the Emperor to consider negotiations with the Sultan.

Peace, treaties for peace, at least the need for peace in one part of Europe or another, were discussed by the politicians towards the end of 1690. In various ways they felt trapped. The Turks retook Belgrade in August but afterwards made little further progress. Leopold's Polish and Venetian partners had not advanced in Podolia, Moldavia or Greece; they too were halted. Nor were Leopold's western allies able to do more than hold their own against Louis XIV. Leopold's forces in Germany and Italy, like those of his partners, would soon require extra manpower as well as money; but both were equally needed in Hungary. These circumstances indicated deadlock as well as exhaustion. They were bound to encourage a notion that, if negotiation brought to an end the strain of war in one region, it could be better fought elsewhere. What also remained to be seen was how this situation affected our soldier of fortune, when he returned to Vienna with the ministers urgently asking for him, after his remarkable experience on both sides of the Danube.

CHAPTER FOUR

Count Marsigli's English Intermezzo

I

In the summer of 1690, recognising that the English ambassador at Istanbul wished to return home, William III decided to send out Sir William Hussey instead. In the normal way he would have travelled by sea on a Levant Company ship.[1] At the last moment there were difficulties, and it was decided – for the first time in English history – to send an ambassador overland to the Sultan by way of Vienna. Hussey had instructions to confer there with the English and Dutch envoys, Paget and Heemskerck, and with the Austrians, and then to attempt a mediation between Emperor and Sultan.[2] William was trying, as he had tried before and would try in future years, to edge the empires at war in eastern Europe to a peace in Hungary. Hussey reached Vienna on 30 November. When he left on 23 April 1691 to begin his journey down the Danube he was accompanied by Marsigli, Leopold's confidential servant.

The loss of Belgrade had dealt a serious blow to the morale of the Habsburg government. This and other losses in Serbia obscured the earlier victorious advance into Hungary; power to wage war offensively seemed to have vanished, and the Emperor's lowered prestige added to the difficulties of those who wanted to negotiate. A settlement on the basis of letting both empires keep what they held at the time, the formula of *uti possidetis** familiar to diplomats, was now less honourable for the Habsburg court than it would have been a year earlier. Too much ground had been lost since then and it was harder to believe that the grand vezir Fazil Mustafa Köprülü, having stabilised the Ottoman government by the glamour of victory, would be prepared to talk of peace, even a peace in which Leopold accepted *uti possidetis*. The Ottoman envoys Sulfikar and Mavrocordato were still de-

---

* This phrase, from a precept of Roman law, indicated to seventeenth-century politicians that the terms proposed for a truce or treaty between warring powers would entitle them to keep regions or strongholds they held at the time, unless exceptions were specified. Exchanges of territories and fortresses were negotiable, but the *fundamentum pacis* would remain: *uti possidetis*!

tained in Austria. They were repudiated by the grand vezir, and therefore posed an additional problem. Meanwhile, after a year of failure in the Netherlands, the Rhineland and Italy, the argument for withdrawing Habsburg forces from Hungary for service in the west seemed irresistible to the Dutch and English and the German princes; but, for Vienna, reinforcements would equally be needed in Hungary in the next campaign.[3] With all this to preoccupy him, Leopold corresponded with his good friend and counsellor father Marco, during the autumn of 1690, in a mood of deep depression. His ministers had discussed the terms on which they could reasonably advise him to negotiate with the Turks, but after a meeting on 5 August the tide of disaster along the Danube practically silenced the debate.[4] Three months later, better news gave the signal for reopening it. Transylvania was saved from Thököli, the line of the Drava north of Belgrade looked secure for the winter. The new English and Dutch proposal for a mediation needed an answer.

Hussey was received in audience by Leopold, and speaking in Italian he handed over William's letter.[5] It referred to the recent pacification of Ireland and a brighter future for the western alliance. Nothing would contribute more to this, it was stated, than a settlement in Hungary, and the king offered his services as mediator. The Habsburg ministers began again to discuss their terms for peace, and to consider how far they should go in authorising the English and Dutch to bargain with the grand vezir on their behalf. Lord Paget was soon writing to London that he expected Hussey's early departure from Vienna. Hussey sent to Belgrade requesting a passport from the Turkish commander. Leopold signed a reply to William on 7 December. From Christmas onwards the wheels turned much more slowly. The reply to William was held up and differing ministerial views were reported. Early in February Paget penned a stiff protest in his best Latin at the long delay, partly because he realised that the approaching thaw would offer an additional reason for putting off a journey down the Danube. As to the political reasons for this pause the English in Vienna could guess a good deal, even if they never saw the paper submitted by Kinsky to Leopold early in March.[6]

In his memorandum the Bohemian chancellor began by stating that the ministers, and Leopold, agreed in December to give the English ambassador powers to negotiate on the basis of *uti possidetis*, and to brief him about the territories in question by showing him 'the Marsigli map'. It was also their intention to associate with Hussey's mission one of Leopold's own servants to advise and restrain the Englishman as discreetly as possible. 'I am aware that your Imperial Majesty is considering Marsigli as the "adjutant"' to go with Hussey, wrote Kinsky; but he nonetheless remained doubtful and suspicious, asserting that the English and Dutch were eager for peace in eastern Europe on almost any terms. They would therefore press to be given the widest possible powers to negotiate and conclude a treaty. A recent conversation with Heemskerck had made this point perfectly clear to him: the mediating states and their agents were insisting that they fully deserved the Emperor's confidence, and they wanted authority to treat in his name. Hussey, once in the Turkish camp or court, would be very difficult to control. Kinsky now suggested, as a precaution, that at least the Habsburg government's minimum demands for a settlement should not be entrusted to Hussey but (until the last moment) to the Habsburg observer in the English mission, the 'adjutant'. He should judge when it was advisable to make a final concession for the sake of agreement. The chancellor went on to express another doubt. Was Marsigli the best or the only possible choice for such a sensitive post? To start with, he had not yet returned to Vienna, in spite of a message to general Veterani in Transylvania to find him. More important was his early misadventure as a prisoner of the Turks, to whom he must now be known as an Imperial officer. In any negotiation they would have 'a well-founded suspicion' of his real function, whatever the English might say in order to protect him. Alternatively, if Hussey came to know of Marsigli's past record he would possibly decline to run the risk of taking him, or indeed of taking anyone acting as an observer for Leopold. Kinsky also emphasised the certain suspicion of the Emperor's Venetian and Polish allies, once they learnt of William III's mediation in what was their own, and not only Leopold's war against the Sultan.

In spite of these objections there was agreement by the end of March. A flurry of letters and other documents launched Marsigli on a new phase of his career.[7] The Habsburg politicians worked over successive drafts of the material to be handed to Hussey for guidance, because from their point of view he started by knowing nothing of Habsburg interests, or of the course of the war and the negotiation of 1689 which failed to end it. They had to brief him about the different principalities and regions which, according to ancient charters, were subject to the kings of Hungary. Above all they had to give him a statement of their present terms for a truce or treaty. In general they stood out for peace on the footing of *uti possidetis* but at certain points asked for more than that, to allow room for manoeuvre. A sacrifice of legitimate Hasbsburg claims on Moldavia and Wallachia could be offered as compensation for requiring from the Turks the surrender of Timisoara. The exchange of outlying or isolated fortified posts, for the sake of a more secure boundary, was also suggested. But the mediators should first propose these terms in their own name; subsequently they must refer them back to the Emperor, who would act in concert with his allies of the Holy Alliance. Finally a new clause was added on 31 March to the earlier draft of these instructions. It says that if the Turks asked for detailed modifications to a settlement *uti possidetis*, the English envoy ought to take advantage of count Marsigli's presence on his staff, in view of his great expertise and knowledge.[8] So Marsigli was accurate enough, when he wrote later that he returned to Vienna in March 1691 to find Kinsky and Stratmann impatiently expecting him.

It took them a week to persuade the English ambassadors that he should now join Hussey's household with the title of secretary, for the journey to the Sultan's court.[9] The advantage offered to Hussey was that he would have somebody at his elbow who knew the unfamiliar world he was on the point of entering; while he needed an interpreter before he met his English colleagues and their dragomans in Adrianople or Istanbul. The advantage for Kinsky and Stratmann was a chance to place their own agent in or near the conference chamber where Habsburg interests would be much at risk. They had already talked Marsigli into a venture which looked dangerous, in certain respects distasteful, as well as politically important. As if to impress him with the need for secrecy, they conferred on one occasion – Stratmann, Kinsky, Marsigli and Werdenberg, who was the permanent secretary of the conference of ministers – in the seclusion of count Harrach's garden.[10] As they knew, he yearned for advancement and reputation. Instead, it was put to him that he must first give up his place in the army and ask for release from Leopold's service. Under cover of employment as William's ambassador's secretary they expected him to report back to them on the progress of the negotiation for peace with the Turks.

His own feelings and opinions emerge from his letters and from his autobiography.[11] His patrons wanted him to suspend, and perhaps end, his military career. They wanted him to join an English envoy's staff, having been honourably dismissed by Leopold, but without giving any publicity to the fact. This finesse troubled him, and he consulted a priest; but if he sighed as a man of conscience and pride he obeyed as Leopold's loyal servant, asking that in due course he might be rewarded. The Emperor assented, and care was also taken to pay off his arrears. Another matter to be settled concerned the use of a cipher and the transmission of letters when Hussey and Marsigli reached the Sultan's dominion. Accordingly Marsigli deposited in Vienna copies of his own seal, so that it could be recognised. Kinsky wanted his agent to communicate with him, when the need arose, by addressing letters to the English ambassador Lord Paget. It was hoped that these, under diplomatic protection, would enjoy immunity from inspection by the Turks; but, because they were first marked by Marsigli with an agreed symbol adjoining his seal, they could then be intercepted by alert Habsburg commanders in the course of their transmission through Hungary, and redirected to the relevant chancery in Vienna. Marsigli made no difficulty. Paget, when he later detected the device, had his low opinion of Kinsky confirmed while his petulance about Marsigli would echo and re-echo for many years in the reports he wrote to Whitehall.

Marsigli's own views in April 1691 on a possible peace treaty were passed on to the ministers. He took for granted the permanence of Habsburg rule in Hungary, Transylvania and nearly all Croatia, but argued that Vienna must aim at the complete domination of Slavonia – the lands between Drava, Danube and Sava – whether by negotiation or by fighting. He reasoned that only this would assure control of the Bácska, that sensitive

area between the Danube and Tisza which would be too exposed to Ottoman power if the Turks held the right bank of the Danube above Belgrade.
He also considered that control over any part of Slavonia depended on
having all of it; Slavonia could not be divided. From this premise he derived
another: in order to keep Slavonia, and with it the line of the Sava, Belgrade
on the river's further shore must first be regained, or there should at least
be an agreement to have its citadel demolished.[12] Just possibly there could
be a demilitarised zone covering the tip of Slavonia, his old stamping
ground of Syrmia. This last idea, which seems to contradict the notion that
Slavonia was indivisible, came prophetically close to the settlement reached
in the treaty of Carlowitz in 1699. At Carlowitz Marsigli would be present,
with Paget.

By mid-April the discussions in Vienna were completed. One last point
to be settled was that if the grand vezir appeared ready to debate seriously
the details of a treaty, Hussey should send Marsigli back to report and
receive fresh instructions before returning to the ambassador.[13] There was
also an understanding about funds, partly to pay Marsigli, partly to cover
the offer of suitable bribes to the grand vezir or other Turkish officials. No
doubt the practical preparations were going ahead but unfortunately details
about boats, crews, escorts, servants and stores elude us. On 23 April Sir
William and Lady Hussey and their company left Vienna to begin the
journey down the river to Buda, Belgrade and beyond. On the same day
Paget wrote a short letter of introduction addressed to Hussey on behalf of
Marsigli, who did indeed leave Vienna two days later and caught up with
the ambassador at Esztergom, just inside Hungary.[14] This was apparently
the first meeting of William's envoy and his new secretary, in spite of the
preceding web of negotiations which concerned their partnership. Perhaps
Kinsky preferred to keep the two apart until the last possible moment.

II

Marsigli's association with the English government lasted about twelve
months, while English diplomats came to vie with one another in their
mistrust of this colleague and 'secretary'. In the performance of his new
duties he travelled unceasingly. He went from Vienna to Adrianople with
Hussey, descending the Danube as far as Ruschuk in Bulgaria; from
Adrianople overland to Belgrade and back to Vienna; from Vienna a second
time to Bulgaria and to Istanbul; from Istanbul north to Bucharest and
through Transylvania to Hungary; then back to Bucharest and Istanbul;
and finally to Vienna from Istanbul. This totals two long journeys down the
Danube, three visits to Bucharest, four traverses through the Balkan passes,
and an acquaintance several times renewed with sections of the direct route
from Istanbul to Belgrade.

13   The Drava joins the Danube. A word to Kinsky: Marsigli suggests building watch-towers on each
of the Drava (1, 2) and, if the ground is solid enough 'something like a fortress' opposite (3). Incid
tally, he is not very well: the food served to Hussey does not agree with him. Compliments to coun
Kinsky.

Hussey's comment on the first of these itineraries was very sweeping: 'tis
a noble country both sides [of the Danube] but perfectly destroyed, not a
house, men, culture, or beasts from Komárom to Nicopolis'; and he was
struck too by the relative absence of river traffic.[15] The immensities of the
waterway, bounded for the most part by broad stretches of reeds or swamp,
blotted out from his memory any image of the smaller inhabited points
outside such places as Buda and Belgrade. His secretary saw little more, to
judge from the tedious diary he kept,[16] although Kinsky received a sprightly
note with a sketch of the region where the Drava enters the Danube.
Marsigli wished to show how best to fortify this important junction.[17] As
they moved on downstream, getting steadily nearer territories under Ottoman control, he also reflected that peculiar dangers faced him in his role as
the Emperor's servant 'among the barbarians', even while enjoying some
security as the English ambassador's secretary. It was a most dangerous
game to play. Yet before long he found the Turks treating him with perfect
courtesy, while he in turn renewed his normally sympathetic scrutiny of
Ottoman institutions. Sir William was first saluted by Turkish guns at Ilok,
so recently in Habsburg hands. At Belgrade there were more ceremonies
and interviews while the transports were assembled for the next stage of his
journey. Marsigli, if not able to speak Turkish with fluency, had to act as

interpreter for a dialogue between the Ottoman commander, or *seraskir*, and the ambassador. Hussey wished him to say things which by no means satisfied Emperor Leopold's loyal servant, who could hardly protest. The commander speedily promised an escort of 150 Egyptian Janissaries, who were returning to Cairo, for the journey down the river.[18] The Turks feared raiding parties of 'heyducks', marauders who were active in the region of the Danube rapids. The prestige of William III stood high in Ottoman circles, and they would not have wished to see his envoy molested.

The travellers moved peacefully from Belgrade down the Danube in the course of eight days, with an occasional twitch of the nerves for Marsigli. He was affectionately welcomed by one or two people at landing stages along the shore. They recognised a familiar figure, the former road builder and surveyor of ancient ruins, and he had to assure a Turkish officer of his status as the English envoy's servant. Once past Vidin the danger receded. He was unknown to the inhabitants on either bank, and the country was new to him; he busily drew sketches of the river's course, and looked out for Roman remains. Hussey meanwhile took note of the information that a journey in the opposite direction would have taken three or four times as long, 'such toil the Turks have to hug up their shores'. Stopping at Vidin he sent two men to Thököli's camp in Bulgaria, where they observed 'the greatest poverty imaginable, poor horses, men almost naked, ragged tents', and the wine sour. Whereas he himself dispensed 'good Rhenish and plenty' to those who visited him.[19] Landing at Ruschuk the little party climbed through the Balkan passes and reached Adrianople safely. They stopped to breathe, and Marsigli went to hear mass in what he calls the 'Ragusan' church.[20] Hussey at last commenced the final stage of his over-land journey from London to Istanbul. But two days further on they met another party of Englishmen coming in the opposite direction. It included merchants, Thomas Coke, who was secretary to the retiring ambassador Sir William Trumbull, and an interpreter named Antonio Peroni. They brought their new ambassador advice from Istanbul that the Ottoman court and a great body of troops were on the move immediately behind them, all bound for Adrianople. Hussey was handed a missive from the grand vezir inviting him to an audience there, and he turned back immediately. A few days later Sultan Suleyman II himself, described by Marsigli as a handsome man afflicted by dropsy, entered Adrianople and went to the palace. Grand vezir Köprülü, less impressive in looks but the ablest man of his time in Ottoman politics, took up residence in a suitably magnificent tent outside the walls, surrounded by the troops of the army. He gave audience to Hussey, with two secretaries and two interpreters, on 11 June 1691.[21] Marsigli himself had never before been so close to the seat of Ottoman power.

The discussion went well. Köprülü was all courtesy. He would not hear of a negotiation at Vienna, proposed by Hussey,[22] but wanted to know whether Hussey himself had authority from the Emperor to negotiate: in that case he offered to call for ink and paper at once. Hussey, speaking through his interpreters, said that this further step could not be contemplated until the grand vezir's own inclinations were known. To this the answer came swiftly that the grand vezir would judge the possibilities of peace in the theatre of warfare, and that he was on his way there at the head of the Sultan's army. The talking went on, and Hussey at length offered to send his secretary back to the Emperor's court, to ask for authority to be given to the Habsburg commander in the field, Lewis of Baden, to treat with the Turks. The English and Dutch ambassadors would continue to do everything in their power to assist the two principals. The vezir finally agreed to this plan.

During the next few months Marsigli travelled amazing distances, and did so at amazing speed. He reached Vienna from Adrianople, after this conference, by the end of June. He was in Istanbul early in August, then in Hungary again, and once more in Istanbul by the very end of November. No other of William III's or Leopold's servants covered so many Balkan miles in the year 1691, threading a way through hostile armies to link together Habsburg and Ottoman politicians in a haggle for peace. Meanwhile both Sultan Suleiman and Sir William Hussey died. The grand vezir was killed in the battle of Slankamen (18/19 August 1691). A venture with possibly broad implications ended in total failure, as many had predicted. One minor figure however, in spite of setbacks public and private, continued to add to his peculiar store of knowledge and experience.

Plentifully provided with instructions, letters from Hussey, and passports in Turkish and Italian, Marsigli had set off from Adrianople in what his own account describes as a fast and triumphal progress.[23] As far as Belgrade it was his old route via Niš, where he stopped to observe the points at which the Turkish assault swept so easily in 1690 through the defences which he had himself helped to design. Crossing the Morava he caught up with a large contingent of traders hesitant to advance through the difficult country ahead, fearful of Christian irregulars on the prowl. But they trusted his own diplomatic immunity, he claims, and followed when he led. Greeted by the cheers of the inhabitants and a salvo of gunfire they entered Belgrade together. The Turkish commander here repeated his former courtesies to the English ambassador's secretary, and expressed his hopes for peace. Marsigli left again, almost at once. Crossing the Sava and passing out of the region under Ottoman control, he felt confident that in the shortest possible time he had seen much of value, and was well qualified to describe to his real masters the strengths and weaknesses of the Ottoman empire. Welcomed in Vienna by Leopold, Kinsky and others, he could consider himself not simply a courier with despatches, but the indispensable and ubiquitous adviser.

There was little time to lose. Out of a welter of discussions and memoranda[24] two main decisions were reached: Lewis of Baden, already on his way through Hungary to the front, should be given powers to negotiate for

peace with the grand vezir; and Lewis must first of all try to defeat the
Ottoman forces in the field. It was necessary also to invite the English and
Dutch to join the negotiation; it was not necessary to inform them that
Lewis had been authorised beforehand to attempt a battle. Behind this
thinking were some of the arguments (but not all) suggested by Marsigli in
a lengthy memorandum dated 10 July.[25] He felt convinced that the Ottoman
army was growing weaker as the years passed, by comparing what he
thought were its numbers in 1683 (when Vienna was besieged) and 1691.
He emphasised the decline of the Janissary corps and overlooked the Ottoman recovery in 1690. At the same time it was his opinion that if the Turks
suffered a really catastrophic setback in battle their disorganisation would
be such that no negotiation could take place; the Habsburg troops would be
pinned down in the Balkans indefinitely. Given the Ottoman collapse in
1687 after the battle at Nagyharsány, it was a possible scenario, and so he
advised a treaty with the grand vezir before he was beaten. This view was
rejected by Leopold's ministers. They were certainly right in thinking that
the grand vezir, on the eve of a campaign which he hoped would recover
Hungary for the Sultan, would be unlikely to negotiate seriously beforehand. Very guardedly, therefore, they authorised further discussion. Carrying letters and instructions from his masters in Vienna, and in the guise of
the English ambassador's secretary, Marsigli set out again.

He was received by Lewis at Vukovar on the Danube in Syrmia, and then
in Belgrade by the grand vezir. The first, having studied his orders, took the
opportunity to write to William III stating that he had authority to negotiate
and conclude a peace, as soon as it could be managed 'avec un peu de
raison'.[26] The vezir, though wonderfully affable, continued his vigorous
preparations for the campaign ahead, and simply sped Marsigli down the
Danube again to the English and Dutch envoys in Istanbul. Having earlier
insisted that the opposing commander in chief should be given full powers
to treat with him, he also required the English and Dutch ambassadors to
attend any conference with Lewis. So he sent Marsigli to fetch Hussey and
Colyer (the Dutch Resident). On this occasion the traveller rode first to the
well-remembered site of Smederevo, where he embarked on the Danube. It
took him ten days to reach the ambassador's house in Pera. He had a kind
welcome, he writes, but was tired: business was for tomorrow.[27]

III

During Marsigli's recent stay in Vienna and his journey back to the
Bosphorus two other events occurred. The one, novel and important,
helped to mould his life. The other was just singular enough to embarrass
him deeply.

Lord Paget's chaplain was St. George Ashe, a Dublin mathematician and virtuoso. He had written a year earlier to Edmond Halley of the Royal Society in London in the following terms:

> Since my last to you, in a long voyage down the Danube I have made several observations on that river, which is most faultily described by all the charts I ever yet could meet with, but my remarks are too loose and unconnected for a letter; I have likewise visited the mines and baths of Hungary and seen most that was considerable in that country. . . . You can scarce imagine how very ignorant a place this Vienna is, among the numerous crowd of priests and other religious here, and notwithstanding their famous and ancient university, there is not one Mathematician to be found, and should I fix my telescope I should fear being seized by the Inquisition as a conjuror. Besides, we are placed in so inconvenient and unastronomical a house that there is no managing an instrument, and scarce seeing a star. I have been forced to send almost to Venice for a glass tube to make a barometer. . . . I have yet enquired to no purpose for some mathematical officer in the Imperial army, in order to persuade him (as you desire), to make a map of the new conquests, but do not yet despair of finding such a person.[28]

Ashe therefore was part of that exciting new network which Oldenburg, Hooke, and Halley had been trying to extend over the known world in order to obtain more accurate data on certain scientific problems. They wanted material for the Philosophical Transactions of their Society, letters from learned men abroad, answers to the questionnaires which they handed to travellers. They wanted data for investigations into history, natural history, geology, for improvements in cartography and astronomy, and for other topics. The Englishmen were contemporaries of Cassini (once Montanari's teacher in Bologna) and his colleagues at the Académie des Sciences and the new Observatory in Paris, who launched in the 1670s a more ambitious cartographic survey of France than had been attempted before. They were now sending out men – together with up-to-date instruments – to check latitudes and longitudes in West Africa and the West Indies. They were partly responsible, also, for the recent despatch of French Jesuit 'mathématiciens du roi' to Siam en route for China, where the missionaries hoped to add to the sum of western knowledge in several fields, and particularly in the making of new maps. Their great Dutch contemporary was Nicholas Witsen, with his special interest in Russia and Siberia. This indefatigable correspondent and collector of cartographic and botanical news from distant regions had published in 1687 his new map of Siberia, to be warmly thanked for his labours by the president of the Royal Society. His volume on 'North and East Tartary' appeared in 1692.[29] Similar in certain respects would be the enterprise of John Jacob Scheuchzer of Zurich, who in 1697 issued his 'Letter of Invitation for Research into the Wonders of Nature to be found in Switzerland', with a formidable list of 186 questions attached for the benefit of those who cared to reply.[30] However Ashe's letter shows that Halley had in mind a different idea: the scientific opportunity presented by the Habsburg armies' advance into lands which had been for centuries a part of the secluded Ottoman empire.

Ashe's communication was read to a meeting of the Royal Society on 6 August 1690.[31] In July 1691 he wrote again:

> I remember in a letter of yours, some months ago, you obliged me to enquire what geographical discoveries and improvements had been made in that vast tract of ground and territory, which before the last year was in possession of the Imperialists, and which is a mere Terra Incognita in most of our modern Charts; and though I have not since been negligent in informing myself, yet I could never meet with any that gave a tolerable account, or took pains in that affair, till by good fortune I became acquainted with Count Lewis Ferdinand Marsigli (the gentleman who addresses the enclosed letter to the Society, by which you will perceive what he has done, and offers to communicate). He is a nobleman of Bologna, but has been for many years employed in the Emperor's service as Colonel of the Engineers, and on that account had frequent occasion to visit all parts of the new conquests, which he assures me are shamefully misplaced in all the modern maps he has seen, and I have reason to believe him by the little of Hungary I saw last year, where (consulting the best charts I could light on) I found often whole rivers ridiculously misplaced. The gentleman has an ambition to be admitted to the Royal Society, to which honour if you think the communication he now promises, and the services he may hereafter do, to be deserving 'twou'd prove no small encouragement to his future endeavours to give him an account he had been elected. You may write to him (if you please) in Latin, French, or Italian, and address your letter to me. . . .[32]

Marsigli was duly elected a fellow of the Royal Society on 25 November 1691.

His own letter, referred to by Ashe, was written during that hectic period of political activity when he had returned briefly to Vienna from Adrianople. He was on the point of setting out again for Belgrade and Istanbul. It is a long screed in grandiloquent Italian but discloses intellectual ambitions of undoubted seriousness.[33] He starts with the Society's wish – described to him by his friend Ashe – for the improvement of maps in the public service. He states that his many journeys on military and diplomatic business have enabled him to make geographical observations in Hungary, Wallachia, Moldavia, Serbia, parts of Bosnia and the whole of Croatia. He has studied the remains of the Roman empire in those regions. He has learnt to disentangle the confusion in the names of places, rivers and mountains due to the variety of different languages in this great tract of country. Above all, he has mastered the 'anatomy' of the Danube, its course, currents, its species of fish and birds, and the natural history of its banks. He wishes that he had used better surveying instruments; he regrets that he has so far omitted solar and stellar observation; and recognises that others will have to refine and supplement his work. But if these labours were considered worthy of publication, he can imagine no better tribunal than the Royal Society in London to appraise and correct them.

Marsigli compiled his great book. The Society remained his helpful patron. What could not be foreseen were the mischances which delayed publication for twenty-five years.

IV

The other matter which thoroughly alienated the English in eastern Europe was broached by Paget to Kinsky on 17 August 1691 at the Favorita, Leopold's residence outside Vienna.[34] He asked the Bohemian chancellor whether he had opened a letter addressed to Paget. Yes, came the reply, because a particular mark on it meant that the letter, from Marsigli, was meant for Kinsky. He imagined that the English ambassador had been already advised of the procedure. Paget, enormously indignant, protested to the Emperor at an audience a few days later: this was not the purpose of the invitation to Marsigli to join Hussey's staff, nor of his title of secretary. It had not been in Paget's mind, but it was in Kinsky's. Paget should surely have learnt enough about Marsigli beforehand to realise that he was an exceptionally zealous servant of Leopold who intended, and was intended, to continue working for his former patron. Paget was also irritated to discover that the Emperor had just granted powers to his commander in chief to negotiate a peace, while declining to give any real discretion to William III's envoys as mediators between the two imperial powers. Consequently he disliked all the more the caperings of Marsigli on his special missions to Istanbul or the headquarters of Lewis and the grand vezir in the field.

Disenchantment about Hussey's secretary soon spread from Vienna to the English in Istanbul. His personality and behaviour reflected other interests rather than their own, and he irritated them. One spark to their annoyance was a letter reaching Hussey which apparently no one in the household could read, because Marsigli had the key of the cipher and was absent on his travels.[35] When he did arrive, 'according to his Custom with much more Noise in my poor opinion than his Despatch required', a conference was called immediately in order to discuss what should be done.[36] Could they do anything if the Emperor had given powers to negotiate solely to his commander in the field? Sir William Trumbull (on the point of departure by sea for England), Hussey, Coke, the Dutch resident Colyer and Marsigli were present, and Hussey posed the question whether it was their duty to leave Istanbul at once, make for the grand vezir's headquarters, offer their mediation, and press for a treaty. In accordance with his instructions Colyer said that he was determined to go. Hussey, nervous that the Dutchman might bring off a significant diplomatic coup and claim all the credit, decided to accompany him although his English colleagues doubted the wisdom of the venture. Trumbull and Coke, with much more experience of the Ottoman world than Hussey, were distinctly less hopeful. Marsigli sided with Hussey, and was sent ahead on the great road to Serbia and Hungary to give notice of the ambassadors' intentions to the Ottoman and Habsburg generals.

Unknown to these diplomats the terrible battle of Slankamen, a few miles up the Danube from Belgrade, was just then taking place in the unbearable August heat. It ended with heavy losses on both sides and the death of the grand vezir. In Ottoman territory there was a report that Lewis of Baden was also dead, which proved inaccurate, and then that Belgrade itself seemed at risk. As Marsigli hurried along through Sofia he began to find, coming towards him, an ever-increasing mass of refugees with their baggage, fleeing from soldiers and robbers on the move in Serbia. There were rumours, then news, of an Ottoman catastrophe. He himself had no reason for going further if the grand vezir was dead; and he retraced his steps to Adrianople to find the Sultan, with a new grand vezir in place, both doing their best to play for time. The English and Dutch ambassadors had arrived, and the vezir expressed a willingness to negotiate with the Habsburg general on a basis of *uti possidetis*. He asked them to accompany him to Belgrade, and Hussey was able to write on 7 September to both Vienna and London giving a hopeful account of the prospects for peace.[37] Prompted, probably, by his adviser, he decided to send Marsigli direct to Lewis with the fullest and latest information from the Ottoman court. Sadly, these were the ambassador's last actions. We are told that outside Adrianople, 'lodged in a garden half a mile from the city in a boggy bad air', he died of fever on 24 September.[38] By then Marsigli was already far away, on his journey to find Lewis.

This time he followed an itinerary through Wallachia and Transylvania, longer but safer. At Bucharest there were some lighter touches.[39] The prince, Brancoveanu, speaking to Marsigli at supper, whispered that he had no real difficulty in distinguishing a servant of the Emperor from a servant of the English king, and then loudly drank a toast in honour of William III. The prince's uncle, the *stolnic* or High Steward Constantine Cantacuzene, took pleasure of a different kind in Marsigli's company; they were both former students of Padua university, both notable collectors of books, maps and manuscripts, and could talk of such matters. The Wallachian politicians underlined their friendly feelings for Leopold, after news of what appeared to be an Ottoman defeat at Slankamen, but as usual they also wished to retain their freedom of manoeuvre. Time pressed for Marsigli, and he hurried on across the hills to Sibiu (Hermannstadt/Nagyszeben)[40] and from there to the town of Lipova on the river Maros, which had been taken from the Turks a few days earlier. Round about was a chaotic region where Ottoman and Habsburg troops, and irregulars, were all present but indistinctly aware of each other's movements. Marsigli alternately tried to speak

German to those he met or flourished his Turkish passport, whichever seemed appropriate. Straying into Turkish-held territory, he then left it again and at last found Lewis of Baden camped in a swamp. In the darkness, he says, the commander in chief heard him speaking outside his tent. 'Is that the count Marsigli?' Lewis asked. 'Si, serenissimo,' was the reply.[41]

After Slankamen most of the Habsburg forces had been withdrawn across the Danube and across the Tisza eastwards. It had been decided not to risk them in a fresh attack on Belgrade; there was not enough shipping and artillery. But the Ottoman strongholds beyond the Tisza, Timisoara and Oradea, seemed sensible and tempting prizes for Lewis. To occupy one or both would consolidate the Habsburg dominion in Hungary, which mattered more than extending it across the Danube. This priority, or preference, echoed the opinion he favoured earlier. When Marsigli arrived to tell Lewis of a possible negotiation with the new grand vezir, he agreed to examine the proposal while continuing to prepare for an assault on Oradea. Marsigli assisted with his sketch maps in the course of a week's hard discussion, and there emerged the 'punti', or points, that Lewis gave Marsigli in the form of a memorandum to take back to the English and Dutch ambassadors for transmission to the Turks.[42] They were put forward as the basis for a settlement between Sultan and Emperor and the Emperor's allies. One of the points was that *uti possidetis* should generally apply. Another was that there should be agreement for the exchange of lands and strongholds; and that unneeded strongholds should be demolished. Lewis believed, mistakenly, that Habsburg forces would occupy Timisoara; and he offered to demolish its defence works if the Turks did the same at Oradea. He added that if the Poles insisted on recovering the fortress of Kamenets in Podolia, the Turks might first be entitled to rase its defences. A further point dealt with the delicate matter of a rendezvous for the negotiation, and Lewis offered to go to Timisoara if the grand vezir went to Belgrade, or to Braşov if the vezir stationed himself in Nicopolis: from these places, preparations for a conference between plenipotentiaries could be arranged. It was for the allied ambassadors and Marsigli to 'elucidate' the response of the Turks. In another document, of 6 October, Lewis wrote informing the two ambassadors that he would respond as soon as they and the vezir reached Belgrade; he had committed his detailed proposals to Marsigli and relied on the 'prudence of the said Count'.[43]

While these phrases were being pondered Marsigli himself wrote a very lengthy account for Leopold, giving the whole narrative of his visits to Belgrade and Istanbul. He described his failure to reach the grand vezir Köprülü in time, and the long traverse via Bucharest and Sibiu to Baden's camp. He said something but little of value about the general issue of war or peace. The Ottoman empire was in a desperate condition, he thought, and therefore the Emperor could choose whether to make peace now, or fight on and win later. More useful was a vigorous sketch depicting a possible boundary. It assigned Oradea to the Habsburgs, but left part of the territory

14 Advice to the Emperor: a page from the memorandum addressed to Leopold, 7 October 1691.

of Timisoara, Belgrade and the Serbian hinterland in the hands of the Sultan. It was a fairly accurate foreshadowing of the settlement of 1699.

These documents were drafted in the midst of an inconclusive autumnal season of fighting and raiding in eastern Hungary. It was Marsigli's business to find his way through it in order to return to the English ambassador at Adrianople; he had yet to hear of Hussey's death. He began well and arrived safely inside the defences of Oradea, where the Ottoman commander gladly provided the king of England's servant with an escort and papers. They moved forward again, but about fifty miles further on were attacked by an armed band.[44] In the confusion it was not possible to see who the assailants were, the Emperor's men, the Sultan's, Tartars, or just thieves. A Turk leading the escort displayed the pasha's passport, and Marsigli – according to his own account – waved another which Lewis had given him. He was wounded with cuts on his head and legs, perhaps not as badly as at first he feared. The Turk was killed but a friendly Serb guided the survivors back to Lipova. Marsigli recovered sufficiently in a few days to be fit enough to travel the next stage in a litter, going east this time into Transylvania. From there, 'with a trembling hand', the result of his wounds, he wrote once more to Leopold and Kinsky.[45] He said that the present difficulties would by no means deter him from his duty as a servant of His Imperial Majesty. He had learnt of Hussey's death, but assumed that he could still act as a member of the English diplomatic staff in Ottoman territory. In almost the same breath he begged for preferment – the colonelcy of a regiment or a chamberlain's post at court – as a sign that his mission was completed.

His health slowly returned. He passed through Sibiu, Braşov and Bucharest, with plenty of time to reflect once again on the possibilities for peace. At Braşov he laid emphasis on the absolute importance for the Habsburgs of that part of Hungary east of the Tisza from which he himself had just come. Conversely, it was now his view that if the Habsburgs could not regain Belgrade, none of their claims on Bosnia or Albania could be enforced. In fact Marsigli was edging closer to a belief that the Danube below Belgrade (and the river Sava west of it, at any rate as far as Croatia) constituted the sensible frontier worth fighting for, and worth a treaty of peace. Everything north of this must be taken and held. Everything further south, probably, was beyond reach. Such a settlement, it seemed, the Ottomans could possibly be brought to accept. Marsigli was far from systematic as a writer of political memoranda. Contradictory, voluble, he rushed across the empty page and filled it. Inconsistent opinions were juxtaposed without any final decision for one or the other. In this particular case the difficulty is to decide whether he or any of the statesmen in Vienna believed that the chances of a peace or truce with the Turks depended on clever diplomatic manipulation of the position. Between July, when he had first returned from Vienna to Adrianople, and his journey to see Lewis in October, Marsigli was certainly hopeful. At the same time Leopold wrote in almost blithe terms to father Marco about the prospect of peace because 'the Turks themselves desire it'.[46] Even Paget, at one moment, felt that there were reasons for thinking an agreement to be not far off. On the other hand the English residing in Istanbul never imagined that there was the slightest chance of a settlement. They spoke of the 'odd, unaccountable voyage', the 'sham journey' to Adrianople led by Hussey.[47]

When Marsigli in turn reached Adrianople, against his expectation he found himself both isolated and becalmed. There was no longer friendly Sir William, ready to agree on how to handle Lewis of Baden's new approach to the Ottoman court. Instead he had to rely on the goodwill of Colyer, and when the Dutchman was given audience by the grand vezir in order to discuss the offer, he was met with an absolute refusal to consider the matter further.[48] Marsigli was present and the vezir expressed sympathy for his bandaged head, but little else. This seemed to put an end to the whole splendid design for a pacification in eastern Europe. Or, as Mr Coke put it more grimly, 'the treaty of peace . . . has the success [that] was rationally to be expected'.[49] The old guard of conventionally-minded Moslem officers and teachers in the Ottoman empire rejected any idea of a settlement, imposing their views on a grand vezir who was now forced to modify his earlier offer to treat. Marsigli reported to Vienna a confrontation between the grand vezir and the *aga* of the Janissaries on the choice of war or peace, and the execution of another vezir who confided to him, Marsigli, in Belgrade a few months earlier his wish for peace. On the other side Lewis of Baden had failed to take either of the enemy strongholds, Oradea and Timisoara.

In January 1692 Colyer and Marsigli, after their failure, could only retire to Istanbul.[50] Coke and his friends of the Levant Company had already rejected what they described as Marsigli's bombastic letters supporting his claim to be secretary of their embassy. He was no longer admitted to the little English 'commonwealth' maintained in the absence of an ambassador. It was Coke, said Marsigli, who spread the rumour that he was a spy. It was Coke, certainly, who called him a 'vain, hot-headed young man'. So he went away, to enjoy what he described as a solitary life in the vastness of the city.[51] However, in April he heard that the prince of Wallachia supported a new plan for uniting Greeks, Serbs and Roumans under the banner of Moscow, and for restoring an Orthodox Christian empire on the ruins of the Sultan's power. Such a dream, already mooted in 1688, still lacked practicality in 1692 and was soon returned to limbo. Then came messages with a different tune relayed by the Dutch envoys in Istanbul and Vienna. William III again pressed for a settlement in eastern Europe; he was sending Sir William Harbord to succeed Hussey, and with similar instructions. The Turks and Viennese replied politely, but Kinsky saw that Marsigli could not possibly play his role a second time and recalled him. So in due course Marsigli slipped away from Istanbul, and without fuss chose a novel route by skirting the Black Sea coast to get to Bucharest. Apparently the ghost of old hopes for a speedy peace, to be secured by some kind of diplomatic artifice, still lingered round him. A Turkish escort was in attendance, he writes, with orders to wait in Bucharest for his own return or for the arrival of letters from the Habsburg court addressed to Colyer in Istanbul.[52] He added that, if a new English ambassador reached Belgrade during the summer, he would find the Turkish authorities willing to negotiate for peace. Marsigli was almost certainly wrong, although William had ordered Harbord to follow his predecessor overland to the Ottoman court, and offer mediation as before. Harbord, like Hussey, was briefed by Paget and by Kinsky.[53] He went on his way to Belgrade and there fell sick and died on 24 September. He was the second English ambassador to die in the Balkans within a year.

By then Marsigli had already crossed through Transylvania and returned to Vienna. During his journey he gave advance notice of his wishes.[54] He wanted nothing more, he declared, than to kneel at the feet of His Majesty and sit at the council table with the ministers, discussing the politics of the Sultan's court. He repeated his request for preferment of a more settled and honourable kind, the command of a regiment or a chamberlain's place near Leopold. It would be colonel Marsigli who stepped into the shoes of a former English ambassador's secretary.

V

That last winter in Istanbul, between January and April, had not been empty. While his wound was healing, he took over 'a little house with a tiny garden', found a servant and turned to the study of natural history.

In the garden he delighted to watch the flowers blooming as the spring came. He was so pleased by the buttercups and their like that he collected ranunculi roots, and had them sent home to Bologna. There they flourished, so that in 1694 drawings could be made for him of half a dozen different varieties.[55] Moreover this second stay in Istanbul was similar to the first in that he spent a great deal of time afloat, or by the shore. He paid less attention to the currents of the Bosphorus, and much more to marine plants, corals and fish. He started asking for the local names of the fish, collecting 120 each in Turkish and Greek.[56] He noted the crabs, lobsters, starfish and shells. Having watched fishermen gutting their catch, he carried out his own dissection (a dogfish on 1 June 1692, and later a brill), taking the trouble to write them up and complete his work with meticulous illustrations. The fishermen ferried him to the Princes' Islands in the Sea of Marmara, and there he examined the different sorts of coral, noting particularly their changes of colour in and out of the water.[57] What interested him most of all was 'the movement of fish', their migrations. He learnt of certain species leaving the Black Sea during the autumn to seek gentler winter conditions in the Aegean, as far south as Smyrna: the narrowness of the Bosphorus made it easier to watch both this and the return movement in spring. He saw for himself that sponges from the Princes' Islands might hold the spawn of those fish which found the Sea of Marmara congenial and did not migrate. He noted with interest, if at second hand, that turbot – 'a big fish with the best flavour' – was plentiful off the Black Sea coasts in summertime as far as the delta of the Danube.[58]

A great deal else caught his fancy. He collected more Turkish manuscripts, including works on chemistry, astronomy, geography and history. His Jewish interpreter during his earlier stay in the city, with whom he got in touch again, introduced him to a renegade from Livorno, another dealer, who procured for him Greek manuscripts, Ottoman maps and other geographical material. Marsigli used some of these to begin a comparative list of placenames in several languages. Nor was this all. '. . . I finished writing my work on the Ottoman army.[59] I went to look at the Arsenal in the Golden Horn.[60] I collected information about beverages. I collected herbs . . .' The list seems to go on and on. One may prune it a little, but not much. These were the remarkable pastimes of Leopold's agent.

CHAPTER FIVE

The Varied Lessons of Danubian Warfare
1693–7

I

The time for armies sent deeply into Serbia or Wallachia, or for daring diplomatic excursions, was over. Until 1697 the Habsburg statesmen never succeeded in breaking free from the limits imposed by the result of the fighting up to 1691, but neither Emperor nor Sultan would settle for a treaty. In each court the militants, aided by the inertia which was immensely strong in both, more than counterbalanced the peacemakers. This continuing deadlock did most to determine the role of Marsigli.

He had to wait until February 1693, six months after the return to Vienna, before promotion as colonel of an infantry regiment came his way.[1] There were by then three vacant colonelcies in the Habsburg army and Marsigli had the backing of Leopold, Kinsky and Stratmann. The president of the War Council, Rüdiger Starhemberg, at first opposed the nomination, preferring to keep such posts for those who enjoyed his own patronage. Marsigli triumphed, thanks to Leopold's earlier commitment, and so did two other Italian officers, Bagni and Corbelli, which understandably caused 'a great stir' in Vienna.[2] Advised by Kinsky and Stratmann, Marsigli presented a handsome jewel to the countess Starhemberg; but reading between the lines of his own account he may have done so with an ill grace, or made too slight an effort to conciliate that powerful family interest. It included not only Rüdiger, who was at the centre of military affairs, but his cousin Guido Starhemberg, one of the most active and talented senior officers serving in Hungary. For the moment all was well. Marsigli appeared securely placed in the hierarchy, and was now better paid. Soon afterwards another, more important change occurred when Lewis of Baden was at last transferred to the command in Germany. The French, he did not forget, occupied his own patrimony. After some hesitation the Emperor chose Charles Eugene, duke of Croy as his successor in Hungary, and under Croy were appointed a general of the horse, a general of the foot, and a staff of fifteen other officers to lead the field army.[3] Marsigli was one of the three brigadiers. No longer on the list of engineers, he still found himself often requested to advise on fortification and transport.

The collapse of talks for a treaty left the Turks holding on to most of the ground which they had recovered in 1690 and 1691. As a Habsburg officer with a passion for Roman antiquities, Marsigli could no longer combine business with pleasure by tours of inspection to Mitrovica in Syrmia or down the Danube to the Iron Gates and beyond. Instead, he was present where Leopold's forces manoeuvred year in and year out north of Belgrade, with the consolation that this allowed him to work on a different aspect of his idea for an Opus Danubiale. Little by little he became knowledgeable about that complex area where the river, after flowing from the north below Buda, bends to follow a more easterly course to the Iron Gates, receiving the Drava and Sava from the west, the Tisza and Timis from the north and north-east. Waters flowing off the Alps, the Carpathians and the higher ground in Bosnia and Croatia all met in what constituted seasonally something like an inland sea below Belgrade. Every military commander and his officers had to accept the constraints imposed by this formidable terrain of marsh, open water, and tracts of firmer ground, with the margins of each constantly shifting. What they could plan to do in part depended on the local knowledge of their advisers. Marsigli was sent ahead of the foremost troops in every year from 1693 to 1697, and in turn added to or modified his concept of the channels and currents of the Danube. As his clumsy but vivid sketches accumulated, the work which he had offered to the Royal Society in London began to take shape.

The original intention of Leopold's government in 1693 was to move the army into Slavonia, as in 1691 and 1692.[4] From a base at Petrovaradin Belgrade would be threatened or, if the Turks marched first and threatened Petrovaradin it could be relieved by the advancing Habsburg forces. This gradually became a game of cat's cradle. Each move prompted a familiar response, with just the possibility of a tactical surprise. Accordingly, in the early summer of 1693 individual units of the army began moving from Buda down the right bank of the Danube towards their general rendezvous near the old battlegrounds of Mohács and Nagyharsány. Croy had not yet arrived when the Austrian command realised that the amount of water coming down the Drava from the Alps, apparently greater than in earlier years, barred their way ahead. The route to Osijek still traversed the marsh before reaching the main channel of the river but other stretches of impassable ground were unusually wide. Marsigli was accordingly asked to look for an alternative route, crossing the Danube instead of the Drava, so that the forces could be moved to its left bank and then down to the Serbian settlement – later Novi Sad – opposite Petrovaradin.[5] At that point they would be able to cross again to the Slavonian and Syrmian side and prepare for action, either by advancing to the Sava to threaten Belgrade, or by defending Petrovaradin if the Turks had taken the offensive beforehand. Marsigli duly prospected, and found a few miles further south a village called Vörösmarton, which stood on one of a row of heights extending through the marshes to the edge of the main channel. There were similar

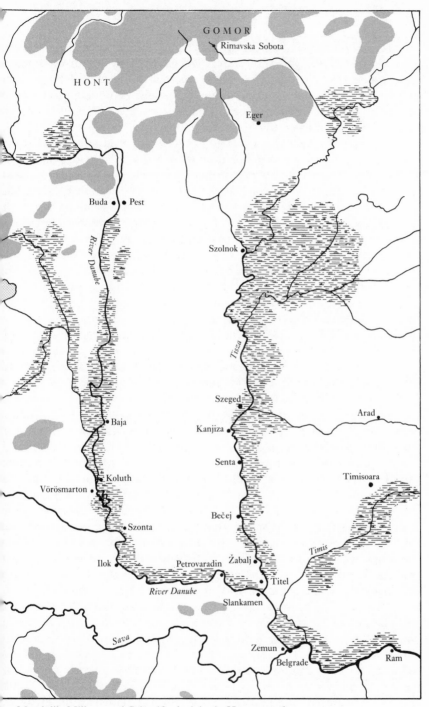

4   Marsigli's Military and Scientific Activity in Hungary, 1693–97

points of higher ground on the opposite shore, which led to the settlement of Koluth. He was given 2000 men for labour gangs, 150 woodmen or carpenters, who constructed a passage across the stream of boats, rafts, pontoons, reed bundles and earth works, in spite of the high water level. There was heavy betting in the army against the success of the attempt, says Marsigli. If he accepted the bets, he won them.

This shift of the main Habsburg force eastwards over the Danube had important consequences for the rest of the war. The response to an emergency, it soon suggested the military advantages to be gained by using the Bácska country between Danube and Tisza, in spite of the derelict economy and communications in that area. Forces assembled here early enough could choose to cross the Danube at or near Novi Sad, or to cross the Tisza to aim for Timisoara, or even to cross the Tisza lower down in order to advance along the northern shore of the Danube. The Habsburg forces would generally be moving on inner lines while the Turks, provided that they were kept pinned to the other shore, had to march and ride longer distances to keep their opponents in check. During the campaigning between 1693 and 1696 the opposing armies tried out every possible stance in this region, helped and hindered by seasonal or unseasonal alterations in the water level and the labyrinth of smaller channels through the marsh, as well as by winds and currents and the pattern of islands in the principal channels. It was not only a world of infantry, wheeled transport and horsemen but of naval flotillas, rafts and boatmen.

The passage across the Danube gave a novel start to the campaign of 1693. Marsigli and his commanders had next to consider a familar problem, their link with the troops stationed in Transylvania. These were admittedly open to attack from Ottoman Timisoara and from Tartars and Turks coming through Moldavia and Wallachia. But discounting such threats, they could be moved westwards to strengthen the main army for a move on Belgrade or another major battle somewhere in Slavonia. So Marsigli, in 1693, while the troops passed across the Danube and descended the left bank to Novi Sad, went east over the plain to find how feasible it would be to bring a reinforcement from Transylvania westwards. What he discovered was the Tisza as swollen, its flooding as extensive, as the Drava. Persisting, he finally chose one point for bridging the river 20 miles south of Szeged, near Kanjiza/Kis Kanicsa; and another 30 miles up the Maros (the large tributary which enters the Tisza at Szeged) for a fortified transit camp. This short cut, bypassing the waterlogged area round Szeged, offered a practical route to and from Transylvania. Unfamiliar names, shocking country: much riding back and forth, much sifting of contradictory testimony from people who claimed to know the neighbourhood, together with a certain obstinacy, must have been called for from Marsigli. However the Habsburg generals, whatever else they thought of him, were certainly happy to use his experience and flair for the job of getting their forces from one Hungarian locality to another. He relates that on this occasion general Heisler again put large numbers of troops, labourers and supply carts at his disposal for cutting through vegetation and building bridges and causeways, as he laid out a military route from his bridgehead at Kanjiza to the bridgehead of Petrovaradin.[6] Swamps and thickets became less of an obstacle to army transport when they had been tamed in this way, or indeed when their location was fixed in Marsigli's memory and plotted on his sketches.

The duke of Croy reached Petrovaradin on 23 July and decided in favour of an immediate advance towards Belgrade. A report that the grand vezir intended to cross the Danube from Bulgaria, and move on Transylvania via Wallachia, offered an argument for diverting him by an assault on Belgrade; but in any case Croy wanted to win back what he had failed to defend in 1690.[7] So another Habsburg siege of the city began; and it failed. The garrison proved too numerous to be rushed by the besiegers. The heavy artillery arriving three weeks later was inadequate. The enemy had more ships, and probably better naval captains. Marsigli, for his part, was never more active. Commanding a sizeable force he cleared the Turkish vessels away from the Sava shore. His own gun emplacement, effective at first, then lost its duel with a bigger enemy battery firing from one of the islands.[8] He shared in the unsuccessful attempt to drive the Turks from their outpost across the Danube, from which they were ferrying fresh stores into the town. Finally he joined in the main assault from the landward side – on 7 September – directed by Guido Starhemberg as general of the infantry. The plan of attack was all wrong, says Marsigli. He protested, to be rebuked then and later by an angry Starhemberg. Heavy losses, after a failure to get through the defences at any important point, soon forced a retreat. The Emperor's troops drew back to Petrovaradin but except for a few Tartar bands their opponents did not press forward. The six-week campaign ended and in retrospect the interest of these encounters of 1693 seems slight; but for the actors and bystanders there was always the chance of triumph or disaster on a much bigger scale, with very serious consequences. The details epitomise Marsigli's professional activity during the following summers.

Early in 1694 he was again sent to the region between the Tisza and Danube, to inspect the angle of ground formed by the Tisza's entry into the larger river. The landmark there was Titel, about 70 miles from Petrovaradin, an old fortified point standing above the surrounding marsh and water. To a slight extent it guarded access to the Tisza, and was useful as a lookout to give warning of enemy thrusts from the direction of Belgrade. Less happily, Titel was vulnerable to water-borne raiders. The Turks nearly took it early in the year, but withdrew before Marsigli arrived to spend some days there.[9] He improved the defences, and a route through the marsh to Petrovaradin was surveyed and made secure. He also explored the side channels winding through the reeds or boskage; they were possible approach routes for enemy landing craft. Then he returned to his regiment. In this campaign the Ottoman leaders took the initiative. Their army emerged from the neighbourhood of Belgrade, got across the Sava and the plain of Syrmia, and laid siege to Petrovaradin. The river's loop here nearly encircled a lofty ridge and created a site with strong defensive advantages.[10] The Turks positioned their front across the neck of the ridge and gradually moved the trenches forward. They brought warships upstream from Belgrade, hoping to destroy the boats guarding the bridge to Novi Sad, and sent Tartars over the water to threaten it from the other side. Marsigli's role was to help in keeping intact the double row of boats constituting the bridge; heavy fire from the enemy ships, and from emplacements on islands in midstream, was fortunately ineffective. With the commander in chief's approval – on this occasion the Bolognese, Aeneo Caprara, ageing and crotchety – he also designed a new fortified line behind the main defences on the ridge of Petrovaradin, facing the Turkish land forces. Here his own regiment was in action. The defence's hope was pinned on the speedy arrival of Veterani's troops from Transylvania, and Marsigli next went up the river to build a new bridge at Ilok, to help them to cross and come round in the Turkish rear. Before they did so, the unexpected happened. The weather broke, rain fell, and fell for a week.[11] It washed the Turks out of their camp, their entrenchments and ships, and compelled their retreat. So this campaign ended, and for a short while the two countrymen Caprara and Marsigli were in close touch and on friendly terms, without a hint of the enmity which developed between them a year later. At the same time Marsigli notes that he accepted Guido Starhemberg's recommendation of an officer named Melchior Salzer von Rosenstein, whom he appointed his lieutenant-colonel. It was a terrible mistake, and Salzer soon became an opponent. These officers, Marsigli among them, found it very hard not to quarrel under the stresses of their dangerous life. If the defence of Petrovaradin in 1694 shows them working loyally together, such a partnership was not too often maintained during the long war for Hungary in either the Habsburg or the Ottoman army. This had been the case under Charles of Lorraine, Max Emmanuel and Hermann of Baden. It remained true under Caprara and his successors.

II

These campaigns, negative in their military aspect, had one satisfying result. The fascination which Marsigli had always felt, in studying the element of water, was intensified by the scale and impact of the hydraulic phenomenon now before his eyes. As bridge builder and fortifications expert he watched the Danubian waters affecting the conduct of a campaign at almost every stage. To solve practical problems he would use the traditional techniques, but his self-appointed task of understanding what he saw was another matter. He began to assemble and add to his working drawings of certain physical features.[12] Not as numerous as those of the Roman sites or the course of the river, and mostly drawn just before or just after the phase of active warfare each year, they helped him to identify another distinctive element in his idea of the Danube. In addition to the cartography, the archaeological surveys, and the studies of fish, there was (to use his word) the hydrography.

He could not build a bridge without first estimating the scale of his task, and sending out orders for so many boats, beams, baulks, rafts, anchors, clamps and pieces of rope.[13] But from the length of the bridge on a particular site he went on to examine the depth of the water there, the force of the currents and the geological character of the river bed. Having solved his engineering problem he looked for a method of describing the physical features under his gaze; an early effort of this sort dealt with the unexpected flood levels which so hampered the Habsburg command. Marsigli's sketches and notes for 1693 and 1964 finally produced the following diagrams.[14]

15 & 16 Measuring the depth of the Danube and Tisza.

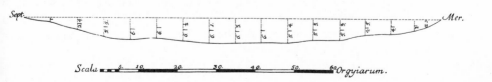

This refers to the main channel, and fails to impart any notion of the flooding which occurred on each side of the Danube, making it so difficult for the field armies to move far or fast until late in the summer. However Marsigli now observed the phenomenon for other than military reasons and two topics predictably attracted him. One was the speed of the current, which he measured with the device he had used in Istanbul. In 1694, in that comfortable lull after the siege at Petrovaradin, Marsigli went back to the bridge there. Edging a boat alongside, he measured the depth of the river in 16 stages equally spaced. At every stage he also dropped his line a few feet down in the water, then to a middle depth, then deeper still. On each occasion he recorded, from a quadrant attached to the side of his boat, the angle made by his line in the current at a given depth. From the angle he calculated the speed. Later he carried out a similar investigation of the river Tisza while bridging it (at Bečej/Becse and then Žabalj/Zsablya), in due course tabulating the data of these three examples.[15]

By 1695 he had extended his enquiries. Taking with him on his military surveys his hydrostatic balance, together with a supply of chemicals – described as alkali, and acids from vitriol, galls, and the rind of pomegranate – he tried in various places to supply answers to a questionnaire on the properties of the local river water, rain water, well water and marsh water; and with his balance he sought to tabulate the varying weights of water.[16] He also defined comparatively its colour, taste, smell and sediment. Whether he discovered anything of value under these headings may be doubted – except perhaps that the drinking water of Szeged was the worst in Hungary – but what he did he thought worth doing.

There was a second novelty in this period. After every campaign a withdrawal to winter quarters followed,[17] and when Marsigli took over his regiment in the spring of 1693 he found it stationed at Rimavska Sobota (Rimaszombat) in the Slovakian hills, 80 miles north-east of Buda. In 1694 his men had to go to Gomor further to the east, and Hont further west. He appreciated at once the richness of this whole area in minerals, known since the most ancient times. In his day there were many exhausted workings of gold, silver, copper, lead and iron. A few mines were still producing ore, and it had always been an anxious question for the Habsburg court and its creditors whether the Turks, or rebels like Thököli, would take them over. That danger receded (for fifteen years) after the taking of Buda in 1686, but the wealth of these minerals had a different significance for Marsigli when he arrived to spend successive winters in Slovakia. Already in April 1693 Malpighi, then in Rome, was replying to a letter which must have described Marsigli's impressions of the opportunity offered for research in this region.[18] At the end of the same year (as he recorded later) he was filling his leisure with a study of mineralogy. At the end of 1694 the iron workings in particular absorbed him, and his account of a search for magnetic iron gives an idea of the pleasure he took in the subject:

17 A mine in Slovakia. There were iron deposits from F to G but the magnetite was found, separated by layers of 'tobacco-coloured' stone at H and I.

Few people have been aware so far that iron loadstone is one of the products of Hungary. . . . Fortunately it happened that a body of troops were assigned winter quarters in the district of Kisun, and I was lodged in this village [Tisovec/Tiszolc] as the commanding officer. Taking advantage of my rank I began to survey the forbidding mountains of the neighbourhood, and in a place called Kissova I found traces of an old iron working now abandoned. Near the shaft I came across several pieces of loadstone which had been there a long time; to a slight extent they were still magnetised. This excited my curiosity, so that at my own expense I had the mine reopened and cleared.[19]

He began a collection of rock samples, crystals and other specimens, and in due course this formed the basis for one of his volumes on the Danube. There is no sensible reason to associate the river Danube with a single small area of the surrounding mountain chains, but what Marsigli learnt in his winter studies led him ultimately to the fruitful idea that he ought to link his hydrography and oceanography with his geology, envisaging land and sea as two parts of a single field of knowledge. The man who looked so alertly at the waters of the Bosphorus and Danube, and at the Slovakian mountains, would in due course be tempted to generalise about the mountain ranges of Europe in relation to 'the natural history of the sea', and to the ridges and ranges under the sea.

At this period, in the 1690s, Marsigli considered the qualities of rock or precious minerals or water in relation to his primary theme, the Danube. He associated the river with both the history and natural history of the Danubian lands, including Slovakia and Transylvania. He even tried to define the limits of his subject in a fragment of composition setting down chapter headings, with short drafts to explain them. It was what he later called a 'first sketch', begun (he said) 'in his tent in Hungary'.[20] He would have to start with the names of the river in different languages. He would explain that his account began at the Kahlenberg just above Vienna, on the ancient boundary between Roman Noricum and Roman Pannonia, and went downstream as far as the confluence with the tributary stream of the Jantra in Bulgaria. These were the limits of his personal knowledge of the landscape. Then, in the third chapter, he would reach his major topic.[21] It was an exercise in the Art of Geography by means of a series of lists and descriptions which depicted the exact course of the Danube, with the windings and reaches of its various channels. He would locate the settlements, islands, cataracts, whirlpools, marshes and areas of flooding. He would name the fishes, birds and animals of the region. He would note the Roman sites along the river, not only for the benefit of classical studies but because the increase in knowledge of ancient military science (he believed) could be helpful in the present war against the Turks.

Another draft turned to the subject of his maps. He pleaded that he had faced exceptional difficulties in spite of modern methods of measurement.[22] What cartographers ask for can no doubt be supplied by sea captains but it is distinctly harder for travellers overland, and soldiers on campaign: they cannot so easily pick suitable vantage points for taking the height of the sun or stars; for them to be at the right place at the right time in the right weather was often a matter of chance. Clocks go wrong. Instruments are not easy to transport. Gradients up and down distort the lineal distance. Such pleas were not too persuasive, and Marsigli himself had second thoughts later, but in this text he described the main obstacles to accurate terrestrial measurement in the landscapes with which he was familiar. A direct traverse across the ground from Vienna to Bratislava, for example, even more from Bratislava to Buda, was impossible. It involved twisting and turning to get round the marshes and woodland, with continual crossing and recrossing the channels of the river; and he described vividly the effect of the currents, the winds, and the direction of the channel, on his efforts to measure distances over the water. Admitting that there must be errors in his work, he went on to his plan for map-making. It was to draw one large map on a small scale – to be entitled IL DANUBIO TRIONFANTE – for which he had used his compass and clock to the best of his ability to give the reader a general concept of the whole region. This would be supplemented by 24 sectional maps of the river giving as much geographical detail as possible, even if his distances and directions were sometimes at fault.

This discussion was his initial effort to give an account of his subject matter, but two more leading ideas occur in other pages of the same fragment.[23] One was a notion, which at that period in his life he found very hard to express, that the enormous Hungarian plain bordering the river and the lofty mountains at a distance belonged to the same geological structure. He was therefore going to attempt some account of the matter in his book. His other preoccuption was certainly the variable nature of the banks or shore of the river. He would want to describe for his readers the higher, more ridge-like edge normally found on the right bank of the Danube, with the muddy, spongy terrain opposite which included wide areas of marshland and strips of ground of great fertility. The bed of the river likewise, and the movement from one channel to another in the course of time, invited comment. For the moment he could get no further.

III

Marsigli never imagined in 1694 and 1695 that he could spend the long interval of winter and spring, between the campaigns, predominantly at leisure. The colonel had a regiment to run, and claimed full responsibility for this body of 1000–1500 infantry struggling to survive against the odds. Quartered on a population poor and malcontent from whom supplies had to be squeezed, they also depended on Habsburg agencies in Vienna which were pitifully slow to find more money, men, and supplies in Austria and Bohemia for transmission each year to the army in Hungary. In any case rival interests and other regiments competed for whatever was sent. All this meant work for a conscientious colonel, and we get a glimpse of it from the registers kept by War Council clerks, as well as from copies or abstracts made by Marsigli's own secretaries. The clerical and bureaucratic component in the Habsburg army had already become one of its significant characteristics, and struck a sympathetic chord in Marsigli's own instinct for amassing and conserving his papers. The written instruction, receipt, referral, judgment, or specification, permeated military life. The flow and counterflow of letters between the perimeter in Slavonia, Hungary and Transylvania, and the centre at court were almost continuous. Accordingly a regimental 'agent' at Vienna, who dealt with the commissariat, treasury and other officials on behalf of a colonel or lieutenant-colonel, had become indispensable. In Marsigli's case, this was the role of one Breitenbucher from 1694 until 1703, a most diligent correspondent.[24]

Gradually he became an administrator, acquainting himself with army rules and practice affecting his regiment. For example, during the first half of each year some of his officers usually returned to Austria or the Bohemian lands to look for recruits, in an effort to replace any losses of the previous year. Marsigli now learnt that it was necessary for him to remind

Vienna of the unwillingness of this or that provincial or municipal authority to co-operate, and ask for help; or that he would need extra money to advertise for personnel good enough to be trained as grenadiers; or that he wanted several hundred new muskets from the Vienna Arsenal; and that careful arrangements were required for the transit of his recruits to Hungary.[25] Then there were the insoluble problems of finance. He was no stranger to the need for a steady barrage of pleas to Vienna on arrears of pay and allowances, and he learnt to do this for his regiment as well as himself. But it must have taken longer to understand the intricacies of regimental housekeeping in Hungary, with troops or companies scattered across a fairly large area, some in Slovakia and others (in Marsigli's case) constituting part of the garrison at Szeged. Company captains each ran the 'economy' of their own company, but were accountable to the regiment, which in turn was responsible to Vienna.[26] Marsigli had to master the rules and tricks of this army accountancy, and appreciate the limits of tolerance for perquisites or profits for himself and his captains. He had to enforce authority and put down fraud, at the same time winning sufficient devotion from his brother officers. It cannot have been easy for them to come to terms with this brusque, eccentric Italian, frequently absent on special missions of reconnaissance or inspection, appearing and disappearing in the course of a single campaign. He depended on his deputy and it was common practice in Hungary, as elsewhere, for the lieutenant-colonel to take full charge of the regiment when its colonel was a prince or general, rarely present with his men. Marsigli differed from princes and generals; he resumed control – and, it would be claimed later, interfered unjustifiably – when he returned from staff duties. He had appointed Salzer von Rosenstein his lieutenant-colonel in the autumn of 1694, but soon gave him leave of absence. He continued to divide his time between supervision of his regiment and enthusiasm for mineralogy.[27] A moment would come when it was Salzer's turn to take charge, with unfortunate consequences.

In the spring of 1695 Marsigli was called back to Vienna. Good news, he must have reflected, on learning of his promotion as a Kammerherr or chamberlain, an honorary title bolstering his status. He took the required oath and speedily returned to Hungary. The painful process by which a new commander in chief emerged to lead the army in which he served was also nearly complete.[28] Neither Lewis of Baden nor William III had agreed to the young Elector of Saxony's request for a command in Germany or Belgium. So Leopold, anxious to satisfy as many of his allies as possible, reluctantly invited Frederick Augustus to take the field in Hungary. He undertook to bring with him 8000 Saxon troops, a badly needed reinforcement; while it was reckoned in Vienna that his authority as commander in chief would be tempered by the advice he received from a council of Habsburg officers led by their senior, Caprara. He resembled that other Elector, Max Emmanuel of Bavaria, as a youthful autocrat in search of the laurels of war, but lacking flair or experience with which to coax the best out of his often divided colleagues. However, long before he arrived in Hungary Marsigli and others were on the move as usual.[29] During May and June infantry moved from Pest along the Danube left bank towards a general rendezvous at Baja; once again Marsigli had instructions to prospect eastwards, and survey the condition of the plain merging into the Tisza's serpentine course. This would help to decide whether it might be feasible this year to plan for an assault on Timisoara. On 4 June he returned from his mission, reporting a 'grosse Inondation' but undertaking to rebuild the crossing at Kanjiza.[30] The sequel could be predicted. For nearly three months the route along the Danube, with Habsburg and Saxon troops finding their way south, fades from our view in Marsigli's correspondence. Instead he was busy building or repairing routes, bridges, ramps and strongpoints along the Tisza. Timber, rafts, rope, guns and corn were brought downstream from Szeged to Kanjiza under his supervision. He rode incessantly from one point to another while his secretary kept the register of his numerous reports to Heisler (his superior until Caprara and the Elector arrived), to count Leopold Schlick, who was in charge of the whole Tisza region, and to other senior officers. Among incoming letters of this period those from Schlick were notable for the frank and friendly postscripts often added in Italian to a formal German text.[31] He was an ally, but did not disguise his low opinion of certain works for which Marsigli was responsible, or of the *ladri* who deprived them all of essential supplies. Yet before the undertaking at Kanjiza had been completed, another was begun. Heisler sent fresh orders to look for a new crossing of the Tisza further south. Intelligence had filtered through of Ottoman preparations for an expedition across the Danube from Belgrade to strengthen Timisoara, perturbing the senior officers who favoured an attack on Timisoara rather than Belgrade. Heisler was one, and consequently he wanted to arrange for the most direct march possible from the field army's rendezvous by Petrovaradin to the area east of the Tisza. Marsigli's bridge at Kanjiza, or even a passage at Senta further downstream, were both too far north. They would involve a long, slow route to Timisoara; there would be less chance of intercepting or anticipating the enemy coming from Belgrade.

Marsigli found what he was looking for at a spot near Bečej.[32] Encouraged by Heisler he assembled labour and materials, and supervised the various operations: above all, anchoring in position the bridge floated down from Kanjiza, and building a causeway across the marsh on the right bank. He states emphatically that there was no difficulty about the approaches on the further shore. Except at one more distant point – for which he had the materials ready – the route away from the bridge and into the hinterland eastward was, in his opinion, dry and stable enough.[33] While the labourers worked under Marsigli's directions, ovens and magazines were set up at Bečej, and troops were detailed to guard them. Schlick's cavalry crossed over and reconnoitred the country south and east, where the waters of the river Bega flowed sluggishly towards the Danube. Marsigli was now well aware of the plan to attack the big Ottoman salient of Timisoara from several directions. Veterani would bring forces from Transylvania. At Lipova, north of Timisoara, artillery and stores were being assembled. If the army from Petrovaradin made use of his new bridge, it would approach Timisoara from the west. In 1693 Marsigli had claimed responsibility and credit for bridging the Danube at a new point. In 1695 he considered his undertaking at Bečej by the Tisza to be on the same impressive scale.

At a council of war in Belgrade on 9 August Sultan Mustafa II – the first sultan to come to the 'domain of war' on the borders of Islam for many years – sanctioned the proposal to transfer his main thrust from the right bank of the Danube to the left. He would take a relieving army to Timisoara. News of this meeting reached the Elector of Saxony soon after his arrival at Petrovaradin. His council of officers was summoned.[34] Heisler advised sending as many men as possible across the new bridge, adding that he was well acquainted with the line of march on the further side. Other views were given. Caprara objected, and wanted to keep the army where it was in order to maintain the threat to Belgrade. Finally the Elector decided to advance as far as Marsigli's bridge, and then look at the position again. In this fashion a deplorably ineffective campaign for the allies began. The troops duly crossed the Tisza at Bečej but a majority of the generals, led by Caprara, then insisted that there was no viable route ahead of them. There was water, water everywhere, they said; Marsigli's advice had proved thoroughly misleading. The Elector allowed himself to be overruled. The army then recrossed the river but crossed back again further north, losing precious time as it did so. During the next three weeks the high command behaved very hesitantly, boxing its forces into a narrow triangle of ground between the Tisza and its tributary Maros. Meanwhile the Turks from Belgrade came to the relief of Timisoara, destroyed the Habsburg magazines along the Maros, and defeated Veterani, who died in the fighting. They also went into action at Titel, which Leopold's flotilla on the Danube failed to protect. Fortunately Ottoman activity then died down and the campaign ended. Sultan Mustafa had been decidedly the gainer, while the disarray of the Habsburg generals and their Saxon commander in chief promised them all a winter in Vienna ablaze with quarrels. Before his return to court Caprara threatened Marsigli with arrest, while Marsigli claimed that Caprara's judgment had been grossly at fault. The Elector sided with Marsigli and Heisler. Heisler also defended the naval commander Assembourg, a Dutchman, who was arguing that his instructions from Caprara were responsible for the defeat at Titel.[35]

The next round of recrimination took a course which the highly personal character of Habsburg government under Leopold I made predictable. Both Marsigli and Caprara looked for allies, who in turn had to decide how far it was prudent to go in defending a client or friend. Marsigli relied on Kinsky, on the Elector whom he plied hard – and the two officers Heisler and Schlick. Caprara expected help from Rüdiger Starhemberg when he filed his complaint against Marsigli with the War Council.[36] However, this body was not allowed to adjudicate in the dispute without referring it to the ruler, and Emperor Leopold very characteristically damped down the affair by a series of intimations to those concerned: first, there would be no official hearing of the complaint which had been referred to him; second, the general and the colonel, if they failed to satisfy one another, would do His Imperial Majesty a disservice; and third, he enjoined mediation by his theologian, father Wolff. Caprara was not easily mollified but realised that he would have to play his hand with some care. Ministerial discussions had been going on to consider the next campaign, and Leopold wanted Lewis of Baden to come back to Hungary and revive Habsburg fortunes there. He would control the Elector more deftly than the existing council of officers. Lewis, declining the offer, suggested prince Eugene of Savoy instead:[37] but Caprara had no intention of yielding his post or retiring in favour of a younger man. Accordingly, if he wanted to protect his interest on this major issue, there was little point in pressing the minor feud with Marsigli. So the quarrel died down until in May 1696 mutual apologies were stiffly offered and accepted. Leopold had intervened once more; and Marsigli received a warning from the War Council expressing the Emperor's wish that he should write in terms of respect to his superior officer.

Even if errors of judgment during the past campaign could be fastened on this or that commander, the worst consequences were due to the belatedness with which the army entered the field. So asserted many critics. It was always easy to say, and difficult to remedy. In 1696 there was an understanding that the greatest effort should be made to have every-thing ready early in the summer for a second, more resolute advance on Timisoara. The Saxons were as good as their word, and by the middle of June the Elector was encamped south of the Maros with a large body of his own troops. Much of the other armament still lagged behind, and while waiting for the Habsburg regiments and artillery he gave audience to colonel Marsigli.[38] It was a friendly and indeed jovial conversation, according to Marsigli's account. He received orders to carry out another reconnaissance to find a suitable site for bridging the Tisza, this time as far downstream and as close to Titel as possible. It was intended, he learnt, to place a sizeable force in that area. His duties would be to supervise the bridge-building, and join with other commanders in organising the defence against any Turkish attacks from across the Danube. After he had discussed these instructions, Marsigli raised with the Elector a quite different matter. It was a scheme of his own, worthy of a virtuoso of the sciences.

IV

As he admitted when writing to the Royal Society in 1691, his innumerable sketches in Danubia, his freely drawn maps and bird's-eye views, made no pretence at measurement to scale. He noted a few distances and heights in surveying fortifications, or sites for which fortification was being planned. He also measured the ruins of ancient monuments like Trajan's bridge. But he had no notion of how to make maps as a cartographer or professional estate surveyor conceived them at the end of the seventeenth century in western Europe, Germany and Scandinavia. He was himself a crude, if vivid draughtsman. In the course of a military inspection he preferred to tell his assistants to produce cleaner copies from his rough memoranda. That was their business, not his, and better drawing did not necessarily imply more useful map-making. This seems to have been his general attitude for a number of years. In 1695, if not earlier, he recognised that he had evaded the problem, which at last he took steps to examine more seriously. He needed first the best possible advice.

On 20 November 1695 the astronomer Cassini wrote to Marsigli from Bologna, evidently in reply to a plea for comments on that familiar contemporary problem, the estimation of longitude.[39] Cassini had been for many years the director of Louis XIV's Observatory, but there is no proof that Marsigli himself knew of Cassini's share in the remarkable contemporary undertaking to construct a new map of France. This, by comparison with earlier work, was based on improved methods of survey on the ground and more refined planetary observation, achieved by using better instruments. Probably the general fame of Cassini as an ornament of the university of Bologna, a city he revisited in 1695 after a long interval, was enough to make him a desirable correspondent in the context of Marsigli's problem at the time. The great man's advice, in his letter to Vienna, sounded both attractive and conclusive. What colonel Marsigli needed were telescopes, clocks, compasses and astronomical tables. With such equipment he would be able to plot the movement of Jupiter's satellites, and thereby calculate the line of longitude passing through the point at which the observations were made. This method of determining longitude had led to undoubted improvements in modern cartography, Cassini continued; there were recently, for example, some startling corrections to the previous location of China on the world map. In fact, such advice was neither novel nor very easy to apply in practice. Galileo suggested using Jupiter's four moons for estimating longitude shortly after discovering them in 1610, Cassini published his account of the method in 1665,[40] while accurate readings required favourable conditions as well as the skill developed by practice. Nonetheless Marsigli was excited and delighted by Cassini's encouragement, and the idea of applying the technique in Hungary was his own. An answering letter to Paris does not survive, but he leapt into action.

During the winter of 1695, in addition to his troublesome feud with Caprara, he had found the time to begin a correspondence with George Einmart of Nuremberg. Einmart was a reputable astronomer, engraver and instrument maker who succeeded Joachim Sandrart as director of Nuremberg's famous Academy of Painters, while also looking after the city's observatory. He was a polymath, craftsman and virtuoso, no genius but alert and anxious to please. The letters he received from Marsigli do not survive, nor his earlier replies, but it is clear that Einmart offered to act as Marsigli's agent for the purchase of books and rarities in Germany.[41] If the noble patron – addressed in ceremonious Latin – desired, he could put him in touch with scholars, booksellers, engravers and instrument makers. The offer was acceptable and Marsigli began to choose, from the printed catalogues and manuscript lists which were sent by Einmart, new items for his rapidly enlarging library in Vienna. Without doubt Cassini's advice, and the link with Nuremberg, prompted the next step and he commissioned from Einmart some scientific equipment. This included a large quadrant, telescopes, a barometer, and handbooks to go with them. Later he asked for a sextant of superior quality and an air pump.[42] Marsigli also decided that he needed someone to show him how to use these instruments, and Einmart supplied the answer. He offered to send his pupil and assistant John Christian Muller, aged twenty-three. Muller left Nuremberg at the end of March 1696, bringing some of the apparatus with him to Vienna.[43]

Marsigli and Muller first recorded their observations of the night sky on 17 April. They examined the movement of Jupiter's satellites on 11, 14, 15 and 17 May.[44] They had made a good start.

Then the pressure on Marsigli to carry out his military duties asserted itself. The stream of letters reaching him from Hungary, which dealt with the business of his regiment, dried up; it was his job to take charge of his men or go on special missions before the campaign began.* The exact dates of his departure from Vienna in 1696, and of his interview with the Elector of Saxony, are uncertain but not far behind him was Muller, ready to use the Nuremberg instruments in the course of a scientific mission. Marsigli's intention was that Muller should stay long enough at selected places to calculate their position correctly, adopting the techniques recommended by Cassini and Einmart. He would take the heights of the noonday sun and the polestar, chart the phases of the moon, and measure the movement of Jupiter's satellites. Marsigli's purse, and seniority in the army of Hungary, secured him all the practical assistance needed. Marsigli also preserved his servant's papers, so that Muller's itinerary can be followed from the diary which he wrote while recording his observations.[46]

His boat down the Danube reached Buda on 23 May, and with his assistants he set up the apparatus next day on St Margaret's island. Cloud, both at noon and night, at first defeated him and it was only on the 27th, after putting off his planned departure, that he had sufficient confidence in his survey of the sky at night to fix and measure the elevation of the pole,

---

*   Another of Marsigli's interests at the time should be noted. During the month of May 1696, he wrote later, he made a collection of all the wild flowers he found growing by the Danube, from Vienna down to the confluence with the Drava.[45]

and the position of the moons around Jupiter. Then he floated downstream to Baja, having stopped at two points on the way where he continued to observe Jupiter. At Baja itself he started well, and after his second day's work felt sure that he had an accurate reading of the sun's meridian. But the weather again turned to wind, cloud and rain, before clearing towards evening so that he could resume work on Jupiter. Next he hastened to a site of the greatest importance in this context, still on the left bank but facing the entry of the Drava into the larger river. On what lines of longitude and latitude should the confluence be placed? It was Whit Sunday, Muller noted, when he set up the apparatus in good visibility, but cloud again appeared too early to let him finish his work, and several days followed (until 14 June) before he declared himself satisfied with all his recordings; these included his assessment of the magnetic variation with the help of four compass needles.[47] Next he crossed the plain to the Tisza. In Marsigli's concept of the geographical problem they wished to solve, this great tributary of the Danube matched the Drava in importance, and to assess its alignment with the main waterway equally required an accurate answer. In Muller's diary Marsigli himself was now mentioned for the only time. It was in 'my Count's garden' at Szeged (which he reached on 17 June) that he placed his instruments, expressing satisfaction that the plains stretched to the horizon on every side, and allowed an unimpeded view of the sun and stars. The garden must have been close to the quarters used by the Marsigli regiment. After a few days' work in fine weather Muller believed that his estimate of the sun's meridian at Szeged was correct, while during the evenings he renewed his intense study of Jupiter's satellites and the phases of the moon. Marsigli, who was probably present, must have debated how much further afield he could send Muller and his precious cargo as the time for fighting drew nearer. Fortunately the military plans afoot offered the two men an opportunity. It may be of no great significance if an eighteenth-century Nuremberg historian records that Muller demonstrated his instruments in the presence of the illustrious Elector of Saxony, 'in the field not far from the Imperial army'.[48] It was distinctly more important that the Elector now ordered colonels Marsigli and Bagni to make a reconnaissance down the Tisza as far south as its junction with the Danube below Titel, before the Turks moved. Marsigli left at once, but on 14 July one of his officers reported from Szeged that he was sending 'the stargazer' downstream to join him.[49] Already on the following evening Muller reached Senta, 30 miles south, and was soon safely in Marsigli's camp in the neighbourhood of Titel. The sententious Latin of his diary refers to the satellites of Mars around him.

On 17 and 18 July clear weather and brilliant sunshine allowed a confident reading of the sun's height. The stellar and lunar observations were made as usual, while Muller had a chance here to become more closely acquainted with his patron's professional universe, the troops maintaining themselves in the desolation of a marshy plain, near the mass of waters where Tisza and Sava join the Danube; such remote-sounding places as Belgrade, Petrovaradin and Timisoara were in fact not very far off. On his side the patron learnt to appreciate Muller's versatile talent. He proved an elegant and reliable draughtsman, and a good secretary whose distinctive handwriting makes a first appearance at this point in Marsigli's military papers.[50] Marsigli himself, having surveyed a wide area, was then formulating his proposals for the Elector. A letter of 17 July describing a site near Titel, where a bridge would allow forces to move quickly east or west, refers to an accompanying map. His own copy has with it two drawings, also dated 17 July and certainly Muller's work. The first, of the whole region between Belgrade-Timisoara-Kanjiza-Petrovaradin, shows how the bridge he suggested building at Žabalj would meet this requirement; and the second depicts the bridge, with the defence works suggested, the adjoining islands in the stream, and a belt of marsh along the west bank. Soon afterwards there was news of a possible Ottoman attack or raid on Titel. On 21 July Muller made a drawing of the shores and islands along this stretch and on the same day, it is interesting to find, all the Habsburg commanders in the area conferred. Admiral Assembourg disagreed with Marsigli and some others present.[51] When the Turkish attack did come, in August, the consequences of their discord were serious.

Warfare was not Muller's concern, and before the fighting began he turned back. He left the camp while Marsigli's men were still at work on the bridge. Passing through Szeged again he halted next at Szolnok, 150 miles north of Titel. The site here was unsatisfactory, buildings and people were in the way, but between 10 and 13 August he succeeded in making his observations. Finally he visited Eger still further north, where a sympathetic commander gave him every assistance. He returned to Buda, on this occasion observing the sun at noon and Jupiter's satellites after dark under good conditions. On 1 September Muller reached Vienna again, and his diary finished on a note of heartfelt Christian piety. He felt grateful to God for the important work he had been able to do.[52]

During the following year Marsigli had a long spell of unexpected leisure, as we shall see, and could reflect on the problem of setting out the result of his enquiries into the geography of Danubia. An intimate personal knowledge of the landscape for several hundred miles of a great river system, and a few reliably recorded celestial observations for a distinctly smaller part of it, were hard to combine in a satisfactory manner. He was unwilling to begin again, throwing in the fire his own sketches of the Danube between Belgrade and Nicopolis, nor could he in Muller's company re-enter the territory now in Ottoman hands. What he ultimately decided was to hand over to Muller his old materials, instructing him to copy them in a more professional and elegant manner. At the same time he asked him to produce a smaller-scale general map, harmonising them as far as possible with the grid of latitude and longitude which their recent observations made reliable for at least part of the whole area. It sounds a modest programme. In fact the general north to south course of the Danube below Buda, its west to east course below Belgrade and the alignment of the Tisza to this, as they appear on modern maps, were the discoveries of Marsigli and Muller in 1696. Certain inaccuracies in the cartography survived, but the two men had eliminated the Danube's diagonal north-west to south-east course rather crudely shown in maps printed before 1700. It was their gift to the European mapmakers of the eighteenth century.[53]

V

After Muller had gone Marsigli appears at first as a bystander of the campaign, supervising the bridge builders at Žabalj while the Elector and Caprara advanced their forces to lay siege to Timisoara. But this was a siege begun, suspended, resumed and broken off in response to faulty intelligence about the movements of the enemy. It provoked more discord between the generals.[54] When Turks and Tartars finally crossed the Danube from Belgrade but then disengaged again, the Elector led his forces south-west into the waterlogged tract of the river Bega to try and bring his opponent to battle. Marsigli received orders from several of his superiors, from the Elector and Heisler on the Bega, Caprara in the north, and Guido Starhemberg, who arrived to take charge at Titel.[55] They each pressed for rapid measures to give them bridging over the Tisza, at Žabalj and also at Bečej (as in 1695), and at Kanjiza (as in 1694). The general idea was to hasten more troops – like the Brandenburgers who had just arrived in Hungary – eastwards to help the Elector. Marsigli evidently objected that his equipment was limited, so that he could only move the necessary bridging materials from one of these sites to another; but soon the Turks gained the upper hand along the Bega and the Elector had to order a withdrawal. Early in September Marsigli was deeply involved. First he went to Szeged, where sadly he found his friend Heisler on the point of death.[56] Next he crossed the Tisza, finding a way through the marshes and helping to screen the Saxons and others as they withdrew. The Elector himself hurried off to Vienna to present his excuses to Leopold.[57] Most of the troops were brought back over the Tisza and the Danube to Petrovaradin in order to protect Slavonia. Marsigli followed. An Ottoman attack was expected, until the threat died away and the campaign ended.

At that moment he quarrelled with his lieutenant-colonel. The clouds gathered for a fresh storm which threatened his standing as an army officer. As so often in his crises, he fell ill. A winter of convalescence in Vienna followed and many months of useful leisure in Muller's company; but one more reconnaissance by Marsigli in Hungary was called for in 1697, which would complete the sequence of these forays into the no man's land of the middle Danube.

The Elector of Saxony, whose offer of manpower for the army in Hungary made him an immovable supremo, in spite of his setbacks in 1695 and 1696 proposed that Belgrade, not Timisoara, was the prize worth winning in the next campaign.[58] Here would be the key to final victory and a victorious peace. For an effective assault on Belgrade he listed his requirements, most of them tediously familiar to his Viennese colleagues. They included more money, the transfer of more troops from Germany to Hungary, an early start, and a bigger naval force to be stationed on the Danube above *and* below Belgrade. The last point was a novelty. Between January and May discussion of the Elector's plans continued fitfully, in parallel with a search for someone better than old Caprara as commander of the Habsburg forces, a search which ended on 28 April with Leopold's decision in favour of prince Eugene of Savoy.[59] A month earlier Rüdiger Starhemberg, as president of the War Council, had attempted a critique of the Elector's plan of campaign.[60] He suspected in a general way that no immediate assault on Belgrade was possible with the resources actually available, and in particular considered that the notion of stationing a naval flotilla below Belgrade was a fantasy. However, an alternative (he informed the Emperor) 'had occurred to him'. The army could certainly march from a rendezvous at Petrovaradin as far as Zemun, the point facing Belgrade from the other side of the Sava, and it could proceed to build there – with the infantry and the local Serbian population both conscripted for labour – a new and substantial fortified base, as the pivot of a line of defence running west along the Sava and east along the Danube. This stronghold, garrisoned through the following winter, would increase the pressure on the Ottoman government to treat seriously for peace, and at the same time improve the chances for an effective attack on Belgrade in 1698. As part of his scheme Starhemberg proposed a new bridge across the Danube close to the new base to be built at Zemun. Opposite, on the left bank of the river – and he says that this was derived from his recent talks with Guido Starhemberg, Lewis of Baden and count Nehem, the commander at Petrovaradin – 'an old route which could take traffic' led inland. He insisted that confirmation was needed but, if forthcoming, this old track and the new bridge (crossing the Danube) would allow the allied command to bring troops much more speedily from Transylvania and elsewhere for an assault on Belgrade. It would also help to stop the Turks sending reinforcements to Timisoara.

In due course the Elector approved this intriguing idea. But was there in fact such a path, or route, leading somewhere south from Titel to that stretch of the left bank which faced Zemun on the other side of the Danube? Was such a bridge feasible? No one in Vienna could be positive, and on 20 May the War Council decided to ask for a survey and report from Marsigli.[61]

With a troop of 300 cavalry and 300 Serbian hussars he set out from Titel across the Tisza, with the immensity of the Danube on their right.[62] They crossed many smaller channels; a guard was left in a ruined fort to secure the line of their return. They continued across the empty and level landscape, until nearly at dusk Marsigli could see Belgrade in the distance across the water. Night was spent in the marsh, and in the clearer light of morning he was able to convince himself that this spot would never serve as the base for a bridge. It was too windswept and unsheltered, while there were no island stepping stones across the width of water, so that the task of bridging and ferrying here could only be extremely difficult or indeed impossible. This was not a route to Zemun fit for an army. Marsigli and his troop turned back, 'my whole reconnaissance finished'. On the way they sighted what looked like a powerful Turkish escort a long way off, with supply carts presumably bound for Timisoara, having crossed the river further down. The usual feints were used by Marsigli's followers, giving an exaggerated impression of their numbers. Fires were lit in several places, bugles were sounded, and small groups of horsemen rode rapidly about. Then they withdrew across the Tisza. What Marsigli had to report to Vienna buried Starhemberg's novel plan, and the campaign which led to the famous victory of Senta/Zenta later in the year took a different course. Moreover, as things turned out, with this viewing of the Ottoman citadel of Belgrade on its height above the Danube, Marsigli ended his career as an officer in the war for Hungary.

VI

The details of his quarrel with lieutenant-colonel Salzer von Rosenstein are elusive; the eagerness in conflict of the two is plain. Marsigli, often absent on special missions, was entitled to leave his lieutenant-colonel in charge of his regiment. Yet if Salzer expected and presumed on this, he was mistaken; his colonel was a zealous officer who did not delegate authority easily. In 1696, obeying the Elector's order, Marsigli took at least part of his regiment down the Tisza and soon afterwards was bridging the river. The unsustained siege of Timisoara began, followed by the Elector's withdrawal. Marsigli moved his bridge upstream; he commanded troops, including his own men, which covered the retreat. It was at this point that the uneasy partnership collapsed, he and Salzer fell out, and Salzer was even placed temporarily under arrest.[63] What happened during the next few weeks is uncertain but Marsigli refers darkly to the role of his lieutenant-colonel's friends, count Nehem, the commander at Petrovaradin, and Guido Starhemberg. He himself was sick. The differences were patched up to the extent that he quitted the regiment at Szeged leaving it in Salzer's charge, and returned to Vienna. The first round of the dispute ended, the second began. He had given strict instructions for controlling the use of regimental funds, and this in effect tied the hands of Salzer and his brother officers. They appealed to higher authority in Vienna, accusing Marsigli of withholding improperly money due to his regiment. They claimed that they could not meet their liabilities and pay the men.[64] When this statement of grievances reached the War Council, it was decided to cancel Marsigli's instructions until a properly constituted enquiry had dealt with the allegation. He himself, convalescent in Vienna, was not consulted. He regarded so hasty, so sympathetic a response to his own officers as an arbitrary suspension of his authority.

The Habsburg War Council, the Hofkriegsrat, had by now a well-worn procedure for dealing with grievances and administering justice. A tribunal of qualified officers would be selected to investigate and determine such cases, with the Council in Vienna and the Emperor himself as superior authorities. It was rare that both sides to a dispute between officers would not be considered at great length, with the help of many written submissions. It was normal in such cases that strong political and personal influences co-existed with an even-handed bureaucratic routine. It was normal, too, that in time of war the campaign each year should interrupt these proceedings. Therefore, they took time: Salzer and the officers of the Marsigli regiment versus Marsigli, followed by Marsigli versus Salzer, burdened the files for nearly five years. From the start Marsigli believed that Rüdiger Starhemberg used his presidential position to pursue a vendetta. More probably, Starhemberg could have protected him fairly easily but chose not to do so. His subordinates, conversely, could not deny Marsigli his procedural rights in defending himself. A few specific traces of this tedious duel survive. Among them are letters from general Schlick, still the senior commander in the Tisza area, to Marsigli in Vienna.[65] Here was someone else who loathed lieutenant-colonel Salzer, and even described him as a Wallenstein, or an 'Attila' harassing honest colonels like Marsigli and Schlick. In his post at Szeged, Salzer (he said) had defied his superior officer, maltreated the commissariat officials, and intrigued with the local Magyar gentry – led by the notable and rebellious count Miklos Berczényi – who exploited this disunion among the Habsburg commanders. Meanwhile Salzer tarred Schlick with the Marsigli brush: both, he alleged to his supporters, were colonels withholding funds due to their regiments. In April 1697 Schlick prudently declined the War Council's request that he should lead the enquiry concerning Marsigli. At the same time he offered his friend some advice, urging Marsigli to come to Hungary as soon as possible to appease his officers, most of whom (Schlick believed) might be won over by a show of courtesy and forbearance.[66] They had been misled by Salzer.

The instinct to conciliate was never Marsigli's strong suit. A month later he passed through Szeged[67] on his way to carry out the reconnaissance which took him within sight of Belgrade, but there are no signs that he made any effort to settle his dispute with the officers. Vienna meanwhile persisted with its scheme for an enquiry, appointing Guido Starhemberg to take Schlick's place;[68] Starhemberg was regarded by Marsigli as an enemy. He found compensation for this, as usual, by trying to canvass at a higher level.[69] He pressed advice on the Elector of Saxony, taking some part in the discussions at Vienna which immediately preceded the Elector's conversion to Rome and his candidature for the elective crown of Poland. He approached prince Eugene, the new commander of the Habsburg forces in Hungary, appointed commander in chief in July when it was known that the Elector had secured the Polish crown. Eugene appreciated Marsigli's expertise in a country where his own knowledge was slight. He knew also that chancellor Kinsky regarded Marsigli highly, that Kinsky's friends were Rüdiger Starhemberg's enemies, and that Starhemberg – but not Kinsky – had originally championed his own appointment in Hungary. Indeed the change in the army command was a setback for Marsigli. While the Elector trusted him as a good staff officer in 1695 and 1696, Eugene had no commitment to Marsigli. They had both come to Vienna in 1683. Both were outsiders. Both favoured concepts of daring, aggressive warfare. Both, incidentally, were collectors and bibliophiles. But Eugene, taking up his new responsibilities in 1697, saw no reason to give particular encouragement to someone who exasperated influential colleagues like the Starhembergs, or who failed to control his own regiment. Eugene left Vienna for Hungary on 7 July; and three weeks later wrote to Marsigli from the camp at Petrovaradin.[70] He said that he wished to take advantage of Marsigli's presence at court, asking him to press for the despatch of supplies which the army needed so desperately. He also hoped to see him soon. This was courteous language of little substance. Marsigli's quarrel was unresolved. He had fended off the official enquiry by asking for Salzer and other officers to be summoned to testify in person, and by delaying his own reply to certain 'quaestiones'. Belatedly these tactics were rewarded when the councillors of the War Council – after hearing from Guido Starhemberg – decided early in August that the enquiry would have to be held over until after the fighting ended. They acknowledged also that Marsigli could take part in military operations.[71]

There followed two parallel series of events, which were intermittently linked: one on the grand scale attracting attention then and since, the other a smaller matter. The first proved to be the preliminaries of a decisive battle. The government had failed to mobilise a sufficiently large army along the Danube, after diverting troops to deal with a popular rising in the country north of Szeged. General Rabutin in Transylvania initially declined to send a reinforcement to the field army. Eugene and his fellow officers concluded that the Turkish armament was the stronger. They feared, to begin with, another Ottoman assault on Petrovaradin. Then they anticipated – it was the familiar cat's cradle – enemy moves across the Danube lower downstream, with thrusts possible at Titel, Szeged, or

Transylvania. To counter these, and hasten a conjunction with the forces approaching from Upper Hungary (where the fractious peasantry were at length crushed by general Vaudemont) and from Transylvania, Eugene marched most of his units to the Tisza. Vaudemont, Rabutin and their array of hussars and other cavalry joined them at Senta during the week from 26 August to 1 September. But on 24 August, shortly before reaching Senta, Eugene wrote to Marsigli and referred to a minor, intensely irritating item of business.[72]

The good colonel had been amazingly tactless. Preparing to leave Vienna, he sent ahead some of the cash due to his regiment while vetoing a settlement of accounts until he himself reached Szeged. Given the extraordinary poverty of the entire army in Hungary, the arrears of pay and lack of finance for supplies, and the need to check dissension spreading from civilians to soldiery, this was bound to worry the command. The supreme Habsburg interest was just then to pacify and encourage its manpower. Marsigli, piling on the tinder, had sent a message requiring the arrest of one of his officers: we cannot prove, we must guess that this was Salzer.[73] In consequence Eugene, as commander in chief, received a petition from the officers of the Marsigli regiment, protesting against an order for the arrest of one of their number and the failure to settle their accounts. Marsigli had not yet appeared. On 24 August Eugene accordingly wrote to say that he was referring the whole matter back to Vienna; he had no intention of antagonising officers or men at a critical moment in the campaign. A week later he sent a major Glowitz to take charge of the garrison at Szeged, which included the Marsigli companies still there.[74] The enlarged army withdrew from Senta back towards Petrovaradin in response to the latest Ottoman moves. Then Eugene found the Ottoman forces moving north a second time. He retraced his steps, and the battle of Senta took place a week later. The other part of the Marsigli regiment served on the left wing of the Habsburg army.

In Vienna, a few days earlier, the War Council and its president considered the report from Eugene and made its decision. Colonel Marsigli, they stated, would be suspended from his post 'in oeconomis et militaribus' until a final judgment was handed down on the complaints against him.[75] He was not heard in his own defence and it was a most damaging blow. It cannot have been softened by the arrival of another letter from Eugene, describing the army's march through the Bàcska, Marsigli's country *par excellence*.[76] It was written before the final collision with the Ottoman troops. Then came to Vienna the news of a victory over the Sultan and grand vezir more startling and complete than any other Christian success in Hungary since the war began, and it was a victory won without Marsigli's guidance or presence. For someone who liked to wear the mantle of an old soldier in these Turkish wars, his personal isolation must have been intense at a moment when the Emperor expressed the relief and excitement and admiration of the court, in sending congratulations to Eugene and his colleagues in Hungary.

Gradually the routine and the mood of ordinary business asserted themselves again. Marsigli, still under Kinsky's powerful patronage, made a direct appeal to Leopold.[77] His petition argued that on the eve of the great battle the War Council in Vienna had proceeded too summarily to observe the rules and principles of justice. It did not hear Marsigli's side of the case, nor investigate fully the colonel's financial accounts, and those of the lieutenant-colonel and the regiment. It favoured unduly and unjustly his subordinate officer. Having thus played his last and highest card, he declined to recognise the jurisdiction of the military authorities. They chose to maintain his suspension.[78] Everything now waited on Leopold's sovereign decision. It was several months coming, until in May 1698 the Emperor ruled that – 'for reasons not disclosed'[79] – colonel Marsigli should be reinstated. The colonel, meanwhile, had found plenty to do in his other universe.

CHAPTER SIX

An Author in the Making

I

From the end of 1696 until the autumn of 1698, aside from one brief military mission to southern Hungary, Marsigli spent his time in or near Vienna. He regarded himself as a senior army officer unjustly accused, defending his interest by negotiation on the spot with officialdom and courtiers. He continued to serve his powerful patron Kinsky in every way possible. The circle of his acquaintances included members of the Emperor's household and resident foreign ambassadors. Yet the check to his military career allowed him to give more time, including the extra summers which should have been spent on campaign, to his literary and scientific activity. If there was a grand design embedded in his many-sided enthusiasm it was probably the work, the 'opus', of bringing together his varied studies of the Danube, and he was encouraged by the presence of Muller, the willing draughtsman and secretary. Intermittently Marsigli dived headlong after a new distraction, a fresh idea for some other enquiry, or for resurrecting an earlier piece of writing. Then he would return to the problem of preparing the biggest, most complex work of all for the press.

One enjoyable stimulus were his incoming letters, which usually replied to the stream of requests and queries sent out from Vienna. What Marsigli wrote to his correspondents has all but disappeared but he kept his own mail, and from this we must learn what we can about him. For example Einmart wrote on several occasions during the winter of 1696–7.[1] The Boyleian air pump which he had been making for Marsigli in Nuremberg was 'nearly ready'. He would try to find examples of Dürer's engravings. As to works on astronomy, he advised that it was always best to consult Riccioli's *Almagestae Novae*; if this could not be found in Vienna, he offered to look out for a copy. He still had some of Marsigli's money in hand and was accordingly searching for a new telescope, but thought that an enquiry should be sent to the famous Roman instrument maker, Campani. Einmart also supplied the names of editors of the *Acta Eruditorum*, the Leipzig journal, who would certainly respond (he wrote) to any proposal put to them. Marsigli had no doubt prompted this because one of his ideas in 1696 was to publish a scientific paper.

The remarkable offer he had made to the Royal Society of London in 1691 included a compliment to Robert Boyle: he wished to dedicate to the great English scientist his youthful essay on luminescence, one of the many topics studied by Boyle. Either Boyle's death, or Marsigli's campaigning, or simple forgetfulness, soon pushed the thought to one side. Meanwhile the editors of the *Acta Eruditorum*, an annual volume of book reviews, had issued a Supplement. It contained notices of books and papers crowded out of their main series, or overlooked since the appearance of their first volume in 1682. Marsigli saw the Supplement, perhaps receiving a copy from Einmart, and certainly he read with pleasure a full if belated critical notice of his piece on the Thracian Bosphorus, printed in 1681.[2] It concluded with an almost elegiac confession of ignorance. We do not know, the reviewer says, whether the author is still alive or indeed whether he ever submitted to public scrutiny the works which he claimed to be writing after his return from Istanbul – on the Ottoman empire, and on the phosphorescent stones of Bologna.

To prove his survival as a virtuoso in a world of warfare harsher than the cosy civic order of Leipzig, Marsigli now used the little geological essay which he earlier thought of offering to Boyle. He got into touch with the editors of the *Acta Eruditorum*, receiving answers from the firm of Gross, publishers of the journal.[3] Everything went well, and the next number of the Acta (September 1697) included a full account of Marsigli's manuscript, together with illustrations. A second notice followed in March 1698. It mentioned that the work was in print, 'with the costs liberally defrayed by the author', the well-born soldier whom the review complimented for devoting himself to the natural sciences. A more restrained account appeared later in the transactions of the Royal Society. After an interval of several years, therefore, Marsigli had the pleasure of seeing his words in print.[4] It was mixed with a little pain. Why should a German printer setting up type for an essay in Italian confuse 'Bosforo' with 'fosforo'? The author happened to be an expert on both. But how gratifying to be described on the title page as 'di S.S.C. e R.M. Cameriere e Colonello d'un Reggimento di Fanteria,' even if his status was just then under attack by his enemies.

His wish to associate with men of science by correspondence or published communication was one facet of this period for Marsigli. Another was an interest in measurements systematically compiled, like his study of the Danube currents in 1695. Towards the end of 1696 we find him recording continuously the atmospheric conditions at his lodging in Vienna. From 11 December until August 1697 he persisted with daily thermometer and barometer readings, together with brief notes on the prevailing winds and weather.[5] When snow fell, therefore, the different forms of the flakes were described. On 7 January he picked out from the Danube a lump of ice, made a drawing to show its parallel series of air bubbles imprisoned in the ice as one freeze followed another. On 19 May he was examining hailstones with a microscope. He tells us that four thermometers and two barometers were used to produce his readings. After the end of July the record is less complete. In August, it will be recalled, the military authorities suspended him, and Marsigli should have had more leisure for his science; but he may have lost interest in what had become – at least for Muller, who probably did the work – a tedious pursuit. On the morning of 3 November 1697, by contrast, Marsigli and Muller enjoyed themselves examining through their telescopes in fine clear weather, for one hour and seven minutes, the conjunction of the planet Mercury with the sun.[6]

The employment of Muller and the purchase of instruments from Nuremberg had to be paid for, but as usual it is difficult to form a reliable impression of Marsigli's income and assets.[7] He and his two surviving brothers inherited their father's property, and in 1693 a division between them had been planned. Marsigli left the management of his share to his brother Filippo until the final distribution could be made. In March 1696 another Bolognese patrician and a family friend, cardinal Tanari, wrote from Rome of an unedifying quarrel between brothers Filippo and Antonio Felice over property matters.[8] He asked Luigi Ferdinando to intervene, and on 4 April Marsigli in Vienna signed a legal instrument which laid the ground for a settlement of their differences. By the following year his own agent Niccolò Maria Guicciardini had begun moving with fair regularity between Bologna and Vienna. Appointed to look after Marsigli's interests at home, he brought or transmitted to Austria the income needed to keep up Marsigli's level of investment as a patron of the sciences, and collector of books or rarities. The unpaid allowances of a suspended military officer were compensated for by this private wealth. Without a family except for servants, he could afford to wait for the arrears of pay due to him from the Habsburg administration. In that sphere he pinned his hopes on the Emperor, and relied on the influence of Kinsky against Starhemberg.

Cardinal Tanari was by no means his only Italian correspondent.[9] One Rinaldo Doglioni, for instance, acted for him in Venice and Padua, receiving funds which he laid out on the books demanded from Vienna: the complete works of Galileo, those of Gesner the old physiologist and naturalist, and Vincenzo Coronelli, the contemporary Venetian cartographer. More important was Marsigli's former tutor in Bologna canon Lelio Trionfetti, that dim but loyal man, keeper of the city's Botanic Garden. The opus on the Danube embraced a collection of plants made in 1696 (p. 135 above); there were sketches, and notes stating rather imprecisely whether the specimens had been found by the river, or in marshes, or elsewhere. Trionfetti was now asked whether he could match these descriptions or drawings with what could be found in other regions, and give their correct nomenclature from the classic botanists. Marsigli also asked him to consult the people in Bologna who could help with the different aspects of his subject. For example, how should the river Danube itself be studied, that extraordinary body of water with both its seasonal and its abnormal changes of level and speed? Trionfetti sounded out Domenico Guglielmini, the most celebrated hydrologist of the day, who taught in Bologna. The professor's masterpiece on the subject, *Della Natura de' Fiumi*, was published in 1697 and he obliged with some informative, helpful letters to Marsigli in Vienna.

II

Also in 1697, from the presses in Venice and Frankfurt a book appeared which surely came to his notice. Paolo Boccone, botanist and wandering scholar, had not long before visited Vienna and relates that he was given specimens of Hungarian plants by colonel Marsigli's German doctor.[10] Then, having collected together all his botanical and geological essays, Boccone declared that he was publishing them as his final bequest to the world of learning.[11] One of three volumes he dedicated to the Englishman William Sherard (who later founded the chair of botany at Oxford) and the others to that supreme patron, Emperor Leopold. Here was a shining example and precedent for Marsigli to follow. He had earlier undertaken to offer his work on the Danube to the Royal Society, of which he was a member; but, undeniably, a dedication to the sovereign of Germany, Austria, Bohemia and Hungary would have the deeper symbolic fitness. The Danube's source was in the Holy Roman Empire of Germany. The Danube carried on its stream troops and transports making their way to Hungary, where Leopold was matching the old empire of Rome (commemorated by the ruins of Trajan's bridge) with a new eastern empire. If Sultan Suleyman's conquests barbarised a vast region, the Catholic Emperor and his army were now reopening it to the civilization of Christian Europe. A great book on the Danube itself would exemplify this new era, in which useful studies of the whole region could at last begin. Such were Marsigli's daydreams, edged with more than a touch of bombast as he set them down on paper,[12] and generally wrestled with the problem of putting his long enquiry into proper order. After much hesitation, perhaps with young Muller's help in discussion, he devised and approved a scheme for publishing the work. He would first draft, and print, a 'prospectus' of his researches addressed to the Royal Society. Later he would complete the definitive volumes, dedicating them to the supreme patron Emperor Leopold I. It was an exciting programe. The *Prodromus*, as he called his prospectus, would be a synopsis describing in detail the arrangement and contents of his work. He would then be committed by its publication, after adding any corrections offered by his colleagues in London and elsewhere to the form and substance of the final version.

The word 'Prodromus' reveals a change of language. It signalled that Marsigli was no longer preparing a text in the Italian used in all his early drafts and notes and maps, including a manuscript booklet of 5 pages intended to clarify his thoughts for arranging the 'opera del Danubio'.[13] Muller always wrote in German or Latin, and both men regarded Latin as the international language of science and scholarship. Marsigli was no doubt pleased to have, and indeed he required, an assistant with this qualification; Latin would give the better currency to his own research. But as time went by he also wanted a bigger book. His appetite, his notion of grandeur as greatness, grew. Between 1696 and 1698 a change of this kind is plain enough. At the start, the Danube was to be described 'geographice, hydrographice: historice et physice' in four volumes, one for each heading.[14] They would contain all Marsigli's cartography, archaeology, geology, and his studies of Danubian fishes, birds and animals. There are draft title pages for these, corrected by Muller. Yet later Marsigli settled in favour of a plan for six volumes: one each for geography, antiquities, minerals, fishes, birds, and a set of appendices. This was the plan which appeared in the Prospectus completed during the summer of 1698.

The enlargement or exaggeration so characteristic of Marsigli must partly be associated with the breadth of his intellectual activity. His own texts for the *Acta Eruditorum* and the Danubian prospectus were being put into order. His scientific instruments were in daily use. He was active as book collector and bibliophile. What he and Muller needed in particular were the publications which would help them to assess the measurements and samples of all sorts brought back from Hungary, but Einmart had orders to look for purchases in a wider range of subjects.[15] Marsigli was also in touch with booksellers at the Hague and Venice. He received lists of titles and hints on book prices, and other incoming letters show that he took an equal interest in binding, typefaces and the qualities and sizes of paper used for the books he bought. This concern developed as he pondered over the publication of his own Prospectus. Einmart, an engraver with an eye to business, encouraged him to think of spending generously on the finest possible format in his forthcoming volumes.

Publishers were at this period specifically looking for anyone who offered them the chance of producing richly illustrated books. In Nuremberg the printing professions had joined forces with the notable artists' Academy founded some years earlier by Joachim Sandrart the elder; and its members – above all Sandrart the younger, Einmart and Christopher Weigel, who were good but not inspired craftsmen – did a great deal of work for the book trade. One recent enterprise had been a new illustrated Bible which appeared in 1691, with no less than 700 illustrations including contributions from both Sandrart and Einmart. A directory of traders and artists appearing in 1698 would have more examples from Einmart's hand. A Nuremberg firm likewise printed the posthumous work of the most famous literary man of his day in Germany: Samuel Pufendorf's gloriously illustrated history of the 'Reign of King Charles X Gustavus of Sweden' in separate Latin, German and French versions, which had come out in 1696.[16] The drawings and plates were older but the Nurembergers had the honour and profit of publishing the work. It was therefore desirable at this stage to look for fresh business, and Einmart's letters to Marsigli in 1697 and 1698 amount to the wooing of a new author. Einmart, as obsequious to Marsigli as Marsigli was to the Emperor, spoke for a whole fraternity of Nuremberg printers, bookbinders, engravers, instrument makers and type founders. The Italian nobleman in Habsburg service certainly looked a likely patron and client. His funds seemed plentiful. He had maps, and drawings of birds, fishes, mineral samples, flowers and classical fragments waiting to be engraved for illustration, all from a region much in the public eye. The despatch of Muller to Vienna, and Muller's journey to Hungary, could now be seen paving the way for another publishing venture of similar kind.

On 18 May 1697, while Marsigli prepared to set out on his reconnaissance in Hungary, Einmart wrote again.[17] He replied in some detail to queries in Marsigli's latest letter. First, it would certainly be possible to arrange for a group of craftsmen to be sent to Vienna to work for his Excellency. Einmart had made enquiries, and found one man who was an admirable engraver, and four or five others – all good people – who could accompany him. They only needed an assurance that there was enough work to keep them there a reasonable time, and that no official restrictions were likely to worry them or limit their pay. However Marsigli seems to have implied that he had plans for economising on both his own money and the men's time. Einmart differed. It was unreasonable to hustle craftsmen of this quality, he wrote; they were disinclined to scramble through six months' work which really needed a year to complete. And whether they were in Vienna or Nuremberg they would do their best.

Second, Einmart was cautious in estimating costs. It depended on the amount and complexity of the whole task, he wrote, but gave an example of what might be required by estimating that the 150 copperplates for Pufendorf's Swedish History, originally engraved in France, must have been worth 8000 Reichstaler. The illustrations for count Marsigli's work could probably be assessed at the same level. He added that the standard of Nuremberg work was as high as any foreign product, if not higher; and craftsmanship 'of the highest perfection' surely deserved a fair reward, etc.

Third, it was essential that a commission of this intricate kind should be supervised by a person of sufficient experience, acting as assistant to his Excellency, and on this point he fully agreed with Marsigli. To a suggestion that Einmart himself was the right choice for this post of supervisor or manager, he demurred; but with the usual expression of his humility and gratitude. Nothing was said about Muller's position, and unfortunately no more letters from Nuremberg survive before April 1698. We have been given just a glimpse of Marsigli's preparations for printing and publishing his work on the Danube.

III

At the same time he was well aware of the need to arrange and organise his materials. It was one point settled if the number of volumes for the Danube had been fixed; it was another to decide in detail on their contents, which in turn depended on the range and character of his collections.[18]

He and Muller never doubted that they must begin by portraying the geographical framework of the Danube lands. The first volume would start with a text describing the course of the river and the points of importance located along its shores. Then came their maps, with the fundamental device of a large small-scale general map combined with smaller large-scale sectional maps. It was gratifying to be able to add Muller's tabulated terrestrial and celestial measurements. Next followed the hydrographic element in Marsigli's enquiries, the method of which had been anticipated by his earlier account of the Bosphorus. He would investigate the element of water in the Danubian context, including its impact on the shape of the river bed at various points, on the character of the shores and marshes and the actual course of the river. This section, originally assigned an entire volume, was sensibly annexed to the geography and cartography in volume I. After that, as he pondered the problem of arrangement, Marsigli visualised placing 'history' and then 'natural history'. History was Roman antiquity, the collection of his drawings and notes which described the ancient sites he had visited along the Danube or at some distance inland. Natural history would include illustrations of the mineral samples he had collected in Slovakia, together with an account of the mines he had seen. It meant as well his material on Danubian birds and fishes and plants, in the form of illustrations or descriptive lists. Marsigli never tries to justify the limits of his general theme. He relied simply on his own experience and travel during the years of warfare, and therefore did not intend to venture upstream beyond the Wienerwald nor downstream beyond Nicopolis in the course of his enquiry. He never reached the delta lands adjoining the Black Sea, or at this stage went upstream into Germany. Yet within the stretch of 800 miles of river known to him, and on broad expanses inland on either shore, almost any topic seemed relevant enough for his purpose. He was likewise attracted by the notion of select 'appendices', which appealed to his ideal of scholarly virtue. He reserved these for a sixth and final volume, although most of the material could have been inserted in earlier sections of the work.

Marsigli and Muller soon changed their minds on one matter. It was resolved to reduce the number of sectional maps from 24, Marsigli's earlier

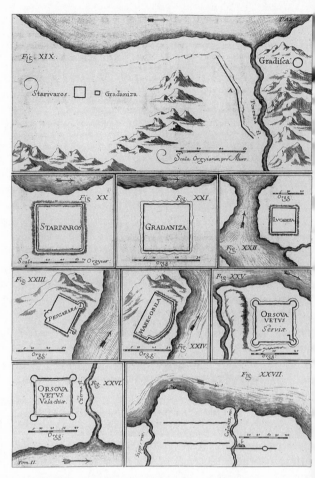

18 Roman sites along the Danube: these can also be located on illustration 12, p. 85.

choice, to 14, which is the figure given in the Prospectus. Muller, told to make the finished drawings which in due course would have to be engraved, had evidently found reasons for suggesting this modification. After studying Marsigli's own earlier maps and sketches of the course of the Danube, he produced a first series of 14 maps. This was examined and reviewed in certain respects, to be followed by a second series, again of 14 maps.[19] Later it would be revised again.

The idea of a general map of the Danubian region, showing the wider frame in which his sectional maps were set, posed other problems for Muller. He had to master the geography of an enormous region which his patron had come to know by dint of countless journeys, marches, or reconnaissances in the course of fifteen years. As guidance, he could use Marsigli's own sketches covering the area. He was then expected to produce more professionally drawn maps from this amateur's treasury of knowledge. His new task was in fact to learn what he could from Marsigli's maps, and modify them where necessary in the light of Marsigli's later observations or is own. Whenever his patron required maps – for his work on the opus of the Danube, or for other compositions, or for illustrating memoranda to be submitted to the Emperor's ministers – he would be able to draw them in a manner regarded by Marsigli as acceptably accurate and elegant. It is fascinating to look at some of the material still in Bologna to see how this was done.[20] There are Marsigli 'originals', and Muller 'copies'. There are maps drawn by Muller with some of the placenames added by Marsigli. Marsigli exaggerated vastly the breadth of his rivers; Muller normally but not always reduced it. Muller realised that, for the course of the Danube below Belgrade his only guide was Marsigli: he might improve the draughtsmanship, but for the physical outline of regions now in Ottoman hands would have to rely on his master's impressions from river voyages long ago. On the other hand, in Hungary Muller was able to use his own instrument readings to correct Marsigli's earlier efforts.

All this involved something more far-reaching. Marsigli had to sift through his massive collection of maps and sketches in order to guide his assistant who needed to study them. This probably explains why a feature of Marsigli's early maps, in many cases, is the annotations; to judge from their wording this was not done when he first drew the maps, nor in his old age. Undated, they are marginal notes for guiding somebody who was using the maps or had been told to arrange them. The somebody was Muller, acting as Marsigli's secretary and mapmaker for six years from 1697. By 1703 this had been done, and many fresh maps and papers were filed by the conscientious secretary in an ever-growing collection. Marsigli in Vienna went through his old maps one by one, adding a comment every now and then.[21] He would say, for example, 'I made this map in 1689, with the help of the best guides I could find', and noting that it was submitted to the commander Lewis of Baden in order to show the region surrounding Niš. Or he noted that a map of the eastern Balkans traced the routes of his successive journeys in 1691 and 1692. Or he explained that a certain map of Croatia dated from 1689 when Leopold sent him to reconnoitre a viable frontier with the Sultan in that area. If Muller was instructed, as happened a little later, to draw a new map of the Balkans showing the medieval dependencies of the crown of Hungary, he could base his work on Marsigli's earlier efforts. The mapping of existing or projected trade routes, of Roman roads, of mineral deposits or mine workings, all depended on his patron's experience, which was revealed partly by conversation but more by his sketches and maps. These were the source of knowledge for Muller.

Marsigli, annotating his maps, uses the past tense. 'Made by me to show . . .' was his usual formula. He is not found saying this on maps drawn after 1695, because his secretary knew the answers; but Muller knew much less of areas through which his patron travelled at an earlier stage. From the moment of his entry into Habsburg service in 1683 Marsigli had tried, as we know, to commend himself to possible patrons by submitting sketch maps and diagrams as well as written memoranda. They showed relevant tracts of

country, or illustrated his ideas for siege warfare. The simple device
apparently came as a pleasant novelty to ruler and ministers, whose concept
of business was normally limited to the written or spoken word. At any
rate they regarded it as one reason for qualifying Marsigli to supervise
the engineers, and also began to give him credit for exceptional knowledge
of the terrain between Buda and Belgrade. Then, after the capture of
Belgrade and the advance into Serbia, this was extended further. Marsigli
emphasised and exaggerated what he had learnt on his journey from
Istanbul through Serbia in 1680, and on his way through Bosnia as a captive
in 1683. He also, as he states so often, consulted the best-informed guides
His drawings as a roving staff officer were consequently respected in the
field and at court, valued in default of anything better. From the closing
months of 1688 until 1692 Marsigli was mapmaker and sketcher in Serbia
Bulgaria and Croatia. On the left bank of the Danube he was active in
Wallachia and Transylvania during the winters of 1689 and 1690. Wherever
possible, as in Istanbul or Bucharest, he collected maps by other hands
which gave him a notion, fantastic at certain points, of the Black Sea littoral
from the Bosphorus as far as the Crimea and the mouth of the Don.

In planning the work on the Danube, as in arranging the collection of
maps, the two men used the river as an internal boundary. 'Cis-Danubia
and 'Trans-Danubia', for the right and left bank respectively, were common figures of speech at the time.[22] Accordingly they put maps showing
Syrmia, Slavonia, Serbia, Croatia, Greece and Bulgaria in one group; and
maps of Timisoara, Transylvania, Wallachia, Moldavia and the Ukraine in
another.[23] Both included examples of Marsigli's own work, those acquired
by gift or purchase and, increasingly as time went on, those drawn by
Muller. It was Muller who numbered them on the back, like a good filing
clerk. A third group comprised drawings which specifically mapped the
course of the river Danube. They were the work of various artists, but
Marsigli's pieces predominate below the point where the Drava and
Danube join. Other maps depicted the Bácska region with its 'Roman
entrenchments and, in great detail, the course of the Tisza. These were
initially Marsigli's, drawn between 1693 and 1695, but from 1696 Muller'
work in the same area accumulated, including the maps which supported
Marsigli's memoranda to ministers on the campaigning prospects for 1697
and 1698. Traces of their arrangement of these rich materials still appear
occasionally in Marsigli's surviving collections, in the sequence of the map
in certain volumes together with Muller's numbering.

The convenient distinction between Cis- and Trans-Danubia was also
used in arranging some of the material for Marsigli's second volume. In the
Prospectus he undertakes to begin his study of Roman antiquity with a list
of the ancient sites he had examined along the river. Starting at Deutsch
Altenburg a few miles below Vienna, he enumerated 38 of these going
downstream to the limit of his travels in Bulgaria. With few exceptions, like
the conspicuous earthworks of the Bácska, they were on the right bank

This was the ancient frontier of Roman Pannonia, to be revived for the seventeenth-century imagination, and Muller in due course prepared to display it in the definitive volume. He would do so by adapting and then reducing Marsigli's clumsy, vivid wash drawings of the sites to fit them into groups of three, four or five on a folio page, suitable for engraving.[24] Having dealt with points along the river the two men turned their attention 'inland', starting at Osijek on the Drava. Ten more places in Slavonia, Serbia and Bulgaria (Cis-Danubia) were listed, to be followed by Marsigli's findings across the Danube in Transylvania, Wallachia and by the Tisza (Trans-Danubia). Fifty inscriptions and 40 other Roman fragments were also referred to summarily; the intention was to arrange them into distinct groups for Cis- and Trans-Danubia. According to the Prospectus another part of the volume would give a full description of the Roman roads in the Balkans and Dacia. Marsigli asserts that the routes from Rome across the Adriatic and along the Via Egnatia to Constantinople, or from Rome northwards to Noricum and Pannonia, were familiar enough. It would be for him to fill in the large segment between, in Moesia and Dacia, using his observation of ancient remains adjoining the tracks along which Emperor Leopold's forces had marched into unknown country. Again it was impossible to visualise this aspect of the enquiry without help from his draughtsman and mapmaker.

The next great block of original material to be used derived from Marsigli's delight in samples of earth and minerals, a counterpart to the attention he paid to the qualities of water, studied earlier. It was mainly a matter of organising his collection of rock samples, picked up during the winter visits to Slovakia, so that he could link them with the account already given of the Danube.[25] For this reason the Prospectus explains that he will begin the third volume with his attempts to investigate the river bed at four separate points. They were in the Danube just above Vienna and at Pest, the Tisza above Szeged and somewhere (not specified) on the Maros.[26] Next would come his list of the large number of different pebbles and stones which he had collected from these rivers. After that, a glance at the varieties of vitriol identified, at cinnabar and the other crystal formations he had seen, would precede his more fundamental study of 'the organic structure' of the mountains in this region. He explains that, fire at the earth's centre tended to force veins of metal through the inner rock towards the earth's surface, and his own exploration in Slovakia took advantage of the mining shafts dug down through this surface (or through part of it), giving him a chance to look closely at the whole structure. When volume III came to be published he hoped to add some maps and illustrations showing the mining areas. Then followed a catalogue and synopsis of the minerals he intended to consider, including the 'imperfect' iron, copper, lead, mercury, and the 'perfect' silver and gold, and such 'related' categories as antimony, gypsum and tartar. It should be noted, he concludes, that the samples were all being sent to 'his Museum' in Bologna, and could be examined there.[27] This is one of the earliest distinct references to another of Marsigli's ideas, of a centre for scientific study to be set up in his old home. It would absorb him in later years; but already in 1698 someone in Bologna compiled a so-called 'general catalogue' of the mineral samples despatched there by Marsigli at various dates: unfortunately, says a note, there was much damage in transit, and they cannot be arranged in a proper order.[28] While drafting his Prospectus Marsigli wrote to the senior mining official at Kremnica (Kremnitz), and asked for help. In a very friendly reply the writer said that he was getting the map drawn for which he had been asked and enclosed an ore body from another district, which seemed to contain gold of finer quality than had ever been found at Kremnica.[29] A phrase used in this letter suggests that Marsigli had been enquiring as well for samples from the mines in Saxony. He certainly intended to hand the map, when received, to Muller, so helping Muller to plot all the information they had about mineral deposits in Hungary on a general 'mappa metallographica'. According to the Prospectus, they would then add copies of the engravings already in Marsigli's possession which illustrated the techniques of mining.[30] Such an example shows our virtuoso hard at work. Correspondence with the best authorities, collecting material, preparing the prospectus, preparing maps and other drawings for the final publication at a later stage, all went together.

There remained three more volumes to organise, for the fishes of the Danube and its bird life, and for the appendices which he called the 'analecta'.

We have already found Marsigli watching the fishermen of New Orsova with their gigantic sturgeon, and dissecting dogfish for himself at Istanbul. Since then he had 'collected' the fishes of the Danube by a series of drawings (with some colour wash) of varying size.[31] By 1698 he could visualise a catalogue of the fish he had identified as a whole volume of his forthcoming work. He conceived that his main task was to name the fish, as they were known to Germans, Magyars and Slavs, and if possible to identify them with the types of fish already known to such scholars as Aldrovandi, Gesner and Rondelet. He duly obtained these works, and also the much more recent *Four Books on the History of Fishes* by Francis Willughby, published at Oxford in 1685.[32] In certain respects this was a volume after his own heart. Dedicated to Samuel Pepys as president of the Royal Society, it had a rich supplement of plates engraved at the expense of Pepys and others as an 'Icthyographia'. Marsigli planned an icthyographia for the Danube. In order to draft this section of the Prospectus, therefore, he went methodically through his paintings of Danubian fish, in many cases finding them described in Aldrovandi, Rondelet or Willughby. Otherwise he considered that they were novelties, his personal observation. Then he used his own lists of German, or Magyar or Serbian names for the fish, and arranged them in an orderly sequence which was duly set out in the printed prospectus of 1698.[33]

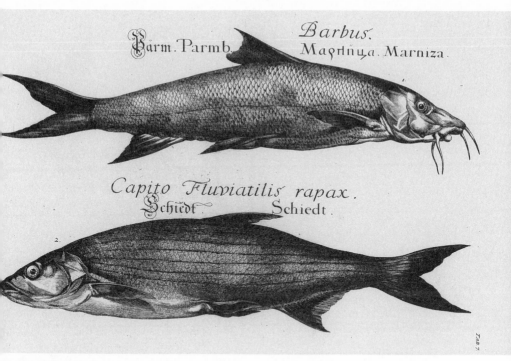

Bárm. Parmb. — *Barbus.* Маρнйца. Marniza.

Capito Fluviatilis rapax. Schiedt — Schiedt.

9 Danubian fish.

The preparations for compiling the fifth volume on the birds of Danubia were very similar; the evidence is less plentiful. Marsigli did not normally parade an enthusiasm for ornithology in his writings, as he does for geology and certain other branches of natural history. All the same he made another 'collection' of sketches, which includes individual species of the birds he saw, and a more original series showing nests and eggs.[34] In due course these were listed for the prospectus. Marsigli, although he once again used the classic older authorities and Willughby's more recent ornithology[35] to identify the majority of his examples, was less concerned than in his study of fish to give the local nomenclature. It was as if the habit of collecting names in several local languages had faltered in this branch of his enquiries; on the other hand his phrases give us some idea of an observer distinguishing what he saw on the open water of the river's broader channels, the different species in the marshes, the native and the migrant birds, those feeding on fish or on insects.

Last came the schedule of 'analecta' with which Marsigli intended to complete his picture of the Danube in the light of his research.[36] He had eight in mind, the first being his catalogue of the plants collected in Hungary before the campaign began in 1696.[37] Topics 2 to 4 were certain physical and hydrographic tabulations in Danubia, the attemped measurement of the speed of currents and qualities of water in the major rivers, and recent barometric readings for Vienna. Then there were to be studies in

Anas Cristata Flavescens
Querquedula Cristata
Colymbis sive Belleny.

20 Danubian birds.

anatomy (of which the sturgeon was one), and the last topic of all promised
a note of 80 or so different insects which Marsiglis had observed during his
travels. His précis of these scattered collections closed fittingly with an
assurance of the physical splendour of the six volumes to come, the quality
of their paper, print and illustration. The prospectus was complete. The
Viennese censor passed it for publication on 1 August 1698.

IV

While searching for and sifting through his early maps, Marsigli could not
avoid confronting the general medley and multitude of his papers. They
included old diaries, letters received and copies of his own despatches or
reports, instructions from ministers, passports, notes, memoranda and
other fragments. He did not think of using them for his opus on the
Danube, having taken what he considered was needed for that purpose, but
the working papers of half a lifetime remained at his fingertips. They
suggested to this proud and superlatively energetic nobleman another
possible venture, an idea for some kind of autobiography.

The memoirs he composed have often been cited in our account of
him. Sixty years ago, working from an eighteenth-century copy of the lost
original, an admirable scholar published them.[38] Lacking firm evidence, he
could not be certain of the date when Marsigli wrote or dictated these pages

of reminiscence and apology, but considered it likely that most of them described in the manuscript as parts I to IV belonged to the year 1705, when we shall find Marsigli in Switzerland and Milan at a particularly agitated epoch of his career. However it seems likely that at least parts I to III belong to his time in Vienna, when he could still consider himself the successful and competent servant of Emperor Leopold, while warding off attacks by his personal opponents. He must have intended to give an account of his own career, written freely in Italian, to satisfy himself and edify future generations bearing the noble name of Marsigli. Muller meanwhile went on chiselling the Latin and drawing the maps required for their joint work on the Danube.

Each of the three parts is a continuous piece of writing with a well-marked unity. The first dealt with Marsigli's origins and early life before he entered his chosen profession in Leopold's service. The second, covering the years from 1683 to 1691, described his share in the Turkish wars as a Habsburg officer. The third part is entirely taken up with the curious and unsuccessful diplomatic episode of 1691–2, until it led Marsigli back to his role in the Habsburg army. In writing he obviously referred constantly to his papers in order to check what he was saying. Passages about his life in Istanbul in 1679–80 and again in 1691–2 simply paraphrase selections from his own collection of manuscripts dealing with this early period.[39] The same is true of the phase when he acted as the English ambassador's secretary. Likewise remarkable are the respect and admiration with which Lewis of Baden was mentioned. Marsigli could never have written in this vein in 1705, when we shall find him bearing a profound grudge against Lewis as a thoroughly unjust commander. What follows in the fourth part, taking the narrative down to 1705, has a quite different character. He here adopts the device of using yearly headings, and writing from memory an entry for each year in turn, while stating from time to time that his papers deal very fully with one matter or another. There is no evidence that he actually consulted them in his account of this period. The fact is that he had already sent his archive off to Bologna; it was not accessible to him in 1705 when he wished to give an account of his career after 1693. There are a few additional hints. For example it would be reasonable for Marsigli, if he was writing in 1696–8 and describing his first visit to Istanbul, to recall a point of interest which also cropped up during his second visit in 1691, 'a few years ago when I was again in Istanbul'.[40] It would also make sense, if he were writing between 1698 and 1701 about the earlier period, to refer to 'my work on the Danube recently brought to completion', or to an account of Trajan's bridge 'which will appear in my treatise on the Danube'.[41] Whereas he refers to a meeting at Vienna in 1698 in the light of papers 'which are among my documents located in Bologna':[42] those are words written after 1702, when he no longer had access to his papers. In 1698 he was still in Vienna, beginning an autobiography with the help of those rich collections which he and Muller were busily arranging for further use.

Meanwhile Marsigli never failed to assert his claim to be an authority on the Ottoman empire and the world of Islam. As a former traveller in Ottoman lands, and a former captive in the enemy army or in Bosnia, he offered his knowledgeable advice to the Habsburg court. Ministers listened to him or read his memoranda even if they did not adopt his views. In his own mind, if not theirs, his reputation was not only justified but reinforced by his long-standing plans for composing a work dealing with the subject, based originally on the material collected during his periods of residence in Istanbul. In 1681 he first referred to it. In 1692 he speaks of having perfected his treatise on Ottoman military forces.[43] But it was after 1696, more especially after the great Habsburg victory at Senta, that he crystallised his view of the Ottoman empire's fundamental, irremediable military decay since Kara Mustafa's retreat from Vienna in 1683. His idea was to demonstrate this by evidence taken from his own papers and by an account of his own experience. He made the attempt in a new work to be dedicated to the 'Princes of the Holy League'.[44] He urged them to profit, in the wake of the last great battle, from the continuous long-term decline in Turkish power. A great opportunity, after a similar victory, had not been taken in 1689 and 1690. The mistake should not be repeated, and the implication was that Leopold should now plan for a fresh attack on Belgrade or Timisoara. Soberly described as a study of 'past and present military structures of the Ottoman empire', book I contains an account of the Sultan's armed forces, as they were revealed by Marsigli's copy of a Turkish set of registers dating from the previous century.[45] In 50 chapters it gives a comprehensive account with a minimum of extraneous material, moving briskly from the Janissaries to the other types of Ottoman foot soldier, and from the feudal cavalry to the distribution of land tenures in the Turkish empire. It describes the auxiliaries, such as the contingents provided by the Tartar and Danubian princes. It concludes with an account of the Sultan's navy, including his galleys, and with a tabulated list of the materials, maintenance costs and personnel required for a single galley. The list is in Muller's unmistakable script.[46] Having demonstrated Ottoman power at its maximum Marsigli proceeded to the focus of his argument: the opening chapters of the second volume described the 'diminution' of that empire, of its army and the army's recruitment. Then he dealt with such topics as weapons, transport, drill and military music, before turning to the Ottoman army's operations in his own day: its procedures on the march, in battle, and in the course of siege warfare. These were considered on the basis of his experience in all the recent campaigns (except 1697). Naval tactics, including the handling of the Sultan's Danube flotilla, were examined at the end. It was a tract for the times.

Unfortunately, we have only Marsigli's copy (with a few entries in Muller's hand), and whether he presented another to Leopold or the Habsburg ministers cannot be confirmed. Many years later he declared that the Viennese authorities objected to the second part of the work, which described military operations which he had witnessed himself, and referred to Habsburg errors of judgment. Consequently he could not publish the manuscript, which was set aside.[47] The project of such a book, which would have appeared before the negotiations leading to the treaties of Carlowitz, had failed. All the same, as it turned out this was a further stage, after his earlier drafts, in the writing of Marsigli's book on 'the Rise and Decline of the Ottoman Empire' which was published, after considerable further revision and after his death, in 1732.[48]

One other of his dreams in Vienna appears as a manuscript. This has a title beginning 'A natural, civil and military description of Moesia, Dacia and Illyria' in fourteen sections, with maps and genealogical tables.[49] It is not much more than a synopsis, with certain fragments written out in greater detail. A preface tells how the writer, having been given a brief rest from his profession of arms, intends to serve the Emperor with his pen and will employ his knowledge to describe the regions lying on the further side of Hungary. In his opinion, because these were situated on a band of mountainous territory from the Adriatic to the Black Sea, they formed the best line of defence against the Turks. The work is patchy. At the beginning, part of Dacia is omitted because it had already been studied in 'my treatise on the Danube', but later he refers vividly to the chaos of peoples found in that particular area: the Magyars, Saxons, Szeklers, Vlachs, Greeks, Armenians and Bulgars, and to the effects of warfare in driving so many of them out of the plain and into the sheltering hills. He relates how he had seen this for himself when the Habsburg army entered the country under Lewis of Baden's command. Next, treating of Serbia and Thrace, he has much to say (not always accurately) of the mountain ranges, and how their configuration influenced events in 1689 and 1690. Illyria and Bosnia get scant treatment but there is a fuller description of the regions from Wallachia to the Ukraine and Crimea. Marsigli was once again making use of his papers, here a map of the fortresses on the river Dniester given him by the Prince of Wallachia, there a report he had himself written recently for Kinsky on what he had learnt of the Ukraine and the Tartars at a meeting with the Muscovite Boris Sheremetev.[50] It was a bird's-eye view of distant places Marsigli felt he should not neglect; but he knew very little about them.

Two or three years later he tried again, when he had the benefit of extra experience and fresh materials. He now planned nothing less than a history of the Hungarian monarchy with all its medieval dependencies; Muller penned the Latin on 70 or so folios of magnificent paper.[51] There were maps of the principalities from Hercegovina round to Moldavia. There were genealogical tables of the cluster of ruling families. There was a sequence of brief essays by Marsigli, with occasional reference to his travels. Then this too he seems to have put aside although Muller, instructed to make a fresh set of the relevant maps as highly finished and free from error as possible, was still working on them in 1702, in the midst of a new war.

ALOYSI FERDINANDI

COMIT. MARSIGLI

D ANVBIALIS

OPERIS

PRODROMVS.

A D

REGIAM SOCIETATEM

ANGLICANAM.

Auſpicio Anni ac Sæculi Novi

cIɔ Iɔcc.

21 The *Prodromus* of the Danube: the titlepage.

Marsigli himself, at this desperate moment, felt constrained to give priority to other business.

On balance, the most ambitous of these literary projects had made the most progress. The plans for publishing six stately and learned volumes on the Danube were maturing, to the extent that a prospectus of the whole work could be laid before the public. Marsigli's concern for the elegance of layout and paper may have held up an agreement to print, and unfortunately this part of the bargaining with Einmart, and Einmart's canvassing of his colleagues, are not described in what is left of the correspondence. They have to be taken for granted. The upshot was that one of the grander names in the history of Nuremberg publishing, the firm of Endter – more specifically the heirs of Johann Andreas Endter – printed the *Prodromus* at the noble author's expense.[52] Copies began to circulate in 1701, when readers everywhere could see for themselves what Marsigli had visualised earlier: a dedication to the Fellows of the Royal Society of London which expressed his gratitude, begging for advice and corrections as well as encouragement, with an admission that he would be dedicating to Emperor Leopold the six volumes whose contents were described in the following pages. There was also inserted a specimen page showing the title of the work to be presented to Leopold, with its lines printed alternately in red and black ink, and using no less than ten different type faces. In Marsigli's judgment, as in that of many contemporaries, great works offered to great men required this sort of ornament. Meanwhile more remained to be done to complete the definitive manuscript volumes and arrange for their publication. Fortunately everything seemed well in hand at a moment when Marsigli came nearest to what he wanted most, an elevated role in political affairs.

CHAPTER SEVEN

The Treaty of Carlowitz
and the New Frontier

I

At last, after catastrophe at Senta and the following swift thrust by Eugene into Bosnia, the strongest interest in the Ottoman government wanted to end the war.[1] It was a remarkable change. For years, those Turks who preferred to continue fighting had been more powerful than the peace-lovers. Led by the Sultan himself, Mustafa II, they obeyed the traditional wisdom forbidding the surrender of any of the 'domain of Islam', or indeed of the 'domain of war' – the borderlands surrounding and protecting Islam. War could properly end, by this view, when the bounds of Islam had been extended. In 1698 Amadja-Zade Hussein Köprülü, recently governor of Belgrade and then with reluctance appointed grand vezir by the Sultan, thought otherwise. He belonged to a new school of thought among Ottoman counsellors and politicians, for whom the empire was big enough as it stood. 'Avoid wars in old age', the old age of the Ottoman empire, became a guiding maxim which they maintained against stiff opposition. So Paget, William III's ambassador to the Sultan since 1693, by royal instructions the ever-willing mediator, was invited to Adrianople in December 1697 after intricate manoeuvres at court. As he travelled up from Istanbul he was made aware of a promising change in a different quarter; he received a message from Kinsky in Vienna authorising him to listen favourably to any serious overtures for peace.[2]

At the end of January 1698 Paget wrote to London and Vienna, giving an account of the position.[3] He had seen the grand vezir and discussed difficult points in a series of interviews with Mavrocordato, who came to Paget with proposals and soundings from the vezir and other officials. He replied, and debate among the Turks continued, but the result was that the Divan and the Sultan at last acknowledged approvingly a proposition for peace on the basis of *uti possidetis*.* This willingness to renounce what had been lost to the Habsburg Emperor was a great step, a fundamental concession. Paget

---

* For an explanation of this phrase, see p. 101.

went on to explain that the Turks still wished to evade or whittle down the principle, by demanding that Transylvania should be restored to its former status under a native prince, and that Leopold should demolish certain fortresses, Petrovaradin, Osijek and possibly others. Paget indicated to London and Vienna that he had refused to take seriously the Ottoman bid to have Transylvania released from Habsburg control. He did suggest to the Turks that, once the principle was accepted, an agreement to fix the boundary between the two empires and to deal with the problem of isolated strongholds, indeed to consolidate a frontier zone, could safely be left until later. It was understood by this that in due course plenipotentiaries could confer together to work out the details of a pacification.

This Ottoman acceptance of *uti possidetis*, and their counter-claims, were duly set out in copies of various documents which Paget forwarded with his own letters. What he himself wrote was of particular importance because the Austrians had to trust his judgment that the Ottoman court would want peace, even if its demand for exceptions to the principle were rejected.[4] But Paget was right. The grand vezir was strong enough to resist his courtier and military opponents, and had a powerful ally in the Khan of the Crimean Tartars, who was fearful of Russian progress towards the Black Sea after the fall of Azov in 1696. In that area, certainly, the Turks could use *uti possidetis* to ward off further claims by the Russians, or by the Poles who had fought so long and won so little ground in Podolia and Moldavia. They also perceived that a negotiation for the exchange of territory or forts, or for the demolition of forts on one side of a frontier in exchange for similar concessions on the other, offered a chance of scoring successes by diplomacy in spite of the withdrawal from Hungary. These would help to mask from the court and popular opinion at Istanbul the major loss. Such considerations were plausible, and Paget never wavered in his opinion that the Ottoman government genuinely desired a treaty. He anticipated greater difficulty in Vienna, fearing 'the scrupulous, irresolute temper of Count Kinsky . . .'.[5] Indeed, when Paget's secretary had completed the long journey via Vienna to London, and then back to Adrianople, this time bearing William's instructions for an Anglo-Dutch mediation, it turned out that the Habsburg government's first response to the proposals – which he also brought with him – by no means satisfied the grand vezir. Sultan Mustafa was restive.[6] The secretary, tireless Mr Schreyer, therefore reappeared in Vienna to seek a fuller commitment. Kinsky and his colleagues, hopeful by then that they could bring into line Leopold's partners, Venice, Poland and Muscovy, were now willing to negotiate.

Marsigli had already given his view of the problem. The first of his surviving memoranda on a settlement for eastern Europe after Senta was written early in 1698.[7] Entitled a 'geographical description of the frontiers of the Holy League' it traverses an area from the Black Sea to Dalmatia, placing heavy emphasis on the precedents: rivers and mountains had always served to limit empires, he says, and the Romans considered the Danube and the Balkan range as their defence against the barbarians. 'As your Majesty knows', that topic would be dealt with in his forthcoming volume on Roman antiquities, and he reminded Leopold of his earlier maps and reports. He concluded that the new frontier of Habsburg Hungary should run from Wallachia[8] along the Danube as far as Belgrade and from there along the waterways of the Sava and Una.[9] He also wanted to keep for Leopold the districts of Lika and Crbava in south Croatia. The difficulty was in the centre. Marsigli first assumed that the Turks would cede the whole territory of Timisoara, but favoured a final military push to recapture Belgrade as well. Then he offered an alternative. Asserting that the Romans built 'artificial' earthworks between the Tisza and Danube, he relied on this example to recommend the construction of a similar boundary-cum-defence across the Syrmian plain to link Habsburg posts on the Sava with the Danube above Belgrade, leaving the city in Turkish hands. He held that the overland boundary could be drawn from a point on the Syrmian side five miles below the meeting of the Tisza with the Danube, and across to Kupinovo on the Sava. Or it could be drawn less favourably between points further up both rivers, giving the Turks easier access to the Tisza from the Danube.[10] One more attempt to take Belgrade before coming to terms was therefore Marsigli's main recommendation; if this was not possible he preferred his first scheme for a boundary across Syrmia to the second. He ended lamely, admitting that another siege of Belgrade meant more fighting, while peace and security would probably be secured by his other proposals. In the best official manner of such state papers the adviser left the august patron and senior ministers to decide for themselves, after he had submitted the material to be used in their discussion. But it was his characteristic touch to add sketch maps, which on this occasion were unmistakably the work of his own servant Muller. The partnership of Marsigli and Muller in drawing the new frontier would be of the greatest interest and importance.[11]

    This survey belonged to a phase when the chances for war or peace still remained evenly balanced. Many Habsburg officials spent the first seven months of 1698 in their normal routine, trying to find men, money and supplies for the next campaign. There were discussions with the German courts in order to bring to Hungary some of the troops released from service in the west by the treaties of Ryswick. In Hungary itself taxation was sharply increased, to the dismay and anger of the Magyar population. Like many commanders before him prince Eugene spoke of a larger army, to be assembled earlier than usual, for yet another attempt on Belgrade: it turned out to be a smaller army, which did not arrive in south Hungary before mid-August. On the Turkish side there is a similar story of fresh taxes and active military preparation, with early successes reported on the Polish front while larger bodies of Ottoman soldiery moved across the Balkans towards Belgrade.[12] From the beginning of August desultory warfare in the Timisoara region coexisted with the activity of peacemaking. By then the

grand vezir, Paget, and the Dutchman Colyer were also on the move to
Belgrade; and Paget's secretary, hurrying ahead, had again reached Vienna
bearing the definite proposal for a conference of plenipotentiaries to be
held at Slankamen, halfway between Habsburg Petrovaradin and Ottoman
Belgrade.[13] The Ottoman delegates to such a conference had already
been nominated, Rami (who was one leader of the peace party) and
Mavrocordato.[14] Meanwhile Kinsky and the Venetian envoy in Vienna,
Ruzzini, reached agreement on their terms for a pacification, which helped
the Austrians to put greater pressure on the Tsar and the Poles. Tsar Peter,
in the course of his great itinerary round Europe, now arrived in Vienna;
but was then compelled to leave for Moscow to deal with his mutinous
guards, after reluctantly giving Kinsky to understand that he would send a
representative if peace talks with the Turks took place.[15] So a conference,
the choice of the Emperor's spokesmen, their instructions and objectives,
as well as the prospects for another campaign in Hungary, all became
important items of discussion in Leopold's court.

Following the arrival of letters from Paget a meeting of ministers took
place on 8 August, to consider the Ottoman terms and to choose plenipotentiaries and other staff to go to Slankamen. It was pointed out that the
delegation would certainly need someone with sufficient knowledge of
the frontier lands to help the negotiators to decide in detail where the
Emperor's interest lay in drawing the new boundary, or settling what places
in Habsburg occupation – with their defences demolished – could safely
be handed back to the Turks. Those present at the meeting concluded
that Marsigli was the most experienced geographer available, and
advised Leopold to appoint him a counsellor to the delegation, but without
any other status.[16] They clearly wanted the benefit of his experience,
while warning the Emperor against the notion of Marsigli as a possible
plenipotentiary. In substance Marsigli's own account agrees with the official record. He says that he was summoned to a series of conferences, at
which the Austrian and Bohemian court chancellors and also count Kaunitz
were among those present; but Starhemberg, as president of the War Council, would always decline to appear if Marsigli was to be one of those
present, and sent a deputy. At these meetings a great deal was done to define
Habsburg terms for a settlement, and his own expertise seemed welcome;
his maps and memoranda were consulted.[17] Yet on the question of choosing
the plenipotentiaries the objection of Starhemberg and his allies was so
intense that Kinsky and Leopold had to abandon the suggestion of appointing Marsigli. Finally they agreed to recommend count Öttingen and
general Schlick, with Marsigli as their technical assistant and councillor. On
this question he surely deluded himself, misunderstanding Leopold deeply
if he thought that the ruler's singular benevolence to him on many occasions
could now stretch to an insistence that he should be appointed to a post of
this character. The Sultan had already nominated two spokesmen. The
Emperor must therefore also find two, at least one of them being a great

nobleman and officeholder with the elevated standing to speak for the Emperor to the Sultan's representatives. Such a person was Öttingen, although it could be objected that he had no previous experience of Balkan affairs. It was all the more important to find him a suitable partner. Schlick, a relative of Kinsky's, sensible, articulate and well-informed after several years in Hungary, met this requirement. At the same time Marsigli's warmest friends were aware of his reputation, not for expertise on the territorial problems of the frontier, but as quarrelsome and tactless, someone dangerously capable of upsetting his colleagues and the Turks, who might indeed refer back to the murky events of 1691. He should not have been surprised, in some measure he was gratified, by official memoranda of 3 and 5 September praising his reputation as a geographer, and defining his duties at the conference to he held at Slankamen.[18] He was promised suitable pay and allowances. By a happy coincidence, a fortnight earlier the Viennese censor had approved the printing of his work on the Danube, the *Prodromus*.

Both friends and critics appreciated the importance of the geographical data to which Marsigli had so persistently tried to draw their attention. The Venetian ambassador Ruzzini describes a conversation with Starhemberg early in August, when Starhemberg referred to a collection of 'topographical maps' (Ruzzini's own phrase) which he had recently commissioned from a number of engineers; these were to show the existing limits of Habsburg authority along the rivers Una, Sava, Danube, Tisza and Maros.[19] The minister asserted that there was no difficulty about Transylvania where 'nature and a chain of mountains' formed the frontier, but it would prove harder to settle with the Turks elsewhere. He hoped that the maps would help to clarify uncertainties and bring the two powers closer to agreement. Later Ruzzini spoke to Kinsky on the same topic; Kinsky seemed to think that the river system made demarcation a simple matter almost everywhere. To explain particular problems he then showed Ruzzini three maps. The first was of Timisoara, with the Maros and the Tisza, the second of Petrovaradin and the Sava, and the third displayed the course of the Una. On the basis of the last of these Kinsky argued that there ought to be certain exchanges of territory in Croatia, while he seemed satisfied with a proposal simply to demolish the military works of Petrovaradin and Timisoara. For his part Ruzzini noted with interest that Kinsky's maps were not the work of Starhemberg's engineers, but of Marsigli, who hoped – 'with count Kinsky's favour' – to be present at the congress of the powers. When this appointment was confirmed, Marsigli politely assured Ruzzini of his own goodwill towards the republic of Venice, reflecting on his gratitude for help given fifteen years earlier in rescuing him from slavery in Bosnia.

More than maps, memoranda abounded. Advice had been asked for and received from such men as prince Eugene, Caprara, Starhemberg, and even Lewis of Baden in the distant Rhineland.[20] They gave their opinion on the best terms for peace within the general framework of *uti possidetis*, while a majority came out against the idea of offering to destroy the fortifications of Petrovaradin in exchange for Timisoara. Eugene hoped to win this place, or at least a part of its surrounding territory, by force of arms before any treaty was signed. One further submission laid the emphasis differently.[21] While Eugene signed his paper on 27 August, en route from Petrovaradin for a crossing of the Tisza with his army, on the 29th in Vienna Marsigli's latest piece declared roundly that, if it was intended to convert the balance of power achieved by arms into a lasting settlement, this justified swift and practical measures. His proposal was to make the new Habsburg frontier impregnable before the peace conference got under way, by building a number of new citadels. The first should be located in the north-east Carpathians, to guard against Tartar raids into Transylvania; another at Brașov in the south-east; and a third in the south-west corner of Transylvania, in order to keep watch on the approaches from Timisoara. It was from here that the Turks, like the Romans before them, had launched so many attacks on the Transylvanian population. His fourth citadel, which he proposed to locate at Szamos (Gherla) in the north-west, showed that defence against foreign raiders or invaders was not the only military commitment. Kinsky would well understand that these four fortified places, with their garrisons of German soldiers, were intended to keep 'that turbulent people' – the Transylvanians – 'in proper subjection'. Marsigli also asked for stronger defences at Szeged. He had evidently come to accept the existing position in this region *vis-à-vis* the Turks, and does not refer to Timisoara or Belgrade. His survey then moved westwards, recommending a number of points on the Danube and Sava as 'first-class' or 'second-class' strongholds. He emphasised the need for usable routes, with usable bridges. Finally, he worried over the problem posed by islands in river channels. Who could claim possession of these, when rivers were adjudged the boundary between two empires?

Marsigli's concern for security in Transylvania did not merely express the long-standing Habsburg desire to eradicate Ottoman claims and Thököli's influence in that part. In June and July the government had been disturbed by serious popular uprisings around Tokay and Sarospatak in Upper Hungary, where troops restored order with some difficulty. Then, in the third week of August regiments stationed in Transylvania took part in a plot to upset the regime and bring in Thököli again.[22] The hardships suffered by soldiers and civilians alike as they competed for the barest necessities, food and fuel and a minimum of coin, were certainly terrible in the whole region. But Marsigli remained a conventional disciple in the school of Italian generals like Montecuccoli and Carafa, holding that repression was nine-tenths of government in all parts of the kingdom of Hungary. Fortunately the Tokay rising had done little more than delay the army's full mobilisation for the Turkish campaign which never took place; nor was the Transylvanian plot exploited by a Turkish grand vezir anxious for peace.

The great Magyar revolution, luckily for Leopold, would be delayed until after the treaty of Carlowitz was completed.

The briefings came to an end as time pressed. At Ebersdorf outside Vienna instructions for the envoys were ready by 28 September.[23] Kinsky and others had given up their more optimistic plans, and what remained was the firm Habsburg demand for sovereignty in Transylvania right up to the mountain frontier with the Danubian principalities, Habsburg control over both banks of the Maros and the lower Tisza (viz. a footing in the territory of Timisoara), the retention of Petrovaradin as a fortress, a barrier of some kind across the tip of Syrmia, and the river boundaries of the Sava and Una. Starting from the basis of *uti possidetis*, already agreed, the negotiation was to begin by seeking an accord on territory where one power or the other was indisputably in possession, before considering areas where possession was partial or disputed.[24] It was for the Turks, if they wished, to propose any supplementary bargains for the exchange or demolition of forts. These instructions were influenced by the generals' memoranda and Marsigli's maps and suggestions. They were finally settled by the judgment of Leopold, Kinsky and other ministers on what was feasible, given their view of the state of Europe at that moment. The crisis of the Spanish Succession could not be delayed much longer, as they and all observers were aware.

II

Not a plenipotentiary preparing to set out from Vienna in the grand style, Marsigli all the same began to enjoy himself. He was the indispensable expert and greater men came to him. 'This evening', he wrote to Kinsky on 25 September,

> as I was going to bed the Dutch ambassador paid me a visit, and suggested safeguarding the rendezvous of the conference with a larger tract of neutral ground than had been considered earlier. I looked at my map of Syrmia and proposed a triangular area with one side running up the Danube from Belgrade, another from Belgrade along the Sava as far as its tributary, the Bosut, while the third could easily be drawn from there to Ilok on the Danube.[25]

Another Dutchman, Jacob Hop, recently arrived in Vienna with William's plea to hurry on the peacemaking, then asked Marsigli about the villages and monasteries within the area; everyone preparing for the conference shared a concern about accommodation and resources on the spot. What Marsigli knew was filtered into the discussion in which ministers, ambassadors and the mediators were all involved. Waiting in Belgrade Paget and Colyer shivered to think of living in tents on the Syrmian plain as the winter came on. This was one reason why the former criticised what he regarded as signs of dawdling in Vienna. Kinsky retorted that the negotiations could, indeed ought to, take place in Vienna or even Debrecen. An enhancement of the Emperor's prestige, certainly, this course would also be more comfortable for the envoys and their staff, making it easier to feed and house them. But the Turks still insisted that the meetings must be held between the frontiers, somewhere – as they conceived the matter before a treaty was signed – on open ground between the effective confines of the two powers. To offset this melancholy prospect, the mediators had to hope that a tacit agreement on all major issues would mercifully shorten the congress: therefore, urged Paget, any intricate plans for what he called 'permutation', the exchange and demolition of listed strongholds, should be discarded. *Uti possidetis*, with as few qualifications as possible included in the treaties, would send them all swiftly home again. On balance the calculation was correct, but the principals were not to be spared part of the winter in Syrmia, described by one of them as a 'Nova Zemblya' of ice and snow.[26]

At length they were ready, their journeys began, and the Danube became the highway down which they floated through Hungary.[27] The Habsburg delegation led the way on 6 October, and in rapid sequence Ruzzini and the Venetians, Malachowski and his Poles, the Muscovite Voznicyn, all departed from Vienna. It took them about a week to get to Futog, on the left bank above Petrovaradin, and here their numerous retinues camped for another week. What posterity would like, but lacks, is an account of the journey by a witness more talented than the author of a diary kept by one of Öttingen's servants. But on the day after reaching Futog he refers to Lord Paget's indefatigable secretary, who arrived to give notice that in Belgrade they were ready for the publication of a truce.[28] This was accordingly proclaimed by the Austrians both at Petrovaradin and Futog, and covered the whole region suggested by Marsigli. Prince Eugene received a message to stop his military operations beyond the Tisza. The allied envoys got ready to cross the Danube, the Ottoman spokesmen crossed the Sava, into the neutral zone; but within that wide, almost featureless plain and the adjoining hills they had to decide exactly where and how to organise their meetings. Marsigli, who spent his leisure moments cultivating the Venetian, Polish and Muscovite personnel, or repeating to Vienna his demand for satisfaction in the affairs of his regiment, was soon deeply involved.

Although the Turks had earlier insisted that their ambassadors would confer only at Slankamen, they now contemplated minor changes of plan. Paget and Colyer decided first to go to Krušedol, an old monastery closer to Petrovaradin than to Slankamen, and some miles inland from the Danube; hoping for accommodation there.[29] They reached it on 22 (or 23) October, and the Ottoman envoys followed them as far as the tiny settlement of Maradik,[30] only a short distance from the monastery. Meanwhile Öttingen,

Schlick and Marsigli together with the Poles, Muscovites and Venetians were still at Futog. Schreyer arrived once more to report the mediators' journey across Syrmia, while at the same time two Habsburg engineers had been sent off to survey the river bank below Petrovaradin. They found, just past the ruined settlement of Karlovci/Carlowitz, what appeared a suitable piece of ground and prepared to put up a timber building for the plenipotentiaries' formal meetings. Nearby they pegged out more ground for the Habsburg delegation, and assumed that the allies would camp in the immediate neighbourhood of the Austrians. An order was sent up the river for a speedy despatch of the timber needed for building.

On 22, 23, 24 and 25 October, by boat and overland the embassy staffs were making their way from Futog to Carlowitz. Ruzzini describes, almost with pride, how he and his *genti, carozze, cavalli e bagagli* crossed the bridge at Petrovaradin, to the salute of gunfire from the Habsburg fortifications above them and from shipping on the river.[31] He was less satisfied by the camp beyond Carlowitz, where the Polish ambassador Malachowski and his officials immediately convinced themselves that the Muscovites were making offensive claims to priority, taking over ground they themselves wanted. The quarrel rapidly looked like becoming a battle. It threatened to disrupt the whole delicate process of coming to terms with the Sultan.[32] The Austrians, after discussion with Ruzzini, suggested that it would be best to make a fresh start somewhere else, and at that moment they received a note from Paget and Colyer stating that they too would have to move: there was not enough water at Krušedol. The Ottoman envoys, with a following of perhaps a thousand men, were reported to be in difficulties for the same reason. Accordingly, the congress of the powers at Carlowitz began with their representatives in erratic movement from one place to another, around the central point on which it was hoped to put up a wooden assembly hall as soon as rafts carrying timber arrived down the Danube.

Marsigli, as might be expected, was in his element. He wrote later that he had always recommended Carlowitz to the ministers in preference to Krušedol, and he came to the fore when it was decided to move the entire encampment of the Christian powers to a site nearer Petrovaradin. On this occasion, to avoid more hard feelings, it seemed essential that all the envoys should agree beforehand where to set up their quarters. The plan was to sidestep the problem of precedence by arranging the four allies on the sides of a square, and it was Marsigli who was told to seek consent from each of them first, and then to make detailed arrangements.[33] He did the job well, even if Malachowski still demurred. After a few days everyone settled down in the new quarters. Rami, Mavrocordato and the Ottoman party took the space left empty by the Christians, and Paget and Colyer rode down from Krušedol. The Dutch quarters were placed close to the river, Paget remained a little inland. In between them was the spot chosen earlier for the conference itself. On 30 October, 200 soldiers were engaged in levelling the ground in order to build, but they still lacked timber. Their progress was slow. During the next fortnight the diplomats were rather more successful, and began moving to an agreement on questions of protocol, while the Ottoman representatives convinced the mediators that it would be possible to commence the major, political negotiation in the tents which they could provide for the purpose. It was necessary, they said, to conclude the treaty before colder weather set in and was not necessary to wait for an elaborately finished building. On 11 November a certain amount of snow and an icy wind proved their point. Paget and Colyer fully agreed, and on 13 November the Ottoman and Habsburg ambassadors met for the first time in full conference, in the presence of the mediators. This took place inside an ample tent while work on an adjoining timber assembly room continued.[34] Later sessions, bringing in the ambassadors from Venice, Poland and the Tsar of Muscovy, would be held in the new building.

During the next few days they all settled down, and happily no incident between the attendant Habsburg and Ottoman guards was serious enough to disturb them. The rules for procedure during the conference were finally agreed[35] and informal approaches, which have left few traces, were made at various levels of seniority. Ruzzini once again appeared before Marsigli to ask for his goodwill in the Venetian interest, and this time Marsigli insisted politely on his overriding commitment to the Emperor.[36] He also assured Kinsky that he would make it his business to forward supplementary and confidential items of news, while the ambassadors' staff were sending him the ordinary report of conference proceedings. He took note of Paget's secretary's opinion on the political situation in the Ottoman court, and of Mavrocordato's alertness to news about the king of Spain's failing health. In fact he was working with his usual intensity. He had not only to gather material and sift arguments in support of the Habsburg case. He also discussed the wishes of Leopold's allies, studying the three problem regions of the Crimea, Moldavia and Dalmatia where the Christian powers each produced claims on territory still in Ottoman hands.[37] In the case of Dalmatia, Ruzzini expected support from Vienna. Within what limits should he get it? A memorandum from Marsigli skirted this issue and was more concerned to locate the point in Croatia – as he had already tried to do in 1690 – where the extension inland of a new boundary between Venetian and Austrian territory should meet the equally new boundary to be drawn between the Venetian and Ottoman empires. He also rehearsed his earlier ideas about the 'artifical' line to be drawn through Syrmia, and discussed navigation rights on the major rivers where these became the new 'natural' boundaries; and argued again that nothing mattered more than the fastest possible improvement in the military defences of sites and regions in Habsburg occupation. This would safeguard the principle of *uti possidetis* to be invoked for the treaty.

The Habsburg propositions were handed to Paget and Colyer on 2 November, for transmission to the Turks.[38] In general they follow the instructions drafted earlier in Vienna, as they were bound to do, and there is little evidence of Marsigli's influence on his colleagues at this stage. One of the propositions was that Emperor and Sultan should share suzerainty over the principality of Wallachia, although ten years of warfare had failed to enforce the once buoyant Habsburg claim to authority across the Carpathians. This was put forward as a pawn for tactical use when the Sultan's servants put forward his inevitable claim to suzerainty in Transylvania. A bargain would be easier to strike, Leopold giving up Wallachia while keeping Transylvania. This was in fact agreed early and easily in the conference, Paget having already settled it in substance earlier in the year, but Marsigli wrote excitedly to Kinsky about the Ottoman envoy Mavrocordato's personal motives.[39] In 1697 his son had married the Prince of Wallachia's daughter, but died shortly afterwards; Marsigli believed that Ottoman policy at the conference would be determined by Mavrocordato's wish to secure the principality for himself, a speculation in which he was quite mistaken. The Habsburg proposals also referred to the question of boundaries in that region. They wanted to keep the old mountain frontier running along the crest of the Carpathians from Moldavia as far as the Danube at Orsova, from there continuing the boundary along the river as far upstream as an old fortified point near present-day Bazias.* After that their projected line was drawn north-east and then west again to the Tisza: it gave Leopold a large slice of the territory of Timisoara, paring down the existing Ottoman salient north of the Danube to a minimum. Thereafter, from the mouth of the Tisza the boundary was taken over the Danube, across Syrmia and along the Sava and Una as far as territory held by the Venetians.

Paget's original plan, accepted in principle by the leading statesmen in Adrianople and Vienna, had been that the basis of a pacification must be agreed first of all, while consequent decisions could be taken by a meeting of plenipotentiaries under the guidance of the mediators. After months of discussion and correspondence, while the normal preparations for a campaign continued – a campaign which each government hoped could conceivably tilt the balance of power in its favour if the talks broke down – such a meeting opened at Carlowitz in November 1698. There, at once, the envoys took the premise of Paget's plan a stage further. They too had important problems to solve in formulating the peace treaties; but, with the winter coming on fast, they believed that subordinate commissioners should be left to settle matters of detail. An unnamed correspondent, writing to Schlick on 9 November, was already proposing Marsigli as a suitable executive commissioner for appointment after the Austro-Turkish treaty was complete.[40] A few days later, in full conference, the spokesmen on both sides began by emphasising their solemn duty to establish a firm frontier

---

*   The present frontier between Romania and Yugoslavia (1993) meets the left bank of the Danube near this point.

between the neighbouring empires on the basis of *uti possidetis*, even if it meant the sacrifice by each party of outlying strongholds and enclaves in order to secure a viable boundary. For this purpose, they went on to suggest, after the treaty had traced out the general direction of the new frontier, commissioners should deal with problems of detail by a careful inspection of the actual terrain. On this topic one can almost hear the drone of Mavrocordato's speechmaking in the record kept by the Habsburg secretariat:[41]

> It is worth notice (he said) that in the past treaties have always laid down the formula for determining the frontiers – *un certo metodo circa i limiti* – but details were always left to commissaries named by the two parties. It would be impossible to look at these details of the settlement in a congress where the plenipotentiaries either have no knowledge of the country or, if they do, might well prejudice the negotiation of the whole treaty by their excessively lengthy debate. The best and indeed obvious solution is to refer the details of the proposed 'artificial' boundaries to mature, expert and sensible men who – proceeding quite differently from people here at the conference – can erect landmarks on the spot, and make the boundary clear and unmistakable. This is the old expedient of our predecessors, and we should pay attention to the precedent.

Schlick agreed with Mavrocordato, adding that the brief for the commissioners must be drawn with the greatest possible care; otherwise, past experience showed, their work ran the risk of causing further disruption in the border countries. With these expressions of official wisdom Marsigli's next major role was anticipated, but first the congress had to run its course.

After five days spent on the treaty between Emperor and Sultan, the mediators invited the envoys from Venice and Muscovy to begin their own negotiations with the Sultan's spokesmen. It quickly became clear that they wanted the cession of ground which was still in Ottoman hands. For them, the idea of *uti possidetis* was a nuisance, for the Turks it was a splendid diplomatic weapon of defence. So, without any progress on either flank of the main massif the conference turned back to examine the frontier to be traced in Slavonia.[42] This helped to fix the pattern of debate during the next few weeks. It oscillated between a concern for the stiff, intractable issues dividing the peacemakers over the Morea, Dalmatia, Moldavia and the Crimea, and steady progress in drafting the clauses of an agreement covering the main Danubian basin. When the Austrians considered that they had wrung as much from Rami and Mavrocordato as possible, even though it fell some way short of their original instructions and propositions, they sent their counsellor Marsigli to Vienna to report.

The description he gives of his interviews with Leopold (who was ill in bed) and with Kinsky may be true, but cannot be checked.[43] There is a great deal of testimony that Kinsky was a spiky, difficult man and Marsigli's account of his smouldering, petulant way of speech on this occasion sounds plausible. His own power of persuasion, by argument with ruler and minister, he no doubt overstates. The Emperor liked the peace terms well enough and wanted the treaty to go forward; he would willingly put pressure on his allies to agree. Kinsky was less happy, blamed Öttingen and Schlick, but then fell in with the Emperor's wishes. He accepted Marsigli's detailed exposition of the clauses of the treaty, and in turn agreed to try coaxing the Venetian authorities into limiting their claims in Greece and Dalmatia. It followed that the instructions which Marsigli took back with him to Carlowitz, at the very end of the year 1698, were profoundly significant in the history of the house of Austria. Peace with honour along the Danube was in its grasp. Such was his own estimate of the occasion.

In the new year there were hitches at the conference, but no calamity. The Ottoman-Habsburg treaty passed through its final stages after Marsigli's return and was signed on 26 January.[44] The Tsar's representative preferred a truce with the Turks to a treaty, and secured it more easily, saving the conference from further worry over the fundamental but distant clash of interests around the Black Sea which the rise of Muscovite Russia certainly involved. Malachowski had to take his cue with infinite reluctance from the Austrians; it became clear that he would settle with the Turks, recovering the dismantled stronghold of Kamenets in Podolia but very little else. Ruzzini came nearest to unsettling the conference. The Venetian conditions for peace remained stiff to the last. The Turks rejected them. The Austrians had reason to fear, that if Venice insisted on bigger surrenders of territory by the Sultan in the south, the Turks would look for compensation further up the Adriatic, uncomfortably close to Habsburg Croatia.[45] This breeze blew over. The treaty of 26 January between the two major antagonists had been decisive and Leopold's allies were compelled to content themselves with moderate rapture and moderate gains. They could not go on fighting without him. The decision was in effect taken in Vienna that a Habsburg agreement with the Turks should not depend on the result of the negotiations between Leopold's allies and the Turks at Carlowitz. There would be no Habsburg leverage to help Ruzzini or Malachowski.

As for Marsigli, his claim to a new post of honour and responsibility was written into certain parts of the treaty of 26 January.[46] In this, the first five clauses describe the new boundary acceptable to both empires. From the standpoint of Vienna it began by confining Habsburg Transylvania within its 'ancient' mountain frontier, without extending it south to the Danube or west into the foothills and plain of Timisoara.[47] Having circled halfway round Transylvania the frontier was then drawn down the Maros to its junction with the Tisza, and down the Tisza to its junction with the Danube. On the further side of these rivers the Ottoman province of Timisoara survived, a region considerably larger – especially along its eastern edge – than had been allowed for in the 'propositions' submitted

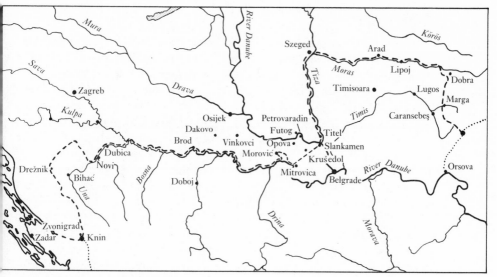

5   The Making of the New Frontier, 1699–1701

originally by Öttingen and Schlick to the mediators. It would involve the
withdrawal of certain Habsburg troops and garrisons. Next, from the
mouth of the Tisza the line was drawn across the Danube and straight over
Syrmia to the marshes adjoining the Sava. On the Ottoman side therefore,
some hours' journey away from the boundary, would be Belgrade; and at a
more or less equal distance the Habsburg fortress of Petrovaradin. Having
reached the Sava the frontier was designed to follow the course of the river
as far as its junction with the Una, and to continue up this tributary through
the Croatian hills. It was all generally consistent with the master principle,
nowhere directly mentioned in the treaty, of *uti possidetis*, but clause V
listed particular sites where this unspoken rule would be modified. Thereafter, the further west and south the draftsmen proceeded the vaguer
became their language, as if the division of that wild and mountainous
country was of slight political importance; they preferred to leave it to the
judgment of subordinate commissioners, whose duties they went on to
describe. For in clauses V, VI and XVIII – while attempting to solve other
difficulties, and ease the transition from war to peace for prisoners, traders,
and clergy – they laid down and described the duties of two commissioners,
Habsburg and Ottoman. Wherever the treaty envisaged an overland or
'artificial' frontier rather than a 'natural' or river boundary, these two were
to trace the actual line across the ground by getting ditches dug or landmarks built, in order to avoid any future disagreement. After due enquiry
on the spot, the commissioners also had the task of determining for each
centre of population near the border the area of land belonging to its
inhabitants before the war began. They were to take this into account before
fixing the actual course of the boundary. Finally, the signatories stipulated
that the commissioners should begin their work as soon as possible, requir-

ing them to be nominated by 22 March 1699, eight weeks later, and enjoin-
ing that everything should be completed in two further months 'or more
quickly if possible'.[48] As it turned out, two months became two years.

Marsigli was soon absorbed by his work on the new frontier. Before the
treaty had been signed he asked Vienna for instructions to be drafted,
feeling secure in the knowledge that Leopold intended to appoint him the
Habsburg commissioner.[49] The ink of the treaty was scarcely dry before he
began discussion with his future colleague, the proposed Ottoman commissioner, to make the arrangements for their joint enterprise to begin
punctually in March.[50] He solemnly informed Kinsky of his conviction that
he would be doing better on the frontier than attending in Vienna the King
of the Romans' wedding celebrations; he was pleased to have been first in
the field on the river Rába in 1683, and to become now 'the last actor in the
peace treaty', placing the Emperor's flag at the limits of his empire.[51]
Rhetoric apart, he was ordered to appear at court to receive his instructions,
and set out in wintry weather by way of Szeged.[52] During the night, sleeping
in his carriage a few miles south of Buda, he was attacked by bandits. They
killed his cook and took the valuables. Marsigli himself had been badly
knocked about and the misadventure delayed his arrival at court. He
recovered, only to suffer a much graver political loss with first the illness,
and then the death of Kinsky on 27 February.

He had come prepared with another 'project'.[53] It gave his view of what
should be the aims and working procedure of the boundary commission,
and was surely intended to influence those who were drafting his instructions. All the documents, the treaty, his own memorandum, and these
instructions dated on 14 March, guided him during a phase of ceaseless
activity. They first defined the task, and then laid down a programme. From
the right bank of the Danube, just below Slankamen (and therefore close to
Carlowitz), the commissioners were to start drawing the new frontier overland or along the rivers as the treaty prescribed, until they reached the point
in furthest Croatia where the Turco-Venetian frontier was deemed to begin. Returning through Ottoman territory to Belgrade they would then start
the second part of their long haul in what the Viennese Latinists termed
'Transdanubia': tracing the western boundary of Ottoman Timisoara up
the river Tisza and its northern edge along the Maros, until they reached
Habsburg Transylvania. They had next to decide where the boundary
between Austrian and Turkish territory left the Maros and ran south again,
the treaty draftsmen having remained cautiously silent on its location.
Marsigli, in his 'project', thereafter visualised a swift journey across
Transylvania to the Moldavian frontier, followed by a survey perambulat-
ing the old Carpathian border between Transylvania and the Danubian
Principalities. For all this he estimated that a labour force of 600 men,
sometimes 900, would be needed to fix and erect the whole frontier, putting
up stone cairns, cutting clearings through woodland, digging ditches and

destroying unwanted military works. But the most interesting requirement of all was laid down in clause 25 of his instructions: a detailed map was to be made of all the routes, ways, rivers, marshes, mountains and forests in order to have complete information regarding them in future.[54] This is indeed the core of Marsigli's own thought, and shortly afterwards he enlarged on it, giving Leopold an account of what he intended to do. He writes that he expected to describe the entire frontier with all possible geographical precision. Where it was a 'natural' boundary and followed the course of a river, for example, he hoped to trace the windings of all the channels, adding observations on the depth of the water and the speed of the flow, together with data on flood levels, bridges and the boats in use. Where it was 'artificial' the boundary would be made 'four hours wide', with two hours in Ottoman and two hours in Habsburg territory, and a line of cairns or other landmarks running through the middle. He would study marsh and forest. He would investigate the language, costume, character, religion and livelihoods of the population. The forts dismantled, and alternative sites for defence purposes, would be listed and described. The whole complex of this information, incorporated in maps and reports, was intended to give a clear account of the needs of the new frontier and of its personnel. It would be Marsigli's tribute, in carrying out his instructions, to the glory of His Imperial Majesty. The usual note of hyperbole ended the discourse; but for his readers – the ruler, ministers and secretariat of a European empire at the close of the seventeenth century – he had not been deploying such familiar wisdom that they took it for granted. Marsigli wanted to convince them that they needed this type of information to ensure the defences of the new frontier, and the prosperity of the new conquests.

There was a secret here, a secret not difficult to guess. In 1696 it had been Muller who gave Marsigli a much improved framework for his earlier studies of the Danubian waterway through eastern Europe. In 1697 and 1698 it was Muller who helped in preparing the big book on the Danube for publication. In 1699 Muller remained in his service, the perfect technical assistant for a boundary commissioner. An important element in Marsigli's plans at the time of the Carlowitz treaty depended on their continuing partnership, and the magnitude of Muller's share in the undertaking becomes clear as we follow the commission on its journey.

On 14 April Marsigli was back in Syrmia again, completing his first report.[55] He wrote from the monastic buildings of Hopovo in the hills of the Fruška Gora, a few miles distant from Carlowitz and Petrovaradin. He was late, but lucky to be there at all. Everyone, above all the diplomats departing from Carlowitz, emphasised the persistent wintry conditions, the thick ice and snow everywhere. There was too little forage available at any price; the local boatmen refused to come forward for service on the river. Furthermore, Marsigli's critics had been trying hard to block or cancel his

appointment as commissioner following Kinsky's death. Their recommendation was that the making of the frontier should be left to the senior
Habsburg and Ottoman officers who were responsible for the frontier areas,
men like general Rabutin in Transylvania, and the Turkish commanders in
Belgrade and Bosnia. They indicated that this was the Ottoman proposal,
and that Marsigli was not of sufficient rank to represent the Emperor in the
company of these highly placed servants of the Sultan. General Nehem, the
old enemy still at Petrovaradin, informed Paget that he had received no
orders to meet the Ottoman commissioner 'and hopes that he should have
none, because Count Marsigli was named Commissioner for the purpose,
with whom he desired not to be engaged in anything'.[56] Nehem was at one
moment expecting Schlick to be appointed instead of Marsigli;[57] while
Marsigli, having arrived at Hopovo, sharply informed the court that
Nehem was unaccountably or inexcusably slow in sending him the promised escort of dragoons and cuirassiers. When it became clear that the
Turkish authorities at Belgrade accepted his credentials, he was able to
denounce as a fabrication a report that the Ottoman commander there
wanted to intervene in settling the boundary.[58] For the moment the critics
were silenced. The commissioner's great enterprise could begin with a full
secretariat and escort in attendance.

An enthusiast can read for himself Marsigli's account of the following
two years. It forms a part of the extraordinary archive brought together as
he and Muller moved across the landscape month by month. They kept all
the papers they received, and copies of everything they sent out. From the
court came, as a matter of course, letters or instructions. In response
Marsigli put together enormous despatches. There were 34 of these, the
copies he retained running to 1600 pages between April 1699 and March
1701; his secretaries also prepared German translations from the Italian
texts.[59] To the commissioner's own letter addressed to the Emperor were
normally added memoranda on particular problems, illustrative maps or
views, and copies of correspondence with Habsburg and Ottoman officials
on both sides of the border. The original Turkish documents, as well as
their translations into Latin or Italian, were kept by Marsigli. Further
material, as might be expected, stemmed from the conferences held with
the Ottoman commissioner Ibrahim, who seems to have been a sweet-
natured and courteous man except under strain. Marsigli was far the more
assertive of the two. Often there were no difficulties, and the Habsburg
commissioner duly reported to Leopold the agreements reached at
successive stages of the journey. At other times compromises were worked
out. Occasionally no agreement was possible on the basis of their instructions, and the negotiators had to refer back to the ruler's advisers at the two
courts. Moreover the provincial authorities, like the Pasha of Bosnia and the
War Council in Styria, were involved; letters therefore came in from Sarajevo or Banja Luka or Graz, to be translated when necessary, copied and
answered. At rarer intervals Marsigli himself branched out by submitting

to Vienna elaborate papers on special aspects of the frontier world: Balkan commerce and the future of Croatia became the themes for a pair of sonorous essays. And while he dictated or wrote, Muller drew. His was the pictorial and cartographic record of their journey, kept as an *aide-mémoire* for mapping the new boundary. It began as a sequence of pen (sometimes pencil) drawings in which he showed, often from day to day, the itinerary followed. To these he often added detailed studies of the frontier line and its landmarks, at the time in contention between Marsigli and Ibrahim. Here also were his earliest efforts at maps or panoramas of larger areas on a smaller scale. In due course he had more than 400 such pages, grouped into what he called 'diaries'. 'Diarium I' begins on 1 May 1699 on setting out from Slankamen. 'Diarium XLVII' shows the western limit of the frontier reached on 12 August. 'Diarium XC' contains a diversion to Zagreb on 1 February 1700. Finally he compiled an index and wrote out a title page. The assembled 'Notitiae Geographicae Originales' became a precious manuscript volume;[60] they had been his detailed impressions of a world new to him.

More highly finished work followed. For example he began a series of larger drawings, after careful inspection, of the forts and fortified places on or close to the new frontier. Marsigli included copies of these in his reports to clarify his discussion of military matters, or to show in detail how he was carrying out the demolition of the defence works of sites to be handed back to the Turks, in accordance with the treaty. Here again Muller arranged the originals (or other copies) in a single volume at a later stage, adding a long Latin title to describe its contents.[61] But more important were his admirably drawn maps. Marsigli asked for these from time to time, clearly encouraging him first of all to view as much of the country as possible. Muller obeyed, and returning from his excursions and studying his notes, his sketches, his estimates of distance or time of travel between one point and another, with an occasional reading of latitude and the testimony of colleagues, he would set to work. Each of his maps became a basis for the next, and copies were kept.[62] They too were submitted to Vienna in order to explain problems and proposals for the benefit of statesmen remote from the scene. They must have helped Marsigli in argument with Ibrahim, and were attached to his copy of the written agreements which finally fixed each part of the boundary, as stage by stage the commissioners moved forward. Then, while the long traverse continued towards the Adriatic and back again to the Carpathians, Muller went a stage further. He began to see how his regional maps could be aligned and scaled down to produce a general map of the entire frontier, as asked for in Leopold's instructions of March 1699. He and Marsigli even visualised maps displaying the frontier, in which a number of symbols were designed to refer to an additional sequence of illustrations: these would be taken from Muller's assembly of drawings to show the appearance of individual landmarks as the frontier crossed the hills and forests in Croatia or Transylvania. The two men, patron and artist, certainly contemplated a meticulous guide to the new boundary of the Habsburg empire.

III

On the day he finished his report from Hopovo Marsigli and his staff moved on to Slankamen by the river. They were followed by their Ottoman colleagues coming from Belgrade. The commissioners met and formally agreed the 'preliminary articles' which would guide their future proceedings together.[63] For example, they arranged for the translation of Turkish documents into Latin and Latin documents into Turkish. They conceded that their teams of labourers, Ottoman and Habsburg, should set up the boundary marks of the new frontier alternately across the country, every 300 paces. Looking ahead, they agreed in requiring the help of a Venetian commissioner at the Dalmatian end of their survey, and of representatives from Moldavia and Wallachia on the Carpathian border of Transylvania. With this preamble behind them Marsigli and Ibrahim plunged into argument. They found themselves differing over the starting point of the boundary through Cis-Danubia.

What did the treaty of Carlowitz say about this? It said, after drawing the boundary of Trans-Danubia down the Tisza to its mouth, that the line should be extended over the Danube at that point, and then again extended across the Syrmian plain to the Sava. This acknowledged the result of the years of warfare, that the practical limit of Ottoman dominion along the Danube was Belgrade, of the Habsburg dominion Petrovaradin, and that the frontier should run between them. To this extent the powers were agreed, but Marsigli spoke for a sovereign whose interests required the line to be drawn *straight* across the Danube from its left bank to the appropriate point on its right bank below Slankamen. The Turks, or some Turks, argued that the treaty entitled them to have the line drawn *obliquely*, so that at least part of the walled enclosure round Slankamen would be in Ottoman hands.[64] On this difference, according to Marsigli, depended the future control of shipping entering or leaving the Tisza, with military and fiscal consequences. Fortunately, aware of the Turkish reading of the treaty, he had already prepared himself to argue the case. He got Muller to help him with sketches which showed the significance of the alternative lines drawn across the water.[65] The quarrel of the commissioners did not last long. Joining with Ibrahim on a trip by boat to survey the mouth of the Tisza, and sharing a friendly cup of coffee, he had his way and the first stone cairn indicating the new frontier was assigned its position on the right bank of the Danube, a short distance below the outer wall of Slankamen. The Ottoman squad of labourers built and then named it 'Joseph', a compliment to the King of the Romans who was king of Hungary. Having made this decision he commissioners immediately began their journey across the plain, and in a few days fixed the sites for 213 cairns to reach the neighbourhood of the river Sava. Muller took the opportunity to locate the cairns, villages, and watercourses of the area in his sketches, and drew experimental maps showing the whole country of Syrmia. He saw for himself the Roman remains at Mitrovica nearby. Ibrahim, nervous of criticism in Belgrade that he was being outmanoeuvred, happily joined with Marsigli in relying on readings from the latter's 'astrolabe', to determine how the line of cairns should be carried across Syrmia in accordance with the treaty.[66]

They were required to draw this line through the country 'to the nearer bank of the river Bosut at Morović', and from Morović down the Bosut to the Sava. But Ibrahim had already agreed to the extension of Marsigli's theoretical line across the Danube 'straight' (i.e. without deflection) over-land and this led, not to Morović, but shaving past Mitrovica and its ruins, directly to the Sava.[67] Mitrovica was considerably closer to Belgrade than Morović: the Sultan stood to lose territory, the Emperor to gain it. Once more Ibrahim faced awkward criticism, and on this occasion Marsigli reported to Leopold that he was making a small concession outside Mitrovica, which was indisputably on Ottoman ground. He proposed to bend the line a little and give the place a wider margin, before continuing it to the shore of the Sava.[68] This still left the Habsburgs a short but useful stretch of firm ground along the river bank. After that a wilderness of marsh and scrub began, which the commissioners and their scouts had to skirt, taking the frontier line inland in a series of zigzags to the crossing of the tributary Bosut at Morović, an almost derelict spot. Thirty more cairns were sited and built. Marsigli and Ibrahim moved forward in relatively harmonious negotiation. Ibrahim had fought off the hawks on his own side, although complaining to his colleague that the Emperor had taken the more fertile regions in Syrmia, leaving the Turks with mostly desert and swamp. This Marsigli contentedly reported to Leopold, enclosing a formal document of 12 May signifying the commissioners' agreement.[69]

So far, in the language of the diplomats the frontier was 'artifical', indicated by the new landmarks. Marsigli and Ibrahim came next to a 'natural' boundary, along the right bank of the Bosut for a short distance to the Sava, and then up the great river for 180 miles to the confluence with the Una in Croatia. They could hope for swifter progress with less debate, and their main problem over this stretch was of a different kind. As a young man Marsigli had merely crossed the Sava, at Mitrovica in 1680, and at Brod in 1683 on his way to captivity in Bosnia. He had now to try moving upstream in this region, where the river was on the scale of another Danube or Tisza, with floods each year inundating huge bands of territory along the shore.[70] Islands and sandbanks grew and vanished in the main channel which in turn, over longer periods, shifted about across the terrain. Here was indeed a natural frontier, which would be retained by the European political system for the greater part of two centuries.

From Morović Ibrahim took his way into Bosnia, and then made for Brod where another rendezvous had been agreed. Marsigli searched for carts and boats to get through Slavonia on the northern side of the Sava. Muller meanwhile explored the course of the Bosut and the many windings of the Sava upstream.[71] When Marsigli met Ibrahim again at Brod, they found a settlement on each side of the Sava, with an island in between, and according to the treaty Marsigli was to arrange for a Habsburg withdrawal from Bosnian Brod after rasing its defence works. The Turks were authorised, again according to the treaty, to revive the Brod staple or market for trade. Marsigli agreed to remove the garrison, but only when the entire frontier settlement was complete. He also claimed that Leopold was entitled to retain his men and his redoubts on the island, arguing privately to Vienna that this would be a way 'of dominating the new emporium and guarding the river Sava'.[72] Ibrahim, predictably, could not agree. The commissioners decided that they would have to refer the problem to higher authority and meanwhile try to hurry on. They went together through sodden country north of the Sava because flooding cut off Ibrahim's intended route across Bosnia. Their next conference was planned for Jasenovac where the Una joins the larger river; but before it took place Marsigli himself crossed the Sava because of inundations on the Slavonian side. From Bosnia they entered Croatia. At Dubica, a little way up the Una, they began their next round of discussion; Marsigli introduced to Ibrahim the colleagues who had arrived to join in the settlement for Croatia, the Croatian Vice-Ban or Lieutenant, and counts Herberstein and Rabatta from the Inner Austrian government at Graz. There was soon sharp debate over Jasenovac. It was another stronghold on the Bosnian side due for handing back to the Turks with its defences rased but Marsigli felt reluctant to accept this. He feared that Habsburg river traffic was at risk if an Ottoman battery were placed there, then or later, in disregard of the treaty. He also chose to argue that his opponent had no claim on a small island facing the settlement, which would offer the Turks an even better chance of controlling the waterway. Ibrahim replied that it was not an island, but a spit of land adjoining Jasenovac for the greater part of the year.[73] Marsigli sent an engineer to measure the depth of the water around the island, but the dispute had merely begun when he moved away to a new encampment at Novi, up the Una. Arrived there and writing hard, he finished a massive report on 11 June. He had much to say to Leopold from this distant spot in Croatia.

IV

First of all he forwarded a provisional agreement for the frontier along the Sava, adding several commentaries, copies of documents, and maps.[74] One of the maps shows the entire boundary from Slankamen as far as the Una at

Jasenovac. Measuring 92" by 19", signed by Marsigli, it was Muller's first big effort at bringing together his perceptions of the Sava.[75] He had noted most of the many tributary streams flowing from the north, and taken considerable pains with the serpentine course of the channel below Brod. His knowledge of the Bosnian shore and hinterland remained imprecise. Meanwhile Marsigli completed the first of his critical studies of the frontier world, a model which he followed thereafter. It began by describing the boundary line, 'artificial' across Syrmia and 'natural' along the Sava. Then he turned to economic and military problems, with a side glance at conditions in the neighbouring border countries of the Ottoman empire. As he wrote, he tried to identify topics which he considered should preoccupy the Emperor's government, and gave relevant advice. In the case of Syrmia he asserted that there was at least no shortage of people: they had recently been moving into the region from other parts of Hungary in order to plant vines and raise cattle, while by contrast a population shrinkage was one of the gravest Ottoman weaknesses in Bosnia. Syrmia was also fortunate in its location; Marsigli visualised it as the entrepot for traders arriving from many directions. There would be increased traffic on the highway of the Danube, Italian textiles brought through Slavonia or Bosnia, and Transylvanian salt and honey floated down the Maros and Tisza. Even in Turkish times the town of Osijek had maintained three fairs a year . . . but he promised a more considered survey of all this later, together with a map illustrating for Leopold the concept of a Habsburg trading empire in Danubia.

The report turned next to Syrmia's military problem. A line of cairns across the plain could not be defended; the fortresses of Petrovaradin and Ilok only offered support from a distance. Marsigli accordingly suggested bringing German settlers to Slankamen, so that some of them could be enlisted as frontier guards.[76] This seemed to him the best way of compensating for the treaty's veto on building new fortresses. Such immigrants would form a suitable militia, capable in peacetime of manning the watchtowers he was planning, and easily trained as soldiers in war. In any case, as soon as war was declared again, it would be necessary to build defences at Slankamen in order to protect navigation on the Danube and Tisza. He then drew attention to the short strip of land along the Sava next to Mitrovica, acquired thanks to his bargaining with Ibrahim: the easy crossing over the river at this point would, in time of war, be valuable for getting a force over the Sava to cut Ottoman communications between Belgrade and Bosnia. But he warned that the Turks – again, when war broke out – would have little difficulty in ferrying their own forces up the Bosut to Morović and then moving rapidly across country to Osijek, that sensitive Habsburg point guarding the Drava. On the other hand this route connecting Osijek to Morović appeared to him one of the most promising links in the new commercial network which he wished to see established in Syrmia.

The boundary along the Sava and its Slavonian hinterland interested him less. There was less he could say. A world of flood, forest and marsh faced hillier but otherwise similar country across the river. In Slavonia there were no fortresses, but no need for them. The population, mostly Catholics in the care of Franciscans from Bosnia, by contrast with the predominantly Orthodox elements in Syrmia, was scattered thinly over the country. To keep an eye on them, as on the Turks and their subjects over the Sava, watch-towers positioned along the shore should prove sufficient. Muller's map shows these 'sardakis' above Brod, and Marsigli asks for more of them to be built further downstream. Otherwise, he wanted only a few lightly armed easily trained forces, and enough stores in suitably located magazines. He had little to say about Slavonia's wretched subsistence economy, save the idea that the state's revenue would gain if better communications brought Transylvanian salt to the region: Adriatic sea salt from over the hills returned most of its profits to the foreigner. These were his first thoughts on the topic, he said, intending to return to it later. Perhaps he was running out of time as he wrote, in his camp at Novi. Croatia, the country in front of him, needed attention; and Croatia, as he described it a few weeks later was 'purgatory'.

The cloudy language of clause V of the treaty, referring to the river Una set the commissioners their hardest problem.[77] They could understand and carry out a ruling that the limit of Ottoman sovereignty should be the right bank, so that Marsigli's duty was to arrange for the withdrawal of Habsburg troops from Jasenovac, Dubica and Novi on the Bosnian side. It made corresponding sense that the islands in the river below Novi should fall to the Habsburgs, as the treaty stated. But where exactly *was* Novi, when it transpired that there was 'New' Novi on the left bank as well as 'Old' Novi on the right? What were the limits of the adjoining dependent territory of the place, the 'terra Novense', and to which of the two did it belong? Much turned on answers to such questions because Ottoman power, after fifteen years of war, still stretched across the river further upstream. In this region the peace treaty had therefore accepted *uti possidetis* by ruling that above Novi, on the Croatian side of the Una, the Ottoman and Habsburg forces should each retain the strongholds which they occupied at the time; while the commissioners were in addition to assign to each place the pre-war boundaries of their dependent lands before finally drawing a line between the two empires. Consequently, if 'New' Novi and the 'terra Novense' on the Croatian side were subject to 'Old' Novi, as the Turks claimed, they enlarged the Turkish salient. If they did not, as Marsigli held, it was diminished.

The issue became clearer as he surveyed the landscape. Writing to Leopold on 11 June he refers to a ride of sixteen hours undertaken to see as much as possible. Muller was in attendance, and drew a map of the Una from Jasenovac upstream, showing the stronghold of Dubica, the important crossing of Kostajnica, and Novi; he was able to outline the 'terra Novense' and its boundaries on the Croatian side.[78] As Marsigli told Leopold, the map was a 'geographical demonstration' of the problem confronting him. Old Novi, he asserted, was a ruin. New Novi was a vigorous settlement of about six years' standing, well built and held by a large garrison and population. The question was whether all or any of the extensive Croatian 'terra Novense' should be assigned to the inhabitants of Ottoman Old Novi when the Habsburg authority withdrew its outposts from Bosnia in accordance with the treaty. He does not say so, but another aspect of the same problem was whether the Turks, by enlarging their salient, would succeed in getting any nearer the plains of the Sava and lower Una: the Habsburgs wanted to keep the boundary on the higher, more defensible ground. Marsigli also asserts that the whole neighbourhood contained as many as 40,000 immigrants who had moved out of Bosnia in the recent past.[79] It was manifestly not desirable to hand them back to the rule of the Bosnians and Turks.

The two commissioners quickly recognised that it would be difficult for them to agree about Novi. Marsigli had the support of both the Styrian and Croat representatives. Ibrahim was under pressure from local leaders in their invulnerable fortress at Bihać and from the Ottoman provincial governor at Sarajevo. Therefore they again decided to ask for further instructions, to continue their journey and return later.[80] Marsigli momentarily foresaw fewer difficulties ahead and left part of his baggage behind. Making a fresh start some distance inland from the Una, well clear of the territory in dispute, from a hilltop called Klepala they began staking a boundary across the country by means of cairns, pillars, even individual trees, and by clearings cut through the woods. From one valley to another they crossed the ridges and placed their marks. Three weeks later, they had enclosed much of the big Ottoman salient.[81] The Habsburg commissioner and his staff camped close to the river Korana, which Muller was soon sketching and mapping. But a new contest threatened when Marsigli claimed land on the right bank, although the course of the river bent (as one went upstream) into the Ottoman salient. Ibrahim refused to consider this, and counterclaimed by demanding a stretch of ground further up on the left bank which included an old fort called Drežnik.[82] Marsigli regretted bitterly that the local Habsburg forces had failed to maintain a footing in a number of places (Drežnik was one) in this region which were in their hands earlier. *Uti possidetis* was a very poor argument to apply to a ruinous empty tower and other deserted buildings, while the Sultan's men more effectively invoked the treaty by claiming ancient tenurial rights in the surrounding land. Ibrahim could rely on the inhabitants' testimony, while the Ottoman command in Bihać was determined to give nothing away. Marsigli seems at first to have been influenced by the general idea he had formed ten years earlier of a viable frontier in this region: the Habsburgs would have the valley of the Korana as far as its source, and from there the crest of the mountains southward as far as Venetian Dalmatia. He opposed every Ottoman claim bringing the Turks nearer the coast, which might help them later to interrupt communications between the Habsburg conquests along the Adriatic and the rest of Croatia. This possibility alarmed him, as he wrote to Leopold on 24 June, and he sent count Rabatta to Vienna to ask for guidance. The despatch included a drawing of Muller's, to show what had been achieved since leaving Novi and what the Turks demanded along the Korana.

After scarcely a pause, accompanied by count Herberstein and other officers, Marsigli toured through a large tract of the neighbouring country. It was hard going, no doubt; he was unlike the travellers in a modern charabanc who could pass in comfort by the headwaters of the Korana, the celebrated Plitvička Lakes in their mountain setting. On his return he wrote again to Vienna. Confident that he had identified a safe and practical route joining Zagreb and Karlovac – the old military centre of Habsburg Croatia – with the newly acquired Habsburg territory in the south, he was less disposed to resist a compromise along the Korana.[83] Unfortunately, he added, he dared not wait to bargain at leisure, having found that his whole party was fast running out of supplies in that empty, desolate country, while the Venetians were expecting him on the Dalmatian border. Ibrahim, anxious to hear from his superiors before discussing the Korana with Marsigli at a further conference, was happy to defer; and so the two commissioners moved forward again, leaving one more question to be settled on the way back.

Beyond the Korana remarkably little had altered since Marsigli had been there in 1690. The coast and the adjoining territories of Lika and Crbava were indisputably lost to the Ottoman empire, but it retained the hinterland further back. In between stood the Mala Kapela and Plješevica ranges, massifs continuing south to the Dinaric Alps, with upland plateaux on either side of varying altitude and fertility. Still further inland the upper course of the Una descended northwards in Ottoman country. The ridge of high ground was the 'natural' frontier, although cut by a number of passes where the commissioners would each try to secure for their sovereign extra ground on the further side east or west, as a forward base offering possible military advantages when war broke out in the future. While Marsigli's personnel hurried on to find fresh stores, he relates that he himself took a detour to the east in order to view the approaches to the main ridge from Bosnia.[84] His draughtsman Muller was active, and made drawings on both sides of the range. They then rejoined the main party in Habsburg territory, Marsigli fixing his camp on the slopes of Mt. Popina, a good way to the south, and making arrangements to meet Ibrahim (who had followed a different itinerary) as well as the Venetian and Ottoman commissioners Grimani and Osman, who were charged with determining the frontier of the Venetian and Ottoman empires in Dalmatia.

The Carlowitz treaty between the two powers anticipated a conjunction of this boundary with Habsburg ground in the neighbourhood of Knin, a famous old fortress, once Hungarian, then Ottoman, and now Venetian.

The terrain was forbiddingly complex, with rugged hills and deep clefts. Knin overlooks the river Krka. Not far off to the north was the decayed stronghold of Zvonigrad, in Habsburg hands. The practical limit of Ottoman power ended further inland, eastwards. So, for a short while Marsigli, Grimani, Ibrahim and Osman harangued and bickered. The first asked for possession of a district which would have brought the Austrians closer to Knin – without any justification, as he admitted to Leopold, except to extend Habsburg territory in that direction.[85] The second was reluctant to cede Zvonigrad: it had originally been Venetian, he said, and it protected the route to their summer pastures used by the herdsmen of Venetian subjects lower down the valley. The Ottoman spokesmen felt less concern in deciding exactly where the Austro-Venetian frontier should meet their own boundary with the Christian empires, and Marsigli may have been justified in reporting to Leopold, with jubilation, that the Turks finally helped him to advance his claims further south and nearer Knin than he had expected.[86] After a few more days the tactical bargaining ended and a plan was agreed, on the ground and on paper, for linking the boundaries at one of the summits – *un bellissimo monte* – of a massif called (like many others) Veliko Brdo, about 15 miles south-east of Mt. Popina.[87] On 12 August 1699 all the commissioners climbed up the slopes to this remote hilltop, to lay the foundation stones of a sizeable triangular pyramid, with its surfaces facing towards the territories of the three empires. They orated, embraced and feasted, not very grandly. Marsigli professed himself immensely pleased with what had been achieved on the Emperor's behalf, and delighted to give assistance to Osman and Grimani. During the next few days he accompanied them some distance south, helping to determine the Ottoman-Venetian boundary drawn round Knin, and down to the river Neretva as far as the region of his former captivity. It was his personal contribution to the peace between Turks and Venetians; and on the way he encountered, as we know, his old Bosnian masters.[88]

Then he retraced his steps, returning to Mt. Popina to complete a long report for Vienna, with two of Muller's maps,[89] and instructing engineer Hollstein of the Inner Austrian service to survey all routes north from the new southern border of the empire. He sent his interpreter Michael Talmann to Ali, the governor of Bosnia, in order to persuade that dignitary to be amenable in settling the question of Novi and other disputes outstanding. Indeed he had hopes of rapid progress, which would be disappointed.

The 'triple' frontier was in fact an isolated achievement. It was still necessary to fix the boundary from this point northward, placing landmarks where they were needed to link together the 'natural' line of the mountain ridges. As Marsigli tells the story he tried once again, in doing this, to secure territory on the Bosnian side of the passes while the Turks asked for footholds in Lika. As before, both parties preferred to differ while agreeing to move on without delay.[90] It seems that Ibrahim then proposed a formal

conference, to be held at Drežnik. When they foregathered there on 2
September most attention was given to the problems of Brod and Novi, to
the fate of Drežnik itself and the Korana river. Less was said of the stretch
immediately behind them, leading back to the triple frontier, before they
were deadlocked again and paused for breath.[91] A few days later Marsigli
heard from Vienna that the Ottoman court had told the governor of Bosnia
to intervene directly, and he was himself empowered to go and negotiate
with Pasha Ali at Novi, the focus of the quarrel.[92] This became the most
pressing motive for the next stage of his journey. Colder autumn weather
and dwindling supplies were other reasons. He duly crossed through the
Ottoman salient and arrived back at Novi.

The Pasha came, saw, and did not conquer. At a first formal meeting
Marsigli, who had been promoted to the rank of general – a wonderful
gratification – in order to negotiate with him, received the splendid gift of
a horse with all its Turkish trappings. At the second, these spokesmen
concentrated on the *terra Novense*. At the third, a private evening session
with few other persons present, they turned to the crucial task of balancing
all possible concessions which the two sides might make; but there was no
hint of progress when they stopped. Thereafter the Pasha handed over to
Ibrahim, who on 15 October at last indicated that the Turks were ready to
accept a general settlement of the boundary in Slavonia and Croatia, if
this were agreed without prejudicing their claims at Novi.[93] It was a chink
of light, provided that the Habsburg government toned down the more
extreme demands which Marsigli had been putting forward for Brod,
Jasenovac, and the mountain ridge in the south. The commissioners therefore persuaded themselves to pay a final visit to the area where the difficulties (after Novi) looked greatest, the Korana valley. When they arrived
the local Moslem worthies of the Bihać salient, anxious to uphold their
private claims on as much land as possible, were boisterous and hard to
tame. At a noisy assembly Ibrahim and Marsigli both played their parts with
some skill, and in the end successfully arranged a 'carve-up' of the respec-
tive claims.[94] Marsigli, conscious of winter's approach and anxious to have
something to show, allowed the Turks a fair-sized wedge of territory on the
left bank of the Korana. He contented himself with the watershed along the
line of mountains up to the triple frontier, and came to terms on points in
dispute along the Sava. Writing to Leopold from his hillside camp on 29
October, he felt that the year's work had ended in triumph. The Croatian
purgatory was almost over. He even looked ahead to the affairs of the
frontier in Trans-Danubia, the other half of his mission.

He could not have been more mistaken. Another nine months passed
before he left Croatia. Their instructions did not authorise the two commissioners to complete the agreement of Cis-Danubia by a compromise on
Novi, or to continue to Trans-Danubia while leaving Novi an open question. Marsigli returned from the Korana to his old camp by the Una and in
January 1700, after a last gloomy and useless conference with Ibrahim and

'the leading nobles of Bosnia', he withdrew to Sisak on the Sava. A place of importance since Roman times, here were some of the stores needed by his men. Food was decidedly short. He waited three months without a word from Vienna, and for some time after that.

V

Such a recital of Marsigli's journeys in 1699 to Syrmia, and from there to Croatia and Dalmatia, gives one side of the story. As usual there was another and we must retrace our steps.

He had chosen the most direct route from Vienna to his rendezvous with the Ottoman commissioner. A few miles along the road into Hungary Muller was soon copying inscriptions, sketching old earthworks, or recording the pieces of a fallen Roman column.[95] At Slankamen, and from there forwards, the busy secretary had to attend first of all to his general survey for mapping the new frontier, or to any diagrams Marsigli needed for arguing with the Turks. However he was also sent off to view and record the ancient sites. Half an hour from the Danube, on the Ottoman side of the new landmarks being built along the boundary, there were clear traces of a Roman entrenchment. Muller duly went to sketch them before riding over the plain to view what could still be seen of the Roman city at Mitrovica. An old drawing of Marsigli's was now superseded by his careful study of 'Sirmium', showing pieces of building scattered over a wide area as well as other sites in the neighbourhood.[96] Later they stopped at Vinkovci, once 'Colonia Aurelia Cibalae', where Roman entrenchments adjoined the waters of the river Bosut. Again Muller got to work.[97]

For many weeks they then passed through country where nothing was reported of Roman sites and stones. This changed on reaching Sisak early in the new year. Muller, presumably under the direction of his patron, put in many hours on an illustrated study of the rich Roman remains adjoining the existing settlement.[98] His view to scale of the whole area located the ancient diggings, drains and surviving foundations, which were then drawn in detail. He examined and recorded individual inscriptions and other stone carving of apparently Roman origin; some were inside, some outside the principal site. He and Marsigli also looked for and found traces of Roman work in the existing tracks and routes centred on Sisak, while a correspondent in Rieka was able to send them a report offering other evidence about Roman communications between the Adriatic and Pannonia and Sirmium. All this was welcomed as extra material for the forthcoming volume on Danubian antiquities. Marsigli even considered writing a separate essay on Sisak, to be illustrated with these drawings. His increasing familiarity with the Roman road system would be used to develop and support his views for improving contemporary transport and traffic in his submissions to Vienna.

There is a similar blend of ancient and modern interests in another of Marsigli's leisure interests during the winter. This was the early history of Croatia, an attractive topic partly because the man best qualified to advise him appeared at his elbow. Paul Ritter Vitezović, the literary son of a Habsburg frontier official, had earlier attracted attention in Bratislava and Vienna by his pleasing Latinity, and now came into contact with Marsigli as an agent of the Croatian Estates; he represented their interest in a sometimes embittered dialogue with spokesmen from the Inner Austrian government during the proceedings of the boundary commissioners. On 25 September at Drežnik Marsigli took note of certain views advanced by Ritter Vitezović.[99] These amounted to an idea that the ancient kingdom of Illyria, with lands in Dalmatia, Bosnia, Servia and Croatia, had become in due course the kingdom of Croatia, which therefore embraced them all. Croatia's legitimate boundaries accordingly extended further than was commonly supposed. More soberly, with his new friend's assistance Marsigli began trying to assemble the names of Croatian rivers and mountains. A fortnight later Ritter Vitezović was back in Zagreb, composing a chirpy letter to Marsigli in Latin verse, which described his recent journey home. In February and March of the following year he informed his noble patron how hard he was working on the genealogies of prominent familes in Croat history.[100] In due course these 'Stemmata' were printed, and Marsigli received copies together with additional manuscript material.[101] It is not altogether easy to decide who gained more from this partnership, but the Italian took seriously the idea of unfolding the histories of Croatia, Serbia, Hercegovina and Dalmatia by assembling genealogies of their old princely families, to which he considered adding maps by Muller to show each of these countries in their pre-Ottoman and early Ottoman periods. His attention was also drawn to the itinerant singers, often blind minstrels, who handed down a record of incidents in the eternal warfare of those parts with recitals in 'the ancient Illyrian tongue'. Unfortunately Ritter Vitezović himself enjoyed little effective support from the Croat nobility and higher clergy in his day. Marsigli took up the subject, collected a few papers in his customary manner, but then dropped it again.

There were other diversions. Our alert virtuoso achieved one startling novelty in the wilds of Croatia. At Drežnik he and Muller had set up their instruments in order to observe the solar eclipse of 16 September. Marsigli asserts that the Turks and the inhabitants seemed amazed, not so much by the eclipse, as by what he and Muller were trying to do. Contentedly transmitting news of this to Nuremberg he advised his printer to add a sentence to the forthcoming *Prodromus*.[102] This stated that observations of the eclipse of 1699, taken at Drežnik in Croatia, would appear in the great *Opus*. Also at Sisak the depths of the Sava and the speeds of its current were measured, for comparison with earlier observations of the Danube and Tisza.[103]

Before the commission retreated from the hills, something else had caught his fancy, one of the features of this frontier landscape. Marsigli did not know of the 80,000 species of the fungal kingdom, as a modern authority describes them, but the mushrooms appearing on the afforested hills took his breath away by their profusion and variety.[104] Perhaps he recalled his teacher Malpighi's opinion of them, as an unusually difficult topic in the general study of plants. Startled by what he saw Marsigli rose to the challenge; and mushrooms, with which he associated mosses and mistletoe, became one of his greatest enthusiasms in later life. From the camp by Novi he wrote on 22 November to tell his old tutor Trionfetti that he enjoyed little leisure for 'the innocent study of nature', while settling the boundary between two great empires, but did regret not having a botanist on his staff to make the most of a wonderful opportunity.[105] He had never seen such quantities of mushrooms: He was doing his best, having ordered his men to bring him samples – picked from the ground and from the trees – of whatever they found. There were 110 varieties collected so far, and he was getting drawings done by his military draughtsmen, while adding annotations. He hoped to employ a more qualified artist to use the rough drawings at a later stage. He asks his correspondent for as much scholarly information as possible; books of reference would help him to produce a reliable account of what he had seen.

The project was carried on at intervals during the next two years and then dropped. What survives are a catalogue and the fragment of a preface for 'A new Collection of Mushrooms . . . , the very long title indicating that these were gathered by the author from the meadows, woods and groves of Croatia and Slavonia in 1699 and 1700.[106] Marsigli begins by repeating in grandiloquent terms the details which he had earlier sent to Trionfetti. He describes the tedium of waiting for despatches in the Croatian wilderness, and the employment of his personnel in bringing together the rich harvest of mushrooms. He adds that Trionfetti responded with a full briefing from the best authorities, although what they said did not always agree with his own findings. The fragment ends here, and nearly all the drawings have long since been dispersed, but another paper shows Marsigli and his secretary trying to classify their material. A synoptic table in Muller's hand illustrates the arrangement they had in mind.[107] They distinguished between field and woodland mushrooms, while deliberately omitting 'garden' mushrooms and tubers. They decided on a number of categories: in the case of specimens growing from wood, they identified the trees (oak, beech, hazel and ash) which harboured them. They distinguished between mushrooms of different texture, colour or smell; between what was edible and inedible. In some of the illustrations it is noticeable that the specimen has been painted on one piece of paper, which was then pasted on to another. A German name was given to the item in one handwriting; a Latin equivalent was added by somebody else.[108] Muller inscribed the running titles at the top of these pages, and also an elegant 'Index Muscorum'. Indeed the mosses were at some stage assigned to an artist who illustrated them with

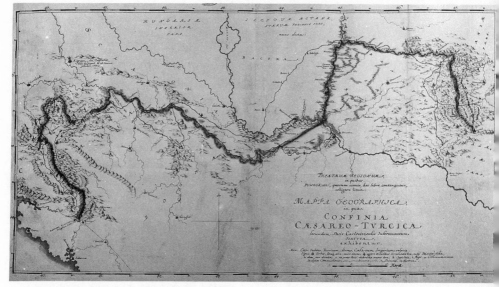

22 The new frontier and its mushrooms, 1700.

great delicacy, using a microscope to show enlargements;[109] another title
page promised a concluding section on mistletoe. In addition, the idea
of listing the mushrooms of eastern Europe, together with mosses and
mistletoe, was still attractive to Marsigli two years later in Vienna during
the winter of 1701–2. There, he decided to add a map to the work, and
Muller duly penned for him a fine version of what was by then his standard
drawing of the new frontier. His patron doubtless approved a title which
ran: 'Panorama of the Regions in which the Mushrooms illustrated in this
Book were collected; Map of the Imperial Ottoman Frontier after the
Treaty of Carlowitz'.[110] It showed the route followed by Marsigli while
making his collections but does not attempt to plot the location of different
species. By this date a valuable contribution to the enterprise had arrived
from Bologna. Trionfetti at last transmitted some comment, together with
fair copies of drawings originally sent from Croatia.[111] After one further
year, in a different country and in altered circumstances, Marsigli would
return to his beloved mushrooms.

At Sisak he also received a long screed from the Hague.[112] It would have
reminded him, if there was any need to do so, that he was not just a botanist
or historian or astronomer, but a book collector of some magnitude. While
on his travels he had kept in touch with Moetjens, a substantial Dutch
bookseller and publisher, and with another correspondent in Holland,
Charles Dumont, who had met him in Istanbul in 1692. From their point
of view he was a useful customer, and possibly an author who could provide them with copy about the Turks, Hungary, and the negotiations at
Carlowitz. Dumont himself was much involved in schemes of this kind for
printing memoirs and state papers of the recent past, and hoped to prise

useful material from Marsigli; while Marsigli wanted from his correspondents in Holland a select catalogue of book titles which might interest him.
He likewise asked for books to be sent on approval. Dumont wrote to say
that these requests were unacceptable: Marsigli would do better to use such
printed catalogues as the *Biblioteca Telluriana* – of the Le Tellier family's
famous library – or that issued by Moetjens himself. If he picked out from
these the titles he liked, and his secretary listed them, his friends at the
Hague would do their best. Dumont offered to bid on his behalf at book
auctions held in the Dutch towns. Marsigli replied two months later on
returning to the camp outside Novi, and continued the discussion. He asked
for the catalogues recommended by Dumont. He asserted that a proper
account of the last rebellion in Hungary was needed. He considered that
treaty documents, such as those published by Dumont and Moetjens in
their recent 'Receuil des Traités', should always be accompanied by proper
maps. As a good customer of theirs he could afford to write a little
stiffly: Moetjens was submitting an account for books despatched to
Vienna in the preceding February, May, August, September, November
and December.

VI

There had been the boundary negotiations with Ibrahim in the summer
and autumn. There was virtuoso activity during the leisure of winter and
spring. Interwoven with both were the memoranda which Marsigli wrote at
the same time addressed to the Emperor, on broad political and economic
issues. As the commissioner surveying the new frontier he believed that it
was his duty to make observations of this kind. His instructions, which he
had helped to draft, enjoined him to do so. The first paper, a 'general
discourse' on trade, was already being written on the way back from the
triple frontier, to be completed at Drežnik in September. Greater leisure,
and other studies, followed later.

In July he had first been asked for his views on the resumption of trade
between the two empires now at peace.[113] The embassy leaving Vienna
shortly for Istanbul needed advice, to be spelt out in its instructions, and
Marsigli was eager to respond.[114] His early travels and his present tour of
inspection seemed to him the very best qualification for doing so. Yet
Marsigli, the Bolognese nobleman who had business experience only as an
absentee landowner and colonel of a foot regiment, knew nothing of the art
of buying goods in order to sell them; and he assumed that an understanding of commerce depended almost entirely on the study of communications. If his memories and notes of incessant travel in Hungary
and the Balkans enabled him to identify the lines of communication along

which trade moved, or could move, he imagined that he would be offering Leopold a master key to mercantile expansion and even fiscal improvement. A government had only to take advantage of this type of information in order to frame an effective policy of bridge building, road mending, locating warehouses and staples, and placing tariffs on merchandise. There would be growing prosperity for all.

He began by setting down on a map, which Muller prepared for the purpose, the 'first and principal' routes from one imperial court to another, Vienna to Istanbul.[115] They followed the Danube to Belgrade and then through Serbia, or to Ruschuk and then through Bulgaria, or to the delta and over the Black Sea. These he numbered 1, 2 and 3. Next came 4 and 5, from either Buda or Baja (60 miles downstream from Buda) through Bosnia to Dubrovnik and over the sea to Smyrna. Routes 6 to 11 all started from Baja; between them they covered Transylvania and the two principalities. After that he linked Buda with Warsaw, and Baja with Warsaw by way of Podolia, with numbers 12 and 13. Finally there were the ancient routes between Hungary and Italy, first overland and then across the Adriatic from Buccari (by Rieka) or the recently acquired Habsburg harbour at Karlobag to Venice and Ancona; these he numbered 14, 15, and 16. After tracing out the itineraries on the map and in the memorandum, and pleading that he had discussed the multiple trade route via the Danube to Istanbul in earlier submissions, he came to his main and rather remarkable proposal. It was that Baja should be considered as the most significant and promising centre for the encouragement of trade in this part of Europe. Its position in the geographical centre of Hungary, where the Danubian route crossed the itineraries which led to and from the eastern principalities, and also those leading to Slavonia and the Adriatic ports, gave Baja an advantage which Marsigli could find nowhere else. At the time of writing he seems to have been more interested in the possibilities of trading east to west, rather than north-west to south-east. He wanted Baja to be the 'emporium' for a 'royal' route, no. 6 on the map, which he traced from Baja to Szeged, Sibiu and then over the Carpathians to Moldavia, while connecting with all his secondary routes through Transylvania. From Baja, correspondingly, ran the Slavonian routes to the Adriatic harbours now in Habsburg hands.[116] He was more cautious about the promotion of trade through Bosnia to the sea, fearing that most of the profit would go to the merchants of Dubrovnik or Venice. He had no wish to encourage the revival of business in Ottoman Bosnia, and recommended that the resumption of trade between Hungary and Bosnia should only be sanctioned if the Turks – in spite of the inevitable Dutch and English opposition[117] – first agreed to encourage a trade in Levantine goods between Smyrna and Dubrovnik.

At this point he drew attention to a peculiar difficulty. If there were efforts made to increase commerce with Ottoman countries, Habsburg exports would be too few for a balanced trade. The Emperor, like the western powers, would have to pay for the surplus of imports with a coinage minted at home and suitable for use in the Ottoman empire. On the other hand he regarded the purchase, import and carriage overland of Levantine silk, wool and cotton wool as desirable, because western techniques of manufacture deserved encouragement in Habsburg lands in order to reduce the current wasteful expenditure on luxuries. If the essential raw materials from the Levant were brought up the Danube, or from Smyrna via Dubrovnik, they might become the basis of a promising new industry in Hungary.[118] As a suitable location for the experiment he suggested Pécs: 50 miles from Baja it was close enough to the main routes for foreign trade already discussed. He went on to repeat his suggestions for setting up fairs and markets, building warehouses and landing stages. Tariffs, tolls and rents would finance the cost of such improvements, although he warned against a level of taxation which killed the goose that laid the eggs. For this reason he advised that any commercial treaty with the Turks should contain a clause barring the double taxing of goods in transit across the frontier. Here Marsigli's memorandum ends, accompanied by a polite plea that the subject was outside his professional competence. He felt sure that Öttingen, the former plenipotentiary now setting out as ambassador for Istanbul, would be well guided by the experts in Vienna.[119]

This discussion, in its essence a series of comments on a map prepared for the purpose, was soon followed by others. While the commissioners encamped by the Una were still at work, Marsigli composed a report on Croatia intended as a sequel to his earlier accounts of Syrmia and Slavonia.[120] Like the essay on trade, it was written in response to the Emperor's instructions, but amplified to suit his own notion of what seemed useful.

He began with a remarkably full historical preface. Learning from his new friend Ritter Vitezović he drew attention to the very large size of medieval Croatia, including those areas which in 1699 were part of Venetian Dalmatia or which remained in the Ottoman hinterland. An accompanying map showed Leopold all the more vividly how much ground there was still to conquer in order to recover for the crown of Hungary its total patrimony in this region. He added that when the next Turkish war broke out, his recommendations would be to make another push first for Timisoara, and second for Bihać.[121] After this prologue Marsigli turned to consider the new frontier which cut through the middle of the old Croatian kingdom. He traced the boundary from Jasenovac to the triple frontier, and included one of Muller's most elaborate maps and a whole series of views showing the fortified places.[122] In his opinion the border here was chiefly remarkable for the length and complexity of the 'artifical' line from Novi onwards, due partly to the mountainous terrain, partly to the Carlowitz treaty's defective drafting, and partly to the malice of the Turks. He dealt next with the inhabitants, of whom he thought a clear majority were immigrants, Orthodox in religion, and ungovernable unless held on a tight rein. They seemed to him an energetic people who generally preferred to live off and cut down the woods to cultivating a crop. In temperament and habits they often resembled the Catholic Croats, but were less trustworthy.[123] That unsteadiness of the 'Vlachs' brought him to his main theme, the need to organise the population of Croatia both native and immigrant into a reliable system of defence.

There were (he had found) 10 existing stone strongholds in the entire region. He wanted these kept in good repair, and manned by German garrisons. Since the treaty of Carlowitz vetoed the building of any new fortresses, he suggests closing the gaps between them by placing Croats in villages specifically planned for a speedy conversion into defensible four-cornered stockades in troubled times.[124] Marsigli defines these as 'military' villages, housing privileged, decently paid, inhabitants and his map duly locates 17 such communities to be strung out between Jasenovac and Zvonigrad. Behind this zone he visualised another, settled by Vlachs;[125] they too would be liable for military service, but in the fortresses and under the eye of a German garrison. An efficient defence depended on magazines and communications; the first must be kept fully supplied, and the second in good repair. It depended on the zeal and ability of the officers in charge of its most vulnerable stretch, the lower part of the Una. Their prime duty was to keep watch on the enemy upstream, in Bihać. Having devised a military framework for the frontier, Marsigli went on to consider its economy. He listed the few places where there were reasonable numbers of people, noting that such villages were small by comparison with what he knew of in Hungary. Conceding that it was in some degree a matter of appearance, he found the enormous size of the Vlach households very difficult to assess. They had latterly been arriving in large numbers but their families looked to him so disordered and confused, their attitude to land and property so nomadic, that his main impulse was to try and tie them down into more settled communities. He wished to see a given number of persons or married pairs in a single district, under the charge of an official. He thought of a reorganisation on this model taking place immediately after the frontier had been consolidated with German garrisons and the new Croat villages. Thereafter, gradually, economic progress and rising state revenues would enable Croatia to pay for its own defence. He reflected optimistically, as he sat writing in his outpost, that soon after the year 1700 the country of the Croats might well be more secure and more stable than the towns and villages immediately east of Vienna had been before 1683.

Later, enjoying his leisure at Sisak, it occurred to him to apologise – at some length – for a notable omission in this report. He had come to appreciate one more local problem which deserved a remedy.[126] According to the treaty the Turks were recovering control of the Bosnian shore of the Sava, but heavy seasonal flooding on the opposite, Slavonian side would always mean that the practical route from Habsburg Slavonia to places like Novi sometimes crossed the Sava into Bosnia. This had been Marsigli's itinerary in 1699. The only alternative open to Habsburg officials or troops, if they were sent from Slavonia to the lower reaches of the Una, was a 'horrible circuit' of many hours' travel north and west. In a visionary moment he therefore proposed the making of a new road on the Roman model, traced at a convenient distance behind the new boundary and offering a continuous line of communication all the way from Slankamen to the triple frontier. It would need three months' work, using conscript labour and local material for the large number of bridges crossing the Sava's tributary streams. He gave particular attention to one region. Drawing the line on his map for the route from Brod and Gradisca to a point just below Sisak (where he planned a pontoon bridge across the Sava),[127] he suggested a branch road to the river bank opposite Jasenovac. Here he wanted a new settlement built, another military village. It was designed to keep watch on Ottoman Jasenovac across the water. He emphasised that his route through Slavonia traversed ground of great potential fertility which awaited new settlers. The usual explanatory map accompanied the proposal.[128]

An infinitely more serious matter worried him, and he responded with the same endearing tendency to attempt a remedy by drawing lines across maps. By mid-January he knew that cases of death from plague were reported in Belgrade and Sarajevo.[129] He feared that traffic of any kind across the frontier would quickly bring infection to Slavonia and Croatia when the spring came. By April he had ready his new project, which adapted to the Danube regions the strict Venetian regime for dealing with disease brought by merchants and other travellers from Balkan Europe. His leading idea was that the political boundary would not be suitable as a barrier against infection.[130] The rivers forming the 'natural' part of the frontier tended to bring together, as much as to divide, the settlements facing each other on opposite banks. River transport, ferries and fishing were indeed hard to control; and the Una was often no more than a pistol shot wide, so that infected straw and bits of cloth very easily blew across. Nor could any trust be placed in Turkish certificates giving clearance to travellers and their goods. Once again, therefore, Marsigli drew his line across a map prepared for him by Muller and suggested a second, medical frontier. It started at Slankamen, ascended some distance up the Danube and was then taken diagonally across the country to Sisak, which was well back from the Ottoman boundary. From Sisak it rejoined the political frontier to follow the mountain barrier south, but he advised that the passes in this remote region should be closed during an emergency. Otherwise he recommended building six *lazzaretti* or quarantine enclosures for people, beasts and goods at the points where the principal trade routes crossed his inner, sanitary barrier. These would be used in times of suspected plague, while other roads crossing the zone separating the two boundaries were kept closed. In another letter he listed all the places along the Sava and in Croatia where travellers should be permitted to cross the frontier in peacable, healthy times, on paying the dues they owed. Other persons attempting to get across elsewhere were lawbreakers who deserved punishment.[131] In general the Emperor's officials on the imperial frontier had a responsibility to protect his lands and his subjects from infection; but for this they needed the reinforcement of a second, medical frontier behind them. He conceded that the problem deserved more discussion. It was still his duty, he liked to think, to offer his ideas to ruler and ministers.

VII

When Marsigli finally moved from Sisak back to Novi it was not because the phase of inertia at court in Istanbul and Vienna had ended, but for reasons of a different kind.[132] As the seasonal floods of the Sava and Kulpa rose, there was renewed sickness. The more water, the worse the air and the more fever. Flooding hampered the arrival of fresh stores. There was no hay left and Marsigli's cavalry escort, which had not been paid, wanted to return to better quarters in Hungary. Also, if he went to Novi in order to negotiate when the word came from Vienna, he would be able to meet Ibrahim and his followers on the frontier. It seemed medically unwise to admit the Turks any distance into Habsburg territory at a time when the plague was certainly spreading in Bosnia. Marsigli's journey from Sisak in fact began on 20 April 1700, after a delay due to the shortage of carts which the Croat authorities had promised, but failed to deliver. His dragoons, on his orders, were now simply taking from the inhabitants what they needed. Happily the encampment an hour's distance from Novi contained sufficient supplies, the ovens which he had had built there earlier were in good order, and he hoped to replace the straw huts with new tents from Austria. It was certainly healthier than Sisak, although the Una was still rising after heavy rains; it flooded the neighbouring villages, and broke down the only bridge nearby.[133] The political pause continued until the Habsburg ministers and the Ottoman ambassador in Vienna at last agreed on what do next.

In the middle of June Leopold's order to Marsigli, and the ambassador's to Ibrahim, required them to complete the settlement for Croatia and then go on to Transylvania.[134] The Austrian garrisons could be withdrawn as the treaty prescribed, except in the case of Old Novi. Rival claims here and over the adjoining territory could be left undetermined, but Marsigli was told that a settlement in Trans-Danubia must still depend on a prior agreement over Novi. Compromise terms of this kind hardly thrilled him, and did not please the Bosnians. Ibrahim warily deferred to Ali (the Pasha) who was some distance off, near Sarajevo; and Ali objected. The commissioners sent notice of the renewed impasse to Vienna, and there was another anxious pause.

After ten days messengers arrived again.[135] One letter briefed Marsigli. The other, from the Ottoman ambassador, contained firm orders that the Bosnian governor should allow the formalities of the settlement to proceed. It emphasised that difficulties over Novi should be disregarded for the moment. Marsigli sent on the messenger into Bosnia, imposing a deadline for the response. After a short delay the messenger returned with good news and on 12 July Marsigli wrote that the Pasha had yielded. The signal was given, and at long last there was bustle rather than delay. Everyone prepared for departure. The transports were loaded. The bridge at Kostajnica was repaired. A last survey of Novi and its ground was made in which Habsburg officers Hollstein and Magni, the commissioners and the local worthies, all joined.[136] Three days were spent inspecting the boundaries, and listing lands and islands. Muller worked over his final map of the area, to which Marsigli added notes analysing the whole dispute for the benefit of the court in any later negotiation.[137] Meanwhile the documents describing the new imperial boundary along the Sava and Una rivers (as far as the gap around Novi), and then through Croatia to the triple frontier, were all but completed. Marsigli had his tent set up across the river on Ottoman ground, and with the customary ceremonies, protestations, last minute objections raised and evaded by both parties, the agreement for the boundary in Cis-Danubia was concluded on 25 July 1700.

What followed were the consequences of this formality. The commissioners inspected the five Habsburg strongholds remaining in Bosnia.[138] From each the officers and their men withdrew, usually with drums beating and flags unfurled. Marsigli then handed the keys of the place to Ibrahim in return for a receipt drafted in the name of the Pasha. Already on the 25th a diminutive guard, a corporal and ten men, gave up a small tower by the Una. Next day the bigger places nearby, Dubica and Jasenovac, were handed back. Neither the senior Croatian officer present, nor the Turks, were happy about the precise terms on which he withdrew the Habsburg garrison from Jasenovac, but the commissioners completed the transfer with little loss of time. Then a course was set east to Gradisca on the Sava, and from there fifty miles inland over wild country to Doboj, which commanded one of the more important routes leading south to Sarajevo. 'A thorn in the flesh of Bosnia', according to Marsigli, it was ceded to the Turkish authorities on 2 August, and he went on to Brod for a last meeting with Ibrahim before they moved over the Danube. The evidence is slight, but a little extra knowledge had been gleaned by our travellers as they passed through Bosnia. Marsigli reported that he was surveying the country with future military operations in mind. Muller did his best to form an idea of Bosnian geography by drawing sketch maps on the basis of what he saw, and what he was told – through interpreters – by such witnesses as a Vlach priest or a Turkish prisoner.[139] The politics of the boundary commission had for the moment become easier, things went faster and more smoothly. As a result Marsigli and his secretary found less time for their own enquiries.

At Brod the usual feints and threats were tried.[140] The treaty required Marsigli (on his reading) to dismantle its military defences before the Habsburg garrison withdrew across the Sava, and he soon claimed to have 1200 men ready to finish this in five days. The Turks wanted as little demolition as possible, and argued stiffly for their version of the agreement. However the work went ahead, and Ibrahim managed to reconcile his final protest with Marsigli's *fait accompli*. On 18 August Bosnian Brod was fully restored to Ottoman sovereignty. Ottoman detachments and Habsburg foot, horse and militia were present when the ceremonial transfer took place in Marsigli's tent, placed deliberately on the site of a levelled bulwark. Two days later Ibrahim was on his way by water to Belgrade. Marsigli, anxious to take a route further off from the area already affected by the plague, halted a few miles north of Brod to bring his correspondence up to date. Leopold and the court, the Croatian Estates, the commanding officers at points along the Sava, the responsible generals in Hungary and Transylvania, the Ottoman dignitaries of Timisoara and Belgrade: all were informed of the Imperial commissioner's recent doings. He took equal care to express appreciation of persons who for various reasons were now leaving him: the experienced official returning to Vienna, Karg, of the War Council; Jackelski, the promising apprentice interpreter; or Paul Ritter Vitezović from the Estates in Zagreb.[141] In certain respects, as he knew, he was leaving one world and entering another when he crossed the Danube on his way to Szeged again.

VIII

Even so, the problems to be solved were similar. During the next six months dispute over a single point, at Arad on the river Maros, merged into the bigger business of drawing a boundary overland between Ottoman Timisoara and Habsburg Transylvania. Behind the commissioner Ibrahim stood a more powerful figure, the 'Pasha' or governor of Timisoara, and this appears to repeat the phase just described when difficulties along the Sava had been overshadowed by the frontier problems of Croatia, and the Pasha of Bosnia overshadowed the more tractable Ottoman commissioner. There was one difference which escaped Marsigli's notice. By the summer of 1700 he had become aware that Moslem landholders in Bosnia and the Croatian border, no less than the provincial governor (or the distant Ottoman court), played a major role in resisting him while he maintained the Habsburg interest. But in the Timisoara region land tenures were not hereditary as in Bosnia, and for this reason it was possible that he would encounter a milder opposition. The Ottoman central administration kept a tighter hold over the distribution of fiefs in Timisoara than in Bosnia.[142] There was another relevant circumstance tending to hasten an agreement. To judge from Marsigli's reports, he and his staff increasingly dreaded the risks of infection from plague in the second, Trans-Danubian phase of their mission. They more urgently wanted to finish work, and get away. One other compulsive influence or interest operated in the European background by the close of the year 1700. The king of Spain's long-awaited death had just occurred, the western balance of power was shifting to Leopold's disadvantage, and Vienna therefore urgently needed a shock-proof eastern frontier agreed with the Turks.

The treaty had determined that the boundary in Trans-Danubia should start (or end) at the mouth of the Tisza, and then follow this river and its tributary Maros as far as the frontier of Transylvania. It was a 'natural' part of the boundary, and the commissioners felt justified in taking for granted the line of these waterways, without any survey or inspection. Marsigli's first objective was to get to the agreed rendezvous at Lipova to meet his colleague again, who had been coming through Ottoman territory from Belgrade. Here was a town on the south bank of the Maros, with a fortress and a history epitomising the concerns of the two men in that area. Ceded in earlier days by the Transylvanian princes to the Sultan, it was then taken by Habsburg troops in 1689. Carlowitz assigned it to the Sultan again, on condition that the fortifications were demolished. Several other places in the territory of Timisoara, between the Maros and the Danube, were to be handed back to the Turks on the same terms. Vienna made Marsigli responsible for carrying out the withdrawal, regrettable as it seemed to him and to the Magyars in Hungary. The commissioner's other task was to come to terms with his colleague on the boundary separating Timisoara from Transylvania, by determining the line of the mountains which the treaty assumed to be 'the ancient limit' of Transylvania. The wording was imprecise but Marsigli enjoyed a working knowledge of the region, from his experience as a soldier and diplomatic agent ten years earlier. His own collection of maps contained many items which displayed the world east of the Tisza, and Muller had studied them while helping with his patron's proposals of 1696, 1697 and 1698 for an invasion of Timisoara.[143] So, confident as usual, early in September Marsigli moved with his staff from Szeged along the road by the Maros to Arad.[144] They crossed here to the south bank and continued 20 miles upstream to Lipova. While waiting for stores to arrive down the river from Transylvania, they gratefully received a modest sum of ready money from the court. Marsigli was less pleased to find himself immediately at odds with the Pasha of Temesvar over Arad. It had been strongly fortified during the final stages of the war, and the Pasha demanded the levelling of the defence works, especially those on the islands facing the town: they would surely disturb peaceful commerce along the river, and menace Ottoman subjects on the left bank. Marsigli disagreed hotly, received a reply in somewhat milder terms and felt able to advance another 30 miles to Faget, a small place with a few Habsburg troops still in possession. He, with Ibrahim, were now close to that border country where the treaty indicated that the overland boundary east of Timisoara would diverge from the river boundary of the Maros. To make sense of this on the ground, to settle what Marsigli called the *terminus a quo* of this next part of the frontier, was the duty of the commissioners.

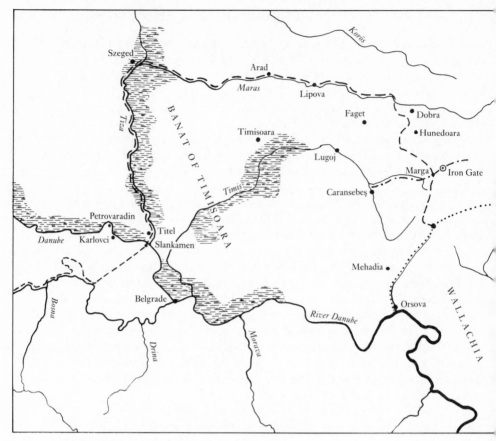

6   The New Frontier, the Last Phase 1700–1701

Lipova was famous for cherries in the seventeenth century, and one day
Faget would boast of its nut trees.[145] Marsigli did not mention such pleasant
items in the massive, somewhat incoherent reports he wrote on his work
and travels in late September and October.[146] In the course of three weeks
he went twice into Transylvania, and twice visited the Iron Gate, which was
the historic pass through the hills 60 miles south of the Maros. First of all
he wanted documentary assistance from the Transylvanian authorities, in
the form of copies of old treaties or charters which might elucidate the old
frontiers of the country. He returned empty-handed, nor was he favourably
impressed by the elderly Transylvanian deputies who arrived at Faget in
order to join in the conferences with Ibrahim and Ibrahim's own team of
spokesmen from Timisoara. Marsigli therefore made a second journey
east, and conferred with general Rabutin in the castle of Hunedoara
(Vajdahunyad), dating from the days of Janos Hunyadi and his son King
Matthew Corvinus.[147] By discussion, reading, and surveying, he gradually
formulated his own idea of the 'ancient' boundary of Transylvania. It was a
frontier obscured in the course of several centuries, as the country's rulers

added to their territory by taking over certain areas from Hungary, which they were later compelled to transfer to the Turks. In this fashion Lipova had become Ottoman, and also Lugoj and Caransebes further south. So much for history: as a matter of geography these towns were separated from Transylvania by the hills, and travellers from Szeged or Timisoara reached Transylvania by continuing up the Maros or by using the Iron Gate through the higher ground. After a first visit to the pass Marsigli was convinced of its importance, and of the need for keeping it inside Habsburg territory. He informed Leopold that his intention, which he conceived as his duty, was to give Transylvania as secure a frontier with Timisoara as could possibly be reconciled with the treaty of Carlowitz. On this point, as on others, he believed that the English and Dutch mediators had leaned too much in favour of the Turks.[148]

He then held a meeting with Ibrahim and the two groups of territorial deputies. This began well when Ibrahim suggested a boundary starting from a certain riverside cliff – called Philippi or Felibe – on the south bank of the Maros, which was acceptable to Marsigli. It crossed the hills east of Faget, but remained some distance west of the first stronghold (the fort of Dobra) guarding the entry along the Maros valley to Transylvania. Ibrahim then traced his line generally south-east for some 30 miles until it approached the higher ground, but next bent it more directly east so that the Iron Gate would remain inside Ottoman territory.[149] Marsigli protested, appealing to his supporters who said, predictably, that the region had always been regarded as their own by the rulers of Transylvania. The Moslem spokesmen, following Ibrahim, disagreed. The meeting broke up, and Marsigli decided on a second and more detailed inspection of the approach to the Iron Gate from Timisoara, a route which leaves the valley of the river Timis and ascends by a tributary, the Bistra, until it reaches the summit of the pass. He hurriedly invited one of Rabutin's senior officers to come and meet him on the spot, and bring along his old partner Morandi Visconti. Morandi, after many years service, was the most experienced Habsburg engineer and cartographer in Transylvania; his superb *Mappa della Transilvania* had recently been printed in Sibiu.[150]

Together these men surveyed the region, imbued with an idea that the Ottoman enemy should always be kept at a safe distance from the pass.[151] They wanted a barrier across the valley leading up to it, a defensible frontier placed decidedly further west than the line proposed in Ibrahim's plan. It could then be traced northward to the Maros, and south towards the Danube. Their first preference was to start from the point where a left bank tributary joined the Bistra; it was 'four hours' distant from the summit of the pass. Less satisfactory, but acceptable, would be a line passing through a site called Marga (by a torrent of that name), only 'three hours' away. Marsigli estimated, if either of these was chosen, that the neighbouring summer pastures and the tillage of the valley were productive enough to maintain the militia which would be stationed there; 'Bulgars, heyducks, and hussars' – quitting the regions further west where Ottoman rule was due to be restored – struck him as the best possible personnel for the military communities guarding the new frontier. In order to brief Rabutin, Morandi was sent back to Transylvania, but before leaving Marsigli's quarters at Lugoj (a few miles south-west of Faget) he gave some assistance to another mapmaker. Muller had been much on the move during these weeks: prospecting north of the Maros and sketching the river in its passage through the hills, or accompanying Marsigli to the Iron Gate. Now, while the commissioner completed his ample report for Vienna, Muller was busy copying maps drawn by Morandi and making progress with his own attempt to express on paper the geography of this large, unfamiliar tract of country.[152]

The commissioners resumed their debate. Unwilling to agree as yet on the Iron Gate, they turned to another aspect of the problem. Marsigli called this the *terminus ad quem*: the point to the south where the line they were trying to fix should meet the boundary of Wallachia with both Transylvania and Timisoara. That second triple frontier was to be located somewhere in the main chain of the Carpathians, as the mountains swung west and south towards the Danube. Marsigli pressed Ibrahim as hard as he could. He had distinct orders, he said, not to withdraw Leopold's forces from any of the places they still occupied until agreement was reached along the entire frontier. He even referred to the need to settle on a third triple frontier, the delimitation of Transylvania with Moldavia and Podolia. Ibrahim coolly responded by suggesting a new rendezvous, nearer the southern terrain in question. Marsigli agreed, and together with the Transylvanian representatives he set out on a fresh lap of his travels. Floods and sickness halted them almost at the start, but once past the town of Caransebeş (where a large Habsburg garrison still resided) they ascended the Timis valley, crossed the watershed and continued south to that ancient Roman site of Mehadia, only 25 miles distant from the Danube.[153] They waited for Wallachian spokesmen who failed to appear, while the weather changed for the worse. The Habsburg party soon returned by the way they had come, and Marsigli's men began to build the wooden huts of a winter camp. They sited it conveniently, close to where the tributary Bistra joins the Timis; and the hope was that the dangers of infection would be less in this relative isolation. Marsigli meanwhile composed a sharp Latin epistle, rebuking Ibrahim for the recent failure to agree,[154] and asserting that thousands of people would suffer from the consequences of Ottoman diplomatic chicanery. During this pause his secretary naturally spent the time drawing sketches of another region new to him. It was bounded by the Timis on one side and the presumed course of a frontier line further east. His notebook shows an intervening country of elusive minor valleys, rising and falling contours, and occasional paths or tracks.[155] Muller was faithfully setting down what he could discover.

Marsigli had been mistaken. Three days after writing to Ibrahim he received, on 10 November, fresh instructions from the Emperor.[156] They ordered him to disregard Transylvania's boundaries with Wallachia and Moldavia, to hasten an agreement covering the boundary from the Maros to the triple frontier, and then begin immediately to level fortifications and remove garrisons in the places to be handed back. This significant decision by Leopold and his ministers was dated 28 October. The case for completing the agreement in Hungary would become even stronger as soon as it became known that the king of Spain had died on 1 November.

From that moment it became easier to come to terms. Marsigli went to see Ibrahim again, at Lugoj, and traded the promise to give up speedily the places still in Habsburg hands against an agreement on the frontier line.[157] The two then rode together up the road to the Iron Gate and on 18 November settled that the boundary between Transylvania and Timisoara should cross the Bistra at Marga, the spot 'three hours' west of the pass. The Turkish claims on the land beyond that point were dropped. From Marga a line would be drawn north across the hills to the rock Philippi on the Maros, the *terminus a quo* decided earlier. It would be taken south, first along the stream falling into the Bistra at Marga, and then extended to reach a triple frontier on 'Mount Murarul'.* Evidently the commissioners were now expecting local witnesses to find them their *terminus ad quem* in the mountains. These must soon have concurred in the view that 'Murarul' was a summit, adjoining other summits, which together formed a massif commonly regarded as the boundary separating Transylvania, Wallachia[158] and the Ottoman territory of Timisoara. Heavy snow had already fallen on the higher ground, as Marsigli reported, so that the commissioners were content to list the names given locally to those heights forming the final section of their boundary. He said that they themselves hoped to start from Marga immediately, tracing the line and setting up landmarks as far south as the weather permitted. Next they would lead a similar survey in the opposite direction, to the Maros. After that, Marsigli pleaded with Leopold, he would like to rest for a few weeks in his camp by the Bistra. It would offer isolation, if not comfort; although the number of reported cases of plague was dropping it seemed sensible to avoid towns like Lugoj and Caransebeş, positioning himself between them and the new frontier. He hoped, finally, to withdraw the Habsburg forces still in Ottoman territory up to the Iron Gate, and from there into Transylvania.

From 10 to 20 November, in a phase of incessant movement, Marsigli and Ibrahim surveyed the line of the new frontier. From one hillside to the next they supervised the placing of landmarks, usually cairns of stone piled high around a tree. Sometimes such marks were described simply as 'in the forest' or 'above the village', but note was always taken of the local names of

---

*   The name Muralui is on modern maps given to a source of the Bistra which flows down from the heights of the south Carpathians: Mt. Gogul rises to nearly 7500 feet.

23   From Muller's diary, 19 November 1700.

adjoining settlements, streams and hilltops.[159] The working parties appear to have penetrated further south than at first expected, climbing far into the uplands used for summer pasture by solitary herdsmen between late June and early September. By then it was November, with snow falling. North of the Bistra Marsigli made the whole journey in person, though skirting the highest ground for the first, very arduous, 20 miles. On the way he was struck chiefly by the immensity of the beech forest providing nuts for the large number of pigs – an 'extremely profitable' business in that area – but he tried to visualise the broader sweep of the landscape.[160] The hills on his left hand descended to the lowlands beyond Caransebeş and Faget, then to the plain and marshes of Timisoara. On the right were more hills, buttressing the Habsburg frontier. Beyond them were the forests and towns of Transylvania. He concluded with satisfaction that he had chosen well his barrier between the two empires.

Further north the line crossed a somewhat easier terrain. The ridges were lower, the country gentler and admittedly more vulnerable to attack from the west. Marsigli turned to the inevitable topic, his proposals for organising a defence of the Transylvanian border in this sector.[161] He satisfied himself that the Iron Gate, together with a single passage near the Maros, were the only routes suitable for wheeled traffic in the entire region. There were six other tracks through the hills, which a horseman could use with some difficulty, 'dismounting to lead his horse'. Accordingly he recommended a large and properly entrenched camp in the central position at Marga, to be held by as many as 10,000 or 12,000 men during an emergency, to protect the pass. At the summit of the Iron Gate he reckoned on the presence of German infantry. To defend the Maros he proposed a string of military settlements along the right bank of the river, and another cluster of these round the fort at Dobra. He considered that scattered outposts would be sufficient to guard the bridleways across the hills. To oversee all this, he asked for an effective chain of command: a Habsburg general in the castle at Hunedoara, an experienced officer at the camp behind Marga, with local headquarters in three of the villages responsible for the separate detachments of militia. He considered that some German troops would always be needed to stiffen the larger body of local forces, which included those shortly to be withdrawn from Timisoara. He saw no point in having more than a few cavalry. With such ideas in mind, and memoranda on paper which included the sketches of his secretary, Marsigli arrived at the water's edge of the Maros. He and Ibrahim must have been thankful: from there, according to the treaty, the left bank of the river was an indisputable boundary. They had only to turn west for a few miles to find themselves back at Faget, two strenuous months after leaving it.

The agreement and the survey were followed by the business of describing them in a formal manner. The commissioners stayed long enough in Faget to give their secretariats time to pen final copies in Latin, Turkish and Italian. On 2 December the settlement of Trans-Danubia was declared complete. Formalities like those which had ended the proceedings in Brod six months earlier were repeated with a similar exchange of legal instruments and of modest gifts to one another, with the same music and official embraces.[162] On the other hand no new Novi haunted the commissioners, the Pasha of Timisoara was for the moment soothed, and neither of the imperial courts intervened or objected. All was concluded in tranquillity. Ibrahim went immediately afterwards to his winter quarters in town at Timisoara, while Marsigli removed again to his camp by the Bistra. They arranged a postal service to keep in touch, but probably the first important messenger was bound for Vienna. He would have carried Marsigli's detailed account of 14 December describing all these transactions, plus the treaty documents, plus a map which illustrated fully the new boundary.[163] The last was Muller's, an achievement surpassing the model of his earlier maps for Syrmia, Slavonia and Croatia. It is in 4 sections, placed end to end to form a rectangle of 8 feet by 20 inches; so that the frontier from mount Murarul to the Maros runs from right to left. It pictures a great deal that Marsigli described in his reports: the landmarks along the frontier, the other line asked for but given up by Ibrahim, the passes, the lesser routes crossing the frontier, the sites suggested for defence posts and the adjoining military colonies or villages. The copy sent to Vienna naturally bears Marsigli's signature. It was a panorama displaying one of his most intensive efforts in Emperor Leopold's service.

Nor could he stop there. While the Turks wanted to take control of the entire territory on their side of the boundary Marsigli had to insist that what he gave back was first stripped of its defences, by the troops and labourers working under his direction.[164] This meant that he required food, tools, explosives, and indeed extra manpower although winter and plague and quarantine checked the flow of goods and the movement of people. As his colleagues were also aware, he tended to exaggerate the difficulties which he hoped to overcome and his plans were soon in train. He wanted to begin the withdrawal at the most distant points, then concentrate the troops and stores at the point with the biggest defences, Caransebes, where there was most work to be done. And from Caransebeş the Habsburg colours would finally move up to the Iron Gate and into Transylvania. The frontier militias, brought back in this manner from the territory of Timisoara and resettled on the other side of the frontier, would be in time to sow their new fields early in March.[165] In one of the transactions at Faget in December Marsigli handed to Ibrahim a copy of his order to certain officers, telling them to start recalling their men from posts still held in the neighbourhood of the town of Timisoara.[166] The commander of the frontier force, captain Ungher, was asked to begin levelling the earthworks and taking down the walls at Faget itself, then to move on and do the same in Lugoj. Marsigli hoped that general Schlick and others in Hungary would speedily send carpenters, engineers and equipment for the bigger jobs of demolition.[167] On their side a consortium of Ottoman officials undertook to continue providing Marsigli's men with stocks of grain.

For three months, until March 1701, the Bistra camp was his usual headquarters. Here he kept snug, giving illness as one reason for staying there, and maintaining his correspondence with Vienna, Timisoara, Transylvania and Belgrade. His reports to Leopold enclosed copies of many of the letters sent and received. Some topics mentioned concerned him at a distance, like the feverish course of court politics in Bucharest and Istanbul.[168] More immediate was his interest in the reports of a link between the Hungarian exiles still led by Thököli, who were quartered across the Danube, with the opposition leaders in Transylvania; and between these and the factions in Wallachia. Marsigli's fear was that the Ottoman authorities of Timisoara intended to settle Thököli's followers in districts from which he would shortly be withdrawing the Habsburg garrisons. In that case he was nervous that the Transylvanian contacts of such dangerous people would be encouraged. It was the more important to protect the new frontier properly, by the measures suggested earlier! Writing to Vienna, he repeatedly made clear his suspicion of the Transylvanians.

In spite of the wintry weather matters moved gradually forward. Not an ounce of extra gunpowder arrived for many weeks, but the defences of Lugoj were dismantled by digging and battering. Then news reached Marsigli which seemed to threaten the frail assurance of Turkish co-operation.[169] The Sultan, he was told, had ordered his ambassador returning from Vienna to take over as governor of Timisoara. Rumour added that this new Pasha, abetted by the senior commander in Belgrade, blamed commissioner Ibrahim for plotting his disgrace at court. Ibrahim believed himself to be in deep trouble and Marsigli felt driven to speak words of comfort to a man 'with the executioner around his neck', as he described him. The asperities of this new chief were almost certainly exaggerated; and Ibrahim survived. But the Pasha shortly afterwards decided to inspect for himself the new overland frontier so recently agreed, even though Habsburg forces still occupied Caransebeş and other points in his province. Marsigli reacted with the deepest suspicion and very little courtesy. Declining to meet the stranger he said that he was ill, and obliged to keep in bed at the Bistra camp. When the Ottoman cavalcade approached, a watch was set along the Timiş and the gates of Caransebes were shut. Late in the evening the Pasha asked to share the ground alongside Marsigli's quarters for his own encampment. This request was refused. He then invited Marsigli to accompany him to the border, and Marsigli again declined. He set out for Marga alone, while the Habsburg frontier guards had been warned and mobilised. The Turk came, viewed the cairns of the new boundary stretching north and south on each side of the valley, returned to his camp, and sent commissioner Ibrahim to parley with Marsigli who lay in bed. The Pasha returned to Timisoara and the gesturing came to an end. Leopold's commissioner had been too quick to take offence; this had been, happily, an unimportant episode.

To some Turks, to many of the civil population, it appeared that their store of winter food was being handed over to feed enemy troops who were destroying the walls or watchtowers required to protect both life and property. Their timber was also being taken.[170] Before the agreement of 2 December intruders from north of the Maros had been cutting timber on the southern side, a few miles from Faget, to be used for repairing the Habsburg defences at Arad, down the river. The Ottoman fiefholder of the woods, supported by the authorities at Timisoara, objected and some awkward incidents occurred. Marsigli, while advising against any attempt to cut more wood, asserted that what had been felled during the Habsburg occupation could legitimately be removed, and again insisted on the importance of strengthening the Habsburg defences at Arad: it was a useful threat to the enemy in Timisoara, kept open one of the main approaches to Transylvania, and guarded the eastern counties of Hungary. But the rumpus over timber, like Marsigli's shrillness at the Pasha's journey to Marga, soon died down. One by one the towers and earthworks and walls, in the places to be given back to the Sultan, were toppled.[171] Muller made careful drawings of places like Lugoj, Faget and Mehadia both before and after demolition.[172] Marsigli might complain that Schlick and the officers at Arad and Szeged gave no help, but two battalions of foot from Transylvania joined in the labour of demolition. Powder and a few craftsmen finally arrived from Hungary. The Turks assisted by supplying carts. There was now confidence that the final stages of the operation approached and

Marsigli gave his instructions accordingly. Captain Ungher was to draw out all his men and the rest of the stores from dismantled Caransebeş. Having crossed the frontier at Marga, they could be stationed in camp sites nearby which had been prepared for the necessary period of quarantine. Marsigli himself hoped to spend the winter in more comfortable quarters beyond the Iron Gate, but the Transylvanians refused to allow this, on health grounds. He wrathfully prepared to sit out his quarantine at a camp in the hills, a few miles from the new frontier.[173]

There was an old stone at Marga with the following inscription:

> DEAE. NEMESI. AEL. DIOGENES
> ET. SILLA. VALERIA . . .
> TEMPLUM . . . FECERUNT
> (To the Goddess Nemesis Alius
> Diogenes and Silla have built
> this temple)

So here, as elsewhere in this region, were the Roman remains needed to fill Marsigli's leisure once again during a winter season.[174] Muller was sent off to make drawings at the ancient sites across the Maros, which would be added in due course to the volume on Danubian antiquities.[175] More attractive still, the notable Roman settlement of Ulpia Traiana (Sarmizegethusa, Várhely) lay not very far distant beyond the Iron Gate. From it, much stone and stonework with fragments of inscription and carving had been taken for use or ornament to the surrounding villages, and to noblemen's houses. Accordingly, after the political negotiations were complete, it was easy enough for Muller – perhaps not so easy for Marsigli – to tour through this neighbourhood, copying what he found and above all sketching the ground plan of Ulpia Traiana's original settlement.[176] The result appears as a significant addition to Marsigli's earlier findings for Dacia. He would have been pleased indeed by the many references to this part of his work in Mommsen's magisterial, much larger collection of Latin inscriptions nearly two centuries later.[177]

One more piece of formal business remained.[178] In December Ibrahim proposed another meeting to be held at Titel, opposite Slankamen, which was the commissioners' starting point eighteen months earlier. He wanted them both to sign a document combining the three regional agreements and giving a complete record of their work together. Marsigli objected, thinking it unnecessary until he understood that Ibrahim's position at home was still a delicate one, after criticism of the versions earlier submitted to Istanbul. The Ottoman commissioner wanted a final fresh copy of the agreement and Marsigli gave way in return for minor verbal changes, to which his partner agreed. On 5 March Marsigli and Ibrahim – not at Titel, but in those familiar quarters by the Bistra – performed the ceremony of publishing their accord by exchanging the documents to be sent to the two courts.

They exchanged in addition valuable gifts, provided by their governments. As was recognised and recorded three matters were omitted or left incomplete. They had not reviewed the boundary of Moldavia and Wallachia with Transylvania. They had not reached agreement over Novi in Croatia. And they had not surveyed the Carpathian mountain area on the frontier between Transylvania and Timisoara. On this last point it was the admirable Morandi Visconti who received instructions from Marsigli a few days later.[179] He and an Ottoman representative were to ascend Mount Murarul as soon as the weather permitted. With the assistance of four senior local residents he was to place in position ten cairns constructed of earth and stone, marking the boundary approved by the commissioners. In due course Morandi replied, describing how they had first blown up unwanted watchtowers lower down, before making their way to the ridges and to a high point – not quite at the summit of Murarul, which was a flat expanse – where there was already a large boulder. This they decided should be their landmark for the triple boundary. The cairns were sited accordingly.

Marsigli had also requested a map showing these details, in order to add them to the rest of his material on the 'imperial frontier'. He seems to have been thinking of his own secretary's final stint for the boundary commission. The new agreement with Ibrahim surely required one more work of Muller's to complement and illustrate it, showing what had been achieved from start to finish by the commissioners. We know that Muller set to work. We do not know when or where he completed the drawing of singular beauty and finish showing the entire frontier, with a title which specifically refers to the ceremony of 5 March 1701, performed by Marsigli and Ibrahim in the camp by the Bistra.[180] In one respect his map represents an extraordinary labour by the large number of people who helped to draw a new frontier across the ground; in another, it is a vision of this part of Europe glimpsed by Marsigli and Muller. It rests today in the Habsburg archives.

The making of the treaties of Carlowitz has never been easy to study because the tangle of texts and languages deters any prudent enquirer. The general consequences are much clearer. William of Orange had at long last the pacification he wanted in south-east Europe. An alliance of powers large and small could confront Louis XIV's government in the west, on the assumption that the Austrian Habsburgs were no longer pinioned in Hungary and Croatia by the Ottomans. At the same time Tsar Peter and Augustus of Poland, by giving up their struggle against the Turks in Podolia, Moldavia, Azov and the Ukraine, secured enough freedom of action in the Baltic region to join with Denmark in a new struggle for dismantling the Swedish empire, and to persist in it for many years. The scenario for the start of a new century was almost in place.

After the treaties were completed in 1699, journalists in the Holy Roman

Empire quickly formulated a fresh model of recent history for their readers. In it the ever-recurrent warfare with the Turks, begun again in 1664 after a longish truce, had continued until peace was made at Carlowitz. An Augsburg publisher offered for sale a large folio of 864 pages, *The Newly Opened Ottoman Gate*.[181] It presented a leisurely account of these Ottoman wars compiled from a wide variety of sources. It was well written with many illustrations, portraits, battle scenes and townscapes. Towards the end Marsigli is mentioned with respect on several occasions, having played his part in war, and in making the peace. The illustrated frontispiece was happily the work of his own agent in Germany, Einmart. In a florid design nymphs give trophies or shields bearing the regional names of Dalmatia, Morea, Transylvania, Ukraine and Azov, to certain goddess-forms who represent the victor states; while a parchment entitled 'Gräntz-Scheidung', or Boundary Settlement, floats in the void. A long string of verses explains the copperplate and includes the lines:

> *Marsigli* hat dem Mars die Gräntz Stein letzt gesetzt
> Lass Himmel dieses Ziel die ew'gen Gräntzen sein!
> (*Marsigli* set this final border stone to *Mars*
> May Heaven grant it marks eternal boundaries!)

It was honourable mention for the Imperial officer but he might himself have disagreed. To draw a frontier line with exemplary thoroughness was not also to wish for its permanence. Marsigli had certainly hoped for deeper inroads into Ottoman territory and still anticipated further advances when opportunity offered. Such a change occurred in his own lifetime when, in 1718, a new boundary accorded far more nearly with his old designs: the territory of Timisoara, part of Wallachia, large areas across the Danube on both sides of the Morava, Belgrade and its hinterland stretching a good way south and west, were all taken from the Sultan after two successful campaigns ending with the treaties of Požarevac. This was what he had wanted, and this Emperor Charles VI and Eugene of Savoy secured. The new boundaries were redrawn again (to Austria's loss) in 1739. So at many points Marsigli's line lacked permanence while his proposals for developing the new Habsburg frontier lands were frustrated by the course of events. In Vienna a commission of councillors had been discussing possible economic and fiscal improvements since 1697. They wanted to improve communications and encourage commerce in Bohemia and Austria as Marsigli did in Croatia and Slavonia. He corresponded with count Kaunitz, one of their number.[182] But their ideas, and his, had very little chance of a hearing in Vienna when a new round of general war in the west began almost immediately, to be aggravated by rebellion and the breakdown of civil government in Hungary. In 1701 and 1702 a beginning was made with the settlement of Serbian militias along the central part of the new frontier, from the Sava to the Maros. However all these new Habsburg territories remained disordered, with recurrent incidents between the new arrivals and the old

nhabitants. The rebel Magyar leaders tried to come to terms with the
nigrants and warriors coming across the new boundary. Prince Rákóczi
nade offers to the Serbian patriarch, and to individual Serbian com-
nanders already commissioned by Leopold. Leopold and then Emperor
oseph I countered by renewing the government's charters to the Orthodox,
vhile raiders on both sides in Hungary were adding to the common misery.
The cause of reform slept for a generation. Marsigli moved elsewhere.

CHAPTER EIGHT

The Downfall of General Marsigli

I

Returning in modest triumph to Vienna in May 1701 when the work of the boundary commission was completed, Marsigli still maintained the dual role of soldier and scholar. There is evidence that in both he saw promise ahead.

Leopold, now an elderly man of sixty-three, who had been granting Marsigli audiences and looking at his memoranda and maps for eighteen years, received him once again and expressed satisfaction with the new frontiers. A few days later Starhemberg died, to be succeeded as president of the War Council after a short interval by Mansfeld, a noticeably softer and easier man, one of the most highly favoured politicians of the Emperor's old age.[1] At the same time a tribunal with a quorum of colonels and lieutentant-colonels met to determine the case of Marsigli against Salzer von Rosenstein. Salzer had shrewdly beaten a tactical retreat earlier in the year by securing his transfer to another regiment, the Longueval, which belonged to the patronage of the Harrach family. Count Harrach, the Hofmeister and therefore senior office holder at court, was as close as anyone at this time to Leopold. The tribunal found against Salzer, and Marsigli asserts that this would not have been possible before Starhemberg's death. Perhaps he was mistaken. Starhemberg was in fact too ill to continue work after January 1701, and there is evidence that the administrative search for those qualified and able to sit on the tribunal had been continuing during the previous year. The delay occurred because the presence of Marsigli in Vienna was essential before the case could be heard.[2] Whether or not the old president's voice had as much influence as Marsigli imagined, the ruler's voice counted for more and on this occasion it did not entirely favour Marsigli. Mansfeld referred, or was told to refer, the tribunal's sentence to Leopold who after two months made known his wish to have the verdict against Salzer suspended. A body of commissioners was appointed to consider this, and devise a settlement.[3] They first visited Marsigli, who says that he was sick in bed; angry, tearful and reluctant he accepted that the wishes of the sovereign were not for him to resist. Then hey arranged that the judgment of the tribunal, with the record of its proceedings, should be sealed up (with the seal of the president, Mansfeld) and placed in the archive but never divulged. On the other hand Salzer was required to apologise to Marsigli in person: the wording he would use, with an admission of guilt, and also Marsigli's response, were drafted by the commissioners. This ceremony of apology and satisfaction duly took place before a select audience, and for Marsigli it represented two things. First, he was not to be given the full satisfaction to which he felt entitled in an affair reflecting on his honour. Second, his greatest embarrassment over the past four years now assuredly came to an end. He recovered his arrears of pay, although nothing extra.[4] He enjoyed full control of his regiment again; his credit stood high.

For Leopold, Marsigli versus Salzer must have appeared gnatlike, a small of troublesome matter. Two experienced officers retained in his service were surely better than one, at a time when the whole future of the Habsburg dynasty was at issue.

A few days before Marsigli's return to Vienna from Hungary, prince Eugene left the city to lead an army from the Tirol into Italy, signifying the start of a new war against the French monarchy. To Leopold's astonished indignation in November 1700 the last will and testament of Carlos II had offered the whole Spanish succession to Louis XIV's grandson, Philip of Anjou. The government in Vienna reacted almost immediately by deciding to send an army to Italy as soon as possible, and thereafter wrestled with the consequences of that decision. It looked for allies, for the components of an army, and for a new head of the War Council as Starhemberg faded away. By June 1701 Eugene was belatedly leading his regiments through Venetian territory to invade Spanish (and now Bourbon) Lombardy; and, to Eugene's regret, Mansfeld was chosen as head of the Habsburg military administration. Then, while tribunal and commission fidgeted over the settlement of Marsigli's suit against Salzer, the Habsburg court moved gradually closer to a major political and diplomatic triumph, its renewed partnership with the maritime powers in the Grand Alliance signed at the Hague on 7 September. A fortnight later a conspiracy in favour of the Habsburg interest, abetted by Vienna, burst into the open at Naples. It was quickly crushed but Leopold continued to encourage a move to his advantage at that distant point. Then came the bad news nearer home, the discovery on 9 November that prince Rákóczi had escaped from his internment at Wiener Neustadt.[5] The greatest of Hungarian magnates, descended from rebels and rulers, he had been suspect for his correspondence with Louis XIV, and the effect of his flight eastward was worrying and incalculable. Such were the matters of state preoccupying ruler and ministers in Vienna after Marsigli's return.

As the European situation altered, so did the fortunes of our two rival officers. The Longueval regiment followed after Eugene to Italy, and Salzer greatly pleased the commander in chief by his mixture of competence and courage in the fighting in May 1702.[6] Marsigli, earlier, when news reached him of a projected march into Lombardy, wrote from Transylvania to sound out whether he and his regiment could join in the Italian venture. His friendly correspondent at court, Kaunitz, sent back a dismissive answer to say that the War Council had already drawn up its list of regiments for the Italian service. Three months later, replying to another letter, Kaunitz wrote to say that Leopold himself could see no reason why Marsigli should not be sent to Italy even if his regiment remained in Hungary.[7] But by the end of 1701 the first Italian campaign in the War of the Spanish Succession was over, Marsigli was in Vienna, and his men were still in their quarters round Szeged. The court continued to regard Hungary as the normal sphere of his activity, and indeed asked for his opinion on the fundamental problem of security there. What did general Marsigli think of the proposition that the garrisons in Hungary could be reduced in size and cost? For if the treaty of Carlowitz offered peace in eastern Europe, Habsburg military requirements for a new war in the west appeared likely to become much larger. In reply to the conference of ministers he said that he would like more time to consider the point, but made clear his suspicion of the Magyars. He wanted his old plans for building good fortresses behind the new frontier carried out, partly in order to safeguard internal security.[8] The government could by no means afford to take this advice and consistently underrated the risks of trouble in Hungary. One consequence was that Marsigli and his regiment were moved in 1702. They went, not to Italy, but to the new theatre of war opening in Germany.

Marsigli himself had a somewhat naïve view of the manner in which this decision was taken. He attributed the choice to King Joseph, who ranked 'my regiment and me' among the best in the army, and who was looking for good regiments to escort him on his forthcoming campaign in Germany,[9] but Marsigli was unaware of another king's important role. William III wanted, as one element of his strategy in 1702, a greatly enlarged force to operate along the upper Rhine in order to divert some of the French pressure on the Netherlands.[10] He asked Leopold to mobilise the German Circles and states for this purpose. He wanted more Habsburg troops to come from Bohemia, Moravia and Hungary. He also proposed, in order to make certain of this enlarged Habsburg commitment, that Joseph (as King of the Romans) should be appointed supreme commander of all the forces in western Germany. From George Stepney in Vienna, the English envoy, we learn how the president of the War Council and then Leopold responded to these ideas. In Hungary, said Mansfeld, it might be possible to demolish many smaller forts and garrison the larger ones with militias, which were cheaper to raise and maintain than the standing regiments.[11] These would in turn be freed for service elsewhere, and in four months it was planned to enlarge each foot regiment by a third to 2500 men and officers, and the mounted regiments similarly to 1000. He advised against bringing these forces westwards until after January. By then the Estates of he hereditary lands would have voted on their supply for the coming year, making it possible to treat them 'with less nicety'. By that time, also, if these forces were quartered along the Austrian and Bohemian borders of Bavaria, they might be used to warn or threaten Elector Max Emmanuel whom all observers knew to be negotiating with France. The same forces would hereafter be available in Germany, as William proposed. On 14 December 1701 Mansfeld gave Stepney a 'Tabella', or statement, listing all the Emperor's foot and mounted regiments 'intended for military operations in the Holy Roman Empire', and among them was Marsigli's regiment of 2500 in Hungary.[12] At the same time Stepney and his Dutch colleague manoeuvred at court to encourage those who wanted Joseph to lead the army in Germany.[13] They had useful allies like Salm, the King's principal adviser, and the Empress; but Leopold was harder to pin down. It was not until 7 March 1702 that he announced publicly his decision to appoint Joseph to the command in Germany,[14] while both before and after that date a few reinforcements were being doled out to Eugene – desperately needing them in Italy – from the nearest available source of manpower, the Habsburg troops under Lewis of Baden along the Rhine.[15] It was this which in the end made it imperative that Marsigli's regiments and Salm's, which were both still in Hungary, together with dragoons and other mounted regiments, would be transferred in turn to the Rhine frontier and not elsewhere. These were the difficult problems and difficult choices for persons more highly placed than Marsigli.

He had been playing the role of a regimental commander with the greatest gusto. After Salzer's departure he required a new lieutenant-colonel; a friend at court warned him not to delay if he wished to choose for himself.[16] Marsigli promoted his major and accepted an outside recommendation for this second vacancy. Soon afterwards both men moved to new posts and he had to start again. He also received the order to enlarge his regiment from 12 to 17 companies.[17] Hence the jostle for commissions and promotions became exceedingly lively, while he had to balance estimates of immediate profit and future efficiency in exercising his patronage.[18] Marsigli used money received from the officers' commissions to accelerate recruitment for the other ranks, while like every conscientious commander in the Habsburg army he pressed constantly for speedier remittances of money, equipment and stores to which he felt entitled. In February 1702 his new companies still needed their muskets. In April he was trying to raise grenadiers in Moravia.[19] Whatever the problems, Marsigli believed as usual that he was within reach of solving them, and was well satisfied when his scattered companies began to pick their way by different routes across the plains of Hungary in May, and then through the gap between Wiener Neustadt and the Neusiedler See, approaching Vienna from the south.[20] The rendezvous was a short distance from Leopold's summer residence, the Favorita, recently restored and redesigned. Not far off was Mansfeld's new villa, one of the first to be built outside the city walls.[21] Marsigli had enquired beforehand whether the Emperor intended to inspect the regiment, and it was indeed one of his proudest moments when Leopold, Joseph, Archduke Charles, and the president of the War Council, all praised the excellent bearing of his troops on parade. They observed, he writes, the companies decently but not showily dressed; they saw no difference between his old, experienced men and the new recruits.[22] The Marsigli regiment then passed on over the Wiener Wald and across the Danube. Other troops, both foot and horse, were already moving into Bohemia; Salm's foot was ahead of Marsigli's; while in Vienna assembled the numerous personnel and transports required to attend the King of the Romans on his journey. His queen, the doctors having decided that she was not pregnant, as she had hoped, wished to go with him as far as Heidelberg. The members of her household got ready. By the end of June, as Stepney reported, they were all on their way.[23] The royal couple travelled via Prague towards Cheb, where the western tip of Bohemia extends into Germany some distance north of Nuremberg and the Upper Palatinate.

Such a roundabout journey from the Danube to the Rhine was intended to skirt without touching the frontiers of Bavaria. As the campaigning season drew nearer, the court of Vienna had to treat Max Emmanuel with the greatest delicacy.[24] Not only did the Bavarians have a long record of intermittent alliances with Louis XIII and Louis XIV, but the Elector was known to have signed a general treaty of friendship with the Bourbon powers a year earlier. It was touch and go whether this would mature into full military co-operation. The Elector, like other Electors, held out for a royal title and additional territory. The Emperor's offers in respect of these had to compete with French offers, and Schlick (Marsigli's old colleague) was sent to Munich to negotiate. In doing so he asked, as a minor point in the discussion, whether Habsburg troops bound for the Rhineland could first pass through Max Emmanuel's lands. Before he returned to Leopold, bearing the latest and stiffest Bavarian demands on the bigger issues, he secured permission for Leopold's foot regiments to march across the Upper Palatinate.[25] It was a small Bavarian sweetener in the bargaining. The matter of King Joseph's itinerary had prudently not been raised.

All this makes Marsigli's own movements the more interesting and unexpected.[26] From Lower Austria he reached Budějovice, in order to lead his troops from there into Bavaria. Then he was told to go quickly north-west through Bohemia to Cheb, in order to guide and guard Joseph as he moved west through Bayreuth and Bamberg. Then these instructions were reversed again, so that his men wearily retraced their steps and moved through the hills into the Upper Palatinate. Their colonel brushed with the Bavarian officials. They queried his papers, he flourished a copy of Schlick's agreement, and some friendly drinking settled the question. His troops continued on their way maintaining good discipline and paying for what they took; they were a model of restraint, according to his own account.

A man riding west through the Upper Palatinate could hardly avoid Nuremberg. It was the focus of the whole region round. It was the city of craftsmen and scholars, printing and publishing, of Einmart and his circle. Marsigli was therefore at the right place, with just time enough to give some thought (as we shall find) to that congenial topic, the progress of the *Opus Danubiale*. A few days later he continued his journey, crossed the Rhine and joined in the siege of Landau, where a strong French garrison was resisting King Joseph, Lewis of Baden and their forces.

II

Another of Marsigli's ventures at this date mirrored a recent change in the European political scene. Prince Eugene of Savoy had taken Habsburg forces into Italy. More and more of Louis XIV's troops were on their way there. Marsigli, equally, turned his attention homewards to Italy, edging towards a cultural initiative of high interest.

On 3 October 1701, Trionfetti wrote to Vienna.[27] He expressed his delight on learning that not only was the *Opus Danubiale* almost finished, but that Marsigli's brother Antonio Felice would shortly become bishop of Perugia. The only unlucky consequence, Trionfetti foresaw, was that Antonio Felice would no longer take an interest in his garden at Bologna, with its holding of rare plants which compensated for the poverty in this respect of the municipality's garden. Marsigli replied with extraordinary promptness:

Yes, the preparations for printing my entire work are nearly complete. The engravers are already busy. New type is on order, which will take time to reach us; when it does, printing can begin. As for my brother's herb garden, don't worry! I will take it over and pay the expenses; but please look for somewhere suitable indoors, in my own apartments, where the more tender specimens – and 'exotica' are always the most precious – can be kept during the winter. Send me a list of what is there and I will then add to the collection through my contacts in Holland and Germany. As for my books, rest assured: I wanted them brought to Vienna in order that they can be bound matching the others that I have here. Together with a great many other things of mine – for which there is no longer room – they will all be returned to Bologna next spring, forming a small but choice library related to my principal interests. Moreover I want to find some young scholar to look after my collections in Bologna, to whom I would offer lodgings. A mathematician named Manfredi has been suggested. Would you make enquiries about him?

A month later Trionfetti replied commending Eustachio Manfredi and another young mathematician, Vittorio Stancari. The difference between them was that Manfredi needed to maintain and house a large family, while Stancari had no such commitments.

24 Marsigli's bronze of Neptune: one of the many items despatched to Bologna from Vienna in 1701.

Marsigli made an offer to Manfredi, who accepted it. This outstanding academic of twenty-seven, and the leading voice in a discussion group well known as the Inquieti of Bologna, expressed his delight at the honour of becoming the custodian of such a 'studio' of books and instruments, which were treasures worthy of a great commander and a great scholar.[28] Marsigli had mentioned installing an observatory. Manfredi therefore hoped, with better apparatus on a better site, to carry out his studies in astronomy to a higher standard than before, asserting that even such men as Cassini in Paris and Bianchini in Rome had so far failed to help him. Marsigli in Vienna was at last pointing the way forward! All these references to the making of a library in Bologna, a studio full of instruments, an observatory, a curator, an augmented collection of plants, begin to bring Marsigli into focus as a patron of the sciences in eighteenth-century Italy, a more important figure than Marsigli the scientist. An inventory of his goods survives, with the heading 'sent from Vienna to Bologna on 22 November 1701'.[29] On this occasion – there had been earlier consignments, and more would follow later – Marsigli sent off most of his Ottoman spoils, including textiles and weapons; most of his scientific equipment including telescopes, microscopes, and his air pump; and certain ornaments, including two fine bronzes and a good deal of porcelain; and a further consignment of mineral samples. The inventory makes it easier to appreciate certain phrases in another letter of Manfredi's. He has now learnt (12 December) that the goods are on their way from Vienna. When they arrive he will obey instructions, taking one of the clocks to the bishop's apartment in the Marsigli residence, and two more to count Filippo. The air pump will be placed in the 'gallery'. When the new apparatus commissioned by Marsigli reaches Bologna from Rome and Nuremberg, it will be essential to discuss the observatory's requirements in more detail, and especially its location. He appreciates that one of Marsigli's ideas was to use part of the roof of the Marsigli buildings. At the same time he referred to his own large family, evidently hoping to secure room for them somewhere in his patron's accommodation, and arguing that his brother and sisters were competent (which was true) to assist in making astronomical calculations. For the next six months Manfredi's letters have been preserved. Often written once a week, they show how Marsigli's great enterprise for his private academy in Bologna got under way.[30]

In due course Manfredi recorded the arrival in Bologna of the goods from Vienna. The air pump was badly damaged, and would be repaired. The azimuthal quadrant was intact. The big Turkish drum could not be found on a first inspection while the English clocks looked splendid pieces. He had signed a receipt for the items which appeared to be his responsibility, handing over everything else to count Filippo. Next, he began to consider the building of an observatory and whether an existing part of the Marsigli quarters, on the existing foundation, could be used; or whether a new tower was needed to overlook the neighbouring structures, giving observers a clearer view of the local horizon. Manfredi, who discussed the matter with fellow mathematicians, with an architect and artists, with Marsigli's business agents and Filippo, at first considered minimum changes but then struck out boldly for a new, specially designed building.[31] For the Marsigli family this would be 'una cosa grande, memorabile e singolare in Italia'; it would also leave as much space as possible for Manfredi, his staff and relatives, as well as for the collections. However, Filippo clearly disapproved of more than a working minimum of the expense and upheaval which his absentee brother appeared to be generating, and Marsigli in Vienna was satisfied by a scheme which amounted to the addition of an extra storey to a small part of the buildings.[32] At its base was a granary formerly used by Antonio Felice. Following this decision Marsigli wrote to his brother in Perugia, assuring him that the building of an observatory above the granary would not harm the fabric.[33] He went on to say that he was commissioning more equipment from Nuremberg, and hoped to have systematic celestial observations started during the forthcoming winter, 1702–3. His library and other goods were arriving shortly in Bologna. They would be practically the last of the consignments for his new institute. He added that a place of study devoted to astronomy was something which their native city sorely needed.

It was indeed true that more cases of valuables arrived from Vienna.[34]

The books, globes and minerals, when Manfredi next reported, were at the customs awaiting a permit from the Inquisition to release them, including modern works in astronomy and geometry. Another piece of news was that the artist Raimondo Manzini planned to go to Germany to work for Lewis of Baden at his palace of Rastatt: he had been living in the Marsigli apartments, and Manfredi wanted to take over his lodging but Filippo objected. Work on the observatory began during the spring of 1702.

Such was Marsigli's novel enterprise while he prepared for the campaign in Germany, but his literary venture also moved promisingly forward. The printed *Prodromus*, introducing his Danube to the public, reached Vienna not long after his own return there from Hungary. Copies were quickly forwarded to friends, princes, scholars and booksellers in various European courts and cities, and comments flowed back. Older friends in Bologna and Venice were predictably ecstatic, but the approval of Cassini, and the thanks of the Royal Society expressed by its secretary Dr Hans Sloane, no doubt gave particular pleasure.[35] Marsigli's letter of October 1701 to Trionfetti sounds exuberant about the whole business. He added a point of detail. At that moment, he says, he was revising volume III on the minerals of Danubia. For, although a detailed list of contents for each volume had been prepared earlier, and announced in the Prospectus, it was still necessary to perfect the Latin text, make corrections or improvements in detail, and prepare the drawings needed by the engravers.[36] In this third volume, Marsigli got Muller to tabulate their findings about the river beds in greater detail than had been planned earlier. Possibly they gathered extra material during the recent journey back from Transylvania, analysing water from the Tisza, Maros and Danube at ten different points. The *Prodromus* gave only four such entries. The account of precious stones, the so-called gems, was shifted to a later part of the text. The maps and views of mines in Slovakia were transferred from one place to another. Transylvanian salt mines were brought into the work, receiving fairly detailed treatment. Above all, Muller had in mind by this stage his magnificent double-page 'mappa mineralographica' of Eastern Europe, which depicts all Marsigli's knowledge and experience of the subject, from his youthful Balkan journeys to the recent mapping of the frontier.

There was more fresh material to add to the account of Roman ambiguities in volume II. The *Prodromus* listed 65 ancient building sites known to Marsigli, which could be described and illustrated by using his original drawings, occasionally modified by Muller. But Muller's new drawings made it possible to recast and enrich several parts of the work when the two men were back in Vienna. In particular, they added to and improved the quality of the illustrations for Mitrovica and Ulpia Traiana, and added those for Sisak. More than once such additions forced Muller to renumber his drawings when he came to group them in the full-page illustrations.[37] Early in 1702 all these 'antiquitates' were ready, and could be sent off to Einmart in Nuremberg for engraving.

Volume IV on the fishes was by contrast hardly touched after the travellers' return. Marsigli told Muller to add, in finishing the manuscript, one new item: that on 5 March 1701, while they were still in their winter quarters by the river Timis, a carp was caught 4 feet long, weighing 27 pounds.[38] The secretary's more important job was no doubt to make certain that the names (to be added to the illustrations before they were engraved) in the various languages and scripts were accurate. The completed volume was then sent to Einmart. Marsigli was even less concerned to alter the contents or arrangement of volume V, the collection of Danubian birds. According to Bolognese testimony he had invited or summoned Manzini, the artist resident in the Marsigli home, to come to Vienna.[39] It seems likely that Manzini, who was a specialist in this form of illustration, made attractive new versions of the original sketches, ready for the engravers to copy. Marsigli concerned himself no further with ornithology and the manuscript of volume V faithfully reproduces the classification set out in the *Prodromus*, Muller prefaced the sequence of drawings and their brief descriptions by one of his elaborately penned synoptic tables.[40] As for volume VI, the miscellaneous observations, he had to work harder and longer. There were now some 700 plants named (but not illustrated) here, and nearly 80 different insects, which included characteristic items like Marsigli's tiny sketches of locusts made on the way to Lipova in 1691, and of a butterfly he saw in August 1688 near the city when Belgrade fell.[41] These too needed arrangement on the page in a manner approved by his patron.

Marsigli was still deep in literary and scientific labours when he left Vienna. At one moment he directed to Venice his enquires about the cost and quality of suitable paper and also of type.[42] At another, he considered buying all the material and apparatus required to have the printing done on his own premises at home in Bologna.[43] Einmart had by then announced that the copperplates for engraving Danubian fish (volume IV) and Danubian antiquities (volume II) were ready. On 30 March Marsigli signed his name on the last page of his text for the birds of Danubia (volume V), while a few days before quitting Vienna with his regiment he signed again – 'Aloysius Ferd. Marsiglij 19 Junij 1702' – at the end of the appendices (volume VI).[44] Paying his unforeseen visit to Nuremberg, while his regiment marched on to the Rhine, he was able to confer in person with Einmart. On 21 July they reached an agreement which settled the terms for engraving the illustrations of volume V, as well as for some additional work on volume II.[45] *Danubius* promised well.

III

With war spreading from north Italy and Flanders to western Germany there was a possibility of more extended trouble. If Max Emmanuel struck out from Bavaria and joined the conflict as Louis XIV's partner, Nuremberg, and correspondence with that city, would be vulnerable. In spite of such uncertainties, amounting to less than a modern condition of total warfare, Marsigli, Muller and Einmart still assumed that their own peacable undertaking could continue. Muller, leaving Vienna after Marsigli and returning to Nuremberg, began on 10 August a new series of letters to his patron, who was by that time with the Imperial army.[46] He reported that he spent his time in Einmart's workshop engaged on Marsigli's various commissions. These were the sectional maps for the Danube which had still to be drawn for volume I, the most important part of the work outstanding; a further series showing the Carlowitz frontier in detail; and a third series intended to map the dependent principalities in Marsigli's phantom History of Hungary. Einmart likewise wrote at intervals, sending copies of the engravings as he completed them.[47] Marsigli on campaign could have every confidence that his Danubian studies were in good hands.

Nor was this all. The production of a book and the command of a regiment jostled with his enthusiastic concern for what was going on in Bologna. Here too Marsigli, Trionfetti, Manfredi and others hoped that their programme could continue in spite of the rumbles of war coming across the not so distant river Po. The observatory building above the Marsigli apartments was making progress. A meridian line, to be inserted in the floor of the Marsigli astronomers' 'sala', was planned. The quadrant on order in Rome was ready, a new clock was coming from Paris, and Manfredi repeated his earlier assertion that he expected to begin systematic astronomical observations by the end of the year.[48] Writing on 9 August he informed Marsigli of the safe arrival from Vienna of nine more cases of silver, porcelain, glass, books and manuscripts, although there were unfortunately some breakages. Water had soaked in, damaging manuscripts as well as the recently bound 'ecclesiastical' volumes. Some rebinding would be necessary.[49] It was a small setback. The news from Bologna, as from Nuremberg, was in general good. Marsigli, firing back criticism and suggestions, had every reason to be delighted by the sequence of confident Italian reports on the advance of his plan for the sciences, which came safely to hand while he found himself plunged ever more deeply into the season's warfare.

By the beginning of August, Joseph and his forces, including the Marsigli regiment, had crossed the Rhine. The intention was to complete the siege of Landau, which still held out in spite of Lewis of Baden's long blockade during the summer. The town fell when the besiegers finally made themselves look irresistible. Lacking direct testimony from others, we may be wise to discount some of the emphasis which Marsigli puts on the importance of his own advice to the King during the last stage of the siege. Yet one after another of the senior Habsburg engineers at Landau had died, or was severely wounded, in July and August; it would have been reasonable to take advice from Marsigli with his acknowledged experience in this sphere.[50] He also refers to his co-operation with 'Keklin', and the chief of artillery during the siege was indeed someone named Kochly.[51] He says that his private message urging a bolder deployment of the available artillery was taken by the royal physician Dr Garelli (his Bolognese countryman) to Joseph, and that the besiegers then determined to concentrate their fire more effectively. This was a success. General Mélac, the French commander, surrendered on 9 September, before he heard of Max Emmanuel's fateful decision to act openly in support of Louis XIV. The Bavarians forced an entry into the Imperial city of Ulm early in the morning of 8 September, and into other places in Swabia immediately afterwards. If Mélac had known this he would probably have resolved to hold out. If Lewis of Baden had known, before Landau fell, he would probably have insisted on withdrawing, in order to cover positions east of the Rhine which were now under threat from the Bavarians. But having taken Landau, Lewis and Joseph wanted to protect it. An order was given for making a fortified line through the wooded country which lay between their new stronghold and the French in Strasbourg. Marsigli found himself, early in October, in the forest of Hagenau carrying out instructions to build these defences. He was busy enough, but in his leisure moments scribbled happily away at a memorandum entitled: 'notes for the Academy, 3 October 1702'.[52] In Alsace his thoughts were still with the household in Bologna and the progress of the sciences.

They took the form of draft rules for 'this institution', his proposed foundation of a select scientific academy. He envisaged a membership of six, with Manfredi, Manfredi's brother and Stancari choosing three more colleagues. First of all, he writes, he is anxious to serve God and the public welfare by having young men trained in the mathematical and physical sciences. In doing so he seeks the blessing of the Virgin, St Dominic and St Thomas Aquinas. The Dominicans, with their church standing close to the dwelling of his family, had always deserved and obtained his devotion; his academy must follow this example. Its teaching was likewise to accord fully with that of the Catholic church on the repudiation of Copernicus and all other matters of astronomy and experimental philosophy. Marsigli proceeds next to a simple statement of his own leading ideas. Astronomy had been neglected in Bologna since Riccioli's death (in 1671); the reason for this might well be lack of funds. Therefore he, Marsigli, 'with the point of his sword' has found money to provide apparatus and books. Experimental physics had been given more attention, he conceded, but it would be beneficial to combine such studies with astronomy. This deserved the labour of the academicians in the long hours of darkness during the winter, while they could do most of their experimental work in the summer daylight. But let research and observation in both subjects begin as soon as possible! Marsigli reminds himself at this point that an 'undigested farrago of observations' is useless, a waste of time and indeed an offence to God. A thesis, to be tested by observation, is always necessary. Observations must be carried through to completion, and the findings published annually in the name of the Academy of Astronomy and Physics. He concluded with certain practical matters. If there were differences between the academicians, canon Trionfetti and count Filippo Marsigli should adjudicate; and one of the six could be chosen as secretary. Moving any part of the Academy's property from Marsigli's house was to be forbidden; and, a point of recurring significance for him, a suitable printer must be found to print the Academy's proceedings. Such was the wisdom of a camp fire in the forest of Hagenau.

Two months later he used his leisure again, having stumbled on something of the deepest interest. On 2 and 3 October the French under Villars had crossed the Rhine a few miles below Basle, hoping that the Elector of Bavaria would send his forces through the Black Forest to join them.[53] Lewis of Baden was compelled to hurry upstream to confront Villars. After the battle of Friedlingen on 14 October the French withdrew again to Alsace, but Lewis decided to pull back most of his remaining troops still stationed west of the Rhine.[54] Marsigli was one of the officers concerned, and was next sent to help in strengthening the defences of the Rhineland and Black Forest against any further thrust by Villars or the Elector. He spent some time in the famous fortress of Breisach, but then went riding up into the hill country behind Freiburg. He tells us that he was first in the Kinzigtal, and after inspecting and improving the arrangements for local defence took a few days' rest at the small place of Elzach (on the Ilz).[55] A fortified line built in the previous war followed here the higher ground of the Black Forest from north to south, and was being used to guard against the Bavarians as well as the French. Falls of snow soon ended any chance of further fighting, the tours of military duty ceased, and commanders turned to deal with the allocation of winter quarters for their men. But Marsigli realised, just before the worst of the winter began, that he had a particular interest in the tract of country above Elzach. The defences nearby ran close to a watershed, not only between the Kinzig and Ilz, tributaries of the Rhine, but between them both and the beginnings of a stream which descended through various pastures to become the little river Donau or Danube, the very subject of his *Opus*. He went as far as the small town of Donaueschingen, accompanied by a secretary and draughtsman who made sketches of the upland country above the town.[56] Barometer readings were taken at various heights. The inspection had little to do with the military situation but brought Marsigli back with a rush to his enthusiasm for geology, for rocks, minerals and 'the structure of the earth', and suggested the idea of preparing an essay on the source of the river Danube, to be added either to the first or the last of his six manuscript volumes in Nuremberg.

At the same time he turned to something different again, but congenial, by composing a letter of New Year greetings addressed to Leopold.[57] To his good wishes he added his usual homily on current affairs, surveying in extravagant language the King of the Romans' recent campaign, followed by a more sober account of the prospects for the coming year, describing

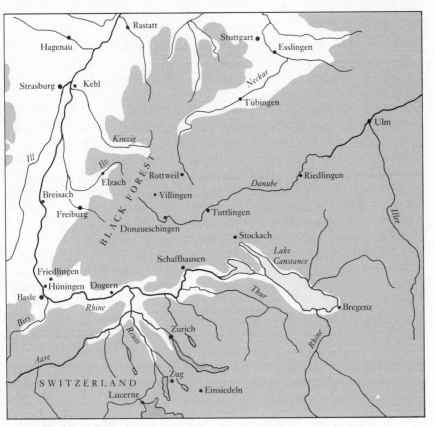

Map labels (reading positions):
Rastatt
Hagenau
Stuttgart • Esslingen
Strasburg • Kehl
Neckar
Tübingen
Ulm
Kinzig
Ill
Ilz
Elzach • Rottweil •
Breisach
Villingen
Freiburg
Tuttlingen
Donaueschingen
Danube • Riedlingen
BLACK FOREST
Iller
Stockach
Lake Canstance
Schaffhausen
Friedlingen
Hüningen Dogern
Basle
Rhine
Thur
Bregenz
Birs
Reuss
Zurich
Rhine
Aare
Zug
SWITZERLAND
Lucerne
Einsiedeln

7   Southwestern Germany, 1702–1703

both the merits and flaws of the existing defence in western Germany. He referred, for example, to Breisach, where he had seen fortifications on the grand scale and of high quality, the work of Vauban himself; but they were certainly weak on the side facing the Rhine, and they were neglected by the responsible authorities. A good commander and a large garrison would be needed there. The advice and the greetings were sent to father Menegatti in Vienna, for transmission to the Emperor at the right moment. Meanwhile Marsigli assumed that he would be one of the senior officers charged with defending a broad stretch of country along the Rhine and in the Black Forest; and was possibly surprised to receive an order dated 10 December from Lewis of Baden, instructing him to join the Breisach garrison 'for the winter'.[58] Second in command after general Arco, he would have special responsibility for the fortifications. Lewis stated that he relied on Marsigli's expertise, telling him to report on the repairs to be taken in hand. It sounded reasonable enough to choose the man who intervened effectively at Landau to improve the defences of Breisach. One of the major strongholds in the entire Austrian Habsburg dominion, it was a watchtower restraining the French in Alsace.

At that moment Marsigli could have looked back over the past year to reflect contentedly on his record. He and his regiment had entered with success a new theatre of war, his professional reputation stood high, while his zeal for learning continued to find outlets in spite of the roving life he led. We can anticipate a year or two, as he could not, to see that Marsigli suffered a peculiar misfortune when Lewis of Baden sent him to Breisach. His post in that important but isolated fortress robbed him of a role in the field in 1703 and 1704, when the upper Danube became the focus of a contest between the expanded Bourbon monarchy and the opposing allied powers. In May 1703 Villars was at last successful in leading his forces across the Rhine and the Black Forest – by way of the Kinzigtal – to give aid to the Elector of Bavaria. Lewis pursued him. The fighting then extended over the Danube lands in Swabia and Bavaria, both above and below the city of Ulm. Indeed the strategic importance of this area acted like a gigantic magnet which brought two more French expeditionary forces from Alsace to assist Max Emmanuel in 1704. It brought Marlborough with the English and confederate troops from still farther off to support Lewis of Baden and prince Eugene, and to fight the decisive battle of 'Blenheim' by the shore of the Danube. If Marsigli perceived so quickly the significance and interest of the streams of the Black Forest which led down to Donaueschingen, we might well conclude that weeks or months spent campaigning by the Danube and its tributaries, like the Iller, Lech and Inn, when the armies moved back and forth while he was hemmed in at Breisach, would have enlarged his vision of his own favourite topic of the Danube. But he played no part there. In Breisach and later he suffered instead a shocking humiliation.

IV

Breisach had been restored to Leopold by the terms of the treaty of Ryswick of 1697.[59] The French hung on for many months thereafter, while constructing new defences in Alsace. When they left in April 1700 plans for repairing and modifying Vauban's work were drawn up by the engineer Fontana but little was done before the new commandant, Arco, appeared several months later. Neither the provincial authorities in Freiburg and Innsbruck, nor Vienna itself, could find extra money. Following an inspection in May 1702 Lewis of Baden gave further orders, and later criticised Arco for not carrying them out.[60] He knew that much was amiss when he decided to send Marsigli as second in command.

Marsigli, obeying at once, arrived in Breisach during the evening of 13 December to find a large fortress with a small garrison and meagre stores.[61] It was a fortified town, with extensive walls and outer works, and a citadel crowning the higher ground at the northern end. He bustled into action, immediately giving his orders for mending the timber palisades where they were weakest, and having flares lit at night to prevent a surprise attack. What he did coincided with some movement by enemy raiding parties in the neighbourhood, and also with an alarm for the security of a powder magazine in the town. Brusque and buoyant as usual, he convinced himself that his arrival had forestalled serious trouble, and a few days later sent Lewis of Baden his detailed proposals. These were acknowledged but then disregarded, and indeed the next eight months would be punctuated by a sequence of appeals from Marsigli and Arco for extra men, artillery and supplies, with an almost total lack of response. Lewis, and Eugene of Savoy, could have said the same of their own correspondence with Vienna: Habsburg fiscal poverty was a fundamental against which every soldier battled with the slimmest chance of success. Marsigli asserted in 1704 that even the arrival of part of his own regiment had not increased the size of the Breisach garrison to more than 2500, while official figures assumed that there were 3500; but in any case Lewis informed Leopold on 20 March 1703 that neither Breisach nor Freiburg, his two major fortresses in the region, had adequate garrisons 'by a long way'. On other occasions he calculated that the former needed a force of 6000, even 10,000 for a proper defence.[62] The actual number of men present certainly fell below any reasonable notion of what was necessary. Nor could troops in Breisach, chiefly drawn from the Baden, Bayreuth and Marsigli foot regiments, maintain their numbers by the normal process of recruitment in distant parts of the Empire. They received little of the pay due to them while food prices rose in the town.

Meanwhile a weak set of defences along the river frontage, where an enemy crossing from the further shore had easy access to islands dangerously close to the town, greatly worried Marsigli. A remedy required both goodwill and hard work on the spot, but when he tried to put repairs in hand by getting the troops to do the work and the townsmen to pay them, there was trouble with the municipality. Arco, slackly, took sides against Marsigli mainly because the two men quarrelled from the moment Marsigli entered Breisach. As commanders they were unable to collaborate, and already in January 1703 Lewis was told that Arco had 'suspended' his colleague.[63] More disputes culminated on 18 March when Marsigli was put under 'arrest'. A predictable appeal in sonorous Italian, part lament and part complaint, went off to Emperor Leopold. It asserts that he has been unfairly accused of overworking the soldiers. In the public interest he accepts the indignity of suspension, but asks for a competent tribunal to adjudicate between Arco and himself. Once again he informed the Emperor of the extraordinary scale of the defence works at Breisach, adding that only someone of outstanding merit and experience deserved to have the command there . . . he, Marsigli, scarcely qualified for such a post.

The hint was not taken, but Lewis of Baden himself was surely at fault in not withdrawing one or other of the two warring officers. Turning down the appeal for a tribunal, Lewis merely patched up the quarrel by ordering Marsigli to obey his superior; he was reinstated on 18 May. To make these matters worse he also failed to win support from a certain captain Heinze, the only experienced artilleryman in the garrison, who resented his interference; but Marsigli was right to warn from the start that a shortage of heavy guns and their personnel would be fatal in the event of a siege.[64] Unfortunately the commander in chief judged that he had no more artillery and manpower to spare for Breisach, and what he did was to try stiffening the defence there by a frail and familiar device. Arco received an order dated 28 February, and repeated later.[65] It prescribed that every officer and man in the fortress must do his sworn duty to His Imperial Majesty by resisting to the end any enemy assault or siege. A negotiation to surrender should never be contemplated. It was dishonourable. It was forbidden. Yet everyone knew that, on occasion, such negotiations and surrenders had to occur.

Gaps in the defence, friction between officers, the disheartening refusal of Lewis in a further letter to Arco (of 30 June) to hold out any prospect of relief in the event of a siege:[66] these all mattered because, in the end, the French chose Breisach as their objective when they might have chosen otherwise. General Villars had crossed the Rhine to go and join his Bavarian ally. General Tallard had another French army on the Rhine's left bank, confronting Lewis of Baden and his forces who sheltered behind fortified lines on the right bank. When Lewis then decided to go in pursuit of Villars, Tallard was left relatively unoccupied; Louis XIV and his advisers could choose between sending him to join Villars in Swabia, or using his forces to besiege either Landau, or Breisach, or Freiburg. But Tallard had to wait for the duke of Burgundy's arrival, his honorary superior, and then for the king's final decision on the plan of campaign. Hence a long period of inactivity during the summer of 1703 for the French along the Rhine, and for Arco and his turbulent colleague inside Breisach. South-west Germany seemed almost becalmed while to the east a tense, uncertain war of manoeuvre went on in which the French under Villars, and Bavarians under Max Emmanuel, and a number of smaller Habsburg or Imperial forces, tried to catch each other at a disadvantage. Still further east, under the banner of prince Rákóczi the Magyars in Hungary broke out in rebellion against Leopold.

V

Marsigli made himself as comfortable as he could. He had much to think about, as his correspondence continued with acqaintances old and new.

First, the letters from Nuremberg. In mid-September 1702 Einmart and Muller had been fortunate in finding a reliable messenger going to the

Rhineland and sent Marsigli examples of their recent work, both drawings and engravings.[67] In return they received what Muller sadly described as a 'vituperation', or sharply critical notes on the discrepancy which Marsigli observed between the originals and their reproductions. Further letters followed while Einmart made renewed efforts to satisfy his patron. Marsigli took a meticulous interest in the symbols to be used on his maps to show features such as marsh, forest or sandbanks, and Muller replied by saying that he modelled his own work on the *Neptune François,* a justly celebrated collection of maps published in 1693.[68] During the autumn, as the campaign continued, there were additional worries in Nuremberg. Where exactly was Marsigli after leaving Landau? Could he continue to pay them? Their stock of paper, and of parchment for the sectional maps of the Carlowitz frontier, was running out. But Muller had been progressing fast with the latter, and would soon begin the more difficult task (he thought) of making final copies of the Danube maps for the first volume of the *Opus.* He remarked in another letter on the peculiar complexity of the many winding channels between Bratislava and Komárom, with which he was struggling. Meanwhile Marsigli moved rapidly across country in the final stages of the campaign, and successive letters failed to find him. At last he came to rest, as he hoped, at Elzach in the Black Forest, writing from there to Nuremberg on 28 November. His artists responded with a full account of their labours, and he learnt that Muller himself hoped to come in the new year, bringing his work with him. When Marsigli transferred to Breisach Muller still expected to make the journey, while admitting that a good deal remained to be done. This was to underestimate a zealous patron, who insisted that he should stay in Nuremberg until he had finished.[69] Einmart and Muller soon found another courier: captain Löffelholtz, of the well-known Nuremberg family of that name, who was going out to join the Breisach garrison.[70] They prepared a package which included the completed manuscript volume of the Danube antiquities (volume II) with copies of all its engravings; in addition there were copies of engravings for two other volumes (IV and VI). Obeying Marsigli's instructions, Muller's own drawings were not hazarded on this somewhat risky journey through unfriendly country. After an unexpected delay, due to family business, the captain set out.

On 12 May Muller wrote again,[71] and sprang a surprise. First he dealt with a familiar problem. In answer to Marsigli, who had found fault with some of the work brought safely to Breisach by Löffelholtz, he again stated that he could not be responsible for checking the accuracy of Einmart's engravings. He listed all his own drawings completed or in hand, adding up the total of Marsigli's outstanding debt. He enclosed a recent book catalogue. He gave an assurance, in reply to his patron's request, that he was looking out for a place of security where all Marsigli's valuables in Nuremberg, manuscripts, copperplates, books, and rock samples could be stored in such dangerous times, with the Elector of Bavaria threatening to knock forcibly on the gates of the city. The Löffelholtz family, for example, had offered room in their house for this purpose. But the surprise, the novelty, in Muller's letter was his admission that he felt tempted by a new offer of employment. The Polish Resident in Vienna was enquiring for the services of a geographer and mapmaker, and Muller – so far denied the chance of joining Marsigli with the Emperor's forces in Germany – described his itch to travel again, reasonable enough (he spoke for himself) in this restless phase of his youth. Moreover, even if he went back to Vienna to take up the post, he could still assist Marsigli. A young engraver working there, Jacob Pfeffel, was in his view a subtle and elegant artist, and the two men in collaboration would make themselves responsible for reproducing the Danube maps. All the same, Muller concluded, he did not think of going without applying first to his generous patron.

It is hard to understand why, but Marsigli was outraged. He wrote to Vienna to inform the War Council that 'his *designeur*, Johann Muller, who had already been in his employment for seven years' now wanted to enter the Polish service.[72] Accordingly he was sending an officer to Nuremberg to escort him to Breisach. If Muller declined to come, Marsigli asked for help in stopping him from taking up the Resident's offer. It sounds brusque enough. Muller duly appeared in Breisach, and in all the troubles of the next six months acted as a loyal secretary and draughtsman to his embattled patron. For example, we have Muller's copy of Marsigli's letter (of 20 July) to Andreas Christian Eschenbach, a gifted member of the Nuremberg intellectual establishment who was well known as author, divine and teacher.[73] In this, he informed Eschenbach that sooner or later Muller would be leaving him, and therefore asked for help in finding someone else to be his secretary, a pupil with fluent Latin and sufficient Greek to help with quotations. This was one of many papers in Muller's handwriting and Muller's Latin which belong to this period of the blockade and siege of Breisach. They were copies of his patron's private or his official letters.

Part of the correspondence was with the court in Vienna. As keenly as ever during the months of enforced leisure, Marsigli wanted to keep in with men of influence who could protect or assist him in high quarters. He tried, and on the whole he failed. Fixed to his post in Breisach, debarred from spending the winter at court and maintaining personally his dialogue with the ministers, or enjoying the occasional gushing audience with the reticent and elderly Emperor, he had indeed lost touch. No successor of Kinsky appeared to defend the Marsigli interest; he might be a colonel of infantry with the title of general, but he now lacked a patron powerful on the political stage or behind the scenes. He wrote letters of compliment to some of the greater dignitaries, like the president of the War Council Mansfeld, and the Vice-chancellor of the Empire Kaunitz, which they politely acknowledged.[74] He wrote also to two influential civil servants, Thiel of the War Council (one of his former colleagues at Carlowitz) and Palm (once Carafa's secretary) of the Treasury or Hofkammer.[75] They learnt of his

ELENCHUS
LIBRORUM ORIENTALIUM
MANUSCRIPTORUM,
Videlicet
GRÆCORUM, ARABICORUM,
PERSICORUM, TURCICORUM,
Et deinde
HEBRAICORUM, AC ANTIQUORUM
LATINORUM, TUM MANUSCRIPTORUM,
TUM IMPRESSORUM
A DOMINO COMITE
ALOYSIO FERDINANDO
MARSIGLI,
SACRÆ CÆSAREÆ MAJESTATIS
CAMERARIO, PEDESTRIS LEGIONIS TRIBUNO,
ET VIGILIARUM CAMPI GENERALI
Partim
In ultimo bello Turcico,
Et partim
In itinere Conftantinopolim fufcepto collectorum,
coëmptorúmque,
OPERA
MICHAELIS TALMAN,
S. C. M. Linguarum Orientalium Interpretis
compilatus
Et
In fex Partes divifus.

◆─◎◎◎◎◎◎◎◎◎◎◎◎◎◎◎◎◎◎◎◎◎◎◎◎◎◎◎◎◎◎◎◎─◆

VIENNÆ AUSTRIÆ,
Apud Sufannam Chriftinam, Matthæi Cofmerovij, S.C.M.Typogr.
Aulici Viduam.
ANNO M. DCCII.

25 The titlepage of the catalogue, printed for Marsigli in Vienna in 1702 while he was campaigning in Germany.

arrival at Breisach, of his prompt remedial measures to strengthen it, and of his problems with Arco thereafter. In return Marsigli was told of the depressed mood of the court and, at one point, of prince Eugene's lack of success in getting reinforcements or supplies for the army in Italy. But he seems to have received no inkling of the grand political crisis of the Habsburg administration during the first six months of 1703 which culminated at last in a change of government. At the very end of June Eugene himself and Gundacker Starhemberg, ardent and efficient, replaced the feebler Mansfeld and Salaburg as heads of the two main offices of state, the War Council and Treasury. This alteration might have affected Marsigli, because there is evidence that Eugene appreciated – as Mansfeld and Lewis of Baden never did – that the divided command in Breisach was an absurdity, but in fact nothing was done.[76] In Vienna Marsigli could rely on his old Italian friends for humbler services, such as Garelli, the Emperor's physician and librarian, or Menegatti, of the Emperor's corps of attendant priests. They were his postmen. Another doctor, Giuseppe Lupi, kept an eye on Marsigli's lodgings; and when he left in order to join the army in Italy Lupi's cousin, a priest, took his place.[77] Marsigli's agent from Bologna, Guicciardini, reappeared in Vienna at this period. He brought some money, if not enough to cover all current expenses. A joiner and other craftsmen, hired earlier to put in new fittings for a workshop or laboratory, had been paid by Lupi. So was a carrier, for taking packages from Vienna to Venice. The housekeeper meanwhile complained that she received nothing for her pains. Michael Talmann the orientalist and future diplomat, who had been asked to examine Marsigli's collection of Hebrew and Turkish manuscripts, returned them: the printing of a catalogue was going ahead, but both he and the printer needed payment.[78] Guicciardini meanwhile went off again. One may conclude that Marsigli himself expected to return to Vienna before too long, to find his *pied-à-terre* dusty but secure, and to pay his debts.

Less news, or fewer letters which have survived, reached him in 1703 from Bologna. After the excitement of the autumn before, when Manfredi proclaimed that everything would be ready in time to start systematic celestial observations on 1 January, a further series of reports to the distant patron was surely owing. These have not been traced, although he heard from Trionfetti, who was evidently working on the geology and minerals of the third manuscript volume of the *Opus*. It seems that Marsigli's wish to have the illustrations engraved in Italy led to a long search for the right artist, and then to uncertainty in assessing the cost. He was already in Breisach when examples of the highly experienced F.M. Francia's work arrived; he approved, and production of the plates duly began.[79] This, and simultaneous progress in Nuremberg, brought the possibility of printing much nearer. Unfortunately only a fragment is left to hint at another lost correspondence: a note in Muller's hand, dated 20 July in Breisach, mentions the great diligence with which type was being prepared in Venice, so that a printing press could soon be installed at Bologna 'in my palazzo', using paper 'as good as the best Dutch, but two-thirds of the price'.[80] An engraver 'for the Sectional Maps and Geography' still eluded discovery. This suggests that the enquiries for type in Venice at an earlier stage had been successful, with Marsigli intending to have the *Opus* printed in Bologna.

His enthusiasm for his library in Bologna persisted. On 10 January he informed Trionfetti that he was having catalogues forwarded from Basle, Nuremberg and Leipzig with items on botany and natural history, and it would be for his correspondent to begin by deleting anything which could be found more easily in Italy;[81] and he referred to the bindings he wanted in white, green, yellow or violet. Trionfetti responded, and in March another letter emphasised how fortunately placed Marsigli felt at Breisach, being so close to a notable publishing and booksellers' centre like Basle.[82] He wanted now to complete his collection of works on mathematics and natural history,

leaving political science, grammar, ancient and ecclesiastical history until
later. As for the books in Bologna, he again asked Trionfetti to see that his
instructions about binding were followed, adding that he wanted to exclude
law books and anything more than a minimum of *belles-lettres* and medicine.
He also tells his old tutor that he has been collecting snails along the shore
of the Rhine, but three months later (20 June) wrote at greater length about
his most enjoyable hobby in Breisach. It was predictable, a return to the
tantalising problems posed for him earlier by mushrooms, their diffusion
and generation.[83] In this Rhineland terrain, by the sandy edge of the river
which was liable to flood, or the drier ground of the earthworks in one of the
bastions, or the small garden in the town which he started cultivating,
Marsigli found a profusion of mushrooms. He examined them with his
microscope.[84] On what particular days he did so, how much time he could
spare, are not stated; but careful drawings were made as he passed on to
other matters. A new friend had introduced himself.

John Jacob Scheuchzer of Zurich, a reader of the *Prodromus* and fellow
student of the sciences, wrote to Marsigli in Breisach.[85] He listed their
interests, such as maps and minerals, stones and fossils, explaining his
particular concern for the natural history of the Alpine region. He did not
say so, but it was a fact that the mountains of Saxony, Austria, Slovakia
and their mineral wealth had attracted a certain scholarly interest over a
long period, while the Alps of Switzerland were from this point of
view hardly more familiar than the ranges of Bosnia or Transylvania.
Scheuchzer, recently a visitor in Germany, was in touch with Einmart.
News of Marsigli's arrival in the Rhineland, as of his visit to Nuremberg,
would have reached him quickly. It was also easy for the two men to grasp
that they both were patricians enjoying scholarly tastes, collecting with
an ample purse fossils, stones and minerals. Their correspondence began
under the best of auspices.

At first Marsigli responded rather pompously. The great Malpighi was
his teacher, and he followed Malpighi's methods of observation to explain
the progress of nature, as could be seen from the *Prodromus*.[86] Then his
guard dropped and he showed genuine pleasure and interest in the scientific
papers which Scheuchzer had enclosed. One was an illustrated essay on
rock samples, *Specimen lithographiae Helveticae curiosae . . .* , published in
Zurich in 1702. Marsigli asked whether he could purchase some of the
samples, adding that he always paid promptly; and in return offered his new
friend a detailed description of the coffee plant, no doubt the little treatise
printed long ago in Vienna. A second piece by Scheuchzer described his
recent journey in the Grisons, including the area where the Inn – a major
tributary of the Danube – rises in the Upper Engadine.[87] This excited
Marsigli, recalling his own survey a few months earlier of the springs
flowing down to Donaueschingen, the place usually honoured as the source
of the Danube. If he persevered with the idea of composing something for
the *Opus* on the origins of the great river, he would want to determine

whether the mountains near the Septimer Pass seen by Scheuchzer had a better claim than the Black Forest to contain its headwaters. This seemed a problem worth discussion, and their correspondence during the summer of 1703 turned on this and similar geological themes. Scheuchzer also introduced Marsigli to a member of his circle, John Woodward of London, a man noted in Europe for his exciting *Essay towards a Natural History of the Earth*. The Swiss had translated this into Latin.[88] Woodward saw the *Prodromus*, and now learnt that Marsigli was in Breisach. The three started corresponding, they exchanged samples, and a little later Woodward would deplore Marsigli's unhappy fate as warmly as he disapproved of Marsigli's views on the distribution of fossils in the earth's strata.[89]

The last letter sent to Zurich before the siege of Breisach began was dated 9 August, and is in Muller's hand.[90] They were trapped in the town together. But the loyal secretary, and the loyal friend in not too distant Zurich, both stood by Marsigli during his predicament. They ensured that in the worst moments of his life – apart from his captivity in Hungary and Bosnia twenty years before – he would not flag in cultivating his favourite sciences.

VI

There had been little improvement in Breisach's defences. It was still tacitly hoped that they would not be tested. On 21 June Arco wrote asking Lewis of Baden to return pieces of artillery which had been transferred at an earlier stage to Freiburg, saying that otherwise it would be impossible to hold out for any length of time if the place was besieged. Lewis refused. His reply of 30 June asserted that Freiburg was equally at risk, and complained that he himself was utterly without resources; in an emergency the defenders of Breisach must rely on their own judgment and valour in doing their best for the Emperor's service.[91] At the end of July it was Marsigli's turn. He tried to raise funds to pay the troops from the government treasury in Freiburg, sending one of his regimental captains with the request. Soon afterwards both commanders became convinced that an assault was possible, even imminent, and Marsigli ordered captain Keyser to go on directly from Freiburg to Vienna with an urgent appeal for help.[92] There was no reply before the siege began. On 11 August the French started crossing the Rhine and general Tallard put in hand his preparations to besiege Breisach, not Freiburg or Landau. By 18 August the town was encircled on the landward side. Bridges upstream and downstream were built, the first more rapidly than the second. Trenches were opened during the night of the 22nd at a considerable distance from the defences, but the besiegers soon started to traverse the glacis. Their numbers, and the number of their labourers employed to dig the approaches, must have looked overwhelming to the 1100 men assigned by Arco and Marsigli to the outworks, the counterscarp and the ravelins.[93] The will to resist ebbed even more when French artillery began breaching one of the bastions; the defenders had sufficient munitions but nothing like enough heavy guns to oppose the enemy bombardment. Vauban himself was now on the scene, viewing his own fortifications, and advising the duke of Burgundy and Tallard to concentrate their efforts on a relatively short stretch at the south end of the town. Marsigli tried to counter the projected assault by placing relatively large numbers (again, just over 1000 men and officers) on or close to the bastion most at risk.[94] In consequence the gaps in the defence elsewhere, with a total garrison of not more than 2500, were enormous.

Arco, in the citadel at the other end of Breisach, felt all the more vulnerable. He decided that they would lose less by trying to come to terms than by continuing a useless resistance. A sortie led by one of his colonels, Tanner, did not stop the French advance to the inner edge of the outworks. They also occupied, one by one, the islands facing the town, and fire from this direction helped to choke the sluice through which water normally entered the moat protecting the bastion under threat, and the others beyond it. The pressure increased. The unpaid troops were dispirited, the civilian population was passive. On 5 September there was coming and going between one location and another in the defences; the discussion between them cannot be accurately recorded from the differing accounts given later. They led Arco to summon next day a conference of 30 available officers, who were not disposed to continue fighting in a hopeless cause. After more discussion, and the handing to Arco of written opinions, another meeting decided to favour a surrender if the enemy agreed to honourable terms. Those present, including Marsigli, were persuaded that Lewis's letter of 30 June – which Arco read out – offered reasonable grounds for disregarding the instructions given earlier to hold out to the last, mainly because the commander in chief's letter denied them any prospect of aid or rescue.[95] Military law, they were told, supported the argument. Accordingly they convinced themselves that resistance, if prolonged, would be a costly and useless exercies which would not save Breisach. They had done their utmost in impossible circumstances before seeking to save themselves, just like the garrison at Kehl which surrendered to Villars earlier in the year or like many smaller Habsburg garrisons in the same area during the previous autumn. They would leave a doomed place with flying colours, and fight again.

The terms of a surrender were quickly settled by the French command, delighted with 'un peu de miracle' in the transaction. The withdrawal from Breisach began on 8 September. The march of the Habsburg detachments out of the town with colours flying after three weeks of danger and tension, and from there south to Rheinfelden on the Rhine above Basle, looked almost like a peaceful excursion; but the result was a military triumph for Louis XIV and a loss to Leopold of one of the most famous fortresses in

Germany. At the same moment French forces were in Swabia. They were in Breisach. They stood outside Trento, on the route from Italy to the Tirol. It proved to be the lowest point to which Habsburg fortunes sank in the whole course of the war.

When Lewis, then in Swabia, was first told of the surrender he guessed that there had been a 'rivolta' by the impoverished garrison. They had been left without pay (he admitted) for such a long time.[96] He felt shocked, not surprised. A few days later he understood that there had been no rebellion, no mutiny, and declared himself astonished that Arco, Marsigli and the other officers should have decided in favour of an early surrender, in view of his explicit orders to defend Breisach to the bitter end. He informed Vienna that he would have an enquiry held, as usual detaining the officers concerned until they were absolved from blame. A fortnight later the Emperor received a further report, and the Vienna authorities sent a commission to general Thüngen, the senior commander in the region, to take action. It instructed him to set up a military court and to preside himself over a full enquiry into the recent surrender of Breisach. The administrative mechanism of the Habsburg armed forces was still working, in spite of the terrible setbacks and evident dangers ahead.

The effects of all this gradually became clear to Arco and Marsigli. At Rheinfelden the much travelled captain Keyser of Marsigli's regiment, who had gone on their behalf to Freiburg and then to Vienna to beg for help, belatedly arrived to hand them replies dated 2 September.[97] These blandly repeated the substance of earlier instructions, while adding a little more encouragement: the garrison must defend the town to the last man; Leopold was aware that they had sufficient forces to stand firm; help was on the way; Marsigli must co-operate loyally with Arco; he should take over sole responsibility if 'the interests of the Emperor' required it.

Such messages from the distant centre of government were past history when they arrived, but were *prima facie* evidence that the two commanders had disobeyed orders by their surrender. They now excused themselves. From separate lodgings in or near Rheinfelden they defended their own conduct and blamed each other. An officer from headquarters questioned them both, and sent back a report which led Lewis to write to Vienna, and Vienna to Thüngen.[98] Marsigli, although his anxiety increased as the weeks went by, at first believed that his position was unassailable. The more searching an enquiry – if there was one – into the tragic course of events, the more effectively his personal archive would protect him. It contained copies of all the relevant documents and had been brought safely out of Breisach, no doubt in Muller's charge. Meanwhile Marsigli was suspended from military duties, and with his usual verve began to use the little village of Dogern – east of Rheinfelden and a few miles from another Habsburg town on the Rhine, Landshut – as a centre for the alternative life of study and research. The faithful Muller took a letter from Dogern to Scheuchzer in Zurich, now so much nearer than it had been from Breisach, and returned with the welcome news that Scheuchzer could read Italian. Marsigli was delighted. From then on he wrote to his Swiss collaborator with all the freedom and emphasis of his ordinary speech, expressing himself as he wished. It became so much the easier for the friendship to ripen and deepen.[99]

Muller also brought back samples of rock to Dogern. Marsigli's prompt thanks (in Italian) spilt over into a geological argument, and he went on to tell Scheuchzer of his museum in Bologna, for which he was busy assembling minerals, shells and fossils. He said that he wished to make it the most complete in Europe, systematically arranged for the true study of nature, and superseding the absurdly miscellaneous collections usually found. He admitted how much a study of the Swiss Alps would help his own work, and in return offered to put Scheuchzer in touch with Trionfetti who looked after the botany garden in Bologna, and with Manfredi who directed 'the astronomical Academy of my new observatory'. This was an institution unparalleled in Italy, he declared, not much less well equipped than the royal observatory in Paris under Cassini, who was an 'old and intimate friend of my family'. Repetitive and boastful as usual, Marsigli also had questions to ask. Was there a good engraver in Zurich? Were paper or type of better quality to be found there, or in Basle? Had Zurich businessmen any correspondents in Bologna? Then he reverted to his problem about the Danube, the Inn and the source of the Inn. The Swiss scientist used a barometer to measure air pressures and fix altitudes on his travels in the Grisons: Marsigli also had been measuring air pressures in the Black Forest, and he suggested that the Black Forest was part of the Alps, but a lower part, whereas the major rivers of Europe – the Rhine, Rhône and Danube – were all assumed to rise in and descend from the highest ground in the central upland of the continent. He was groping for some sort of symmetry, and for this reason it also seemed to him appropriate that the Rhine found a way through the mountains (including the Black Forest) above and below Basle, and the Danube passed through the Carpathians, with a zone of cataracts indicating the passage of the river. The Falls of Schaffhausen illustrated the same geological pattern as the Iron Gates of the Carpathians in eastern Europe. Marsigli was busy forming his convictions about the 'structure' of mountainous country, craving and finding an element of formal symmetry in the pattern of creation. Scheuchzer himself accepted a somewhat similar solution, with an emphasis implied in the title of the work he published in 1709, *Geographia Sacra*. At a more practical level, Marsigli informed Scheuchzer that his draughtsman Muller was engaged in drawing a 'profile' which showed the watershed separating the river systems of the Inn and Danube from the Rhine. He wanted to include it in the *Opus*, now nearly complete.

This must have been almost the last occasion when Marsigli and Muller worked on papers in each other's company, because Muller took his leave on 8 January 1704, a solitary traveller on horseback going to Nuremberg.[100]

He took advantage of the warring forces' entry into winter quarters. Lacking further evidence about his departure, we cannot be sure what Muller had in his baggage: certainly his drawings for the source of the Danube above Donaueschingen, and the 'profile' of the Alps and Black Forest; certainly the sketches made of those mushrooms Marsigli had examined in Breisach, together with an instruction to Einmart to engrave them; possibly also a number of other papers dealing with the *Opus Danubiale* and with the collections of Swiss and German geological samples then being assembled by his patron.[101] On the other hand it is easy to see why Marsigli on this occasion allowed Muller to go; a member of the Scheuchzer family was already engaged to replace him. John Jacob from Zurich had enquired earlier whether one of his younger brothers stood a chance of a post in Marsigli's service.[102] John George, a medical student then in the Dutch army, was anxious to move and the Royal Society of London declined – in spite of his elder brother's plea – to appoint him a research assistant. He was a good virtuoso with a knowledge of Greek and Latin. Marsigli, still looking for a successor to Muller, immediately expressed interest and in a reply from Dogern stated his terms. He offered 100 Rhenish florins a year, meals at his own or the officers' table, and travelling expenses. He would expect young Scheuchzer to write letters for him to fellow scholars, keep the catalogue of his expanding library up to date, and assist in enlarging his scientific collections. He had no prejudice against a Protestant secretary, as the example of Muller showed. The answer was a letter from Maastricht. John George was pleased and grateful. Early in the new year he arrived at Dogern to enquire for his patron.

From Dogern, it may be added, a short and easy journey for an officer on parole led to the ancient town of Schaffhausen. Here Marsigli could examine for himself the celebrated falls of the Rhine, and become acquainted with like-minded people, members of a little patrician group collecting 'rarities' and patronising a competent local artist who depicted their finds and purchases.[103] They were pleased to meet a famous soldier-scholar such as general Marsigli. Schaffhausen was modest, not a Zurich or Nuremberg, but offered the stimulus of conversation which supplemented his correspondence. Meanwhile the storm clouds gathered round him, as they gathered round Arco who was at least his colleague in misfortune. At the end of October Marsigli informed Scheuchzer that he would shortly be going to Vienna, without saying why. He repeated this on 7 November, but wrote a week later that he was on his way to Freiburg where general Thüngen would hold an enquiry into the causes of the disaster at Breisach; in his own opinion, he said, this would have made better sense in the previous April. Evidently something serious was afoot but no more details were forwarded to Zurich until just before Christmas, when Marsigli wrote that he had now to go to Bregenz at the eastern end of Lake Constance for Thüngen's enquiry. Even from there he continued to ply his friend with questions and answers on a wide range of intellectual problems.[104] On 25

February 1704, finally, he revealed the full and calamitous story of his fall from grace. Its ending was his sentence of dismissal with dishonour from the Emperor's service.

Marsigli never ceased, as long as he lived, to consider the proceedings of the tribunal at Bregenz a mockery of justice, but they fit easily enough into the grim framework of Habsburg history at the time. So far he had been left amazingly unscathed, free to pursue his private interests while holding his post in Leopold's army. This still seemed the case when he was pinned month after month in Breisach, until Louis XIV finally decided to besiege the place. But Lewis of Baden, to whom Vienna could never afford a large enough force sufficiently equipped, at first put more emphasis on defending the country further north than on strengthening Breisach or its hinterland, and he was diverted to Swabia and Bavaria during the summer. The French besiegers looked overpoweringly strong, the defending garrison looked trapped without any hope of a relief. Arco and Marsigli, whatever their differences and mutual dislike, seemed to have agreed in accepting the case for an early surrender on good terms. They were saving themselves and precious manpower to fight for the Emperor on another occasion. But this was not Eugene of Savoy's view of the matter nor, after a few days of uncertainty, the view of Lewis of Baden.[105] Eugene, as the recently appointed chief of the military administration in Vienna and the commander recalled from Lombardy, angrily contemplated the shrinkage of Leopold's control in one area after another. In 1703 there were not many more battles or fortresses which the House of Austria could afford to lose without a catastrophic sequel, and the tribunal appointed to sit at Bregenz was a tiny part of the official riposte to that possibility. When Saint-Simon later compiled his Memoirs and described the French siege of Landau, in November 1703, he wrote that the defence was vigorous because the garrison had learnt its lesson from the Habsburg government's sentencing of Arco and Marsigli.[106] The trial in fact took place after Landau fell, but the attitude of their chief critics was already clear. Eugene in particular wanted a rigorous enquiry. He informed Thüngen that unless they were absolved by the tribunal, he would hold responsible the two commanders and every other officer who had voted for the surrender of Breisach.[107] There was to be strict and speedy justice. There was to be no fudging, no appeal, no pardon.

It did not help Arco that he belonged to the great clan of the Arcos, of which other prominent members served at the time in the Bavarian court and army.[108] It was also easy to suspect Marsigli's loyalty when news spread that he had been presented to the duke of Burgundy on the day he left Breisach. The critics did not press these points of kinship or decorum vaguely linked with suspicion of treason. The two men had a more specific charge to answer.

Marsigli was first thoroughly alarmed when he learnt that the commanding officer of Freiburg, on the orders of Lewis, had published a notice denouncing the surrender of Breisach as an irresponsible and infamous transaction. The officers and men concerned had disobeyed instructions and betrayed their trust.[109] Similar phrases were broadcast in two other Habsburg posts under threat from the French, Philippsburg and Landau, no doubt as a warning that further half-hearted resistance and quick surrender would not be tolerated. Marsigli realised also that in certain quarters he and Arco were believed to have been corrupted by the enemy. Deeply disturbed, he addressed appeals to the Emperor and the War Council, in which he referred pointedly to the published condemnation appearing before a court of enquiry had considered the case and delivered its judgment.[110] Leopold was begged not to misunderstand his previous silence: if Marsigli's 'principal correspondents' in Vienna had heard nothing from him since the fall of Breisach it was in order not to prejudice an enquiry which would certainly demonstrate the neglect – by higher authority – of his own repeated testimony since December 1702 of the pitiable state of the town's defences. He therefore asked for an impartial investigation in which the issues were not prejudged by the same higher authority.

Then he went further. He said that one of the hardships attached to military justice was the customary delay between a tribunal's decision and its publication. In the long period used up by referrals to Vienna, the 'very fundamentals' of a soldier's honour and reputation were often unfairly prejudiced. He asked that this should not occur on the present occasion, in the present emergency, when such large numbers of loyal officers were at risk. Let judgment be as speedy as possible! He sent also a more personal plea to Leopold, written in Italian. He wished the ruler a happy New Year, recollecting his similar message from the Black Forest in easier circumstances a year earlier, and alluded as usual to his record of faithful service, his nineteen wounds, and his Turkish fetters. He begged, after the enquiry was over, for the privilege of a final interview behind the closed doors of His Majesty's study, in order to make certain disclosures which would never emerge during the formal proceedings. After that, he stated, he wanted to retire, giving up the command of an infantry regiment which he knew to be among the best in the army. One other letter, addressed to prince Eugene, informed him that Lewis of Baden was prejudicing a fair trial for the officers who had been at Breisach; and that Marsigli, after acquittal by an impartial tribunal which would have received his irresistible proofs of what had occurred there, intended to resign honourably from the service.

In his earlier feud with Starhemberg, Emperor Leopold's goodwill, however slow to declare itself, had been of the greatest ultimate importance to Marsigli. He still courted and perhaps relied on this element of absolute discretionary power, while preparations continued for the court of enquiry requested by the president of the War Council. It was decided that the tribunal should meet at Bregenz, a place not too remote for the personnel concerned. Duly constituted, it had to include two representatives of each military rank, from lieutenant up to general, to act as judges of their peers who were the thirty accused. Members of the Breisach garrison would be

equired to testify in favour of the official view of their numbers during the
siege, and the adequacy of their armament. An auditor-general would study
he papers and act for the enquiry. General Thüngen, as the senior
Habsburg officer in that part of Germany, would preside. By the end of
November, while forces in the field were going into winter quarters, and
general Villars returned (by way of Schaffhausen) to France, and even
Lewis of Baden withdrew northwards,[111] the inquest was nearly ready to
begin. Marsigli then left his quarters at Dogern. He and Arco had been
summoned to Bregenz.

The proceedings opened on 29 December in a room at the 'Lion' inn. An
outline of the case against the defendants was given, and by the end of the
day it became clear that charges of treason or corruption, as motives for the
surrender of Breisach, would not be pressed.[112] It was also accepted that
Arco did not receive Leopold's final order to hold out to the last; captain
Keyser of the Marsigli regiment had not arrived in time. Nor had a similar
letter, of a slightly earlier date, from Lewis of Baden. The court then
adjourned in order to give time for Arco, Marsigli and the rest to prepare a
written submission. It began work again on 7 January 1704. Meanwhile
another letter had been on its way from Vienna to Bregenz, from Eugene to
Thüngen, to say that he was forwarding to the Emperor his own recommendation that the court's sentences should be carried out immediately after
judgment, without further delay or appeal; and he hoped to inform
Thüngen of the Emperor's consent to this before the tribunal ended.[113]

Arco seems to have given up the struggle very early. Exhausted and
apathetic, he spent little time in preparing a statement. When the court
reassembled he put up the less resistance to the auditor-general, Johann
Maldoner. This expert on military law had discussed, in his published
work, the question of the mitigating circumstances which could be pleaded
by an officer who surrendered a fortress, in spite of instructions not to
do so.[114] He now confronted Marsigli, always so prompt and effusive in
defending his own conduct, and someone who made a lifelong habit of
keeping drafts or copies of the papers passing through his hands. Having
earlier submitted 99 written questions and objections to the court, Marsigli
also produced the detailed statements made by Arco and himself in the
course of 1703, showing how they had been given too few men and too little
artillery to defend the fortifications of Breisach against a powerful enemy.[115]
The garrison numbered 2500, not 3500 or 4000, let alone the force needed
to meet an assault with any chance of success. He could likewise show how
the council of officers held in Breisach on 6 September, after considering
the text of Lewis's letter of 30 June,[116] unanimously voted in favour of an
honourable capitulation, believing this to be the best service they could offer
the Emperor in the circumstances, since there was no prospect of help or
relief. The French command had agreed to the garrison's withdrawal on
favourable terms. Naturally, the auditor-general countered all this by pointing to the categoric orders of the commander in chief that Breisach should

be defended 'to the last man and the last drop of blood', and to official testimony that the troops and supplies of the garrison provided a sufficient force to defend it for a reasonable time.[117] Whether the accused were given a fair chance to show that the actual figures differed from the force on paper is not clear.

The discussions lasted several weeks and then each of the judges was called on to hand in a written opinion.[118] By 4 February these had been sifted and assessed by the president and auditor; behind its closed doors the court formally concluded that all the accused were guilty of breaches of the law and regulations by which they were bound. The judges differed, in a number of instances, on the degree of reponsibility shown by the accused and therefore on the severity of the penalty required; but the final result was a sliding scale of guilt and punishment imposed according to rank. In fact they had judged in accord with prince Eugene: they 'made an example' of those who had faltered at Breisach. Guilty were two generals, two colonels, two lieutenant-colonels, four majors, 8 captains, 9 lieutenants and 7 ensigns. Arco was sentenced to death. Marsigli, the court declared, merited death as the second in command but it settled for the lesser sentence of expulsion from the service with the stigma of degradation, *cum infamia*. The others were dismissed, although in a number of cases without incurring dishonour. The costs payable by the defendants were graded according to rank. All, without any exception, were to promise on oath never to enter the service of enemies of the Emperor, the Empire and allied powers. The remaining officers of the Breisach garrison, who had not been indicted, would have to swear that they took no part in the decision to surrender. Such were the verdicts and sentences, agreed at first in confidence, of the military court at Bregenz.[119]

Its president, Thüngen, hesitated. On 4 February no word had reached him confirming Eugene's message, so on the following day he sent a copy of the proceedings to Lewis of Baden in Germany, seeking authority to publish the sentences. The tribunal was asking for 24 officers, apart from Arco, to be dismissed from the army and he did not venture to move without clear instructions. Before Lewis replied, the expected document arrived from Vienna. On 2 February the War Council secretariat had recorded that the findings of the Bregenz tribunal were not to be subject to further confirmation or appeal, and it noted that count Marsigli himself was asking for a speedy decision.[120] The Emperor therefore signified his agreement with Eugene's wishes, and this essential notification was sent off to Bregenz. However, Thüngen still hesitated; he wanted to hear from Lewis, who then informed him that he was sending the papers to Vienna. Once he learnt this Thüngen hesitated no longer. He relied on the Emperor's ample authorisation to publish the verdicts and impose the sentences. On 14 February the fate of Arco, Marsigli and the rest was sealed by his decision to proceed, which was confirmed by the tribunal.[121]

Four days later the sentences on the two generals were carried out.

Marsigli's disgrace at Bregenz: he asked for this drawing to be added to his own account of his ⸍e.

According to a pamphleteer the weather was very cold, with flakes of snow drifting down at eight o'clock on the morning of Tuesday 18 February 1704 on the public square of Bregenz, close to the lakeside.[122] First Marsigli was brought out for the execution of his sentence, looking pale but staring alertly at the bystanders. These surrounded the guards who in turn were placed in a semi-circle round Marsigli. A sick man – suffering from gout, according to another account – he had to be brought there in a litter.[123] No drum or piper sounded as the auditor-general read out the sentence of dismissal and dishonour. Marsigli's sword, which had been in the keeping of the court, was produced. The executioner stepped forward and snapped it in pieces; it was said to be worth forty talers. Next, Marsigli was made to recite a promise on oath never to take up arms against the Emperor, the Empire or allied powers, and did so. The pamphlet states that his intention in future was to give up wearing a sword of any kind; and since that day he had worn semi-clerical dress like an abbé. It adds that he was preparing for a journey to Vienna, and hoped to defend his honour by appealing to the Emperor. Count Marsigli, concluded this narrative, is a bibliophile with a fine library, a linguist in the Turkish and Slavonic tongues, and a famous engineer.

The reporter next turned to his main theme, the 'tragic action' of Arco's execution as a public spectacle. At one moment in the ceremony Arco asked Marsigli for forgiveness, to which Marsigli responded; and Arco made a Christian oration to the crowd, before exchanging the splendid full wig he was wearing for a white sleeping cap. The executioner stepped forward again and his life was ended at a stroke.

Another description of Marsigli's bearing on the sad day at Bregenz, a statement sent by Thüngen to Lewis of Baden, differs in one significant respect.[124] According to this, because of his sickness, it was decided to let him take the oath pledging continued loyalty to the Emperor in his own quarters. Marsigli took the oath, and was then helped down the steps or stairs to the street, and carried outside to the square where the Saxon guard surrounded him. The sentence of dismissal was read out. His sword was broken into pieces by the executioners. Then, this version continues, 'without being asked to do so', he repeated aloud the oath of loyalty, advising every soldier present to take notice of his example. As another variant, one year later Marsigli printed his own story, which asserts that before his public humiliation he was compelled to give the pledge of loyalty, and then to repeat it, but adding that he protested in the presence of spectators in the square at Bregenz.

A terrible end for Arco. A terrible day for Marsigli, who may have deceived himself about the way he behaved and what he said, in a moment of illness and degradation. Certainly on one point he was mistaken. His sense of indignity and loss of status, he must have thought, followed an unaccountable loss of support at the highest level of Habsburg authority. Leopold's discretionary power, the affection once graciously offered to the eager, faithful, map-making, risk-taking and knowledgeable servant, had no longer operated to help him. His enemies were even stronger than before. Yet the Emperor did intervene to soften the judgment of the tribunal of Bregenz, if with peculiar feebleness.[125] When Thüngen sent the tribunal's papers to Lewis, who sent them on to the imperial court, Leopold reconsidered the matter in spite of the ruling already made. Leaving intact the sentence on Arco, he still thought of removing the stigma of dishonour from Marsigli's dismissal, and also from that of colonel von der Eck, another of the cashiered officers. He had Lewis informed, and Mansfeld – now vice-president and acting president of the War Council in Eugene's absence – wrote to Thüngen. Both commanders protested, and Thüngen explained how Marsigli had already publicly accepted the sentence by taking the oath of loyalty. After further correspondence the possibility of amending the sentence in Marsigli's case was left *in suspenso*. This accorded with Lewis of Baden's 'considered opinion', the minute noted. The rest was official silence. Marsigli himself heard not a whisper. He never knew that he was nearly spared the insult which drove him to frenzy, and dictated his actions for several years to come. If he had managed to summon up the boldness to protest more loudly on 18 February, and declined to swear submission while suffering the misfortune of dismissal, he might have survived more easily. For the oath, the 'Urfehde', was highly controversial at Bregenz in 1704. Thüngen had been perplexed to find, when the verdicts were announced, that all the officers concerned (except for Marsigli and one other) protested against the decision that they must take an oath of loyalty to the Emperor as well as submitting to dismissal from his forces. Their profession was the profession of arms, they said, and they must earn their bread from one master if not from another. Much discussion followed, and at length Thüngen expressed the hope that Leopold's prerogative of pardon could be used to solve the problem.[126] Certainly some of these men found their way back into the Habsburg service, where they were badly needed.

The shock of dismissal from the army, the insult of his degradation and the slight margin of his escape from Arco's fate, must have hurt Marsigli horribly. Three days afterwards he composed another letter to Leopold, in which a soliloquy on twenty-four years' service brought unjustly to a close prefaced an account of his present plans.[127] He was selling off his baggage and clothes to pay for the costs of litigation, and sending to Italy for more money. Once he had been released he would go to the Capucin house in Bregenz, before travelling to Vienna. His sword was taken from him; he would dress as an abbé. He wanted to appeal to the Emperor in person because the trial had been irregular. In this world, it might be, Lewis of Baden could use the sentence to cover his own gross neglect of the fortress of Breisach but in the next he would surely suffer a just judgment. A few days later Marsigli duly went to the Capucins.[128] There, in the presence of father Marcus Jacob and count Königsegg, the senior civilian office-holder in Bregenz, he protested formally against his conviction. He writes that they advised an appeal to the Emperor for clemency and justice. On 11 March count Marsigli (he enjoyed his military title no longer) received a passport authorising the journey to Vienna.[129]

He had also written to Scheuchzer, sorrowfully comparing himself with Emperor Justinian's general Belisarius.[130] Like that great man he was vilely treated although his life had been spared. Like him he would in due course recover honour and fame when the truth prevailed. He differed from Belisarius, perhaps, in continuing to fill up his time with discussions on science, and for this he could in part thank his new secretary. The younger Scheuchzer, reaching Bregenz after a journey from Maestricht to Dogern, made the acquaintance of his new patron during the dark days before the trial ended. They settled down together, and Marsigli was soon engaged again with congenial topics. Could the Zurich booksellers help him, he asked, by finding works on ancient and modern history for his library, for example Glotzius on coinage and the best editions of the Church Councils? He had already eight volumes of the *Hortus Malebarus*, but wanted the last four. And he was studying Woodward's work in the Latin version with great attention. Above all, on 8th March he reported making up his mind about the future. After Vienna, Bologna; and Guicciardini was sent orders a few days later to raise sufficient funds at home to pay all Marsigli's debts in Germany, Alsace and Switzerland.[131] He himself appears to have been confident that the material problems were fairly tractable. Habsburg pay and allowances, so often belated or incomplete and now suspended, were not necessities for him. What had been lost at Breisach and Bregenz was less tangible but more important, his occupation as Leopold's officer with which he associated honour and fame. In March 1704 he might be recovering a little from the calamity of his degradation. He could prepare for his journey to Vienna. He could pay his debts, and go on adding to his library. Yet if there was to be no reprieve he had still to decide whether he really wished to go home as a dishonoured commander.

VII

Vienna was not a placid or attractive city in the spring and summer of 1704. The spectres of the year before now had more substance. In January Passau surrendered to Max Emmanuel, opening a passage down the Danube for the combined French and Bavarians in the direction of the capital. It did not help that a furious row broke out between the cardinal-bishop of Passau and general Gronsfeld, the Habsburg commander who allegedly failed to defend the castle and town: the cardinal, it was reported, wanted the general to be brought to trial and, if found guilty, 'punished like Count Arco'.[132] More important, the revolution in Hungary was in these months encroaching into ever wider areas on the right as well as the left bank of the Danube, so that Styria in addition to Moravia and Lower Austria became vulnerable to raiding forces. For security's sake the bridges across the river at Vienna had been dismantled and prince Eugene was busy having new fortified lines built round the outskirts of the city. For many people these depressing items of news were overshadowed by a fresh attempt to screw up the state's finances. Church silver was taken to melt down, a new property tax was imposed, tolls went up on a diminishing supply of goods. At court the ageing Emperor, however frail and at his own slow tempo, still ruled as well as reigned.

Marsigli arrived safely on 1 April.[133] For the next dreary phase of his life not much evidence survives. This part of his correspondence may be lost but more probably he preferred to lie low, as if at last lacking the buoyancy to continue exchanging his views with scholars abroad and his own scientists in Bologna. He was a crestfallen hero and wanted first a vindication, but as the weeks passed his hopes diminished and then vanished. On 16 April he still wrote sturdily to Zurich.[134] It appeared to him that the Emperor and the entire court joined in condemning the proceedings at Breisach; significantly Leopold had not awarded the colonelcy of his regiment to any of the contenders. There would be difficulties ahead, because he wanted both an honourable dismissal and a settlement of his rrears, but he felt determined not to compromise. One move he made, therefore, was to assemble a dossier of his case and submit it to Moles, the Spanish diplomat in Vienna with a reputation for enjoying the Emperor's confidence, someone who could sidestep the ministers.[135] After that there is silence, as if nothing was happening. Nothing did happen, except that behind the doors now closed to Marsigli Leopold must have accepted Lewis of Baden's advice not to reconsider the Bregenz verdict. In consequence he stood no chance of securing permission to present himself to the ruler. Another month passed. While other sources show Leopold concentrating, wearily no doubt, on the growing tensions in both Germany and Hungary, Marsigli found the bailiffs raiding his apartment on 3 June to appease his creditors. He learnt also that his regiment had been assigned to one of the influential Jörger family. On 27 June he therefore wrote a 'last' (it was not the last) letter of reproach and farewell to the Emperor, which Dr Garelli undertook to pass on.[136] This was a threadbare gesture and he began to consider a new line of action.

The manuscript volumes of the great *Opus* had now arrived in Vienna; probably Muller, in Nuremberg, was following instructions to forward them. So, with some pleasure Marsigli handed the work to his new assistant.[137] It was ready for printing, he asserted, and in one way or another this could be arranged. In saying this he certainly deceived himself. Guicciardini, expected shortly in Vienna after paying off the debts owed in Germany and Switzerland, could also satisfy Marsigli's Viennese creditors. He could not find funds at this date for a very costly publishing venture. There was also the delicate, important question of the dedication to Emperor Leopold. The symbolic climax of the work, spelling out Marsigli's linkage of the River and the Sovereign, could it really be sustained in the face of such a shaming denial of the ruler's grace and favour? Reflecting on these matters Marsigli began to look at the problem from other aspects. The *Prodromus* was already the detailed statement which made a fuller publication desirable but not urgent. It had alerted the European public to the nature of his enquiries, and emphasised his priority in respect of them. More important was his present predicament, the degradation so unreasonably and unfairly suffered; and at this point the idea of an appeal against his sentence took on a new form. He would broadcast his own story in a manifesto which declared the injustice of the Bregenz tribunal and the nullity of its verdict. He would somehow give the world the truth about the fall of Breisach. Or, as young Scheuchzer put it in writing to his brother, if there were too many difficulties in getting an apologia of this kind published in Germany or Italy, theatres or war under Habsburg influence, would it not be possible to print and publish in Zurich a multilingual manifesto addressed to princes, nobility and scholars who formed the public conscience of Europe? This was Marsigli's latest inspiration.[138] By the end of July 1704, after the allied storming of the Schellenburg on the upper Danube just before the battle of Blenheim, he was working hard in Vienna on the draft of his appeal. The Danubian volumes were set aside while he turned to justify his record in the Emperor's service. This remarkable project inspired most of his journeys and consumed his energy during the next two years.

A part of our study ends here simply because Marsigli's chosen career had been cut off. The Habsburg authority disowned him. The Habsburg lands, east and west, were throwing him out. Under this heading there appears no more to say: we have learnt what we can from an uneven, if intermittently detailed narrative. But Marsigli's later adventures in territory new to him, while he tried to satisfy himself that he had cleared his name, contribute certain extra touches to the history of the early eighteenth century. He was far from idle and his achievements were considerable. Indeed, after many a summer it becomes possible to approach once more the printing of his work on the Danube.

CHAPTER NINE

A New World

I

On 12 August 1704 Guicciardini and Scheuchzer left Vienna together.[1] In their baggage were probably the manuscript volumes of the *Opus*, and certainly the draft of Marsigli's manifesto about the fall of Breisach, with copies of the documents supporting it. They went to Innsbruck, over the Brenner pass – sparing a glance for the Alpine vegetation – and then to Bologna, where the young Swiss found himself enjoying discussion with the scientists at work in the Marsigli household. Obeying his patron's orders he translated the German material on Breisach into French and Latin and, with some help from his new friends, into Italian. Meanwhile Guicciardini joined with Manfredi in submitting the manifesto to that oracular authority on Italian literary style, the Bolognese count Gian Giuseppe Orsi.[2] Orsi may be responsible for the sonorous and pathetic opening words of the final version. This too had to be translated into French, German and Latin. Almost more important, Guicciardini dealt with Marsigli's finances.[3] He brought from Vienna instructions (dated 3 and 12 August) to auction valuable silver ornaments which had previously been pledged, to sell land and raise money on the security of the count's property to the extent that the family entail permitted. He put this in hand, selling silver, porcelain and glass to a number of purchasers both in Bologna and Venice, after Marsigli's brother Filippo had persuaded their cousin Giorgio Duglioli – who was himself residing in Venice – to advance the funds needed to redeem the pieces already pledged at the *monte di pietà*. More desperate remedies had been considered, but were avoided by these loyal associates, who did not find it necessary to dispose of 'lo studioso' or the Turkish textiles and weapons 'to which the General was specially attached'.

On 13 August, the day after Marsigli's two servants departed from Vienna, the battle of Blenheim was fought. Before news of this reached him he may still have hoped for some revolution in court and government. For example, if Leopold had died and Joseph become Emperor – Joseph, who took note of Marsigli's advice at the siege of Landau two years earlier – while at the same time the Austrian presence in south Germany collapsed, the chance of an upheaval at court conceivably justified his long wait in Vienna. After the victory of Blenheim there could be no such change. The position of prince Eugene as the strongest man in the ministry and army was now unassailable, and Marsigli's further stay becomes harder to understand. He finally took his leave on 22 November, behaving like an ordinary traveller in quitting the town. He did not wish to appear a fugitive, he says, although the last box of his papers went with him.[4] After fifteen years he re-entered Italy, but without going to Bologna or even to Venice.[5] Somewhere on the Venetian mainland he waited for young Scheuchzer to come and join him. Rather sadly, it looks as if he lacked confidence at this stage to face or outface the old circle of his contemporaries at home or his relatives, clients and friends. Moreover Italy was no longer the land of his youth. He can have known relatively little in detail about the recent course of events there, or indeed about certain novelties in its intellectual climate. Yet the impact of both on his future would be considerable.

II

After the childless Carlos II of Spain died in November 1700, in accordance with his last will the Bourbon claimant Philip, duke of Anjou succeeded him. With astonishing speed the French government sent forces to protect Philip's inheritance in Lombardy. By the spring of 1701 they were in position along the eastern edge of the duchy of Milan, the left bank of the river Adige. They had a garrison in Mantua, with the reigning duke's consent. They were in Cremona, and across the Po. That famous Habsburg riposte, Eugene's descent into Italy from the Tirol, came too late. His victories gave Vienna the ability to maintain troops in limited areas, which were scattered between south Piedmont and the lands of Ferrara far down the Po, but Eugene was not at first strong enough to endanger the new Bourbon sovereignty. He did his best in the following campaign, but superior forces barred further progress. King Philip himself arrived from Spain during the summer of 1702. From Milan he went to Cremona and from there to Modena, which was occupied by French troops. Its ruler became a refugee in Bologna.

Duke Rinaldo II of Modena was always a firm Habsburg ally.[6] When the Emperor wanted a bride for his son Joseph the choice fell on the duke's sister-in-law, the Hanoverian princess Wilhelmina. She and her widowed mother resided in Modena, so that the betrothal had taken place with due festivity in the ancient Este stronghold on 15 July 1699.[7] Rinaldo's diplomacy, which prepared the way for this, was coloured partly by his inheritance of an enduring family vendetta with the Roman court, a feud aggravated a hundred years earlier when Pope Innocent VIII took back the papal fief of Ferrara from its Este rulers. Papal government in Ferrara during the seventeenth century, in Este eyes, appeared a usurpation. The territory of Modena, another part of the patrimony, was by contrast a fief of the Empire. Rinaldo, acquiring his title in 1696, had been quick to cultivate friendly relations with Vienna, and was aware that the presence of Habsburg forces in north Italy (before 1696), helped to renew the latent tension between Rome and Vienna. The chanceries of the two governments, Este and Habsburg, therefore began to rehearse once again the historic jurisdictional arguments for the Empire and against the Papacy. A general war over the Spanish succession would see this conflict carried further, with the duke of Modena and even Marsigli playing roles at the front of the stage.

Involved also was Marsigli's younger contemporary Muratori, at the start of his remarkable career. A youth in Modena in the 1690s, his inspiring teacher, the Benedictine scholar and journalist Bacchini,[8] and some discerning patrons, all encouraged him. Count Orsi, who had been long in duke Rinaldo's circle, and our Marsigli's elder brother Antonio Felice, helped Muratori to secure a post at the Ambrosian Library of Milan, where he first dipped deeply in the waters of early church history. But in 1700 Rinaldo – as duke of Modena – summoned back his erudite young subject: he wanted a curator to look after his library and archives. There had been neglect, it was alleged, ever since many Este papers and charters were hastily removed from Ferrara to Modena a century earlier. Rinaldo needed efficiency and scholarship in his archive to help in maintaining his hereditary legal claims against Rome and other neighbour states. Muratori took up his new post in August 1700. Then the new war began and by August 1702 the French were in the town. Rinaldo removed to Bologna, while the books and charters which Muratori needed for his work had been hidden away. He turned his attention to themes for which he could more easily find material; sometimes he worked in Bologna and took holidays in Orsi's villa.[9]

Among other famous writings of this period Muratori composed the 'Primi disegni della repubblica letteraria dell' Italia'.[10] Its argument expounded with verve and fluency several of the ideas which attracted our Marsigli. The experience of the two men may have been very different. Their conclusions were in approximate harmony, but with Muratori displaying in addition a strong vein of literary patriotism. Like Orsi, he reacted vehemently against recent French critics of Italian literature. Like his master Bacchini he was greatly impressed by the collective scholarship of the French Benedictines and the Belgian Bollandists, as well as by the organised patronage of experimental science in the Académie des Sciences and the Royal Society. Muratori lamented that the predominant intellectual habit of educated Italians, by contrast, was merely to attend gatherings in which the entertainment was 'verses, and still more verses'. He declared that these were academies in little more than name. They dealt in trifles, without a proper study of the great Italian writers or of the significant historical and scientific questions which increasingly absorbed the learned world north of the Alps. Muratori's notion of the true 'literary republic of Italy' therefore became a plea for a new approach and a new organisation, a nationwide academy of knowledge in which the membership was select, the topics for study were critically appraised, and the connection between all branches of useful knowledge had been grasped by everyone involved. Italy, if the Italians accepted these 'first proposals', would soon be able to hold up its head again among the progressive nations of Europe. Muratori was advisedly Baconian, intent on both the dignity and the increase of learning. He criticised the frivolity and sloth of his countrymen in their universities and academies, whereas true knowledge deserved to be taken 'seriously'. Hence the case for union and reform.

This manifesto was published in Venice early in 1704 under a pseudonym, and met with a varied reception. Bacchini, not surprisingly, welcomed it and pointed out that in Bologna, thanks to the enlightened generosity of general Marsigli, a group of serious men had recently started to co-ordinate their work in just the spirit recommended by the author. He thought that Marsigli himself would be a very suitable director, or 'archon', of the organisation with which Muratori proposed to reform education and learning in Italy. But after stimulating a good deal of discussion the scheme gradually faded from the view of contemporaries. Muratori's suggestions were overshadowed by the continuing, more attractive rival appeal of 'Arcadia' in the early eighteenth century. This Roman literary academy had been founded in 1691, and a host of other academies in towns all over Italy were affiliated to it in the course of a few years. The Arcadians felt satisfied by the ideal of writing and declaiming in a purer style of prose and poetry than that practised by their immediate predecessors. They looked backward to an older, allegedly more glorious, commonwealth of Italian and Latin literature. Notions of intellectual progress, of historical and ecclesiastical debate, rarely concerned them as they did Muratori, and he stood apart from Arcadia. His interests increasingly veered towards historical scholarship and religious experience, but when the war of the Spanish succession began he shared with Orsi a heartfelt desire to defend the best of Italian literature against foreign critics. In a work published in 1703 the count's heavy artillery began to thunder against the stylistic judgment of certain French authors.[11] Muratori adopted the same patriotic view in an essay of 1706 on a similar theme, 'Della perfetta poesia italiana'.

One of the Arcadians was Manfredi the mathematician and astronomer, but equally the gifted poet. Curator of Marsigli's apparatus and books, in 1704 and 1705 he seems to have withdrawn from the palazzo Marsigli, leaving his colleague Stancari to direct the group who met there.[12] The larger scientific society of the Inquieti also moved into Marsigli's rooms, with Stancari as secretary, and several of the most promising university lecturers or readers appeared at these assemblies, including Jacopo Beccari – another polymath and experimentalist – and the young physician Morgagni. In 1704 Morgagni had persuaded his colleagues to accept new, stiffer procedures for testing any work submitted to them. This followed the example recently set by Académie des Sciences in Paris, and echoed the thoughts of Marsigli in Germany on this topic in 1702. So Arcadia, however attractive, had by no means smothered the impulse of a chosen few to persevere in other fields as well.

The warfare, the politics, the literary movement, the group of natural philosophers at work in Bologna, present together a confusing scene north and south of the river Po. In 1708, after Habsburg forces had recovered their predominance in Italy, while the causes of friction between Emperor and the Pope led to open hostility between them, Marsigli intervened directly. Having done so, he joined (in his own fashion) the intellectual debate. Before this remarkable homecoming, a zigzag course took him to Switzerland, Paris and Provence.

III

Scheuchzer duly brought back from Bologna the precious text of the manifesto on Breisach, revised and complete.[13] Then he was sent to Venice to ask the Spanish ambassador for a passport to enter Bourbon territory, and other places occupied by French or Spanish forces. We must guess that Marsigli never considered travelling directly from Vienna to Switzerland; the route across the Vorarlberg was rarely used in this period. Nor could he go from Venice via the Grisons, because Habsburg troop communications blocked the way. Instead the two men, patron and secretary, set out towards the end of the year 1704 across the plains on each side of the Po and went first to Ferrara and then Modena. Here the French officers of the garrison looked attentively at the passport, and allowed Marsigli to continue his journey on his promise to report in Milan to the duc de Vaudemont, the Lorraine prince who was governor-general for the Spanish king. He welcomed the opportunity. Indeed Vaudemont treated him with the greatest courtesy, condemning the injustice of the Austrians and approving the idea of a published apologia. After this interview Marsigli hurried on, leaving us no details of his winter crossing of the Alps which ended surprisingly at Zug. This little capital of the canton of that name had doubtless been recommended for its position, between and conveniently close to Protestant Zurich and Catholic Lucerne. Zug enjoyed what Marsigli called a popular democratic constitution which allowed him to reside there, and come and go freely. It was ideal for reconnaissance in unfamiliar country. On 11 January 1705 he wrote to the elder Scheuchzer that he had just arrived; he was already making friends, among them members of the Zurlauben family who were influential people in the town and canton. From this moment the web of his preoccupations in Switzerland becomes gradually visible. A year of the greatest activity began.

His first concern was for printing and distributing his manifesto.[14] The texts he had with him took the form of a personal account of the siege of Breisach, followed by a set of documents and diagrams. There were versions in Italian, German, French and Latin. The part played by Marsigli between December 1702 and August 1703 was described, with heavy emphasis on his repeated warnings to Lewis of Baden and the court in Vienna. The defences of Breisach were in ill repair. The garrison was too small. Count Arco behaved in the most arbitrary manner possible to his second in command. The author then tried to show that the Bregenz tribunal had been misdirected, while his final appeal against its decisions was choked off by malice. He professed a deep respect towards the Emperor whom he had served so long with such slight reward, but nonetheless wished to clear his name in the minds of honourable men. Like so much of Marsigli's literary work it was a curious compilation, disjointed and by no means complete. He showed flair in retrieving and preserving materials but used them with some awkwardness. The fall of Breisach, after even a short interval, had proved relatively inconspicuous in the general history of the period, though Marsigli and his good friends in Bologna and Switzerland tried hard to revive interest in what happened there. It was only in Zug that he learnt what he might have anticipated. Scheuchzer (the elder), having read the manuscript and taken soundings, could not believe that the city fathers of Zurich would allow it to be printed anywhere in their jurisdiction.[15] The untidy frontier between the Empire and the Swiss Cantons posed problems enough in 1705, and Zurich saw every reason to avoid giving more offence than necessary to the Habsburg court. Momentarily Marsigli was aghast to hear this, and wondered whether to alter all his plans and return to Italy. Then his friends in Zug pointed out that their municipality had far less control over and responsibility for the press than might have been the case in Zurich, and put him in touch with the local printers. Marsigli quickly came to terms, while deploring in his finicky way the poor quality of the paper and print available, and the men of Zug set to work.[16] Within a month the curious amalgam about Breisach and Bregenz entitled *Informazione*, *Information*, *Exposé* or *Relatio* according to language, was ready for distribution. In each version the narrative ended with an engraved emblem, showing a large capital 'M' entwined with the two pieces of a sword broken in half and with the two words: 'Fractus Integro' 'although my sword is broken, my spirit revives'. Then followed the documents, printed in double columns. On the left-hand side of a page was the German original, on the right a French, Italian or Latin translation. At the end were five diagrams showing the town of Breisach, its fortifications and the progress of the siege. These look like Marsigli's own work, touched up or redrawn here and there by a better draughtsman in Bologna.

Copies of this strange little composition were addressed to a large number of people of note in various countries. They included foreign ambassadors in Switzerland, the reigning princes of Italy, the cardinals and

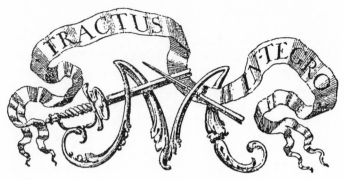

27 'Fractus Integro'.

other members of the Roman court, the Académie des Sciences in Paris, the Royal Society of London, and certain booksellers. In some cases quickly, in others slowly or not at all, acknowledgments flowed back to Marsigli.[17] Their bland expressions of goodwill gave him pleasure, but were counter-balanced at an early stage by news of a hostile pamphlet in circulation denouncing his conduct. He tried for several weeks to lay hands on a copy, believing it to be the work of the auditor-general of the Bregenz tribunal and inspired by Lewis of Baden. In Zug on 14 May he was still baffled, but two days later reported in high spirits that he now possessed the 'famosa risposta anonima'.[18] Enclosing a copy he asked Scheuchzer in Zurich to make him a Latin version of the German original. He himself began a detailed and spirited reply. The anonymous opponent, justifying his title of 'the Pretended Innocence of Generals Arco and Marsigli', had methodically assembled eighteen points on which he held that Marsigli's apologia was erroneous, and derided the idea that the two men were unjustly sentenced. Marsigli, adapting or repeating his earlier pleas while adding new material, drafted a reply under each of the eighteen headings.[19] In a few days these answers, together with the Latin translation of the obnoxious pamphlet, were assembled and sent to Italy for the comments of his relatives and advisers in Bologna. Marsigli also persuaded himself that his family would wish to have a finely printed copy of his work, as a record to hand on to posterity.

As usual, business did not absorb him entirely. There are traces of his presence in Zurich, of meeting Scheuchzer at long last and seeing the sights of the city,[20] but he paid the first of many visits to Lucerne before the end of March,[21] and went off to see the great abbey of Einsiedeln, east of Zug. The abbot had acknowledged receipt of the manifesto, and Marsigli for his part displayed interest in current plans for rebuilding the abbey church. Another place visited was Altdorf on the Achsenstrasse at the south end of the Lake of Lucerne. Its remarkable scenery fired his enthusiasm, and as a geologist he could hardly have done better than take note of the spectacular rock formations near Altdorf. When he tried, in later years, to elaborate his ideas about the principal types of stratification in mountain country, what he had seen and sketched by the lakesides of Uri and Zug provided him with some splendid examples.[22] A related matter, in 1705, was his awareness that

Scheuchzer in Zurich had ideas for a journey through the Bernese and St Gotthard ranges during the coming summer, accompanied by some virtuoso friends. It was part of his programme for a scientific survey of the Alps, and attracted Marsigli's interest.

In spite of these diversions, the thought of redress or revenge was still his current obsession. A published statement proclaiming his honourable conduct at Breisach was one thing. Another was some sort of legal instrument by which he might annul in a formal manner the oath arbitrarily imposed at Bregenz. Marsigli associated this idea with the more daring and dangerous proposition that he would then be lawfully free to offer his services to the Emperor's enemies, the Bourbon crowns of Spain and France. When he went from Zug to Lucerne it was to visit the Spanish ambassador to the Catholic cantons, count Beretti. When he explained to Scheuchzer his anxiety to lay hands on a copy of the 'Pretended Innocence' it was because he had already arranged to make a sworn statement to notaries in Lucerne repudiating the Bregenz oath: in the statement he wanted a mention of his latest rebuttal of the false accusations against him.[23]

The correspondence during June has much to say about the arrangements in Zug for printing this second multilingual blast of Marsigli's trumpet. He still pined for an elegant 'volumetto' fit for the gaze of future generations, which the Zug printers were unable to provide. On the other hand he gave up the plan of attesting a formal statement in Lucerne. A summons from Vaudemont – who remained the governor-general in Lombardy – had arrived, asking him go to Milan.[24] If all went well the offer of a commission from the Spanish crown was anticipated, and the legal formalities were to be settled in Italy. Marsigli also wanted to arrange for young Scheuchzer's future employment, and the offer of a commission in one of the Swiss regiments in Bourbon service appeared possible. It was felt advisable, however, that he should present himself to the right people in Milan as well as in Lucerne.[25] At the end of the month, therefore, they got ready for their next journey across the Alps. Marsigli, in one of his letters, spared just a moment's thought for another world remote in space and time; he wondered whether a final package of engraved copperplates for the Danubian *Opus* had reached Bologna from Nuremberg.

They set out for the pass of St Gotthard. Their timetable, the urgency of business, did not allow for a meeting with the elder Scheuchzer who crossed the St Gotthard route a few weeks later, his party moving from east to west in the Bernese Oberland to carry out their survey. Emulating his methods, however, Marsigli measured barometric pressures at intervals between Altdorf and the summit of the pass, unfortunately breaking the instrument on the way down.[26] In Milan the scene changed, and he was quickly alert to reports that Austrian troops under prince Eugene were leaving their quarters near Lake Garda for the summer campaign. He evidently hoped to have his share in the fighting but – evidence is unfortunately sparse at this point – something went seriously wrong. Perhaps Beretti in Lucerne had been misunderstood by Marsigli, but when he actually appeared before Vaudemont and his advisers they objected, cautiously, that the question of employing a former Imperial officer ought first to be referred to Madrid.[27] *O fata, O fata,* he groaned in a letter of 19 July, as he faced the prospect of an indefinite delay without securing any commitment to make him a suitable offer. Then his mood changed again. Someone must have intimated that the duc de Vendôme, commanding Louis XIV's forces in Italy, would be able to accept him. This was the reason why, only a few days later, he was able to bring his autobiographical writing up to date in a mood of optimism and satisfaction. To paraphrase the closing words of this moving fragment:

> *I am here in Milan on 4 August 1705. Vaudemont, the French ambassador, and Beretti, have all approved my wish to take up arms again, this time in the French service. When I leave it will be the beginning of a new era, to be described at a later date.*

Nine days later, on 13 August, Marsigli duly read aloud to an assembly of Milanese notaries, protonotaries and witnesses a solemn statement cancelling the oath which barred him from the service of princes who were in arms against the Emperor or his allies. It was an oath extorted by a Habsburg tribunal after an unjust verdict and sentence. He took it in the threatening presence of 30 Saxon fusiliers. He referred to his original protest at Bregenz, to his appeal in Vienna unheard, and to his published manifestoes. Immediately after the ceremony copies of a notarial document attesting the statement were made, amd then posted via Venice to ministers and chanceries in Vienna.[28] It was a further decisive move in Marsigli's singular defence of his honour and freedom, and he believed that he now had the fullest possible right to offer his sword to whom he would.

The elements of exaggeration and delusion in this stance were tested at once. Neither Vaudemont nor Vendôme really knew what do with the awkward soldier of fortune on their doorstep until a French diplomat, the abbé de Pomponne in Venice, suggested an answer which looked attractive and sensible to everybody concerned except Marsigli. Surely a man so experienced in the warfare of eastern Europe, the hero of so many campaigns against the Turks before Carlowitz, should go back to Hungary. In that kingdom prince Rákóczi's insurrection was a potent auxiliary of the French resistance to the Grand Alliance, and a point of weakness in the Habsburg defences. Louis XIV, although unwilling to recognise the prince as a lawful sovereign, had already offered him funds and technical aid.[29] Early in 1705 a French political agent and a group of French officers including engineers were sent; Rákóczi badly needed experts to assist his forces in the capture and defence of fortified places. Marsigli seemed to the French just the person suited for such a posting. He himself was aghast to hear this. To go back to Hungary in order to join the rebels, and to do so without necessarily holding any regular commission from the king of France, looked to him as repulsive as it was dangerous. He wanted something better from his new patrons, and resisted. At that moment the Bourbon forces under Vendôme and Vaudemont were directly threatened by Eugene's latest advance towards Milan. The campaign absorbed the commanders' attention, and they had no more time for Marsigli. He was advised to return to Switzerland while their excellencies reconsidered his case. It was a dreadful disappointment, while he prepared hastily for another journey. Their excellencies, it can be added, did not know what else Marsigli had been doing. In Milan he found time to commission a painting of the Annunciation which he wished to present to his friends in Zug, to hang in the council chamber of their Rathaus. He also showed a professional architect (unfortunately not named) the current plans for rebuilding at Einsiedeln; he wanted comments, in the form of a detailed recommendation, to take back with him to Switzerland.[30] In Milan it was likewise a pleasure to have the news from Zurich. Marsigli replied with congratulations to Scheuchzer on completing his great scientific 'Bergreise', the tour of the Bernese Oberland, and judged it a wonderful stimulus for more surveys of a similar kind.

He mentions a single incident during his own traverse back to Lucerne.[31] After passing through Bellinzona in atrocious weather, a horse fell into the swollen stream of the Ticino and his luggage was damaged. Luckily, as he wrote to Einsiedeln, among his papers the Milan architect's drawing for rebuilding the abbey was spared. The loss of a wig mattered less! But safe in Switzerland again, upset by what had happened or failed to happen in Milan, Marsigli began to consider a new plan. It jostled for a while with the earlier proposals that still engaged his hopes. Then it triumphed and swept him off on a different course.

On 11 September Beretti in Lucerne wrote to the French ambassador Puysieulx, resident at Soleures: count Marsigli, having returned from Milan, was now saying that he intended to go next to France on the duc de Vaudemont's advice. Puysieulx and Beretti both understood well enough that Vaudemont wanted above all to get rid of him,[32] but Marsigli in fact felt unwell and was in the hands of a doctor.[33] That certainly justified the new brainwave: if neither the Spanish nor the French government offered him a suitable post, and Vienna ignored his final warning duly sent from Milan, he would make his way to Montpellier in Languedoc. There, as he knew, the physicians were good, the climate was warm and serene, and the distinguished scientific company in residence would attract him. With this thought in mind he applied to Puysieulx, who played the courteous diplomat in responding. He regretted that Marsigli would not consider a mission in Hungary, declared that going to Montpellier for any other than strictly medical reasons was 'bizarre', and warned that a passport would be necessary. He also wrote to the French minister, Torcy, who duly had a passport drawn up for Marsigli, but added a summons in the name of Louis XIV that he should come first to Paris.[34] The Hungarian project was to be aired again at the French court.

There was another thread to be untangled. During the autumn nothing caused Marsigli more vexation than what he thought of as young Scheuchzer's incompetence. He had been sent to Zug again to see that the text of the formal repudiation of the Bregenz oath was translated and printed like the earlier documents of Marsigli's case. There were delays, and Marsigli himself made several journeys from Lucerne to hurry things along. His grumbling echoed the younger man's complaint to their common correspondent, the patient elder brother in Zurich: count Marsigli might huff and puff but he, John Scheuchzer, a Protestant, simply could not interfere with the priority given by the Zug printer to running off propaganda material for Catholic missionaries, who were just then trying to stir up the faith of the local population. They came first.[35] In the end Marsigli's latest appeal as an aggrieved officer of Leopold's army was printed and published, and his business in the little town was nearly complete. He handed over to a well-known architect, Caspar Mosbruggen, the proposal he had been given in Milan for the building at Einsiedeln. This in effect transformed Mosbruggen's own earlier design and influenced a partial reconstruction of the abbey church some years later.[36]

Every time Marsigli returned from Zug, observers in Lucerne wondered what he would do next. He said that he had to go back to Milan. He referred to Montpellier. He felt ill but dashed away again to Zug or Altdorf. His restlessness bewildered them, but for several weeks his own view seems to have been that he should watch and wait a little longer. The French or the Spaniards must make him a proper offer; the new Emperor, Joseph, might still reward his persistence. Beretti and the papal nuncio finally came round to the notion that he meant to go to Montpellier if nothing else turned up, while he himself decided on one more trip to Milan. Another guess made by those who knew him was that he wanted to go to Milan to pick up remittances from Bologna.[37] Funds usually reached him via Zurich. Anticipating that he would join the Bourbon forces in Italy, may he have given fresh instructions for the money to be sent to Milan? Whatever the motive, a wish to serve in Italy, a need for funds, or his usual itch to be on the road, Marsigli crossed the St Gotthard again at the end of October.

Unfortunately no letters to, from, or about him give an account of the next few weeks. He reappears, writing from Zug on 29 November, and the diplomats revert to him in their correspondence.[38] At last Marsigli's path forward became clearer to all. He intended to make for Soleures to meet Puysieulx, and then for Paris. The Swiss chapter was nearly over.

IV

Marsigli spent January and February 1706 in Paris. One of the most interesting and enjoyable periods of his life, it was compounded as usual of various elements. First, he had to learn what the French government proposed for him, and decide how to respond. As a commander who believed himself wronged and dishonoured by the Habsburg court in the eyes of the world, there was a wonderful balm about the welcome given him in France. Writing back to his friends in Switzerland and Italy he magnified all the marks of courtesy and exaggerated his own role.[39] Summoned to Versailles he first caught a glimpse of Louis XIV while standing in the gallery with Philippe Amontant (that notable designer of improved chronometers); the king looked vigorous enough for his sixty-eight years. Then occurred what the French diarist Dangeau calls simply 'une petite audience', but Marsigli describes a scene in the course of which he made a long statement defending his conduct at Breisach. The king interrupted him, expressing his own conviction of the count's integrity and the enemy's injustice. The irrepressible Italian resumed, and once more Louis broke in with the same emphatic statement. An audience of courtiers and other nobles was quick, immediately afterwards, to congratulate Marsigli. For the next day or two he lived happily in the world of his imagination, in which the greatest of kings led a chorus of the good and great to wash away the filth of the Bregenz tribunal. He informed Scheuchzer that he no longer felt it necessary to ask for a hearing in the *tribunal des maréchaux*,[40] where the marshals of France normally adjudicated in affairs of honour. The king's verdict was sufficient. He had considered taking his case to the courts of honour in England and Holland but now he would stop worrying about the good name of Marsigli. It was secure, and the manifesto of 1705 was obsolete. A hideous injustice, at least outside the Habsburg dominions and the Empire, was rolled away.

In this atmosphere of royal goodwill he had to show the greater fortitude to resist pressure from Louis XIV's advisers. After the audience Marsigli had been entertained to dinner by Torcy in a company which included the Spanish and Venetian ambassadors. There followed a private interview of 'two full hours' with the minister, who gave a general survey of European affairs before bringing the discussion round once more to the question of Hungary. He quoted recent messages which emphasised the firmness of the Magyars' will to resist.[41] Then Torcy moved on to refer to the new fortifications needed at Turin, and to the latest plan for protecting the harbour at Port Mahon in Minorca. To judge from the first of Marsigli's surviving letters, after this conversation there was no definite offer of a mission to Hungary, and therefore no positive statement by Marsigli in reply. A second letter, probably written a week later, has Marsigli roundly affirming to Torcy that he would not accept any commission which failed to associate him with troops bearing the French colours. If he fought in Hungary it must be on the understanding that he was enrolled among the regular forces of Louis XIV: 'I would rather be a humble musketeer in the standing troops of the Most Christian King than serve with rebels and hold the rank of a general'.[42] The letter added that he was shortly going again to Versailles 'to test the depth of the water', in order to decide whether to stay longer in

Paris waiting for something suitable, or to leave and go to Montpellier while placing himself at the king's disposal. At first he still hoped for an honourable posting to the French armies in Italy, Spain or elsewhere, as the war moved from one climax to another in different areas of western Europe. On the other hand he is unlikely to have formed a realistic idea of the sharpness of competition, during the winter of 1705–6, for commissions in the French armed forces.[43] Patronage counted for much in the selection of senior officers, and Marsigli himself had no friends in France except for the virtuosi of Paris with whom he was spending his leisure.

Indeed, while waiting first on the goodwill of Versailles and then for a seat in the diligence going to Lyon, en route for Montpellier, the civilised pleasures of Paris enchanted him.[44] For a moment he was even the conventional traveller. He went to Notre-Dame, viewed the Bastille and the Invalides, walked in the garden between the Tuileries and Louvre. At Versailles he thought poorly of the staircases, admired the Hall of Mirrors, but reserved higher praise for the stables. He was much impressed by the manner in which the collections of coins and medals were displayed: the design of the cupboards and drawers, the juxtaposition with mirror glass and carving. However he also followed his particular bent by seeking out the scientists of the capital. They included the younger Cassini, who showed him the Observatory with its rotating telescopes, and discussed the famous meridian line through Paris which French astronomers had been plotting north and south across France since its inception in 1679. He visited Jean Méry the anatomist and Homberg the chemist, but passed as much time as possible with Joseph Pitton de Tournefort and his splendid collections of fish, shells, fossils, fruits, seeds, minerals, corals and marine plants. The last two of these, Tournefort's corals and plants, may have helped in attracting Marsigli towards a fresh concern for what he called 'the natural history of the sea'. It echoed his earlier work on the straits of the Bosphorus and the Danube, and merged with ideas absorbing him more recently. Writing from Paris in January, he reminded Scheuchzer in Zurich of their common concern with the structure of the mountain ranges of Europe, and for the first time extended the argument to the Jura (recently crossed on his journey from Soleures to Besançon and Paris), and to the Pyrenees.[45] A fresh conjunction of interests was evidently taking hold of his imagination: the geology of mountains, coasts, the sea shores and the sea bed, the nature of marine plants and of coral formation, and the possible relationship between them all. This would engross his studies in the south of France. But while he was in Paris something occurred which made the plan of a journey to Montpellier still more attractive. By chance, and for once, Marsigli's timing appeared perfect.

For several years past an enlightened group had been trying to set up an officially authorised scientific society in Montpellier.[46] Their patrons included Colbert, bishop of the diocese, and Lamoignon de Basville, the intendant of Languedoc, but most of them were intelligent and prosperous officeholders in the provincial 'Cour des Comptes, Aides et Finances', who wanted to encourage experiment and fieldwork of a kind which did not normally attract professors in the town's university faculties. Their opportunity came, it seemed, when Cassini had arrived in Montpellier in 1701 with a mission of astronomers, surveyors and cartographers. These experts lodged with a counsellor of the Cour des Aides, and their business was to resume work on an enterprise suspended during the recent war, and plot the Paris meridian as far as the Mediterranean coast. An old argument that the clarity of the atmosphere in the south recommended this region as a centre for astronomical study, together with the high reputation of Montpellier's medical faculty and its botany garden, were no doubt urged on Cassini to justify the foundation there of an officially sponsored academy. The enthusiasts with whom he came into contact, and Cassini himself, appreciated that the secretary of state responsible for arts and sciences, Pontchartrain, took this part of his duties seriously. Not long since he had reorganised the Académie des Sciences in Paris, his nephew abbé Bignon was its new president, and Fontenelle its new permanent secretary: both wished to encourage the ties between scientists in Paris and those elsewhere, in the French provinces and abroad. If a literary academy in the neighbouring town of Nîmes could be associated with the Académie Française, as was the case since 1692, a useful link between the virtuosi of Montpellier and Paris was surely acceptable.

Cassini promised to help but the war of the Spanish succession broke out almost at once. He either could not or did not press the matter. Then in 1705 a further plea from Montpellier reached Paris. The intendant of Languedoc again used his influence to urge the project, and in February 1706 Louis XIV finally issued a foundation charter for the 'Société Royale des Sciences' of Montpellier. This was modelled on the reorganised society in Paris with which it was formally associated, and at 8 o'clock in the morning of 12 May the inauguration took place in a garden adjoining the city wall.[47] Everybody who was anyone in Montpellier had turned up to watch, while the astronomers of the new society manipulated their instruments, and the sun was duly eclipsed by the moon. It is hard not to believe that Marsigli was there, because he had already written two interesting letters from Montpellier on 28 and 30 March.[48] The first states that members of the new society desired to open a correspondence with Manfredi and his colleagues in Bologna, and asserted somewhat rashly that the people there would be more worth cultivating than the similar group in Paris. The other letter simply says that he both enjoyed and suffered from too much company, and felt that he needed to get away, and do some work. He was as good as his word. In the year of the battle of Ramillies and of prince Eugene's victorious march with the Austrian forces across Lombardy to Turin, when the whole balance of power in Europe received its most violent shock since the beginning of the war, Marsigli made for the Mediterranean.

He intended to observe natural phenomena along the coast and carry out experiments.

During the next two years the search for news about him is often like looking for cowrie shells on a beach among the stones and sand. He was busy but apparently wrote no letters to his older correspondents, until at last a surprising apology for the long silence reached Scheuchzer, dated from Lyon in January 1708.[49] You will be astonished to hear from me, it says, but I have travelled widely and worked hard. Money has been safely coming through from Italy month by month; letters from Zurich can be forwarded through the French ambassador to the Cantons; my agent at Marseille is M. Bartoli, Castiglione my banker in Lyon. Much more important, Marsigli announces that he has now written in French an 'Essai physique de l'histoire naturelle de la Mer' expounding his notion that the geological structure of the European continent continues under the sea bed. A work in five parts, the fourth included 'the brilliant discovery' that corals produces flowers; the fifth was not yet complete. What Marsigli told his friend in 1708 anticipated by many years the publication of his *Histoire Physique de la Mer* in 1725, but the printed volume in turn lets slip certain details about his time in Languedoc and Provence. Documents from the Montpellier academy have recently been added to these,[50] and a sketch of his travels by land and sea along the Mediterranean shore becomes possible.

His first excursion took him westwards to the coast of Lower Languedoc, that extraordinary littoral of sand and marsh which lies on either side of Cette.[51] Guided by a knowledgeable colleague and naturalist from Montpellier, a member of the new academy, he was certainly fascinated by a scene new to him, and after taking advice determined on a second venture. Accordingly he was in Provence in May and June, moving from Marseille to the little harbour of Cassis where he quickly came to terms with the local fishermen.[52] He paid, and they took him with them for a cruise of nine days, and told him what they knew. Probably they went along the riviera as far as Hyères and returned again, so that by 18 June Marsigli was analysing the constituent elements of sea water off the islands of Ratonneau and Pomèges, not far from Marseille.[53] On 15 July he made a further analysis at Port-de-Bouc, and the following day was opposite the Rhône's main outlet. His boat continued westward as far as Cette where he went ashore and with a vast haul of shells, sponges, coral and other fragments returned to Montpellier. Here the 'Société Royale' had settled down to an orderly programme, meeting weekly. Its members were accordingly happy to listen to Marsigli (now speaking sufficient French) when he addressed them on 12 and 19 August. His lectures concerned that long-disputed problem, the vegetable or mineral nature of coral.[54]

Coral greatly excited Marsigli. It often overshadowed his general theme of geological continuities between land masses and the sea bed, and what he had to say on the subject provoked hot debate. He himself felt convinced, after this first inspection in Provence, that coral was formed like crystals: branches of coral were what he called 'concrétions marines pierreuses . . . sans semences', and on this premise he examined what was shown him by the fishermen. The alkaline sap in the substance of coral was simply a part of the phenomenon. This view bewildered the Montpellier botanists. In particular Pierre Magnole (whose name the magnolia celebrates) followed the teaching of his Paris colleague Tournefort; he could not bear to think of the vegetable kingdom being deprived in this way, if coral was denied the status of a plant simply on the basis of Marsigli's assertion. In a contribution of 2 September he dissented, and other speakers joined in until everyone sensibly agreed on the need for further research. Marsigli was still in Montpellier early in November, busy calculating the weight of samples of local river water, but from there he set out for a second visit to Provence. On the way he took more samples of water from the Rhône,[55] but reached the sea again, and after a spell of bad weather moved on to Marseille. Here he made more friends and continued to discuss the properties of coral, before returning to Cassis to set up what he called his 'laboratory'. It seems that he paid no attention to the current rumours of armies and navies preparing for an allied attack on Toulon, Louis XIV's naval base further along the coast. A spell of intensive work began.

Marsigli went first with his boatmen on an expedition to the 'Grande Chandelle', a point off the shore where conditions were normally favourable for the coral searchers.[56] What he particularly wanted was to examine the milky sap which coral produces, and to do so immediately after pieces or branches of it were broken off and brought aboard the boat. On this occasion, or perhaps on a second trip – apparently without further thought – he put some of the pieces into containers filled with sea water, and carried them to Cassis. Greatly to his surprise these mysteriously produced or grew 'flowers' by the next morning, which he had never seen before. Nor had the phenomenon been mentioned by anyone in Montpellier. It disproved his own assertion that corals were mineral, not vegetable. He considered this so remarkable that he wrote at once (on 18 December) to Bignon, as president of the Academy in Paris.[57] In his letter he discoursed at length on his plans for research in Provence and Languedoc, gave a detailed account of his discovery and added some sketches. Montpellier, and M. Magnole in particular, received the welcome news at the same time, and Marsigli continued to collect as much data as possible. The study of coral and marine plants would in fact fill much the longest section of his book on the sea.

Nonetheless he still persevered with a wider programme of marine research. The neighbouring elements of land and sea at the Bosphorus and the river landscapes of the Danube had tempted him, long since, to measure the speed of currents, analyse the qualities of water, describe rock formations, and flora, fauna, and fish. Next he considered the geography and geology of southern Europe while moving stage by stage from the Carpathians to the Black Forest, the Alps and Jura. His present object, in

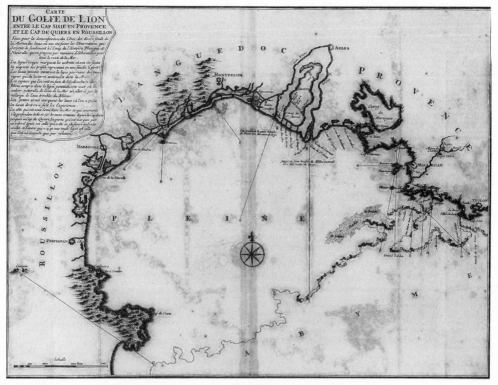

28   Marine research: a map from Marsigli's *Histoire physique de la mer* (1725).

examining the littoral of the Mediterranean between Provence and the Pyrenees, was accordingly to enrich his understanding of the earth's structure. He intended to compose one 'essay' on the earth, another on the sea. A good deal of the research was complete, with a framework fixed by what he had learnt previously by travelling west as far as Cette and Agde on the Languedoc shore, and east to La Ciotat in Provence. He determined not to venture beyond those working limits; confining his observations to a single sector of the Mediterranean he would offer it as a sample for the rest. In this area he could also rely on excellent maps, which he owed to the kindness of the intendant at Montpellier and to Charles de Chazelles in Marseille, the cartographer who instructed officers of the royal fleet of galleys. Chazelles, a pupil of the Cassinis, was the best contemporary authority on the mapping of the Mediterranean.[58]

In his own 'laboratory' at Cassis these marine topics absorbed Marsigli's attention as they had not done since the distant days in Istanbul. Outside, he cherished his partnership with the local fishermen. He used their tackle and his instruments to take soundings, or to carry off samples of rock, sand, coral and vegetation. Indoors his observations were located on his maps and charts, and he arrived at the procedure described in the first chapter of his published work: from selected points along the coast on his map, he drew lines out to sea, and along each of these lines – using his soundings – he attempted to draw a profile of the sea bed. Some of this was guesswork, and his research at sea off Languedoc was certainly minimal. From the Rhône eastwards he made more expeditions with the fishermen, his findings were much more numerous, and his published map shows him tracing with some confidence the outer edge of the shelf, the shallow 'plaine' off the coast of Provence, which then falls away to the greater depth of the 'abîme' further out to sea.[59]

With these and other enquiries he was kept busy throughout the year 1707. For the first three months, until 7 April, he maintained daily records of the temperature at Cassis, and of the direction of winds and currents.[60] The fishermen helped, but they did not go out on feast days; the data is therefore curiously incomplete. He likewise continued to work at his corals, completing another piece on the subject in February. This and its predecessor would be printed in the *Journal des Sçavans* for the year 1707, to his intense satisfaction.[61] He spent many more hours trying to measure the salinity of seawater taken from different depths and in different locations, comparing the results with freshwater wells or springs near to or further from the coast; and in this context he was the earliest authority to report on a subterranean river which reaches the sea immediately west of Cassis.[62] He added meanwhile to his collection of samples and specimens, and made drawings of them. Some of the time was passed in visits to Marseille and Aix; his life in Provence was not quite so solitary, nor perhaps so idyllic as he came to recall it later, but the interruptions in this mainly placid phase of his career have gone unrecorded. Exceptionally, on 30 June, in an outing to sea his thermometer broke. He says that he had managed to lower it to various depths at 4 am, 6 am, and 9 am, when an enemy brig suddenly appeared.[63] His own boat withdrew as quickly as possible, but in the confusion he lost his precious instrument. The brig was a warning of something more serious. The effort of the Allied powers to combine an English fleet with an army from Piedmont, for an attack on Toulon by land and sea, approached its climax. A fortnight later, and twenty miles east of Cassis, the assault on this major French stronghold began. Marsigli, for his part, wrote tersely to Scheuchzer: 'I found myself involved in the war in Provence without knowing how it happened', and a not too reliable text hints that his presence close to the action provoked suspicion.[64] He was said to have declared that the defences of Toulon were too weak to be defended against a powerful attack. But his friends in Montpellier and Aix stood by him. Toulon held out and admiral Sir Cloudesley Shovell, prince Eugene, the duke of Savoy and their forces all retreated. As far as we can tell, Marsigli spent the rest of 1707 composing a full account of his marine observations. His manuscript was still not complete in the following spring, he admitted, but he was pleased, having done a great deal of work. As much as ever before he felt himself to be someone of consequence.

V

Among Marsigli's papers is a diploma in Pope Clement XI's name, of 1 June 1708, appointing him colonel of a regiment of grenadiers. The regiment was still to be raised, recites the document, adding that the title of 'sergeant-general' commanding the Papal forces had also been conferred on him.[65] It seems therefore that in the spring of 1708 Marsigli was sucked back into warfare and politics, and years later he gave a summary account of the matter to a young friend.[66] An urgent message had reached him in his quiet retreat, appealing to his conscience as a Bolognese citizen for whom Clement was both Pope and prince. He felt reluctant but Louis XIV's ministers, the king himself, and the company whom he met in the provincial intendant's household, all urged him to respond as a good Catholic, a good subject, and a professional officer of great experience. At length he agreed and, having made the decision, transformed himself at once into a swiftly moving soldier on tour. It is not suggested in this account that he had the least qualm about taking arms against the Emperor, only that a simple and studious life was disturbed by necessity and his sense of duty.

A good Bolognese patriot, writing of Marsigli nearly seventy years later, looked at this quite differently.[67] He thought that Clement's decision to resist prince Eugene's army by force of arms was unwise; while Marsigli made a mistake by playing any part in this one-sided warfare. Paolucci, secretary of state in Rome, and the Bolognese cardinal Gozzadini, had sent letters bidding and requesting him to rally to his prince in the hour of need. He hardly hesitated and was soon on the way, after writing to Louis XIV to explain his departure. The miserable fiasco of the Pope's 'war' against the Emperor followed in October and November 1708, and in 1709 Marsigli returned to Bologna with his credit not enhanced. Another author, of this century, offers a stout defence of Marsigli's military achievement in 1708 against overwhelming odds, and adds the suggestion that he went back to Italy for two principal reasons: his feud with the Habsburg court, and his desire to win a place of honour among the Bolognese nobility.[68] The first was certainly calculated to rouse him,[69] but it is hard to believe that he cared as much for his particular status in Bologna as for prestige and recognition elsewhere in Europe. More potent was surely the normal rhythm of Marsigli's impulse to swing back and forth between his zest for study, and for a certain type of commitment in public affairs which he could never resist. It involved rapid journeys, contact with great persons, and confidence that what he was doing was immensely important. For this reason the Pope's invitation had to be accepted and he at once got on the move again. It was pleasant meanwhile to anticipate that his enemies would suffer further discredit by this show of his energy and competence.

From Marseille he went first to the papal city of Avignon where the vice-legate gave him a suitable passport.[70] He discussed here the recruitment of

soldiers for the new Roman army, possibly without appreciating that a
shortage of manpower was noticeable everywhere at this advanced stage of
a great European war. During the next six months the French ministers and
intendants, the bishop of Marseille and marshal Villars all objected to the
efforts of Rome to raise troops in southern France.[71] Marsigli, moving with
his usual speed through dreadful weather, next went up the Rhône valley to
Switzerland and his old haunt at Lucerne. The nuncio had received instructions to ask the Catholic cantons for 3000 men,[72] at a moment when
Swiss Catholics were preparing for war at home in defence of the abbot of
St Gallen's rights in the Toggenburg valley, a matter of hot dispute with
Protestant Zurich and Berne. They would not want to offend their natural
ally on this issue, the Habsburg rulers of the Tirol, or send away to central
Italy their own men of fighting age. It was likewise hard to see how Swiss
mercenaries could reach Papal territory except by way of the Grisons and
Venice, and no one expected the cautious politicians of Coire and Venice to
risk a quarrel with the new Habsburg masters of Lombardy, after their
recent stunning victories. Marsigli, although he found time to visit old
friends in Zug, hurried on to discuss recruitment with count Ulysse de Salis
in the Valtelline, one of a family frequently involved in the business of troop
raising. His circuitous route then took him to Brescia and Venice. Continuing rapidly, he approached the several channels of the Po. In that region the
marquis de Bonneval (one of several French officers whose sense of injured
noble pride matched Marsigli's, leading them to change sides) had recently
occupied the papal town of Comacchio in the Emperor's name. It was the
first muscular sign of Habsburg enmity towards the Pope. Marsigli crossed
the river and entered Ferrara. Cardinal Lorenzo Casoni was the newly
appointed legate there, with the task of defending papal sovereignty in the
former Este principality.*

Marsigli, from this moment onwards, tried to play the role assigned him
by Rome. He was the general commanding his master's troops while an
enemy stood at the gate. Casoni and his vice-legate were more disposed to
consider him a technical adviser, who would tell them how to improve
Ferrara's obsolete fortifications or where to place garrisons outside the
town. The higher authority was theirs, not his. To settle the point, and
indeed other matters, Marsigli was anxious to get to Rome as quickly as
possible. He continued his journey and reached Bologna on 10 July.

It proved a brief, unpleasing visit after twenty years' absence. The legate,
cardinal Grimaldi, woundingly received him as a private citizen. His rank
and authority were not published and only in the palazzo Marsigli was the
return of the native celebrated, by a party in which he could claim acquaintance with certain elderly ladies and nobles of Bologna. He also found time,

---

* By this time the Este ruler Rinaldo was safely back in Modena, thanks to the Habsburg
triumph in Lombardy. Muratori's first published defence of the Emperor's cause against the
Pope also appeared in 1708.

we shall see, for a glance at his collections but moved on after five days to
rejoin the highway through Emilia and Romagna. Stopping at Imola,
Faenza, Cesena and Fano, in each town he made a quick inspection, trying
to instil a due sense of emergency with his proposals for repair work, and for
supply. He visualised Faenza as the centre of a defensive system protecting
the whole region.

At Rome, by contrast with Bologna, he was well received by Pope Clement and other dignitaries, and in a whirlwind of activity prepared plans for
raising an army, devising a strategy, and organising the defence of the city
and its provinces. An elaborate state paper was addressed to the Pope[73] and
he appeared before the relevant 'congregations', or committees, in order to
comment on his own and other proposals. If Clement XI's fundamental
error had been to believe that a military defence of the Papal States would
be more effective than diplomatic manoeuvre or ecclesiastical censure in
resisting the Emperor, Marsigli in turn built a grandiose paper structure on
the basis of this mistake. It called an army into existence by revising old
Roman rules for paying, clothing and disciplining troops, and assumed that
the weapons and munitions they needed could be found. Fortunately or
unfortunately, in Rome there was none of the military-cum-administrative
expertise which had developed elsewhere in western Europe during a fairly
long period. For several generations the Roman lands, however disorderly
the internal policing, enjoyed peace with their neighbours. So Marsigli,
punctuating his writing and discussion with a tour round the walls and gates
of Rome, found that guard duties were universally neglected (as he informed Clement).[74] Fears of an early attack by Habsburg troops from
Naples next prompted him to survey the border south of the Campagna. He
recommended putting there a force of 12,000 men; but it was only a force
on paper. As to the Adriatic side of the Appenines, he never varied in his
view that the available manpower should be concentrated in the few fortified places: but these, Ferrara, Forte Urbano in the hills north-west of
Bologna, Faenza, and Ancona on the coast, were all in fact very weakly held.

Marsigli's original appointment appeared to give him command of the
Pope's forces. By the time he left Rome on 5 September some of the
limitations of this senior post were becoming plain. There were now two
other officers with the title of sergeant-general. They stayed in Rome while
Marsigli became responsible for defending the realm across the Appenines,
where he depended as before on the goodwill of cardinal legates in the
provincial governments. Earlier there had been just a possibility that Clement would persuade Louis XIV to allow one of his own generals to take
command of the forces raised – or to be raised – by a league of Italian
princes and republics against the new Habsburg domination.[75] Rome asked
for the duke of Berwick. The name of marshal Tessé was mentioned. Such
commanders would have found it somewhat easier to overrule provincial
governors in the Papal states. But Louis then drew back because his losses
in Flanders were too great. He could no longer consider intervening south

of the Alps and the suggested league of Italian states faded rapidly from view. However hard Marsigli worked, the defence of Clement's territory against a stronger opponent was frankly impossible. He was a commander perhaps without talent, certainly without the necessary troops.

Leaving Rome he went to the Adriatic end of the boundary with Naples, before retracing his steps along the main road to Bologna. Here he was dismayed to find how little had been achieved by those to whom he had given (he thought) such clear instructions six weeks earlier. Yet his greatest misgivings were about an initiative planned by the legate of Ravenna, and his provincial commander Rasponi.[76] The Rasponi family had been dominant – rather like the de Salis family in its corner of Switzerland – for several generations along the coast between Ravenna and Comacchio. After the seizure of the town of Comacchio by enemy troops, the local population was willing enough to try and drive them out again: as the Pope defied Emperor Joseph, so they were prepared to defy the Habsburg commander. According to one account Rasponi put together an expeditionary force of outlaws and smugglers; and papal edicts of the previous July, requiring the conscription of one man for every hundred inhabitants, certainly allowed 'banditi' to get safe-conducts by volunteering for service.[77] These recruits, or volunteers, were led northwards to the edge of the lagoon which almost surrounded Comacchio, and began to dislodge isolated Habsburg detachments. The legates in Ferrara and Faenza collaborated eagerly but Marsigli, arriving on the scene, dissented and considered that Clement's government stood no chance of resisting its opponent except by concentrating the tiny forces available in a few chosen strongholds.

Worse followed when he returned to Bologna. General Marsigli was not well received, nor did he behave with tact. He took offence at the legatine protocol, and irritated the senators to whom he tried to give orders. For the defence of the city, he told them after a tour of inspection, some sort of glacis – 'a mile round' – was imperative. In his opinion, if they were to enjoy any chance of resisting a siege, the buildings abutting or close to the town gates and walls would have to be demolished; including a mill, an inn, and part of the colonnade leading up to the shrine of S. Luca. In addition a ditch or moat should be dug. 'But who is to pay for this, signore generale?' Marsigli was asked. He answered that the public treasury must provide, to which a senator responded: they were and would remain friends of the Germans, French and Spaniards alike, and as loyal subjects of the Holy See they had no cause to arm themselves in the manner suggested, unless His Holiness specifically empowered them to do so.[78] An appeal was sent off to Rome. The contemporary who tells the story admired Marsigli's tireless activity but considered that his truculent manner, which had been his ruin in Germany, was evident enough in Bologna. His countrymen, while now giving him the style and title of a general, did not seriously intend anything other than a negotiation with the Habsburg commanders. If and when these demanded quarters and supplies for their troops, it was comforting to assume that they would only be on their way through Emilia to Naples.

Marsigli went next to Forte Urbano and to Ferrara, where he found the legate apparently more sympathetic. Workmen were taken on to improve the defences of the town. Recruits were assembled to wait for clothing and arms, and for the arrival of officers to train them. While Marsigli on the whole respected the legate Casoni, Casoni disapproved of Marsigli. Informed that the Austrians were preparing to recover the ground they had just lost near Comacchio, he continued to think ill-judged the general's advice to abandon it in order to bring all their forces together for the defence of Forte Urbano.[79] This would demoralise the rural population, believed Casoni, commenting that Marsigli was too rigid in his maxims: the sergeant-general's head had been turned by too much applause in Rome.[80] In fact the legate insisted that the outlying places should be garrisoned, while from the end of September to the end of October Marsigli moved restlessly about the country. At one moment he was on the Po, at another in Faenza. The Habsburg commander in Comacchio meanwhile got ready for action, and marshal Daun began moving part of his field-army from Piedmont down the Po, the preliminaries of a serious attempt to force the court of Rome to give way.[81] Another Habsburg representative made ready to go south from Milan to hand Clement the Emperor's terms for a settlement. The pressure suddenly became intense.

Marsigli no doubt convinced himself that what happened next proved that he was right. Bonneval in Comacchio easily recovered his control of the lagoons and villages in the north-east.[82] Places further west, between Ferrara and Modena, fell to the Habsburg troops; and then Cento nearer Bologna. The light scatter of manpower at many points had been a complete waste of strength and energy, so that Marsigli could only hurriedly withdraw and leave Ferrara under blockade by the Austrians. Casoni, having insisted on measures with which he disagreed, wrote unkindly that the sergeant-general left for the south after doing nothing but offer useless excuses. Marsigli moved the regiment of the young Albani, Clement XI's nephew, forward from Faenza to Bologna.[83] After a single night in town Albani withdrew again. It was clear that the city intended to bargain as politely as possible with the Habsburg authorities. The legate left matters to the senate and on 15 November the Emperor's forces marched through the city with drums beating and colours flying. They were reviewed in the piazza but quartered outside the walls. In the second half of November Daun moved quickly along the road to Faenza and Forlì, and some of his troops reached Rimini and Fano a little later. Marsigli preceded them. One account describes how he and Albani took with them the Roman government's money chests, and were followed on the march by some hundreds of recruits, while behind these came a disorderly baggage train carrying clothing and weapons not yet distributed; other stores were left behind, a bonanza for their pursuers.[84]

The uncertainties were still great enough. Marsigli feared an immediate enemy approach to Rome, and tried to guard the various points of entry leading through the Appenines. He sent most of his men into the hills but removed himself, rather unaccountably, to Ancona. Here on the coast he was able to observe Daun from a safe distance, while the Austrian general stood his ground in papal territory waiting impatiently for the politicians in Rome to patch up a settlement, thanks to the pressure he exerted.[85] Clement agreed to a pacification on 15 January 1709. Amid weather of memorable severity this news was slow in crossing the hills but Marsigli's last campaign now ended, without any credit to the former Imperial officer. Peace in Italy, and his own unexpected presence there, more or less compelled him at last to go home.

CHAPTER TEN

The Later Works of General Marsigli

I

Marsigli returned from Ancona in May 1709. Entitled general but without the prestige of a successful military command behind him, at home where he always felt uncomfortable, Marsigli never flagged.[1] A new idea caught his fancy and gradually took shape as his greatest achievement. Danubia might remain an inaccessible region, *his* Danubia a set of unpublished manuscripts. Even Provence was elusive. Bologna meanwhile acquired through his insight and generosity two novel institutions of permanent importance, its public academy of sciences, and its public academy for the fine arts.

He said later that when Clement XI unexpectedly summoned him to Italy in 1708 he found his collections 'disordered, diminished and damaged'.[2] This sounds exaggerated, and a different testimony refers to Marsigli's delight at finding his own studio at work, surrounded by his Turkish stuffs, his glass, porcelain and other rarities. More probably things were in good order in July 1708, but less so when he returned nearly a year later to find that the admirable, conscientious Stancari had died recently, leaving no one who acted as curator or director of studies in the Marsigli apartments.[3] After returning, Marsigli himself wanted to go back to Provence, but could hardly avoid feeling concern for those working under his own roof. His new scheme was accordingly to give the collections to the Senate of Bologna, provided that in recompense and gratitude the senators built a proper observatory and agreed to fund permanently the study of astronomy and mathematics.[4] Moreover, in a notable memorandum (of 9 November 1709) he tried to broaden his proposal by a wholesale critique of the contemporary decay of Bologna University, comparing it with what he believed to be the greater progress of learning in European academies outside Italy.[5] To arrest this decline, which he believed to have occurred during his own lifetime, and not before, he sketched out a bold set of reforms for almost all the university faculties. His emphasis was placed on the need for fewer teachers who would be better paid, for lectureships in new subjects, and for larger libraries. He wanted in particular the more thorough study of oriental languages, experimental procedures in the sciences, and the prompt publication of any findings. The generous offer of his own books, apparatus and collections would help to make these improve ments possible: he does not say so directly in his paper, but implies it. This 'Parallelo' or 'comparison' with other universities, in many ways a splendid and sensible manifesto for academic reform, was duly received by the city fathers of Bologna.[6] There is no evidence that it was ever seriously dis cussed; and the new university statutes of 1713 show very little change from those published in the previous century. Marsigli might have learnt from the failure of his brother the archdeacon, ten years earlier, how difficult it always is to remedy the perceived decay of learning. The ideas of the 'Parallelo' attacked so many entrenched interests in the city and university that no prudent municipal politician could have followed him in thinking that this was the way forward. The more practical course, the compromise negotiated during the next few years, was to add a new institute or academy – not very different from the one already at work in Marsigli's house – to the unreformed structure of the old university, leaving the two to co-exist and even to co-operate. Educational improvement, as so often, would come in through a side door.

Matters were made more complicated because Marsigli, at the same moment, exuberantly widened the span of his patronage.[7] A grouping of the principal painters and sculptors working in Bologna was just then canvass ing the Senate for recognition as a public academy. Their colleagues in certain other Italian cities had preceded them in doing this, because it arguably offered the artists higher status and higher rewards for their work Count Niccolò Fava, a painter himself, was their sponsor and patron in Bologna but they now approached Marsigli. He seems to have responded with enthusiasm. Inviting representatives to meet him on several occasions in November and December 1709 to consider a draft constitution for this academy, he fervently offered his support. Somebody present recalled – at a much later date – the powerful impression made on the gathering by this sonorous military man. Marsigli lobbied for these artists, as well as for his own team of scientists; and he blithely offered them accommodation assuming that in due course they would be found official quarters in which to teach painting, sculpture and architecture to the pupils who enrolled The Senate accepted the scheme for an academy, as indeed it had already done in outline before Marsigli intervened, and he next proceeded to mount a gala occasion at the palazzo Marsigli to inaugurate the new society, the 'Accademia Clementina' which the Pope was honouring with his name.

It proved an extraordinary function, and the spark igniting yet another of Marsigli's quarrels. The celebration took place in the family residence which included apartments belonging to Filippo and the absent bishop of Perugia, with other quarters let or lent, as well as the accommodation of Marsigli's scientists and collections. The disturbance matched the frenzy of preparation, before torches were lit and music began on the evening of

2 January 1710. Earlier in the day there had been a church service in which the academicians took S. Caterina dei Vigri for their protectress. Later, the new legate Casoni (transferred recently from Ferrara), the vice-legate, the Confaloniere and many others climbed up the principal staircase of the house to find a salon not large enough for all the academicians and guests, who then overflowed into neighbouring rooms. They could admire the pieces of antique sculpture acquired by Marsigli in Rome during the previous winter, which he intended to put at the disposal of the new academy. They could view the quarters offered for its temporary accommodation, for modelling and teaching during the winter months. They listened to speeches, and there was dancing. After the festivity came the unhappy sequel.

If this were a family saga there would be more to say in unravelling the dispute. The senior branch of the Marsigli family, senator Alessandro and his brother Giorgio Duglioli, were by no means pleased with their overbearing cousin's airy ideas, which threatened to alienate part of the family assets at a moment when the marriage had been arranged between Aurelia, daughter of Giorgio, and Marsigli's brother Filippo.[8] It duly took place on 22 January. By then, certain of the Clementine artists had begun work 'upstairs in the house adjoining general Marsigli's palace'. Others were perhaps in his own apartment. At the very least, in spite of disclaimers afterwards, we must surmise that in January 1710 there was more bustle and upset in the family residence than at any other time in the past few years. The artists were there at work, together with the men of science and mathematics already introduced by Marsigli. Consequently, one morning, long-suffering brother Filippo erupted with rage and protested that he would no longer stand such disorders – 'questo bordello nel Palazzo'.[9] Marsigli, ever quick to take offence, was affronted and another of his quarrels began. As the contest developed, the elder man threatened to remove all his collections to Provence. At Marseille, he added, he could have passports entitling him to go wherever he liked in Europe or even north Africa. The younger Marsigli threatened to litigate at home: Luigi Ferdinando's possessions, Filippo asserted, were a pledge to the rest of the family for his indebtedness following the disaster at Breisach and the disgrace of Bregenz, and could not be allowed to leave Bologna.

Both stances were overdone. Marsigli did indeed go to Provence but left everything intact behind him. Having reached France he soon learnt that his other brother, the bishop, was dying; and hurriedly had to return by felucca across the sea, taking care first to forward to Paris the fair copy of his still unfinished marine researches. When he reached Bologna the bishop was dead.[10] Then, gradually, peace was restored. The legate, some of the senators, Pope Clement, lawyers representing the embattled principals, and the brothers themselves, edged their way towards an agreement on many intricate points. Happily, as it turned out, the negotiation of Marsigli's original offer of his collections to his native city had only been delayed and rendered more complex by the misadventure. The Senate gave a formal, favourable answer on 15 May 1711 to the general proposition, and serious discussion began. It is worthy of note that already eighteen months earlier one Bolognese citizen, Ghiselli the chronicler, had been deeply impressed by what he saw of the Marsigli treasures.[11] A visit in October 1709 left him amazed by the splendour and range of what he could appreciate: the porcelain, statuary, books, printing types and manuscripts. Canon Ghiselli evidently thought that the removal of this valuable endowment abroad would be a loss to the city of Bologna, and that giving it to the city would also add much to the honour and credit of the Marsigli name. If others agreed with him, these ideas may have made it easier for the members of the family to come to terms with each other as well as with a majority of the Senate.

One problem was to find a suitable building for the new foundation. If the public accepted Marsigli's collections, it seemed reasonable and indeed necessary that the city should provide the accommodation which Marsigli himself could no longer dream of offering in his own house. After enquiry someone suggested that a palace in the via Donato (now via Zamboni) which had been enlarged and frescoed for cardinal Poggi in the sixteenth century, and then occupied successively by the Cellesi and Banchieri families, would have room for all the collections, for the astronomers and experimentalists and their pupils, together with the teachers and students of the Clementine Academy.[12] This ambitious and attractive scheme posed its own problems. There was doubt at first whether the owners of the Poggi palace, even if they felt disposed to sell, were lawfully entitled to dispose of the property. It was far from clear that enough money could be found to pay for the buildings, for repairing and altering them, and for other parts of the whole enterprise. Was the city of Bologna, at the taxpayers' expense in a depressed post-war economy, to buy or lease a palace and find salaries for the teachers who used it, and not only for the advancement of learning but for count Marsigli's greater glory? Not everyone thought so. However the response depended on the sovereign as well as the Senate. The Pope's overriding prerogative gave him sufficient authority, if he wished, to vary the interpretation of the trust under which the building was occupied, and to find the extra funding to pay for the project. This possibility suited Marsigli, who leapt at the perfect excuse for a journey to Rome in June 1711 to make a direct appeal to Clement.

In the last of his surviving autobiographical fragments this negotiation is described in the same rapt language which he had used years earlier to describe his mission from Emperor Leopold to Pope Innocent XI.[13] It was now Clement XI's turn, and Marsigli experienced his usual thrill from the ambience of sovereignty vested in a single person. The audience – 'four hours in the gallery' – dealt with a number of topics which the legate in Bologna had entrusted to Marsigli for discussion. One was the deployment of papal authority to relax the trust under which the Poggi palace was occupied, and find future revenue for building an observatory and maintaining a new scientific academy, as proposed by Marsigli. It was Marsigli who now effectively communicated to the ruler his own enthusiasm for the project, explaining how the palace could be used for the study both of arts and sciences. He produced plans drawn by the painter Franceschini – a Bolognese very active in Rome and much favoured at this period[14] – to illustrate the fitting up of rooms and halls, he listed the apparatus which he intended to donate for the advancement of learning, and rehearsed the terms of a draft agreement between the Senate and himself. The other matters Marsigli was empowered to raise dealt with individual items of patronage, and as it turned out Clement demurred to these while approving of Marsigli's 'vast and novel idea'. It was Casoni and the papal advisers in Rome who then resolved the legal and financial difficulties; so that part of a recent public loan could be used to fund the undertaking. After the audience Marsigli himself fell ill, but was treated by the papal physician Lancisi who soon became his collaborator and friend. He compensated for one of Marsigli's 'atrocious' enemies at the papal court, Aldrovandi the official Bolognese envoy, who did not lightly tolerate Marsigli's claim to a special relationship with the Pope.[15] It seems that Aldrovandi spoke for those at home who resisted the scheme for transferring a private collection and a private study group to the state, at the state's expense.

In August 1711 the Senate in Bologna finally accepted the proposals for a new foundation which would have professors demonstrating and experimenting in six subjects: chemistry, physics, natural history, astronomy, geography and military science.[16] During the autumn Marsigli began drawing up the enormous schedule, divided into a series of inventories, of what he intended to transfer to the Senate.[17] It was his assumption that he already possessed material of value contributing to the study of these subjects, while admitting and emphasising that more books, apparatus and samples would be needed later. Lawyers arranged meanwhile for the purchase by the Senate of the Poggi palace. At the beginning of 1712 and on the basis of many earlier drafts and documents, Marsigli and the Senate accordingly concluded a formal treaty. It recited how the noble Count had nurtured during a long period of his distinguished military career an intention to advance learning of the modern kind in his native city, and with this in mind had collected books, instruments, maps, models, samples, print types, and many other objects of value; how he wished to present them to the Senate; and how the Senate, in accepting the bequest undertook to find, and indeed had found, a building suited to accommodate these treasures for the professors and students who would make use of them; how also His Holiness the Pope had authorised the employment of certain taxes and funds to pay for the building and maintain the professors. The agreement then recited a document (of 12 December 1711) laying down a constitution for the new scientific foundation, with its officers and their duties, its professors and their rights and duties, its chapel, library, annual programme, and festivities. This new 'Institute' would form a body working in association with the old, unofficial academy of the Inquieti – which had been merged earlier into the group supported by Marsigli in his own lodging between 1703 and 1709 – and also with the recently founded Clementine Academy of artists. All three would be brought together under the roof of the same building, the palace acquired by the Senate. Other clauses promised the construction of the new observatory, and the fitting out of rooms and studios within one year. Over the entrance of the palace would be inscribed the words: *Bononiae Scientiarum et Artium Institutum ad Publicum Totius Orbis Usum.* The final paragraphs of the long screed have the text of the Senate's vote of the previous 5 August, which gave authority for what was now concluded in its name.

Such was the agreement confirmed at a ceremony in the presence of the legate on 11 January 1712. More bargaining followed before the formal inauguration of the Institute in 1714 and of the Clementine Academy in 1715. Teaching and demonstration had already begun, and would now continue. During the next fifteen years Marsigli himself was often dissatisfied with what he believed to be indifferent support from the Senate for his foundation, and slackness in research on the part of its members. At other moments he felt proud to think, and it was true, that the Institute and the Academy had become a very notable part of the cultural existence of eighteenth-century Bologna.

II

This has been a long traverse from Marsigli's old Balkan world to the refuge in Provence and the opening of the Bologna Institute. Yet elements of that more distant past were still embedded in his mind, and in this later period they reappear from time to time. He might be busy negotiating with the Senate, on 9 November 1709 putting a date to that radical critique, the 'Parallel'; but on 3 December he wrote to the historian Pietro Garzoni to say that recently he had found among his papers the translation of a Turkish account of the siege of Vienna which he wished the reading public to enjoy.[18] This became the dedicatory letter of a little work on the siege which duly appeared in print. More significantly, in the 'Parallel' itself which compared Bologna adversely with other universities, he gave an example of the defects he was deploring: he could find no one in the town with sufficient expertise to help him with a critical scrutiny of his volume on Danubian antiquities.[19] Later, he included the six volumes of the whole work in the great inventory of what he was handing over to the Senate for the future institute.[20] Another item transferred was the metal types used for the printing in 1700 of the *Prodromus*, the lettering of which had given him so much pleasure at the time.[21] A clause in the agreement also stated that

obody, except for Marsigli himself, would be permitted to remove books
r anything else from the buildings of the foundation. He soon made use of
ie privilege of borrowing what he needed, and in May 1713 wrote to ask for
ie loan of his copperplates (Einmart's work) illustrating the mushrooms of
reisach. He wanted to send them to his publisher in Rome, and added that
ie procedure for these loans should be formalised because in due course he
ould ask for the plates of his 'voluminous' account of the Danube, which
as likely to be printed elsewhere.[22] No more was heard of this for the
ioment. Writing to inform the Royal Society of the new foundation
i Bologna, he simply advised it that Englishmen who came to Bologna
ould be able to see for themselves the completed text of his Danube in the
brary there.[23]

Marsigli turned instead to his more recent work. On cutting short his
:cond stay in Provence, in 1710, he brought home the original notes and
ther relevant papers describing his research at Cassis. In leisure moments
e now prepared a summary which was ready for the printer before he went
) Rome to see Clement. The general aim of the little book, published in
711, was to give the Italian reader a concise account of what he had
iscovered in France. It takes the form of two letters, one dedicated to an
ld Venetian friend, the other to a more eminent acquaintance Antonio
'allisneri. The second letter straightforwardly discussed the origins of the
ye which produces cochineal, but the first is something of a mosaic.[24] It
egins by expressing (once again) the author's fundamental preoccupation
rith 'the structure of the earth', and possible continuations or counterparts
f this structure in the sea bed. Then followed Italian versions of Marsigli's
bservations on coral – including a little new evidence supplied by
shermen in Ancona at his stay there during the recent war – and of a note
:om Fontenelle, secretary of the Académie des Sciences, which acknowl-
dges the safe receipt of Marsigli's account of his research in Provence.[25]
'he content of this was then summarised, and he pointed out that his
overeign's peremptory summons in 1708 had called him back to Italy
efore finishing the fifth, concluding section of the work; he hoped to find
ime later for the stay in Provence needed to complete it. But at the end
/larsigli reverted to Fontenelle's note. It surely expressed the high regard
f the Parisian authorities for his enquiry and could be accepted as a
?stimony of his own good faith. He was anxious (he wrote) not to have the
eputation of a boastful would-be scientist who never produces what he
promises: ten years had passed since he sent to London the printed pro-
pectus for the *Opus* on the Danube, but the completed work still remained
1 manuscript in Bologna. The *Natural History of the Sea* was likewise a
nanuscript in Paris. In neither case, he claimed, should he be censured for
he delay in publication.[26]

These were literary echoes from his past. They were unfinished business.
/lore remarkable was a different sort of reminiscence dating still further
•ack, which he now stitched into the concerns of his new academy. Had he

not seen for himself in 1680, as a young man in Istanbul, the miserie
suffered by the Christian galley slaves of the Porte, and enrolled himself i
a Bolognese charity concerned with the redemption of the these men?[27] Fc
the rest of his life he took an interest in the charity, after his own captivit
paying the costs of an oratory in the fraternity's modest chapel of S. Mari
della Neve. Now, thirty years later, this was associated with his new plans
In 1712, when agreement had been reached for the installation of th
Institute in the palazzo Poggi, Morsigli requested a meeting with his com
panions of S. Maria della Neve in order to secure their approval for
petition to Clement XI: he wanted an oratory for the charity to be placed i
the same building as the institute of scientists and the artists' academy, wit
indulgences for those who came there intending to give generously toward
the redemption of Christian slaves.[28] It was suggested that the fraternit
would always celebrate the feasts of the Assumption and the Annunciatio
in this oratory. How much was done immediately is far from clear, but
letter written in Marsigli's old age by his good friend Lambertini, the futur
Pope Benedict XIV, indicates that the 'chapel of the Institute' was at las
fitted up in 1725. Two years later, Marsigli, sick and fading, signed
document dated 22 March 1727: the fraternity of S. Maria had agreed wit
His Excellency that on the day of the Annunciation they would come ever
year in procession from their own chapel to the chapel in the building of th
Institute of Sciences. They would pray there for the souls of Marsigli an
other former captives, and receive the money deposited in the chapel durin
the year. Three days later, on the feast day itself, this celebration duly too
place. Marsigli, carrying with him the fetters of a slave, was present to gree
the brethren. Even more remarkable, publishing the agreement in the fol
lowing year he added a long account of his experience as a prisoner in 1683
4, and of his encounters afterwards with his former captors. He wrote, h
said, to encourage his colleagues by recalling the wonderful protection c
the Blessed Virgin which had brought his own ordeal to an end on the Da
of the Annunciation long ago.

He wished to associate this concern with his other works. In his view the
all belonged together, so that a delay or reverse at any point tended to upse
him the more deeply. Unfortunately the complex affairs of the Institute le
him to brush repeatedly with the committee of Senators which dealt wit
them. Marsigli would therefore often combine his outbursts of indignatio
with a threat to abandon Bologna 'for ever', by going back to Provence. O
in 1711 he angled for an invitation from Augustus of Poland (his ol
commander as Elector of Saxony) to join in the current warfare against th
Turks, and made enquiries of his former friends in Vienna – Mansfelc
Schlick, father Miller and others – whether the new Emperor Charles V
would be willing to revoke the injustice done at Bregenz.[29] In August 171
he informed the Jesuit general, Tamburini, that his departure 'dalla patri
e dall'Italia per sempre' was imminent.[30] Fifteen years later he still used th
same language of despair, together with abuse of his opponents in Bologn

to which they had long since become accustomed, and he still intended to leave Bologna 'for ever'. In fact Marsigli remained in Italy from 1709 until 1721, before he took one more distant journey of the greatest importance, visiting England and Holland in 1722 and 1723. He went to Provence in 1728 but suffered a stroke, and soon returned. Against expectation and against the grain, from 1709 onwards he settled back into Italian society.

A sign of this was the cultivation of his friendships new and old. One was with Giovanni Maria Lancisi, the Pope's doctor, who looked after him when he fell ill in Rome. This celebrated man, like Marsigli, opened his own 'museo' to the public; they shared not only scientific interests, but enthusiasm as collectors of sculpture and other classical remains. The result was the joint authorship of their 'Dissertation' published in 1714, a stately folio oddly put together,[31] which explains why Marsigli wanted his old copper-plates of mushrooms sent from Bologna: he had returned to the topic with an illustrated mycological paper, addressed to his friend and collaborator Lancisi. After surveying the progress of scholarly discussion on fungi, it reasserted his theory (already proposed in 1700) that soil, combined with other matter like timber, straw, or dung, was the agent which in certain conditions of humidity produced fungus; he did not think that a fungus developed from 'seeds', as many other observers held. Lancisi's lengthy comment followed, expressing approval, and he was echoed by a polite review in the *Giornale de' Letterati* for 1715. However, historians of mycology tell us that the authentic study of this topic begins, not with Marsigli but with another investigator very close to him in period and place. It was Pier'Angelo Micheli, in the Boboli gardens at Florence in the year 1718, who first positively identified the spores of a mushroom.[32] Marsigli, in spite of his persistent study, belonged to a more primitive stage of the enquiry. The other half of the Dissertation of 1714, Lancisi's work, was a careful description of the ruins of the naturalist Pliny's famous villa. To this Marsigli did not contribute, but the visits he paid to Rome were certainly associated with the pleasure he took at this time in adding to his own collection of ancient inscriptions, lamps, urns, carvings, all the fragments constantly up for exchange or sale in one of the busier periods of Roman excavation. He justifiably enjoyed discussion with such enthusiasts as Lancisi and Francesco Bianchini the astronomer, who was also Pope Clement's official archaeologist. He wrote brief little essays of his own on some of the objects acquired, and addressed a letter on Trajan's bridge over the Danube to Bernard de Montfaucon the Benedictine scholar.[33] (But in Rome, he says, he could not consult his manuscript volume in the library at Bologna.) The pleasure of collecting antiquities was possibly enhanced by his notion that he would hand them over to the Institute, and in 1715 he seems to have added many new items to those given earlier to the Clementine artists.[34] One of his prizes, greatly admired during the eighteenth and nineteenth centuries, was a laughing satyr carved in marble found near Cecilia Metella's tomb on the Appian Way. It would in due course travel

29 Marsigli's Roman
satyr.

back to Rome from Bologna, then to Paris in Napoleon's day, and from
there to Munich. Other finds, like the Etruscan remains coming to light at
the time, excited him equally, while occasionally he considered going to
Egypt to study the river Nile and look for ancient artefacts.[35]

One of those who accompanied him on his excursions from Rome, to
Gandolfo or the Etruscan remains of Veio, was a French cleric named
Hébert de Quincy. They had interests in common, and the younger man
conceived a deep admiration for Marsigli, who little by little during his last
years must have realised that he had found not only a disciple but a biographer.[36] He offered him relevant documents to copy, and in conversation
gave his own version of past or contemporary transactions. De Quincy,
receiving and conserving this material, was a wonderful discovery for someone so proudly aware of and anxious about his reputation.

He had two other good friends. Both Antonio Vallisneri and
Giambattista Morgagni were by then notable professors of medicine at
Padua. The first shared his passion for geology and botany.[37] Morgagni was
younger, one of the most active scientists with Manfredi and Stancari in
Marsigli's residence while he worked for the principal hospital in Bologna,

before moving to the Venetian university. By 1720 he was a treasured correspondent; and in 1723 Marsigli wrote promising to act as godfather to a forthcoming infant in the large Morgagni family.[38] Men of this academic standing gave him the extra support he needed from outside Bologna, as he grew older and still continued fighting the battles he judged necessary to maintain his Institute. For he remained displeased.

III

The inventory of Marsigli's gift to the Senate of Bologna itemised his collections in 101 pages but they were listed briefly in the constitution of the new foundation. This referred to:

> Apparatus for the study of mathematics, astronomy and science
> A collection of fossils
> Materials for the study of terrestrial and marine plant life
> A collection of shells
> A library of the best editions
> A large number of Arabic, Persian, Turkish and Greek manuscripts
> A collection of classical artefacts
> Many antique marble statues
> Apparatus and models for the study of fortifications and gunnery
> Armour
> A collection of types for printing[39]

Several of the layers of Marsigli's past experience in the course of thirty years are displayed here, but in addition to oriental manuscripts were the volumes of his own papers, with records of journeys to Istanbul, Rome, Belgrade, to Serbia and Romania, to Carlowitz and along the frontiers. Among the instruments were those used by Muller to survey the course of the Danube in 1696. Beside the shells and fossils were corals from the Bosphorus and Provence, and mineral samples from many regions in central Europe. One and all were to be deposited in the new institute of arts and sciences for 'the benefit of mankind'. The practical problem was how to use them as instruments of teaching and research. It meant fitting up the building recently acquired for the purpose, installing suitable officers and teachers and, perhaps most difficult, setting them to work in a manner which satisfied the noble founder.

Those responsible, in the relevant Senate committee, had first to think of distributing the large but diverse endowment between different rooms or halls of the old Renaissance palace.[40] They distinguished the branches of study mentioned in the constitution, and accordingly assigned them the material or apparatus concerned with astronomy, the history or science of war, experimental physics, medicine, and natural history; these became the original *stanze* of the eighteenth-century Institute in addition to a library and a showroom for ancient sculpture. They likewise had to find space for the Clementine Academy, giving the painters, sculptors and architects those apartments which enjoyed the attraction of fine sixteenth-century decoration by admired masters. They even had to consider the right of the old academy of the Inquieti to a place of assembly for their meetings. A chapel, a workshop for Marsigli's projected printing press and other craftsmen, together with lodgings for at least some members of the Institute and for the custodian, were also requirements.

An outstandingly important matter was the appointment of officers and teachers. In most cases they were already chosen before the building was ready. Among the witnesses present with the Legate on 2 January 1712, when Marsigli and the Senate confirmed their agreement, were Lelio Trionfetti the future president of the Institute, and Messrs Rondelli, Bazzani, Beccari, Corazzi and Laurenti, who in due course reappear as principal instructors or officers in the early phase of the Institute's history.[41] Bazzani, from a family much involved in the city's administration, a professor of medicine, was appointed as secretary, with a particular responsibility for keeping a record of the Institute's proceedings and maintaining contact with foreign academies of science. Rondelli, a mathematician and member of the Inquieti, became librarian. As to the professors, it must have seemed appropriate that Manfredi, whom Marsigli had placed in charge of his collections in 1702, became the first professor of astronomy in the Institute, and that old Trionfetti should not only be president but preside over the study of natural history, and the care of a new botany garden adjoining the palace. The choice of Jacopo Beccari as professor of 'physica' was a great success. Reader in logic in the university, and one of the Inquieti, he was known as an enthusiastic experimentalist; he installed the apparatus he wanted in the Institute.[42] Whereas Marc' Antonio Laurenti, a highly experienced physician in the city hospital, proved disappointing in his department of 'spagyrical' or medical chemistry. The topic was an admitted lacuna in university studies and the post at the Institute was designed to fill it, but Marsigli would complain later that Laurenti never obtained the proper equipment. As for another witness present at the ceremony in January 1712, father Ercole Corazzi was a Benedictine mathematician, well known as an excellent speaker, who was made responsible – he held the office until 1720 – for expounding the principles of fortification and making use of the military collections. Marsigli himself took an interest in equipping the professor with suitable wooden models of fortified towns and the differing systems of fortification.[43]

The original rules emphasised that the professors were not to lecture, but to demonstrate by experiment, or by illustrating the practice of methodical observation; and each professor had to have an assistant to act as his technician. This last point followed the example set in the Academies of Paris and Montpellier.

In due course the *stanze* would be rearranged or altered in order to accommodate new topics or classes, or receive further gifts and collections. The great Bolognese Pope Benedict XIV assumed the role of a second munificent founder, and later in the century some of the professors became European celebrities like Galvani and Volta. But the first founder, Marsigli himself, who lived until 1730, while intensely proud of his achievement in converting a private academy into a public institution open to all, had remained dissatisfied. His intermittent ructions with the Senate concerned the problems of funding, both the income available and the capital needed for building. He found it equally disappointing that the instructors and officers of his Institute often seemed unaware of the stimulus to reform or innovate.[44] They held posts in the university, were anxious about extra stipends, were local men with allies or enemies in the municipal administration or the city churches, and in several cases they were Marsigli's old acquaintances. He had been happy to have his dear mentor appointed president of the new foundation, but Trionfetti was far too feeble to bear efficiently the presidential responsibility for devising an annual programme of the Institute's work and seeing it carried out. Nor was it foreseen that Bassani, the respectable university professor appointed as secretary, would fail to keep in touch with foreign academies or to publish the Institute's findings in matters of scientific interest. Yet these were the secretary's duties, about which Marsigli cared passionately. It also scandalised him that the librarian Rondelli was succeeded in rapid succession by two other persons, often absent, who neglected to correspond with booksellers or librarians abroad. Above all there was Manfredi, the natural and obvious choice as professor of astronomy, the copious correspondent of years ago who had brought the Inquieti to work in Marsigli's house, and supervised the building of an observatory there; he proved the greatest disappointment. It seemed to the Institute's excitable founder that Manfredi had become too grand and fashionable, and too much involved as the government's adviser on hydraulic problems, to carry further the astronomical research of his earlier days. Nor did he press hard enough for the construction of the new observatory, which the Senate had earlier agreed with Marsigli should be built for the Institute within twelve months. It rose from the ground very slowly, and looked nowhere near completion for a number of years.

At certain points, things took a turn for the better. For example Trionfetti resigned as professor of natural history in 1717, if not as president, and after an interval was succeeded by a truly first-rate scientist, Giuseppe Monti.[45] But for Marsigli, in his moments of depression, his whole creation must have seemed no more than a little universe of interacting flaws and grievances, like a Habsburg regiment or the government of Breisach under siege.[46] As usual, other people, in this case a party of senators with their attendant bureaucrats and academics, were to blame if *his* foundation, with which he had hoped to modernise the study of the sciences, became a mere appendage of the unreformed, decaying university of Bologna.

IV

All the same he found plenty to do. In 1715, under orders from Rome, he spent several months touring the Adriatic coast north and south from Rimini, advising on its defence in view of Ottoman threats during the new war between the Sultan and Venice. As he examined the shoreline, with the normally level beaches and shallow water alternating with sandbanks or deeper channels where the rivers enter the sea, his military and geological interests joined in partnership again.[47] He wrote at length to Lancisi about the sea bed of the Adriatic, and mentions finding evidence of subterranean streams and springs near Rimini which recalled the phenomenon he had seen at Cassis in Provence. When the emergency ended he reported to cardinal Paolucci on the production of plaster in Romagna, and this led him to write another of his accounts of gypsum, this time in connection with the sulphur workings of the area. Returning to Bologna, he and a colleague from the Institute went on to make an extensive tour in August 1719 of the hills behind Bologna and Modena. They climbed Monte Cimone, the highest point of the northern Appenines, and Marsigli's notes show him anxious to establish an upper limit or 'line', above which the extensive marine deposits found lower down no longer appeared; and he continued to look for a 'linea gypsea' running south and east as far as Ancona. But he was also offering advice to the Senate on that highly disturbing hydraulic problem, then in a new phase, the growing area of floodland between Bologna and the channels of the Po; and sent his botanist friends to examine the flora where the marshes were gaining ground.[48]

It looks therefore as if Marsigli spent less time in Rome after 1715, and less energy on ancient history, while exploring the natural history and geology of the countryside. A quite different interest brought his attention sharply back to the Institute: those metal types which he had given away with his collections! He wanted them used, and because the activity of printing intrigued him he started to compose notes for a history of typography and the famous printers of past ages.[49] Then, when there were few signs of the Institute's officers or professors showing any concern in the matter, he decided to set up a press himself with the thought of handing it over to them later. In 1719 he appointed a Frenchman from Besançon, a printer, to take charge of three presses which had been installed for him in a house (in the via Centotrecento) not far away from the Institute. As usual he appealed for help from Rome, this time for what he called his 'stamperia bolognese', and secured a privilege to print certain official documents and news sheets. Unfortunately it conflicted with another printer's well-established right. Moreover the Frenchman departed. In spite of such problems, in November 1720 Marsigli was writing hopefully to his old friend Scheuchzer that he had a number of works to be printed 'when, God willing, there exists a Bolognese press of a quality high enough to surprise the world outside Italy'.[50] A few months later he changed his mind on one point by deciding that it would be best to transfer his presses, not to the Institute but to his old neighbours the Dominicans, for whom he felt ever-increasing respect and affection. This was in turn associated with yet another project, the publication of a new catalogue of all his Persian, Arab, Turkish and Hebrew manuscripts deposited in the Institute.[51] He had already asked the great Maronite scholar and librarian at the Vatican, Joseph Assemani, to complete the work begun long ago in Vienna by the interpreter Talmann, and Marsigli himself finished writing an introduction for the catalogue on 6 May 1721. It gives a lively account of his life and adventures in Istanbul, Buda and Belgrade, and of his long continued search for oriental documents. On the following day he formally handed over his presses to the Dominicans, but never entrusted them or anyone else in Bologna with the printing of his own major works or the catalogue of his oriental manuscripts.[52]

In writing to Zurich he reported happily on the success of a more momentous negotiation with Rome. He had won a promise of substantial help to complete the building work at the Institute; and prefaced this good news with the remark that shortly he intended going to Livorno to start on a long voyage. Indeed he was pondering a new idea, in which his confidence that the financial problems of his foundation would shortly be solved fused with his design to travel outside Italy again.

Few other papers survive to guide us here: no letters to or from the port of Livorno, or invitations from Holland or England, with details which disclose the origins of Marsigli's last great journey. Preparations were certainly needed and in May 1721 he was still saying that he would soon be leaving Italy; but it was 26 September, ten months after writing to Scheuchzer, before he went on board an English ship at Livorno bound for London.[53] The sequence of dates tends to confirm what he said later, after returning to Bologna to plunge back into his quarrels with the Senate of the city: that in 1720 he was confident, having received an assurance of fresh funds, that building could now go ahead at the palace of the Institute.[54] He had therefore taken the opportunity to consider what additional books or material would be worth acquiring for his foundation, and whether to go abroad to seek the best advice on what to select and how to organise teaching and research. This led him to make the journey to London, Leyden and Amsterdam. He added a revealing remark which cannot be true: he was unable to travel overland because his dispute with the Habsburg government had never been resolved. On the contrary, there would have been few difficulties in passing through Switzerland and the states of the Empire, but in 1720 and for the next three years navigation in the western Mediterranean was complicated by the terrifying outbreak of bubonic plague in France. Journeys via Marseille and Paris were out of the question, while nervousness in England and Holland provoked severe quarantine regulations for ships, passengers, and goods arriving from Mediterranean ports like Livorno. It is therefore probable that he was considering, before the epidemic reached Marseille, the idea of a long sea journey to countries previously unvisited. This tempted our inveterate traveller with his specialist marine and aquatic interests, while in Holland and England he would be able to collect the information he needed from the most eminent scientists, attract goodwill for the Institute, and look for new books and other material.

This was Marsigli's programme, but a note addressed to the English botanist William Sherard and written shortly before he landed in England, shows how he was forced to alter his plans.[55] His original intention had been to go first to Holland, and then to England in the summer when he could see for himself, in good weather, the famous tin and lead mines of the country. However, at Livorno the only boat preparing to sail to the north was the 'Harley', bound for London, and the quarantine regulations were as strict in Holland as in England. He would only lose time by waiting, and duly embarked. It was now his intention to stay just a few days in London, meet Sir Isaac Newton, Dr Sloane and a few others, and look at the collections of the Royal Society before leaving for Holland. At Amsterdam he had already arranged a forwarding address. So Marsigli settled into his 'frigate', under captain Richard Harley (or Harle) who informed our traveller that – in view of the epidemic – he hoped not to touch land anywhere until they reached London. This proved to be the case. It meant that there was much less coast to be seen, or cliffs or dunes or river mouths, than the geologist Marsigli would have wished.[56] What he could and did do, each day when the time came for Harley to take the sun's altitude, was to follow suit by making his own observations on the weather, wind and the salinity of the water: these, with the location and date, he noted down; perhaps the captain assisted him, as his secretary Muller did long ago. Marsigli greatly admired the efficient arrangements for navigation on the ship, and the methodical logging of its progress and position day by day. Everything went smoothly as they ran ahead as fast as possible through the Straits of Gibraltar and into the Atlantic, in order to anticipate the winter storms of the Channel. They arrived at the mouth of the Thames off Sheerness and then – although he knew what was coming, it did not please our impatient traveller – were delayed for six weeks in quarantine, together (he says) with 40 other ships.[57] He finally came ashore at Rochester and travelled on to London. The narrative depends on his own testimony, but a laconic entry in the *London Mercury: or, Great Britain's weekly Journal* supports him. In its issue for 28 October (OS), a long list of ships includes the 'Harle', under captain Harle; it was reported to be off the Downs, having arrived from Livorno. The letter penned a little later by Marsigli to Sherard, when he began his period of quarantine, begs for medicine and the loan of any new book on the

ciences in Latin or French, to while away the time. The bearer of this plea
vas one Franchi, a Jew from Livorno resident in London who would be
mployed by Marsigli as his English agent.

A week after landing Marsigli's bold signature was entered in the 'charter
book' of the Royal Society.[58] Several years later he described to his friend
Quincy the splendid welcome he received from Sir Isaac Newton the president, and the fellows, and the speeches and ceremony of this great occasion
n his life.[59] In 1691 he had been 'elected' and now, in 1721, he was admitted
n person to the fellowship. Such an account was echoed, also a few years
ater, by the historian of the Clementine Academy who wrote that count
Marsigli, 'greatly loved and esteemed by Sir Isaac (who, to speak as a
painter, is the Raphael of philosophers and mathematicians), was presented
by him to that celebrated and learned Society'.[60] Unfortunately the formal
ecord of the meeting on that day, 14 December (OS), notes merely that Sir
Hans Sloane presided, and thanked Marsigli for his treatise on the *Funghi*
vhich had been 'formerly sent to the Society as a present'. At the same time
he welcomed him as a member. The minutes next refer to Marsigli on the
following 22 March, when the contents of a letter from him were reported
by Halley, with Newton presiding.[61] Marsigli had written from Holland,
and among other things transmitted the welcome news from Bologna that
he new observatory would be completed by September; thereafter the
Society in London might expect to receive details of the observations made
at the Institute.[62]

The high colouring of these Italian accounts of the first meeting when
Marsigli was present in the rooms off Fleet Street, is itself of interest. He
assumed that his prestige in Italy was to some extent due to his association
with the Royal Society and the Académie des Sciences. These 'royal' academies enjoyed and conferred a status south of the Alps which the patronage
of dukes, princes or republics did not equal. At the same time the lively
discussion of Newtonian ideas in early eighteenth-century Padua, Naples
and Rome magnified the portentous image of that distant figure who presided in London. Marsigli, in determining to visit northern Europe, surely
anticipated some advantages by appearing in person to confirm his membership of the Royal Society. It was already an honour of long standing. It
was commemorated by the dedication of his *Prodromus*. Publicly confirmed
and reported, it promised extra leverage in Bologna while dealing with the
senators on behalf of his Institute. It would raise his prestige as an author if
he chose to publish his researches old or new.

In substance his recollections of London were correct. The botanist
Sherard was outstandingly welcoming. Others, Sloane and Halley, were
friendly enough. Sherard took Marsigli to see Newton privately and they
conversed on physical problems, if briefly, because Marsigli had no English,
Newton knew no French and found difficulty in speaking Latin; he was
then 82 years of age.[63] There was also a second meeting between the two,
but on a more formal occasion. Such is Marsigli's earlier description of his

contact with Newton. More moderately phrased than the story told a few years later, it appears in a report to members of the Institute giving them his impressions of the Royal Society.[64] He began by admitting that the buildings and collections of the Society in London were unimpressive. He then observed with approval that the Fellows paid little attention to distinctions of birth or religion, and described the protocol and setting of a meeting. 'It was easy to go from one seat to another to speak to somebody'; in discussion English was spoken, and 'formal argument of the scholastic kind was forbidden'. Experiments were performed in the neighbouring room after a paper had been read to the company and discussed, but the apparatus and implements always belonged to the individual, not to the Society. The account goes on to describe the reception of Marsigli on 14 December: the vice-president's speech of welcome, given in French, referred approvingly to the Institute at Bologna and the mutual benefit to be expected from a correspondence between the two learned societies. The vice-president also begged for speedy publication of his colleague's work on the Danube, hinting that the Royal Society might be ready to give financial assistance, and then asked Marsigli to sign the Society's great book, containing the names of all its members since the foundation. Afterwards Marsigli replied by turning these compliments round, with no more than brief aside on the misfortunes which had delayed the appearance in print of his work. He ended with a tribute to the memory of the English scientists' Italian hero in that period, Malpighi, his own teacher.

Later in the same session a point arose which greatly preoccupied him. In an anatomical paper offered to the Society it was observed that his own young friend, Morgagni, claimed a discovery that had in fact been published in the *Philosophical Transactions* several years earlier. After some debate the vice-president, and also Marsigli, argued that this could happen easily enough because the printed proceedings of the Royal Society were always in English, 'a language (said Marsigli) very little known in Italy'. The conclusion he drew was that a translator would be needed in Bologna, to make the *Philosophical Transactions* and other works in English available to members of the Institute . Somewhat later he thought of commissioning an Italian translation of the general index, which he understood was going through the press, for all volumes of the Transactions between 1662 and 1715. Other stray pieces of information show how he was entertained by Sherard and his brother, and by Sir Hans Sloane in his 'anatomical' cabinet. Dr Mathew Mead and Rev. William Derham gave him copies of works they had written; Halley gave him a book and also maps. 'The Count of Marsigli was here at Christmas', wrote Woodward the geologist, 'and had all the civilities shown him that he gave me opportunity'.[65] Marsigli remained six weeks in London – not five or six days, as he had planned earlier – and spent part of his time with the booksellers, many of whom kept their stocks in the houses round St Paul's churchyard, half a mile away from where the Royal Society held its meetings. He made it his business to list all the English

books which he thought the Institute should have, including a complete run
of the *Philosophical Transactions* and those written in Latin by Englishmen,
paying special attention to the works of Newton and Ray.[66] It is pleasant to
imagine him browsing in the city of London's paradise of books and booksellers' catalogues, before setting off for Holland on 23 January 1722.

This was a miserable voyage. He resumed his marine observations, but
quarrelled with the captain when ice floes trapped the ship at the mouth of
the Maas.[67] With vivid impressions of what was, for him, a novel type of
shoreline he reached Rotterdam. A letter to Sherard describes his difficult
journey. Then, gradually, it became clear to Marsigli that he had in front of
him a stay of the greatest felicity in the United Provinces.[68]

He was absorbed there by almost the whole span of his interests, war and
politics apart. Evidence is patchy, but suggests that an important and novel
stimulus was his acquaintance with Herman Boerhaave. Sherard's letter of
introduction took him from Rotterdam to Leyden, where the great man
gave him the very warmest welcome. Almost equal in fame to Newton or
Leibniz, Boerhaave pursued interests which were distinctly closer than
Newton's to Marsigli's at this period, and he gave him every encouragement. What this Italian traveller and amateur scientist wanted, what he
could do in Holland, and what Boerhaave could do for him, all came into
focus. When the professor first confirmed Marsigli's arrival to Sherard, he
noted somewhat cautiously that 'your Homer' seemed a man of far-reaching
ideas, but was possibly unaware of the great effort required to make anything of them.[69] Marsigli, writing on 23 March, applauded Boerhaave's
lectures on chemistry, while hoping to return to Leyden in May to hear his
course on botany. He was meanwhile making a round of the natural history
collections in Amsterdam, mostly shells and insects mounted for display,
and privately owned, but seems to have preferred the rarities he found in
the botanical garden of the city.[70] He heard of a forthcoming sale of such
items; and wanted to buy the marine plants listed in the catalogue if they
were reasonably priced, to include them in a new 'herbarium' which he
would give to the Institute in Bologna. Not everything about Amsterdam
impressed him; he regarded it with some condescension as more commercial than intellectual in atmosphere. Nor does he tell us anything about the
many Italians living in the town, people like his banker and his priest. What
he admired were the extraordinary Dutch drainage systems which maintained such a heavily populated city in a delta country. These led him to
observe, indeed to study, the peat diggings of the neighbourhood and he
associated this topic with what he had already seen and still wished to
explore, the dunes and dykes of the coast. Peat, sand, and seaweed were the
ascendant elements in the newest version of his 'structure of the earth', part
of which was the 'natural history of the sea'.

In the summer he returned to Leyden, saw Boerhaave again, and then
went on a tour of the Dutch coast which took him as far as the island of
Texel. He made notes and sketches as usual, and collected specimens of

seaweed and other marine plants. In this context it seemed natural enough that Marsigli and Boerhaave should meanwhile have discussed together a new plan for publishing the manuscripts of Marsigli's earlier marine researches. These had already been sent back from Paris to Bologna and, with a view to publication there, were apparently translated from French into Latin before Marsigli left Italy.[71] As the days went by in Leyden and Amsterdam he probably learnt to appreciate, more fully than before, that Boerhaave was a scholar and teacher at the height of his fame, writing a great deal and assured of a wide public both among students of medicine and the more serious virtuosi. His current project was the preparation of a new edition of Vesalius. It followed that booksellers and publishers loved Boerhaave; and to have his recommendation was good enough for the bookseller-publishers of Amsterdam, Leyden or the Hague in the 1720s, the most enterprising of their kind in Europe. A commendatory preface of Boerhaave's was better still, for them and for the author he befriended. So Marsigli, grasping the opportunity, asked for the manuscripts of his marine research to be sent from Bologna. They arrived. Boerhaave approved, even though there was still missing that 'fifth' part which Marsigli had been hoping to write for fifteen years. In its place he offered now to write up his more recent observations, on the voyage from Italy and along the coasts of Holland and Zealand, in the form of a letter to Boerhaave added to the original work. It was even suggested that the new publication could include a reprinting of Marsigli's first marine study, on the currents and vegetation of the Bosphorus.[72] By November, a group of publishers had come forward. It was understood that a notable literary figure in Amsterdam, Jean Leclerc, would edit the work. The principal engraver to be employed was Mathew Pool, also well known. Difficulties were surmounted as they arose: Marsigli apparently assumed that a Latin translation would be printed but the publishers preferred the original French, and they declined to wait for his proposed continuation of the work. He had returned to Italy when the printing of the text was complete by the summer of 1725. The publishers pressed Boerhaave to compose his preface,[73] the great man obliged at once with a most eloquent tribute, and the *Histoire Physique de la Mer* appeared in the same year.

One thing led to another. As Marsigli wrote to Sherard in 1722, there was a bid to republish his essay on fungus; but he intended first to arrange for a copy to go from Italy to London, in order to submit it for approval and comment from members of the Royal Society. More important, he had managed to bring to the notice of the Dutch his other manuscripts in Bologna, above all his opus on the Danube. The subject was noble, he must have told them, and the text was comprehensive and complete, carefully written out in six manuscript volumes; there were hundreds of copperplates ready, with only a few illustrations still to be drawn and engraved. A Prodromus or prospectus of the year 1700, dedicated to the Royal Society, had won praise from scholars and other well-placed persons everywhere. Abandoning his plans for printing the work in Bologna, with encouragement from Boerhaave he now offered it to the publishers of the United Provinces, confident in the knowledge that they had a particular interest in projects of the kind. They were similar to Einmart and his friends in Nuremberg twenty and thirty years earlier, but traded on a bigger scale after the pacification of Europe by the great treaties of 1713, 1714 and 1721. One line of their business was to satisfy the richer customers, patrons who had to fill the shelves of handsome libraries recently built or recently enlarged by fashionable architects. They wanted to satisfy a specific demand for gorgeous folios, finely bound, fully illustrated. Marsigli had long ago entered this world as an unusual client – he wanted suitably bound books, but cared less evidently for their architectural setting – and was now again offering to enter it as an author. First there had been the Sea, now there were his volumes on the Danube, with perhaps the Turks and other good things to follow.

During the autumn of 1722 the discussions advanced, and on 8 December reached a further stage when Marsigli went to a notary in Amsterdam in order to empower his banker in that city, Cesare Sardi of Lucca, to negotiate with the publishers who had come forward.[74] On 1 January 1723, he wrote again to Sherard saying that shortly he hoped to sail back to Livorno via Lisbon; he was busy making collections of exotic plants, fossils, samples of timber and of minerals, with the needs of the Institute in mind.[75] He related how generous Boerhaave had been with material from Ceylon, and mentioned (not for the first time) the name of his agents in Livorno in case Sherard and his English colleagues could send samples or specimens from the English colonies overseas. At the same time he finished drafting his detailed reports to the Institute, describing his reception at and the procedures of the Royal Society in London, together with long lists of scientific books he recommended for purchase, and an assurance that Dutch and English booksellers' catalogues would in future be forwarded.[76] It therefore seemed that the physical world of Asia, Africa and America, in samples or transplants of rock and vegetation, and the intellectual resources of northern Europe, would all be reaching Bologna by way of Amsterdam; while coming in the opposite direction, from Bologna to Amsterdam, were his own manuscripts for publication. With such an achievement behind him, he was returning to Italy.

Yet from this point onwards uncertainties multiply, and Marsigli's biography looks more and more tenuous a topic. It is hard to be quite certain when and by what route he returned to Italy. During the last seven years of his life, up to 1730, it is sometimes equally difficult to say where he was at a given moment, or what he was doing. The biographical evidence becomes sporadic. By contrast Marsigli's principal interests have left some remarkable traces.

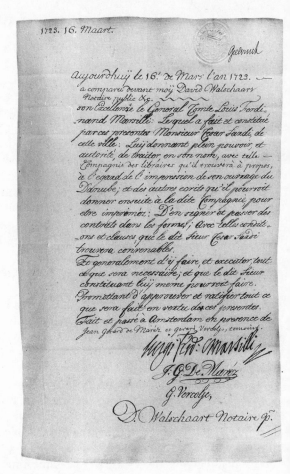

30   Marsigli in Amsterdam:
he authorises his banker to act
for him.

V

Marsigli stayed on in Holland. Although reported to have been ill, what
kept him there was probably the process of coming to an agreement with the
publishers who intended to print his work on the Danube. By no means all
the details could be left to an agent's discretion, and it was necessary for
Marsigli to become at least noddingly acquainted with certain complexities
of the Dutch book trade. The businessmen concerned – occasionally Huguenot or German in origin – usually formed partnerships to diminish the
risks of their bigger ventures, and in this instance the two Amsterdam
publishers principally concerned looked to three others at the Hague. Discussion between them, and with Marsigli, indeed took time but on 16
March 1723 the agreement was ready. In Amsterdam that day Marsigli once
again empowered Sardi to act for him, and in the presence of a notary and
witnesses Sardi signed the principal contract, together with the Amsterdam
publishers and two men from the Hague (the third was also a party, but
absent).[77] They were 'the Company', and the document defines their re-

uirements and those of 'Monsieur le Comte Marsigli'. For example, the Company insists on speed: as soon as Marsigli arrives back in Bologna, without any delay he must put together everything belonging to his work on the Danube, the text, engravings and plates, ensuring that they all follow in the right sequence, in six bound manuscript volumes. He should report on the progress of these preparations to Sardi, who will in turn inform the Company. To save time, the larger maps which still needed engraving should be sent on ahead. When the volumes are ready, their packing must be done with extreme care, transport must be overland to Holland (and not by sea) at the publishers' expense; and Sardi, on receiving them, will hand everything to the Company. Those were Marsigli's obligations. His own wishes were mirrored in the corresponding clauses. Paper of the highest quality and the largest size, with a quality of texture matching the splendour of the engravings, and type of similar excellence, must be used. Then, when the publishers had finished with the manuscript and plates and drawings, they were all to be sent back promptly, carriage paid, to the Institute in Bologna. Marsigli excepted from this provision only the frontispieces, vignettes, and initial letters preceding each of the volumes: he wished the publishers to keep these, partly as a token of his own good wishes, partly as a memorial of the merit of Bolognese artists in his day. He also excepted, as he had to, the plates actually engraved in Holland for his work. But Marsigli's concern for the Institute appeared again in the stipulations about payment. The sum of 10,000 Dutch florins was mentioned; but he waived this on condition that the Company substituted for it books to that value, chosen in the first instance by Marsigli as suitable for the Institute. His list of preferences would be sent to Bologna for revision, and then returned to Amsterdam. The members of the Company undertook to draw up their own list of what books they had, or were easily found elsewhere, before a final selection of works for the Institute in Bologna to the value of 10,000 florins was made. The price of each book included would be 'reasonable', the current price. Finally Marsigli was promised 20 free copies of his work, and the Company very naturally insisted that the manuscript and plates they returned to the Institute should not be used to print another edition 'in Italy or elsewhere' for a hundred years.[78] An additional agreement was signed by Sardi on behalf of Marsigli, and by the publishers, at the same time. It had nothing to do with the printing of the six volumes on the Danube, but again emphasises Marsigli's preoccupation with the Institute. He gives the Dutchmen priority in the printing of any future proceedings, memoirs or other work to be published in the name of the Institute, on certain conditions. The volumes are to be of quarto size, finely printed on fine paper, with the illustrations engraved by the best Dutch masters; the arrangements for paying editors and authors are described; the publishers will hand over 25 free copies. For his part Marsigli, 'after his happy return home', has pledged that the Institute will ratify this agreement.

If the opening clauses of the main agreement were taken with any seriousness it was to be expected that Marsigli would next go speedily to Italy by travelling overland. Before he did so, his publishers can have had little difficulty in persuading him to help them with a 'puff' of his name and reputation among the reading public. He was put in touch with a Huguenot journalist and author usually based in Utrecht, de Limiers, who was commissioned to write up the topic of Marsigli and the foundation of the Institute in Bologna.[79] De Limiers refers to Marsigli's silent modesty in conversation, which sounds most improbable; but he gave de Limiers certain papers describing events in Bologna in 1711 and 1712, the purchase of the Poggi palace, and the foundation of his Institute for the sciences and the Clementine Academy. Using this material, de Limiers wrote a slim, fluent little book which also drew attention to Marsigli's work on the natural history of the sea, then at the press, before describing in some detail the contents of the six volumes on the Danube. The 'puff' appeared later in 1723, and in the following year de Limiers himself produced two more books on very different topics. On their title pages he was described as a 'member of the Academy of Sciences and Arts of Bologna': perhaps the founder had conferred this title on the helpful journalist.

By then Marsigli was in Italy. In August 1723, writing from Ferrara, he expressed high hopes to his friends in Padua of soon being done with the Danube, and going off to enjoy the gentler climate of Marseille. On 1 December Boerhaave reported to Sherard: 'the Count is drowning in his Danube', so that he must have heard from Marsigli how hard he was at work on his revision.[80] In May 1724 Marsigli was gratified to hear that the printers were getting some new type; the result would be 'magnificent'. In November, while pleasurably residing by the shore of Lake Garda he received proofs of the text of the first volume, and announcing this to Morgagni added that the text and plates of the other five had now reached Amsterdam. But in February 1725 a further letter shows that the great venture was entering another phase in its progress towards publication. Marsigli hoped that the next post would bring him copies of a new Prodromus.[81]

The Amsterdam prospectus turned out to be completely different in style from the ponderous catalogue printed for Marsigli in 1699.[82] The brochure of 1725 was part of the publishers' attempt to reach a scattered market through their European network of booksellers. The technique, familiar to the trade, was to invite subscriptions for a limited edition of this magnificent and comprehensive work, by an author to whom a brief but glowing tribute was paid. Specimen illustrations accompanied the brochure, sent out in January 1724 to a long list of booksellers trading in cities as far apart as Riga, Edinburgh, Prague and Rome, with a concentration in towns of the Empire and the Low Countries. Subscriptions of 30 Dutch florins would be received between 1 April and 1 September, but not later. The total cost to subscribers for this limited edition of 625 copies would be 150 florins, while any remaining copies would cost 200 florins. It was intended to distribute the volumes in pairs, the first before December 1725, the second six months later, and the last before December 1726; on each occasion 40 florins would be payable by subscribers. These terms were also advertised in several issues of the main Amsterdam newspaper in July and August 1725.[83] At the same time – between the end of August and the beginning of October – we find that a library of unusual fame and importance was being auctioned at the Hague, the collection of books originally assembled by the abbé Bignon, mentor of the Académie des Sciences in Paris. It had passed through the hands of John Law to cardinal Dubois, who died in 1723, before coming on the market in Holland. The printed catalogue of this *Bibliotheca Duboisiana*, in four volumes, contains 29,922 entries.[84] But one of the auctioneers was de Hondt of the Company, Marsigli's publishers. He and his colleagues proceeded to honour their engagement and pay him his royalty in books, by buying these in from the volumes up for auction.[85] The items were transferred to the agent Sardi. Marsigli, then in Italy, was delighted to learn of their splendid provenance and anticipated transmitting them to his Institute.

In the years 1723–6 the long-neglected work on the Danube was certainly in capable hands, those of his Dutch publishers; we have caught at least glimpses of his and their activity.

VI

Marsigli, wrote Boerhaave on 23 March 1723, has been ill but hopes shortly to leave for Livorno.[86] There is no further mention of such a voyage, while Marsigli's eighteenth-century biographers relate that on his way home from Holland he first visited Aachen and then Bourbon, which lies due south of Aachen and Luxembourg.[87] From there he went across Switzerland to Lake Garda, and in due course to Bologna. This is a plausible itinerary. It was attractive enough for a geologist like Marsigli, if he took a fancy to test the mineral waters of Aachen (with Spa not far distant) and the famous springs of Bourbon, or to revisit the Alps after a long spell on the plains of the lower Rhine and Meuse. But certainly he was in Bologna by the end of August 1723, writing from there to his friend Morgagni: he was completing the piece for Boerhaave, he said, already begun on the way through France, and hoped to go soon to Livorno to fetch the goods coming by sea.[88] He was referring first of all to the work, in the form of a letter to Boerhaave, to be added to the forthcoming publication of his marine researches; and then to his understanding that in Livorno, arrived by sea, were his purchases from Holland of material for the natural history collections of the Institute. A fortnight later he mentions the other main task ahead, the preparation of his 'Danube' for the printers. What he told the public a little later in the preface to that work was therefore true: returning to Bologna from Holland, he had drawn the six manuscript volumes from the dust where they had lain for such a long time.[89] This dust, for the last ten years, was in the Institute where Marsigli's bequests were kept, and he must have treasured the thought that the publication of his work on the Danube, and further benefits for the Institute, were written into the recent agreement with the 'Company' in Holland.

He laboured through the winter. Here and there he revised, or inserted extra material, or found that what he had thought complete was unfinished. For example, his contract refers to the whole-page frontispiece of each volume as an example of the skill of the Bolognese artists. The truth seems to be that there were no such frontispieces in 1723, and if Marsigli hoped to enlist at short notice the services of leading artists of the Clementine Academy, like Franceschini or Manzini, he was disappointed. Instead he commissioned Franceschini's young and untried pupil, Antonio Rossi, to produce suitable evocations of his subject matter.[90] The published volumes III–VI reproduce Rossi's work but those for I and II are the more accomplished work of Dutchmen commissioned by the publishers; and the Dutch engraved all six of the frontispieces. A good many of the original drawings still needed engraving, perhaps more of them than Marsigli had realised, and the accuracy of the new Dutch plates – especially those of Muller's maps – was clearly one of his concerns when proofs of the first volume reached him.[91] With his current interest in the development of Roman archaeology, he felt it desirable to add to his references in volume II, to expand his accounts of the Roman presence in the Balkan region and Dacia, of Trajan's bridge and the Roman network of communications. A plate showing the use of elephants in Roman warfare,[92] for example, looks like a later addition to earlier ones of elephant bones dug from the Danubian marshes. Equally, it is not possible to be certain at what date – in 1704 or 1724 – he fixed the order of the appendices in his final volume; alterations may have been made at both times. Certainly Marsigli now asked his friend Morgagni to correct and amplify his remarks on the anatomy of the sturgeon. The result was a closer, more professional look at sturgeon taken from the river Po, not from the Danube, with some extra illustrations.[93]

By March 1724 he felt able to announce that the text of the Danube and all its plates were ready. Repeating the statement two months later he certainly toiled on through both spring and summer before sending off the last manuscript volume. Other work preoccupied him as well; the promised supplement for the History of the Sea was completed in the course of 1724[94] and he began re-examining his account, set aside long since, of the Ottoman empire. No formal agreement with his Dutch colleagues to publish it has yet come to light, but they must have encouraged him. In September he claimed to be 'engulfed' in the Turks, and six months later reported that he had finished, except for certain statistical tables. These would need another four or five days' work, he thought, if someone with a good head for figures could be found in Padua to help him. Marsigli asserted confidently that his

friends would enjoy the fruits of his Turkish labour! So another segment of
the early experience of eastern Europe, in part dating further back than
anything to do with his studies of the Danube, appeared almost ready for
the publishers, printers and illustrators waiting in Amsterdam.

Many of the letters about his progress in perfecting these works for the
press were written from a lodging by Lake Garda.[95] The attraction here,
ever since he first saw the lake during his journey home from Holland, had
been the usual magic conjunction of a stretch of water with the surrounding
hills or cliffs, revealing the truths of geology as he understood and studied
them. While the Turks were driving him 'mad', he explained, it was a
delight to look out of the window at the scenery outside, and walk every day
for an hour or two by the shore of the lake. A geological and hydrological
study of Garda, together with a certain amount of mapping, was finished by
October 1725.[96] But at the end of the year he was in Venice, to receive there
copies of the *Histoire physique de la Mer* just published.[97] He commented
that the printing and engraving appeared of high quality, while the praise
expressed in the great Boerhaave's prefatory remarks left him gratified,
even bemused. It was a glorious moment. Later he discovered some inaccu-
racy in the engravings of this book, and errors in placing them in the text.
On the other hand, on a different occasion he regretted that his account of
Ottoman military institutions could not be printed in Italy, saying that
unfortunately one had to go nowadays to publishers abroad for the beauty
of their type, speed in doing the job, and generous dealing with the author.[98]
It was another instance of Marsigli's readiness to be critical of his own
countrymen, convinced as he was of ultramontane technical and scientific
superiority.

The fact that the Dutch were willing to print and publish his works
confirmed another of his beliefs: that he was himself a scientist, a scholarly
investigator, who deserved recognition. The learned men of Paris, London,
and Leyden, and the libraries and booksellers of Europe, were welcoming
him into the Republic of Letters even if the senators at home, in his opinion,
remained too grudging. He had gone to northern Europe and returned,
revised and prepared his manuscripts for publication, and pressed forward
with some new research: but what were the consequences in Bologna?

VII

In 1724 and 1725 one can visualise this ageing military man spending as
much time as possible on the riviera of Garda. He praises the food and the
excellent local society. He treats the fishermen, and from their boats takes
soundings, and draws profiles of the shore from the lake, and then carries
the fish to his lodging for careful anatomical examination. From Garda
Marsigli also went to Chioggia where the Venetian lagoon makes one of its

entries to the open sea. Again he studied the water and the fish, as enamoured as ever of marine research. Very reasonably, his earliest biographer therefore entitled this part of his hero's career 'the journey to Salò [on Garda] and Venice'. It had followed the travels to England and Holland. It preceded a 'second journey to Marseille'. He also went with his friend Monti to Livorno in 1723 to fetch the fourteen large cases or chests arrived by ship, which held his new collection of botanical and zoological material from the Indies;[99] they were stored in a house rented by Marsigli not far from the Institute. He appeared in Rome, reporting to the new Pope on the excellent results of his mission to England and Holland. Marsigli's later years look like a sequence of journeys away from Bologna, rather than a phase of residence there which was interrupted from time to time. Yet these travels in Italy were in fact no more than excursions. He had always to return to business in Bologna.

At first everything appeared to be going well. He is said to have been satisfied in 1723 to find the observatory of the Institute 'almost finished'; and in May 1724 Marsigli composed a Latin letter to Sir Isaac Newton, advising him that the building was now complete and commending it very highly; but adding that he hoped to venture next to Provence.[100] He did not do so, returning instead to the territory around Garda. This halcyon period, with the revision of his manuscripts, the continued exploration of rock and water, and occasional visits to his academic friends in Padua, lasted into 1725 when he was again pulled back to Bologna. Marsigli would shortly endure the last and most distressing of all his quarrels with the Senate over the affairs of the Institute.

What incident or remark started it is nowhere made clear, but the appointment of a new librarian who was not Marsigli's chosen candidate – although 'with the most humble and respectful letter I begged the committee to consider Dr Bianconi' – certainly enraged him.[101] An underlying grievance after 1723 gradually became the principal irritant, while Marsigli's personal dislikes resulted from or fused with the main problem. This was, in his opinion, the failure of the Institute's officers to look after the Institute's property, aggravated by the failure of the responsible committee of senators to intervene. The founder of the Institute had a real sense of injury on this point, which was distinct from his other and older grievances over the Senate's failure to get on with the building and furnishing needed for the work of teaching and research. While he was abroad in 1722 there had been progress in that respect, as he admitted. However he also held that the many bequests and additions of material of different kinds, which he had given since the foundation in 1711, were never properly catalogued. Nor were they properly secured. The failure of the librarians to list and describe the books in their charge, to have them suitably bound, or to correspond with booksellers abroad was simply the most obvious illustration of a failure in several departments of the Institute. Trionfetti, the president until his death in 1722, his good old friend and teacher, set a bad example. Marsigli realised this but could not blame him. The next president (who had been secretary), all the librarians, and all the senators involved, were considered by him with much less forbearance. The problem looked the more serious when he returned from Holland with what he viewed as the wealth of the Indies, those fourteen cases of exotic material brought by sea to Livorno. It was magnified when he reflected on the wonderful royalty secured from the Dutch publishers for his 'Danube', the new collection of books on the sciences destined for Bologna. Would 'a second donation' to the Institute be neglected, with its precious items remaining unscheduled, with its new volumes uncatalogued, as so many other gifts of his had been neglected? He wanted to find some way of safeguarding his bequests and, in the course of negotiation, of insisting on improved conditions at the Institute in spite (as he thought) of the Senate's continuing niggardliness and obstruction. These were his wishes for his foundation in Bologna. They were emphasised when he was present in the town and not forgotten by the shores of Garda. On 22 June 1725 he gave instructions to his lawyer, arming him with copies of the original 'Instrument' of the foundation and Pope Clement's patent confirming it.[102] He threatened to demand the transfer of responsibility for the Institute from the Senate to the Legate, or to sell off everything he could for the benefit of charities.

When more papers come to light, more details may be worth giving. We can say that in the course of two years Marsigli reduced himself to despair. An old man, with hair now 'grey' and not 'chestnut', he again decided to leave Bologna 'for ever'. Finally he agreed to transfer to the city, on behalf of the Institute, the rewards of his journey to Holland. A settlement was reached partly because the Roman government intervened, and because its agent was the sensible Bolognese churchman and patrician, Prospero Lambertini.

By the spring of 1726, with Lambertini working hard to resolve the difficulties in a series of meetings, agreement was first reached on certain points. There were promises to make a detailed inventory in each department of the Institute; the professors would be held responsible for any losses. Marsigli's dislike of certain members of the staff, which he had broadened out into a sweeping attack on the practice of confining appointments to citizens of Bologna, and giving way to senatorial patronage in the process, was met by an anodyne declaration. 'Foreigners' were not to be excluded from such posts. On that point Marsigli had been right in general, but was less than fair to individuals. The librarian appointed by the Senators in 1723, Francesco Maria Zanotti, one of a large Bolognese clan with several exceptionally gifted members, proved a splendid and loyal servant of the Institute. He wrote up its early history, collected and published its papers, and became president forty years later.[103] His half-brother Gianpietro would likewise write the history of the Clementine Academy. Moreover, while Marsigli had given extraordinary support to Eustachio

31   The observatory of Marsigli's Institute: a century later.

Manfredi earlier, and approved his appointment as a professor of the new
foundation, in the 1720s he wrote him off as an absentee who simply drew
his salary. He disliked equally Manfredi's brother Gabriele, a distinguished
university mathematician who acted as secretary for the Senate committee
in charge of the Institute. In doing so he underestimated two very able men.
Certainly it was Manfredi's work, associated with the newly built observatory, that did most to give Bolognese astronomy its good name in Europe in
the eighteenth century.[104] Between 1720 and 1740 the Institute also appears
to have been the only place in Italy where experimental work in the natural
sciences was carried out.[105] Marsigli tended to judge his creation and its
personnel too harshly.

When he reclaimed the manuscripts of his 'Danube' from the Institute
and sent them to Amsterdam, he felt fully entitled to do so. There was a
rumpus when his critics afterwards claimed that these were the Institute's
property, which should not have been taken without formal permission, and
that if the manuscripts were printed any profit belonged to the public
authority in Bologna.[106] This authority, similarly, alone had the right to
instruct the agent in Amsterdam, Cesare Sardi, about the books received as

a royalty from the publisher. Marsigli was furious; and there was a related point of difference. He might admire the mass of African, Asian, and American specimens or samples sent from Holland, which were still in store in the accommodation he rented and used; professor Vallisneri from Padua might come to examine them, and testify – as he did in March 1726 – to their extraordinary value. But the opposition circulated a printed sheet addressed to the citizens of Bologna, scoffing that such estimates were exaggerated. Marsigli had on his hands and was seeking credit for a miscellaneous, second-rate collection of strange birds, butterflies and plants. Again, he was furious and requested the Legate's permission to publish his own account of the matter.

Perhaps no one took Marsigli as seriously as he took himself; many doubtless admired him, but were derisive as well. So things dragged on, and in March 1727 he made a number of significant gestures, by signing within a few days a whole sheaf of legal documents.[107] They concerned his gifts to the Dominicans, the fraternity of S. Caterina della Neve and the Clementine artists, but most important was a so-called 'second' donation to the city for the Institute. It signified his final consent to the transfer of the books received as a royalty for the *Opus Danubiale* and of his new natural history collections, for the benefit of the Institute. The men of S. Caterina were to keep their offertory box in the chapel of the Institute. The Dominicans were to come to the Institute in solemn procession every twenty-five years, bearing the standards given them by Marsigli depicting the life of St Thomas Aquinas. The Clementine artists, having received some extra funds from Marsigli, would award annual prizes in future to their best pupils. For its part the Senate, having received the 'second' donation, conceded certain points. It recognised Marsigli's ownership of what he intended to give them, by accepting his right to instruct Sardi to have the books in Amsterdam sent to the Institute. He also formally handed over the key of the house where the botanical and other collections from Holland were stored, and undertook to return his Danubian manuscripts and plates to the Institute. The Senate's officials had to promise not to impose fees on incoming holders of posts at the Institute, and there was a general undertaking to admit citizens of Bologna and outsiders to these posts on equal terms. The cardinal legate, Ruffo, presided over the whole transaction. Roman influence behind the scenes had pressed for a compromise but the Senate's constitutional responsibility for Marsigli's foundation was not impaired.

The shape of things to come, as Marsigli visualised them, now became clearer. In July 1727 he wrote to senator Alessandro Marsigli, his senior cousin,[108] whom he disliked as much as anybody in Bologna. One of his own family, here was a member of the Senate committee responsible for the shabby treatment of the Institute, as also for past and present insults to its founder. Marsigli again announced that he intended to depart for good. Moreover he was going to give up the family name and the family crest. He was inclined, he said, to surrender his status as a citizen of Bologna.

Preparing to leave the city in the course of the following year he devised one more gesture. For this purpose copies were assembled of documents which embodied the transactions of March 1727, and to these he added a few more. One contained the terms of the first foundation of the Institute in 1712. Another was the text of Pope Benedict XIII's letter of grateful thanks for Marsigli's gift to his Holiness of the printed volumes of the Danube, which were coupled with a specific and glowing reference to the Institute, and its enrichment by Marsigli's latest benefaction. There were also the old agreements, transferring his printing presses to the Dominicans, together with details of a recent bequest to them of July 1728, of the types for a number of oriental languages, which Marsigli had acquired from cardinal Albani in Rome.[109] All these documents were handed over for printing to the Dominicans and Marsigli solemnly prefaced them with the very last of his manifestoes.[110] It was entitled 'Farewell', and addressed to 'the Ecclesiastical and Secular Orders constituting the Republic of Bologna'. It solemnly begged them to take note of the enactments for the foundation of the Institute of Sciences and Liberal Arts, and to heed his final words on departing from the city. Once again he told the story of his youth, of dreaming first to set up a military academy in Bologna, and later to extend its interests into natural history, mathematics and good modern philosophy. He referred to his collection of useful material and equipment, to Pope Clement XI's help, and to stiff opposition overcome. Accordingly he intended to distribute copies of the present work containing these documents to every university in Europe, in order to preserve for posterity a reliable memorial of what he had tried to do for Bologna. He wished to announce that he was preparing to leave, to go right away to live a little longer and then die quietly. He accordingly encouraged his compatriots to protect the future of the famous Institute of Science and Art in their city.

The time had come for his journey, so long planned, to Provence. Quincy, who listened to Marsigli after his return, tells us something about it and probably romances a little more.[111] The old man – who now, renouncing his name, wishes to be known as the count d'Aquino and uses a seal stamped with a Dominican emblem[112] – is pictured again in Cassis and Marseille precisely recreating the life he had lived twenty years earlier. In Cassis, in his fisherman's cottage he has his simple furniture, his work table on which the fish and the samples of sand or rock are examined with all possible attention. He takes pleasure as before in chatting with the fishermen, while on visits to Marseille the archbishop and nobility entertain him. This idyll ended when Marsigli suffered a stroke and his physicians advised a return home. News of his brother Filippo's death helped to persuade him to go. He wanted to help his sister-in-law and invalid young nephew to handle the settlement of their family problems. So the noble d'Aquino became count Marsigli once more.

After the homecoming, about six months later, he faded and knew that his time was running short. At that point, one of Quincy's recollections is distinct and memorable.[113] He was present when Marsigli summoned the president and professors of the Institute to visit him. They arrived, and found him with certain of his manuscripts arranged on a table nearby. He explained that he had been working on these, but regrettably could not finish. They would be given to the Institute. Quincy confesses that he could not remember the subject of one of the papers, but another was certainly an addition to the History of the Sea; another, an addition to his early essay on the Bosphorus; and also there was his account of Ottoman military institutions, together with its illustrations. So Marsigli worked to the end; having found, perhaps very recently, the drawings of Janissary insignia he wanted to add to his manuscript about the Turks.[114] That notable book on the Ottoman empire was published after his death on 30 November 1730. It was the end of a long story, to which the Imperial officer contributed the unusual diversity of his experience.

The life Marsigli led has more to show us than the books he wrote or tried to write. In his travels he collected with unwearying zest samples of nature living or inanimate, and illustrations of these samples, in order to examine and describe them. Unfortunately he did so before it was understood how to classify such richness and variety in a truly rewarding, adequate manner. In the taxonomy of plants, rocks and minerals, or the study of birds and fishes, astonishingly greater progress would be made during the half-century after his death. In certain other respects he was a useful pioneer, possessing a wider view than anyone else in his day of the Ottoman empire's military framework, of the former Roman foothold along the middle Danube, and also – viewed in a different aspect – of the Mediterranean shoreline of France. These insights can be found in what he published. Yet they are modest, if measured against the energy and idiosyncracy that filled his days with a span of interests so wide that he was not just a soldier, not just a dabbler in the sciences or antiquities, but a personage quickly attracting notice wherever he went. Perhaps he enjoyed such superlative energy because other things were missing. We have not found evidence of his sexuality or lack of it; of any wish to father a family or maintain a noble household. We could not – others may do better – discover where his lodgings were in Vienna, during the winters he spent there augmenting his collections and pondering how to use them. It seems likely that he had no wish for an establishment of his own, for fine rooms and social graces or the pleasures of the table. He had other things to think of and, if sometimes quarrelsome, impressed sufficiently the Emperor and some of his ministers who employed him on business of undoubted political or military significance. He therefore embodies a curious blend of achievements which the political and intellectual and social circumstances of his period made possible. The relative lack of specialisation needed in the separate branches of learning, or indeed in military science; the relative ease with which the European nobilities climbed into preferment under ordinarily favourable conditions; the ease of transfer from service in one court to service in another, a trait specially marked in Imperial Vienna's reception of gifted men coming from the princely courts of Germany and Italy: all this helped Marsigli along. At the same time his fellow enthusiasts in the sciences and arts, with whom he corresponded, were beyond dispute an important group of men; and he equalled the best of them in his determination to devise a framework which would make more possible than before the continuous study of certain fields of knowledge. For these reasons he mirrors several decades of Europe's history in a style worthy of record.

Abbreviations

A: *Autobiografia di Luigi Ferdinando Marsili*, ed. Emilio Lovarini (Bologna, 1930).

BL: British Library, London, Additional MSS, etc.

BT: Transcripts from foreign archives in the Bundesarchiv, Berne.

Corrispondenza   *Corrispondenza epistolare tra Leopold I. Imperatore ed il P. Marco d'Aviano*,
epistolare: ed. O. Klopp (Graz, 1888).

DBI: *Dizionario Biografico degli Italiani.*

Fantuzzi: G. Fantuzzi, *Memorie della vita del generale Co. Luigi Ferdinando Marsigli* (Bologna, 1770).

FE: *Die Feldzüge des Prinzen Eugen von Savoyen* (Vienna, 1876–92).

Feldzüge: *Des Markgrafen Ludwig Wilhelm von Baden Feldzüge wider die Türken*, ed. P. Röder von Diersburg (Karlsruhe, 1839, 1842). This contains documents separately paginated: *Urkunden.*

HHSA: Haus-, Hof- und Staatsarchiv, Vienna.

KA FA: Alte Feldakten, Türkenkrieg, in the Kriegsarchiv, Vienna.

KA HKR: Registers of the Hofkriegsrat, in the Kriegsarchiv, Vienna.

Memorie: *Memorie intorno a Luigi Ferdinando Marsili* (Bologna, 1930).

MIÖG: *Mitteilungen des österreichischen Instituts für Geschichtsforschung.*

MS: Marsili MSS nos. 1–146, Biblioteca Universitaria di Bologna [BUB], codex 1044, catalogued by L. Frati in *La Bibliofilia*, vols. 27–30 (1925–8).

OD: *Opus Danubiale* or L.F. Marsigli, *Danubius Pannonico-Mysicus, observationibus geographicis, astronomicis, hydrographicis, historicis, physicis perlustris* (6 vols, The Hague and Amsterdam, 1726).

Prodromus: L. F. Marsigli, *Danubialis Operis Prodromus* (Nuremberg, 1700).

Quincy: L.D.C.H. de Quincy, *Mémoires pour la vie de M. le Comte de Marsigli* (Zurich, 1741).

R: Luigi Ferdinando Marsili, *Relazioni dei confini della Croazia e della Transilvania a sua Maesta Cesarea (1699–1701)*, ed. Rafaella Gherardi. Società e Cultura del Settecento in Emilia e Romagna: Studi e Ricerche (Modena, 1986).

RS: Royal Society, London.

Scritti inediti: *Scritti inediti di Luigi Ferdinando Marsili*, ed. A. Sorbelli (Bologna, 1930).

SP: State Papers Foreign, Public Record Office, London.

Stato militare: L.F. Marsigli, *Stato militare dell Imperio Ottomanno, incremento e decremento del medesimo* (The Hague and Amsterdam, 1732), reprinted in 1972 (Graz, ed. M. Kramer and R. F. Kreutel).

T: Haus-, Hof- und Staatsarchiv, Staatenabt. Türkei I.

ZB MS: Scheuchzer MSS, Zentralbibliothek, Zurich.

Notes

Note: Where no place of publication is mentioned, Bologna can be understood.

CHAPTER ONE

1. A. Bellettini, *La populazione di Bologna dal secolo xv all' unificazione d'Italia* (1961), pp. 26–7.

2. R. Zangheri, *La proprietà terriera e le origini del Risorgimento nel Bolognese* (1961), i. 99, n. 22.

3. S. Muzzi *Annali della città di Bologna*, vii (1864), pp. 23–5.

4. At another level, the extensive privileges of the 'German nation' in the university and city of Bologna had been safeguarded by Emperors Frederick Barbarossa and Charles V in 1158 and 1530: these were significantly diminished by the Senate and Pope Gregory XIII in 1575–6.

5. For the links between Roman and Bolognese public finance, L. Nina, *Le finanze pontifiche sotto Clemente XI* (Milan, 1928), 565ff.; G. Orlandelli, *Due relazioni sulla erezione dei monti di pubbliche prestanze in Bologna (1665–1714)* (Milan, 1968), *passim*; G. Orlandelli, 'Nota di storia economica sulla signoria dei Bentivoglio', *Atti e Memorie*, Dip. per la st. pat. di Romagna, NS 3 (1953), 207–14, 239–40.

6. A. di P. Masini, 'Forma dello stato e del governo presente politico della città di Bologna', *Bologna Perlustrata*, ii (1666), pt. 3, pp. 4–9; G. Zucchini, *Edifici di Bologna* (Rome, 1931, 1954), i. 112; P. Colliva, 'Bologna dal xiv al xviii secolo: 'governo misto' o signoria senatoria?', *Storia della Emilia Romagna*, ed. A. Berselli, ii (1977), pp. 13–34. As late as 1725 the legate banned an issue of playing cards (for the game of tarot) which indicated that Bologna had a 'mixed government'. L. Frati, *Il settecento a Bologna* (1923), p. 94.

7. M. Fanti, *Basilica di San Petronio*, s.d., p. 425. The marble facing of the 'west' front remains incomplete.

8. A. Sorbelli and L. Simeoni, *Storia della università di Bologna* (1944, 1947), ii. 7–25; F. Cavazza, *Le scuole dell'antico studio bolognese* (Milan, 1896), pp. 202–10, 230–78; G. P. Brizzi, 'Le istituzioni educative e culturali', *Storia d. Emilia Romagna*, ii. 443–61.

9. Lists of these officeholders in G. N. P. Alidosi, *I signori Anziani Consoli, e Confalonieri di Giustizia . . . di Bologna 1456–1670* (1670), but *cf.* 'Le insignie degli Anziani del Comune dal 1530 al 1796', *Pubb. d. Archivi di Stato*, vols xvi and xxxvi (Rome, 1954, 1960).

10. For the Confaloniere's banquets, Frati, *op. cit.*, pp. 72–9 and further succulent information in V. Tanara, *L'economia del cittadino in villa. Libri vii* (ed. 1648), pp. 539–41; the setting

of these feasts is shown in G. Cuppini, *I palazzi senatorii a Bologna. Architettura come imagine del potere* (1974), figs 60–61 and pl. v.

11. Muzzi, *Annali*, viii, 42–8.
12. A. M. Matteucci, *Carlo Francesco Dolci e l'architettura bolognese del settecento* (Rome, 1968), p. 102; G. Mezzanotte, 'Gli architetti L. Binago e G. Ambrosio Mazenta', *L'Arte*, 60 (1961), pp. 231–71; E. Feinblatt, 'An unnoticed ceiling by Franceschini', *Burlington Magazine*, 101 (1961), pp. 312–13.
13. A. M. Matteucci, *op. cit.*, pp. 5–6, 70–84, 158.
14. Cuppini, *op. cit.*, p. 306.
15. The principal early authority remains G. Fantuzzi, *Memorie della vita del general Co. Luigi Ferdinando Marsigli* (1770) and his *Notizie delli scrittori bolognesi*, v (1786), pp. 286–327. Fantuzzi used the manuscript now printed as *Autobiografia di Luigi Ferdinando Marsili*, ed. E. Lovarini (1930), together with papers from the surviving Marsigli collections and others now vanished; P. S. Dolfi, *Cronologia delle famiglie nobili di Bologna* (1670), pp. 340–41; G. B. Guidicini, *Cose notabili della città di Bologna*, ed. 1869, ii, 202ff. My general guide will be the autobiography, but checked as far as possible against other sources.
16. The marchese Riario Sforza (who died in 1676), played an interesting part in the economic rivalry of Venice and Bologna. Venice barred the import of manufactured goods, but imported raw hemp from Bologna. Riario was a spokesman in Venice for the manufacturing interest in Bologna which protested against this bias. U. Marcelli, *Saggi economico sociali sulla storia di Bologna* (1962), p. 26.
17. For some examples, *The Baglivi Correspondence*, ed. D. M. Schallian, (Cornell, 1974), pp. 9–19.
18. Fantuzzi, *op. cit.*, p. 5.
19. B. L. Additional MS 22, 190, ff. 153–4. The explanatory note from Octavian Pulleyn to John Covel precedes this Italian letter of introduc-

tion to Marsigli.
20. H. B. Adelmann, *Marcello Malpighi and the evolution of embryology* (Cornell, 1966), i. 423, 426–7; M. Malpighi, *Correspondence* (ed. Adelmann, Cornell, 1975), n. 384.
21. L. F. Marsili, *Scritti inediti* (1930), p. 195; L. D. Quincy, *Marsigli* (Zurich, 1741), ii. 28f. The dating of Marsigli's earliest geological interest depends on a letter to Malpighi (n. 390A).
22. S. Muzzi, *Annali*, viii. 165–284.
23. C. C. Malvasia, *Vite di pittori bolognesi*, ed. A. Arfelli. (1961).
24. Fantuzzi, *Notizie*, v (1786), pp. 276–8.
25. *Rime degli Accademici Gelati di Bologna*, 1597; *Prose de' signori Accademici Gelati di Bologna* (1671), pp. 299–318, 365–92. According to a note on the flyleaf, the copy of the 'Prose' in the BL was sent to Henry Oldenburg by Malpighi in 1672.
26. D. Guglielmini, *La meridiana del tempio di S. Petronio* (1695); Cassini's letter to Sig. A. P. (BL. 532.k15.).
27. A. F. Marsigli, *Relazione del ritrovamento dell'uova di chioccole . . . in una lettera al sig. Marcello Malpighi* (1683).
28. E. Costa, 'Contributi alla storia dello studio bolognese durante il secolo xvi,' *Studi e memorie per la storia dell'università di Bologna*, ser. i. 3 (1912); *Memorie intorno a LFM* (1930), pp. 386–403.
29. A. Caprara, 'Introduzione alle lezioni morale da leggirsi nel pubblico studio dell'università di Bologna', *Prose*, pp. 118–32.
30. G. Fantuzzi, *Memorie del maresciallo Enea . . . Caprara*, 1783.
31. *Cf.* M. Torrini, *Dopo Galileo. Una polemica scientifica (1684–1711)* (Florence, 1979); W. E. Knowles Middleton, *The Experimenters . . . the Accademia del Cimento* (Baltimore, 1971); M. H. Fisch, 'The Academy of the Investigators', *Science Medicine and History: Charles Singer* (Oxford, 1953), i. 521–63; M. Cavazza, *Settecento inquieto* (1990) chap. 1; G. Spini, *Ricerca dei Libertini. La teoria*

dell'impostura delle religioni nel seicento italiano (Rome, 1950).

32. G. Campori, 'Notizie e lettere inedite di Geminiano Montanari', *Atti e memorie . . . per le prov. modenesi e parmiensi*, viii (1875), p. 75.

33. J. M. Gardair, *Le 'Giornale de' Letterati' de Rome (1666–1681)*, Acc. Toscana di scienze e lettere, 'La Columbaria', *Studi* 69 (1984); W. E. Knowles Middleton, 'Science in Rome, 1675–1700, and the Accademia of Giovanni Giustino Ciampini', *British Journal for the History of Science*, 8 (1975), pp. 138–54.

34. U. Baldini, 'Un libertino accademico del cimento, Antonio Oliva', *Ann. dell'Ist. e museo di st. della scienza* (Florence, 1977).

35. Leibniz, visiting Rome in 1689–90, found that Ciampini's academy was still active, which encouraged him to hope for a cancellation of the decrees against Copernicus and Galileo. A. Robinet, *G. W. Leibniz. Iter Italicum*, 'La Columbaria', *Studi*, 90 (1988), pp. 43–5, 96–100.

36. G. P. Brizzi, *La formatione della classe dirigente nel sei-settecento* (1976), pp. 169, 181, 231–4.

37. A. p. 4.

38. DBI, sub Civran: two of his brothers had died in rapid succession.

39. T. Bertelé, *Il palazzo degli ambasciatori di Venezia a Costantinopoli* (1932), pp. 214–21.

40. C. Magni, *Quanto di più curioso, e vago ha potuto racorre Cornelio Magni . . . per la Turchia* (Parma, 1679); G. Agop (Agaub), *Rudimenta della lingua turchesca. Grammatica Latina Armenice explicata* (Rome, 1675).

41. G. R. Carlì, *Cronologia historica scritta in lingua Turca, Persiana, et Araba da Hazi Halifé Mustafa* (Venice, 1697).

42. *Viaggi a Costanopoli di Gio. Battista Donado . . . dal fu. Dottr. Antonio Benetti* (Venice, 1688); *Della Letterature de Turchi . . . da G. B. Donado* (Venice, 1688). Cf. *Storia della cultura veneta. Il Seicento*, 4, ii (1984), pp. 335–41.

43. For the journey to Istanbul and back, in addition to A. pp. 9–29, L. Frati, 'Il viaggio da Venezia a Costantinopoli del Conte Luigi Ferdinando Marsili (1679)', *Nuovo Archivio Veneto*, N.S. 8 (1904), pp. 63–94, 295–316 and Malpighi, *Correspondence* n. 390A.

44. L. F. Marsigli, *Stato militare dell'imperio ottomanno* (1732), ii. 168–9.

45. *La schiavitù del generale Marsigli sotto i Tartari e d Turchi da lui stesso narrata*, ed. E. Lovarini (1931), p. 29. The wheels turned slowly. The captive secured his freedom three years later, thanks in part to this 'Compagnia del Riscatto [Archiconfraternità] di S. Maria della Neve di Bologna', of which Marsigli became a fervent and lifelong supporter for a reason that will become obvious. Cf. pp. 21, 284 below.

46. C. J. Jireček, *Die Heerstrasse von Belgrad nach Constantinopel und die Balkanpasse* (Prague, 1877).

47. Frati, *art. cit.*, pp. 310–12; S. Runciman, *The Great Church in Captivity* (Cambridge, 1968), p. 389.

48. OD ii. tab. 62, 63; T. Mommsen, *Corpus Inscriptorum Latinum*, iii. pt. 1, nos. 746, 1685–9 *passim*.

49. *La schiavitù*, pp. 66, 71 et seq.

50. V. Coronelli, *Conquiste della ser: republica di Venezia nella Dalmazia, Epiro e Morea* (Venice, 1686).

51. K. Jurišić, *Katolička crkva na Biokovsko Neretvanskom području u doba turske vladavine* (Zagreb, 1972), pp. 24–5.

52. D. Fabianich, *Storia dei fratri minori . . . in Dalmazia e Bossina* (Zara, 1853–4) ii. 294; C. J. Jireček, *Die Handelstrassen und Bergwerke von Serbien und Bosnien während des Mittelalters* (Prague, 1879), pp. 49–51.

53. M. Prembrou, 'Serie dei vescovi romano-cattolici di Beograd', *Archivum Franciscanum Historicum*, 17 (1924), pp. 498–9, and 18 (1925), pp. 56–9.

54. *La schiavitù*, pp. 85–90.

55. L. F. Marsigli, *Stato militare*

dell'imperio ottomanno (The Hague and Amsterdam, 1732, reprinted ed. M. Kramer and R. F. Kreutel, Graz, 1972) and below, chapters VI and X. His early collections and drafts are to be found scattered through MSS 51 and 81. They were used by H. Wurm, *Der osmanische Historiker Hüseyn b. Ga'fer, genannt Hezarfenn, und die islamische Gesellschaft in der zweiten Hälfte des 17. Jahrhunderts* (Freiburg, 1971), a very valuable work. It remains difficult to distinguish with precision between the materials assembled by Marsigli in his two visits to Istanbul, in 1679–80 and 1691–2. The Ottoman registers used by Hezarfenn and Marsigli originated at various dates between 1660 and 1680.

56. The translation of the whole work was apparently complete in 1679. *Imago Mundi*, i. (1935), art. F. Taeschner, pp. 45–6.

57. MS 51, f. 670.

58. *Osservazioni* (see note 62), p. 107.

59. Malpighi, *Correspondence*, n. 390A. Marsigli was associated with Corraro and the virtuosi of the Accademia Sarotti in Venice (MS 53, f. 410).

60. *Osservazioni intorno al Bosforo Tracio ovvero Canale di Constantinopoli....* (Rome, 1681); G. Bruzzo, *Luigi Ferdinando Marsili. Nuovi studi sulla sua vita* (1921), pp. 19–28. Christina also received from Marsigli copies of the horoscopes of Sultan Mehmed and his son. For a modern summary describing the currents of the Bosphorus, J. Freely, *Istanbul* (Blue Guides, ed. 1983), p. 314.

61. *Osservazioni*, pp. 62, 87; L. A. Porzio, *Lettere e discorsi accademici* (Naples, 1711), pp. 106–9.

62. M. Deacon, *Scientists and the Sea 1650–1900* (London, 1971), pp. 147–9, 153.

63. Halley made his remarkable calculations on this point in *Philosophical Transactions*, nos. 189, 192 (1687, 1691).

64. For this subject, A. M. Belli, 'Variazoni idrografiche della pianura bolognese', *Riv. Geo. Ital.*, 49 (1942);

C. Poni, 'Aratri e sistemazioni idrauliche nell'agricoltura bolognese', *Studi storici*, 5 (1964); and D. Corradi d'Austria, *Effetti dannosi che produrrà il Reno se sia messo in Po di Lombardia* (Modena, 1717).

65. G. Montanari, *Il mare adriatico e sua corrente, esaminata* (ed. 1723).

66. G. Baruffaldi, *Dell'istoria di Ferrara ... 1655–1700*, (Ferrara, 1700), pp. 255–316.

67. MS 24, no. 129. For the threat to Cremona from the Po in the years 1672–80, D. Capra, *Il vero riparo, il facile, il naturale per ovviare, ò remediare ogni corrosione e ruina di fiume, e torrente, abbenche giudicata irremediabile* (Bologna, 1685).

CHAPTER TWO

1. A, pp. 4, 31; Marsigli's letter of 13 August 1681, *La schiaviitù*, pp. 166–7; *Osservazioni*, p. 108.

2. Nicolo Erizzo (4 November 1702) in B. Cecchetti, *La republica di Venezia e la corte di Roma nei rapporti della religione* (Venice, 1874), ii. 328.

3. De Luca had recently published *Il Cardinale della S. R. Chiesa pratico ... nell'ozio tusculano della primavera dell'anno 1675*. For Ricci's ecclesiastical importance, B. Neveu, 'Culture religieuse et aspirations réformistes à la cour d'Innocent XI', *Accademia e Cultura* (Modena, 1979).

4. L. Pastor, *History of the Popes*, xxxii, 414–5.

5. Ricci's scientific influence is illustrated in *Le Opere dei discepuli di Galilei, Galileo*, ed. G. Abetti and others (Florence, 1942, 1984).

6. *Queen Christina of Sweden*, ed. J. M. V. Platen (Stockholm, 1966), pp. 134. 365ff.

7. Halley, arriving at Rome in October 1681, was somewhat contemptuous of the astronomy practised there. On the other hand the Roman cometary observations of November 1680 certainly featured in the fundamental discussion between Newton and

Flamsteed on that topic.

8. The Pope treated Marsigli's contemporary and fellow countryman Giovanni Antonio Davia (1660–1740) rather differently. Also a disciple of Montanari, his early travels took him to Paris and London. He was a volunteer in the Morea (1684) but Innocent then offered him a diplomatic post in Brussels. He took orders, became a bishop and cardinal, and was an active Roman envoy at several European courts (DBI). Marsigli is reported to have attended Davia's 'academy' in Bologna in the 1680s. *De Bononiensi Sci. et Art. Instituto . . . Commentarii*, i (1733), p. 34.

9. R. Bengel, *Der Palazzo di Venezia in Roma* (Vienna, 1909), pp. 122–3.

10. For this episode, MS Gozzadini 184 (Archiginnasio, Bologna), ff. 119–20: 'Manifesto sopra il Trattato intrapreso dal Co: Luigi Marsigli . . . alla Reppublica di Venezia', 6 December 1681, *cf.* MS Gozzadini 75, no. 10; and Marsigli MS 52, ff. 643–66.

11. A, pp. 32–33. I have not been able to find direct evidence of Marsigli's early training in fortification, but his interest was already clear in Corfu in 1679.

12. *Cf.* A Peyrot, *Casale nei secoli* (Turin, 1969), pp. 19–20 and plates 30–3.

13. MS 53, ff. 70–7.

14. N. Steno, *Geological Papers*, ed. G. Scherz (Odense, 1969) and A, p. 35.

15. V. de Vic, *Memorie storiche di Borgomanero* (Milan, 1859) and O. Redlich, *Weltmacht des Barock* (ed. Vienna, 1961), pp. 240, 248ff.

16. MS 53, ff. 80–115 for a draft of the report on Alsace.

17. E. Veress, *Gróf Marsigli Alajos Ferdinánd jelentései és térképi Budavár 1684–1686 iki* (Budapest, 1907), p. 8.

18. Ibid., quoting MS 81, ff. 49–54 (8 March 1683).

19. MS 53, f. 157; F. Theuer, *Verrat an der Raab* (Salzburg, 1976), p. 11.

20. Röder v. Diersburg, *Des Markgrafen Ludwig Wilhelm von Baden Feldzüge wider die Türken*, (Karlsruhe, 1839, 1843) [=*Feldzüge*], i. 86; *Vertrauliche*

Briefe des Grafen E. R. v. Starhemberg, ed. V. Renner (Vienna, 1890), p. 36; Veress, pp. 20–2.

21. Malpighi, *Correspondence*, n. 454; Veress, pp. 25–6; *La schiavitù* pp. 19–20, 38–42, 84, 161.

22. Veress, pp. 17–19.

23. Ibid; Vienna: Kriegsarchiv: Feldakten [= KA FA], 1684–8–7; Lewis of Baden approved of the project but criticised the siege works (*Feldzuge*, i. 101–4).

24. Veress, pp. 8, 11, 20–2.

25. *Vertrauliche Briefe*, p. 45.

26. For González, A., p. 67; *An Account of the Imperial Proceedings against the Turks . . . the siege of Neuheusel*, under 11 July 1685; *Journal de la glorieuse conquete de la ville de Bude* (1686), p. 6; *Vertrauliche Briefe*, p. 107.

27. J. Bérenger, *Finances et absolutisme autrichien* (Paris, 1975), pp. 470–1.

28. Malpighi, *Correspondence*, n. 490.

29. Veress, pp. 25–33; MS 53, ff. 386–9, 460–1, 531–2, 627–30; KA FA 1687–13–7.

30. *Bevanda Asiatica, brindata all'eminentissimo Buonvisi, Nunzio Apostolico* (Vienna, 1685). For Marsigli's conviviality with Buonvisi in 1685, Malpighi, *Correspondence*, n. 529. It is worth notice that another Italian author, Lucantonio Porzio, published in Vienna in 1685 his *De militis in castris sanitate tuenda. Oder, von dess Soldaten im Lager Gesundheit Behaltung*, dedicated to commissary-general Rabatta.

31. The negotiations leading to the marriage treaty remain an obscure topic. *Handbuch der bayerischen Geschichte*, ed. M. Spindler (ed. 1974), ii. 423ff.

32. MS 53, ff. 460–1: M to Hermann of Baden, 12 May 1685 [not 1698, as in Frati's Catalogue].

33. *Mitt. d. K. K. Kriegsarchiv*, 1885, p. 212; Veress, *op. cit.*, p. 11.

34. *An Account of the Imperial Proceedings . . . the siege of Newheusel*, pp. 5–6.

35. A, pp. 68–9.

36. The 'asciugamento' of the channel is mentioned in the well-informed se-

ries of Milan newsletters of M. Pandolfo Malatesta (n. 16, of 15 October 1685) reporting on this campaign. Another account says that an engineer named Mesgrigny suggested cutting a new channel on 23 July, and that his work was spoilt by a Turkish sortie on 1 August (*Feldzüge*, i. 135).

7. *An Account*, pp. 17–22; *Feldzüge*, i. 138.

8. HHSA. Grosse Correspondenz, 63 (fz. Marsigli) ff. 15–27: Rabatta to Marsigli, 9 Feb. 1686, and 'punti dell'esame . . . di . . . Rabatta'.

9. P. Wentzoke, *Feldherr des Kaisers. Leben und Taten Herzog Karls V, von Lothringen* (Leipzig, 1943), pp. 255–7; A, p. 71.

0. For the negotiations in 1686, Redlich, *op. cit.*, 297–8; K. Staudinger, *Geschichte des kurbayerischen Heeres unter Kurfürst Max II Emannuel 1680–1726*, i (Munich, 1904), 206ff.; *Monumenta Vaticana Hungariae*, Ser. II. ii (1886), pp. 80–105.

1. J. Richards, *Journal of the siege . . . of Buda* (London, 1687), pp. 1–8.

2. F. Zieglauer, *Die Befreiung Ofens von der Türkenherrschaft 1686* (Innsbruck, 1886), p. 82.

3. *Mitt. d. K. K. Kriegsarchiv*, 1886, p. 39; *Avvisi del Cavaliere Federico Cornaro . . .* , ed. S. Bubics (Budapest, 1891), p. 13; *Monumenta Vaticana Hungariae*, II. ii. 117.

4. Ibid., pp. 128, 144, for the sketches he sent to Vienna in July and August.

5. For the sequence of events between 29 August and 2 September, Zieglauer, *op. cit.*, pp. 161–3.

6. *Feldzüge*, i. Urkunden pp. 47–8.

7. A, p. 75.

8. V. Rosen, 'Remarques sur les manuscrits orientaux de la Collection Marsigli a Bologna', *Atti. Acc. dei Lincei*, Ser. III, 12 (1884), pp. 165–73; *Scritti inediti*, pp. 179–80.

9. D. Kaufmann, *Die Erstürmung Ofens* (Trier, 1895) and his note on 'Les victimes de la prise d'Ofen, en 1686', *Revue des Études Juives*, 21 (1890), pp. 133–40.

50. L. Frati, 'Della biblioteca Corvina', *Rivista delle biblioteche*, iv (1893), pp. 7–16; C. Csapodi, *The Corvinian Library* (Budapest, 1973); *Bibliotheca Corvina*, ed. L. Zambra (Budapest, 1927), pp. 33–4.

51. T. Pflugk, *Epistola ad V. Seckendorff* (Jena, 1688).

52. For the campaign of 1687 the best general guides are Redlich, 358ff. and Staudinger, i. 227ff.

53. HHSA. Grosse Correspondenz, 63, ff. 51–71 and also ff. 1–30 *passim*.

54. Ibid., f. 73. They concluded that the letter in question was a forgery, highly injurious to Marsigli. On the other hand the brothers La Vigne remained in Habsburg service.

55. *Mémoires de Villars*, i. 66, 354–7; and a hostile judgment on Lorraine at this point, quoted in M. Strich, *Das Kurhaus Bayern im Zeitalter Ludwigs XIV*, ii (Munich, 1933), p. 605; Staudinger, i. 230; *Feldzüge*, ii. 20.

56. A, p. 77–8.

57. M's account does not differ significantly from other authorities, except that he calls the tributary Karasizca the 'Carazza', and an adjoining placename 'Prognovar' instead of Baranyvár.

58. *Feldzüge*, ii. 26–30; Staudinger, i. 233–4; Redlich, p. 310; A, p. 80.

59. The booty of this victory included, for Marsigli himself, a few more Turkish manuscripts ultimately taken to Bologna. *Scritti inediti*, p. 181.

60. Villars, i. 375–7; Staudinger, pp. 240–1.

61. A, pp. 32–6; Hammer, *Histoire de l'empire ottoman*, (Paris, 1838), xii. 252. The stronghold with a Genoese commander was Szilágy Somlyó (Salagiului).

62. His arrival in Rome on 7 February 1688 was reported to Vienna by cardinal Pio on the same day. HHSA. Rom. Correspondenz 66 (Berichte).

63. Odescalchi was born in 1659. For his relations with Vienna, R. Guèze, 'Livio Odescalchi ed il ducato del Sirmio', *Venezia, Italia, Ungheria fra Arcadia e Illuminismo*, ed. B. Köpeczi

318   Notes

and P. Sárközy (Budapest, 1982), pp. 43–50.

64. Marsigli's account of Arva – in MS 54, ff. 70–84 – is dated 12 May 1688. *Cf.* A, pp. 106–7.
65. According to Pio, Marsigli 'fu trattenuto lo spazio di quattr'ore continue' by Innocent on this occasion. (26 June 1688, Correspondenz, 66). For the papers removed from Bologna in 1688, see his own *Dissertazione epistolare* (1698), p. 1. Marking the close of this phase of Marsigli's life Innocent XI died in 1689, and so did Queen Christina. A great many of her valuables were purchased by Livio Odescalchi. Platen, *op. cit.*, pp. 21, 27.
67. For the military history of 1688, *Feldzüge*, ii. 52ff. and Staudinger, 250ff.; on Lorraine's role Redlich, p. 321 is more convincing than O. Klopp, *Das Jahr 1683 und der folgende grosse Türkenkrieg* (Graz, 1882), pp. 414–20 or Wentzcke, pp. 248–9.
68. A sign of the recent advance was that a bridge across the Danube now linked Erdut on the right bank, a little above Petrovaradin, with the furthest point on the opposite shore reached by Lorraine and Marsigli late in the previous year. This new crossing was used in 1688 by Habsburg forces proceeding to the rendezvous from Transylvania. *Leben und Abenteuer des Dolmetschers Osman Aga*, ed. R. F. Kreutel (Bonn, 1954), p. 20.
69. *A true Relation or Journal of the Siege and Taking by Storm of the famous City of Belgrade* (London, 1688) summarises the events of 8 and 9 August by saying that 'while the foot continued to pass over in Boats, the Bridge was laid for the Horses'.
70. The matter was surely decided on personal grounds but Leopold excused himself to his private adviser Father Marco with the hope that Belgrade would fall before Lorraine arrived. A well-placed observer, however, stated that Leopold allowed Lorraine to go, 'tout faible qu'il

estoit', because he received news of the grand vezir's advance with a larger relieving force than anticipated. Another messenger contradicting this report was in Vienna before Lorraine reached Buda, but Leopold did not recall Lorraine *Corrispondenza epistolare tra Leopoldo I. imperatore ed il P. Marco d'Aviano capuccino*, ed. O. Klopp (Graz, 1888) p. 169; HHSA. Lothringen-Habsburg MS 51, f. 252.
71. J. Weiss, 'Berichte über die Eroberung Belgrads', *Ungarische Revue*, 15 (1895), p. 88.
72. *Corrispondenza epistolare*, pp. 169–70
73. A, p. 103; *Feldzüge*, ii. 65; *Corrispondenza epistolare*, pp. 171–2.
74. M. Héyret, *P. Marcus d'Aviano .. 1631–97*, iv (Munich, 1946), pp 164–5 and Weiss, *art. cit.*, pp. 88, 94 The location of Lorraine's camp and the allied cavalry beyond Belgrade is obscure: it was 4 hours or 2 hours downstream, according to conflicting reports.
75. G. P. Zenarolla, *Operationi di Leopoldo Primo* (Vienna, 1689), p 232.
76. L. A. Maggiorotti, *Architetti e architettura militari* (Rome, 1933–9) ii. 125–6, fig. 27 and plate xx.
77. MS 50, n. 31, with an annotation beginning 'Primi Embrioni de Mappe della Servia . . .'
78. *Feldzüge*, ii. 89; W. Fraknói, *Paps Innocenz XI. und Ungarns Befreiung von der Türkenherrschaft*, (ed. Freiburg, 1902), pp. 273–4.

CHAPTER THREE

1. *Österreich und die Osmanen* (National-bibliothek, Vienna, 1983), pp. 177–80; W. Jobst, *Der Gesandschafts-bericht des Zul' Fiqar Efendi . . . 1689* (Vienna, Nationalbibliothek: diss 1980), pp. 205, 213 ff. Carafa interviewed the envoys at Petrovaradin, who guardedly stated a willingness to discuss peace. It emerged later that they had formal authority to do so.

2. Leopold's declaration of his intent to negotiate a new alliance with the Dutch was dated 20 September 1688. *Österreichische Staatsverträge. Niederlande*, i. ed. H. Srbik (Vienna, 1912), p. 254. It was the response to Louis XIV's ultimatum, which set a terminal date (1 January 1689) for the expiry of the Twenty Years' Truce or its conversion into a permanent settlement in Germany.

3. *Documente privitóre la Istoria Românilor*, ed. E. Hurmuzaki, v (i) (Bucharest, 1885), pp. 162–70; L. Höbelt, 'Die Sackgasse aus dem Zweifrontenkrieg: die Friedensverhandlungen mit den Osmanen 1689', MIÖG, 97 (1989), pp. 329–80, emphasises the influence of Stratmann, who favoured the western alliance and held that, at the worst, only one more campaign would be needed to end Ottoman resistance to Habsburg demands.

4. The terms of the truce of Vasvar of 1664, it was believed afterwards in Vienna, did not adequately reflect the preceding Christian victory at Szent Gotthard which was won a few days earlier. In 1688–9 Leopold's government did not wish to repeat the alleged error.

5. J. Radonitch, *Histoire des Serbes de Hongrie* (Paris, 1919), pp. 148, 153, 169; J. Fiedler, 'Die Union der in Ungarn zwischen der Donau und Drau wohnender Bekenner der griechisch-orientalischen Glaubens', *SB d. Phil-Hist. Kl. Akad. d. Wiss.* 38 (Vienna, 1861), pp. 284–97; A. E. Picot, *Les Serbes de Hongrie* (Prague, 1873), p. 61; Hurmuzaki, ibid., v(i), p. 150.

6. J. Radonić, *Prilozi za istorijy Srba u Ugarskoj y 16. 17. i 18. veku* (Novi Sad, 1909) docs, 21–30.

7. L. Hadrovics, *Le peuple serbe et son église sous la domination turque* (Paris, 1947), pp. 122–48; R. L. Veselinović, *Vojvodina, Srbija i Makedonija pod turskom vlascu u drugoj polavini xvii veka* (Novi Sad, 1966), pp. 101–30; S. Kahné, 'A proposito della lettera del patriarca di Peć Arsenio III all'arcivescovo Andrea Zmajević', *Orientalia Christiana Periodica*, xxii (Rome, 1956), pp. 41–58; C. Gianelli, 'Lettere del P. di P. Arsenio III . . . all' arcivescovo A.Z.' Ibid., xxi (1955), pp. 63–78; P. Bogdan, *L'infallibile verità della fede cattolica . . . necessaria a Greci, ed a chiunque vive sotto il Gioco Turchico, per ben vivere . . . spiegate in due copiose lingue Italiana, e Schiava* (Venice, 1691), above all the letter printed after the paginated text. For Bogdan's earlier career, I. Dujčev, *Il Cattolicesimo in Bulgaria nel sec. xvii* (Rome, 1937), pp. 70–1; and for Raspassan/ Raspasanović, *Zbornik Matice Srbske*, 12 (1956), pp. 60–2.

8. A cross associated with St Vladimir on the mountains near Bar (60 miles south-west of Peć was a common pilgrimage centre for Orthodox, Catholic and Moslem into the twentieth century. S. Hafner, *Studien zur altserbischen dynastischen Historiographie* (Munich, 1964), p. 43.

9. H. Uebersberger, *Russlands Orientpolitik in den letzten zwei Jahrhunderten* (Stuttgart, 1913), i. 42–7.

10. *Acta et Diplomata ragusina*, iv.1 (Belgrade, 1941), p. 665.

11. J. Tomić, *Crna Gora za Morejskog rata (1684–1699)* (Belgrade, 1907), pp. 323–4.

12. A. Ivić, 'Ansiedlungen der Bulgaren in Ungarn', *Archiv für slavische Philologie*, 31 (1909), pp. 416–7; cf. M. Macdermott, *History of Bulgaria* (London, 1962) and Dujčev, *op. cit.*, pp. 68–9, 157–9. Already in 1686 the region round Turnovo, further east than Ciprovets, had been in turmoil. The dissident leader here was another 'pretender', claiming descent from the fourteenth-century Tsar Stratsimir.

13. HHSA. Turcica I [=T] 154. ff. 29–33; A, pp. 106–9; MS 54 *passim*.

14. He refers to a place called 'Komolini', which is Gumuljina. *Handbook for Macedonia and surrounding Territories* (H.M.S.O. London, 1920).

15. J. Hofer, *Johannes Kapistran* (ed. Heidelberg, 1965), ii. 446–57; for Ilok on the eve of the Ottoman invasion of Hungary, *Statutum Civitatis Illok, anno MDXXV*, ed. R. Schmidt (Zagreb, 1938).
16. MS 54, ff. 90–106.
17. MS 50, n. 26 is Marsigli's copy of the map, with his annotation: 'Mappa del ducato di Sirmio . . . con il mio proietto delli limiti da assegnarli'.
18. MS 54, ff. 174–5, 180, 185.
19. MS 8, nos. 2, 3, 4 are copies of Marsigli's plans for the refortification of Belgrade. *Cf.* A, p. 108.
20. The following account is based on A, pp. 103–9; the maps and their annotations, MS 50, nos. 30, 31 and 36; MS 54, ff. 216–34; KA FA 1689–13–1: Annotationes und Reflexiones'.
21. Generallandesarchiv, Karlsruhe: Türkenkrieg, vi. 33 (n. 1179). This was the work of Marsigli's gifted colleague Morandi Visconti.
22. P. L. Veselinović, 'Die "Albaner" und "Klimenten" in den österreichischen Quellen zu Ende des 17. Jahrhunderts', *Mitt. des öst. Staatsarchiv*, 13 (1960), pp. 197–214, 227–30. For an account of Albania in the Ottoman period, including the Klementi tribe of highlanders, *Encyclopaedia of Islam* (ed. 1960), *sub* 'Arnawutluk'. Cf. E. Durham, *High Albania* (ed. Boston, 1987) *sub* 'Kilmeni'.
23. Hurmuzaki, v. 1. 153 ff.
24. Ibid., pp. 162–70.
25. Ibid., pp. 189–91; O. Brunner, 'Österreich und die Wallachei . . . 1683–1699', MIÖG, 44 (1930), pp. 265–323 (p. 301, n. 4).
26. The Ottoman envoys were willing to discuss this concession within the framework of an armistice, not of a permanent treaty. Hurmuzaki, p. 261; Höbelt, *art. cit.*, pp. 354–60; Jobst, *op. cit.*, pp. 285–8, for the 7th conference with the Ottoman envoys at the Landhaus, 18 March. One notes at the same time Leopold's resolution in February to offer the Spaniards and Dutch his fullest support. *Lexington Papers* (London, 1851), pp. 342–3; H. Srbik,

'Adriapolitik unter Kaiser Leopold I', MIÖG xi. Erg. Bd. (1919), p. 637.
27. *Feldzüge*, ii. Urkunden, nos. 15, 17, 19 (for Lewis's query about Marsigli, ibid., p. 8); Hurmuzaki, p. 272.
28. Malpighi, *Correspondence*, nos. 740–1. For the elder Marsigli's 'academies', p. 14 above.
29. According to Guêze (*art. cit.*, p. 107) Marsigli, after this second inspection of Arva, advised Odescalchi not to interest himself further in that project. Syrmia was preferred.
30. The route followed the south bank of the Danube for a short distance before turning inland through the woods to Palanka. A. Boué. *Receuil d'Itineraires dans la Turquie d'Europe* (Vienna, 1854), i. 13, 54 ff.
31. For the correspondence of Lewis of Baden and the Emperor, *Feldzüge*, ii. Urkunden 20 *passim*. *Cf.* M. Angeli, 'Der Feldzug 1689 in Serbien', *Mitt. der K. K. Kriegsarchivs*, 1877, 36, ff., and G. P. Zenarolla, *Trionfi di Leopoldo Primo . . . nell'Anno 1689, sino alli 6 Marzo 1690* (Vienna, 1690).
32. *Feldzüge*, ii. Ur. 20, pp. 48–51.
33. MS 54, ff. 408–18; KA. FA. 1689–8–ad2a; A, p. 110; Angeli, *op. cit.*, p. 157.
34. *Feldzüge*, ii Ur. p. 87.
35. A, p. 111 and Marsigli's *Stato militare dell'Imperio ottomanno*, ii. 127.
36. Marsigli called it 'la via maestra di Belgrado'.
37. *Feldzüge*, Ur. pp. 91–7; *Stato militare*, ii. 93–5, 127–9.
38. *Feldzüge*, Ur. p. 97.
39. *Umständlicher Bericht aus dem Feldlager bei Batokin den 3. September 1689* is a printed version of the despatch. No place or date of publication is given. BL. 8010. b. 1(73).
40. L. Marinelli, 'LFM uomo di guerra', *Memorie*, p. 10.
41. *Feldzüge*, ii. Ur. pp. 147–51.
42. '. . . so weit Er kann, gegen den Meer disseits dess Haemus, und Albanesischen geburgs zu erweitern, umb dadurch Bosnien . . . Einzuschliessen.' Ibid., p. 149.

43. Ibid., p. 148.
44. 'vermittels Einer haubtstrassen, die ich längst der Donau hinauf von Fetislan auf Vidin, Calamos, Ram und Semendrian vor Armeen practicabl zu machen, gesinnt bin . . .' Ibid.
45. 'Orsova . . . welcher gegend Ich sodann vermittels Einer bruckhen mit dem Jenseitigen landt Eine beständige sichere Communication stabiliren . . .' Ibid.
46. MS 50, no. 38.
47. A, p. 116.
48. *Feldzüge*, ii. Ur. pp. 154–8; A, pp. 117–9; Veterani, *Memoiren*, pp. 56–62.
49. It soon became clear to Lewis that Vienna favoured the occupation of Wallachia. *Feldzüge*, ii. Ur. pp. 173–4.
50. For the geography of the Iron Gates and the defiles upstream the *Handbook of the River Danube* (London, Admiralty, 1915), pp. 357–75 and plates, is closer to Marsigli's experience than more modern accounts. *Cf.* his own *Opus Danubiale*, vol. i and Boué, ii. 316–20.
51. *Feldzüge*, ii. Ur. p. 177. Nothing had irritated Lewis more than the failure of 'the pontoon bridges' to arrive, causing a fortnight's delay. *Feldzüge*, p. 174 (7 December).
52. Ibid., pp. 181–98.
53. She was the daughter of the duke of Sachsen-Lauenburg. A. M. Renner, *Sybilla Augusta Markgräfin von Baden* (ed. Karlsruhe, 1938), pp. 23, 25.
54. A, p. 119. For the Roman history of this region, E. Swoboda, *Forschungen am Obermoesischen Limes* (Vienna, 1939); F. Kanitz, *Römische Studien in Serbien* (Vienna, 1892); J. Sašel, 'Trajan's canal at the Iron Gate', *Journal of Roman Studies*, 63 (Vienna, 1973), pp. 80–5.
55. OD i. tab, 37, 39; C. Patsch, 'Der Kampf um den Donauraum unter Domitian und Trajan', *SB d. Phil-Hist. Kl. Akad. d. Wiss*, 217 (1937), p. 90.
56. OD ii. 143–5: 'Haec et duae sequentes inscriptiones, Anno 1680

Bizantio Venetiae profiscentibus' referring to a site at Bela Palunka 30 miles south-east of Niš. He revisited it in 1690.
57. R. Fabrettus, *De columna Traiani syntagma....* (Rome, 1683, 'ex officina Nicolai Angeli Tinassi'), substantially the re-publication of a work by A. Ciaccone (1576). In a letter to Bernard de Montfaucon of 27 April 1715 Marsigli simply says that 'in Vienna' he saw illustrations of the reliefs on Trajan's Column. 'Lettera . . . intorno al Ponte fatto sul Danubio', *Giornale de' Letterati d'Italia*, Venice, 22 (1715), p. 118.
58. A, p. 119; OD ii, 27 (Pons Traiani).
59. A, pp. 119–20.
60. *Feldzüge*, ii. Ur. p. 197.
61. A, p. 121.
62. OD i. sectio 14, and the following *Geographica*, p. 28.
63. OD vols i, ii, v, *passim*.
64. OD ii. 30.
65. R. Syme, *Danubian Papers* (Bucharest, 1971); Paoly-Wissowa, 'Limes (Donauprovinzen)'; C. Daicoviciu, 'La Transylvanie dans l'antiquité', *Acad. Roumaine*, ii. *La Transylvanie* (Bucharest, 1938).
66. The finished result may be seen in the lines marked 'via incisa rupe facta', and 'via lapidibus strata. Ant. Romana' in OD i. sectio 14, tab. 16.
67. OD i. tab. 2, 16, 37, 39, 40; OD ii. pp. 17–20, tab. 7.
68. Swoboda, *op. cit.*, pp. 69, 71. Swoboda is a severe critic of Marsigli's attempts at transcribing the inscriptions.
69. OD vi. 15.
70. MS 54, f. 362; A, p. 122.
71. *Feldzüge*, ii. Ur. pp. 183, 193–8.
72. F. Veterani, *Memoiren* (Dresden, 1788), pp. 64–5.
73. *Mitt. des KK Kriegsarchiv*, 1877, pp. 134–58.
74. C. Gianelli, *art. cit.* and p. 56 above. The Venetian authorities, who had wanted him first of all to accept the Republic's protection, deplored the patriarch's return to Peć where he was out of their reach. *Acta et*

Diplomata ragusina, iv. 1 (Belgrade, 1941), p. 659.

75. *Mitt. des KK Kriegsarchiv*, 1877, 164 ff.

76. KA FA 1690-7-13; Hadrovich, *Le peuple serbe et son église*, p. 138.

77. A, pp. 110, 120; Ant. Stefanov to Marsigli, 23 June 1689, in *Spomenik* (*Srbska K. Akad.*), 2nd Ser. 37 (1905), pp. 41-2.

78. *Feldzüge*, ii. 76, 78. According to Marsigli, Brancović met Lewis 'pomposamente'.

79. *Enciklopedija Jugoslavije* (1982), ii. 402. *Cf.* T 156, f. 2.

80. *Feldzüge*, ii. Ur. pp. 198-212.

81. A, p. 122; Veterani, pp. 78-9.

82. HHSA. Illyrico-Serbica i (1611-1738), ff. 15-18.

83. *Acta et Diplomata ragusina*, iv. 1, pp. 571-3 (19 December, 1688). The Habsburg agent in Dubrovnik was instructed to have the patent distributed in Hercegovina. He commented that there would be no rising until a Habsburg force reached Mostar. HHSA. Ragusa 1690-1701, f. 4 (6 Feb. 16), 89.

84. *Serbische Privilegien von 1690-1792* (ed. J. Radonić and M. Kostić, Belgrade, 1954), pp. 19-20, 26 ff. An old index of official papers (T 157 fz. Index', nos. 58-60) makes the connection of Marsigli's memorandum on Albania with the issue of the patents very plain.

85. Radonić (1919), p. 168; *Prilozi*, nos. 31, 32; Illyrico-Serbica (1611-1738), f. 14.

86. T 156, ff. 29-33; MS 54, f. 249 (29 April). For the disturbed history of the region Lika-Crbava in the 1690s after the Habsburg re-conquest, G. E. Rothenburg, *The Austrian Military Border in Croatia* (Urbana, 1960), pp. 94-80.

87. T 156 (March-April 1690), ff. 109-14.

88. A. Blanc, *La Croatie occidentale* (Paris, 1957), pp. 84-95.

89. HHSA. Kartensammlung, ix. It is endorsed: 'Map, made by count Marsigli after his inspection of the Croatian frontier, showing where the frontier line with Turkey could be drawn, and submitted to the Emperor ad finem Ma. 1690'. A second map was prepared for Kinsky and a survey of the Adriatic coast was promised. T 171 fz Varia, f. 10 (undated).

90. T 161 (Kinsky's correspondence), ff. 2-10 (undated); T 156 (May-June 1690), ff. 54, 128-9.

91. *Feldzüge*, ii. 124 and Ur. pp. 222-4.

92. KA FA 1690-7-4. It should be noted that Marsigli took the opportunity, while en route to Sofia, to look again at the ancient inscriptions he had already seen in 1680 (OD ii. Tab. 62, 63). KA FA 1690-7-6: in this report (of 4 July) on Niš he describes progress with the ditch, covered way etc. and asserts that the place will cost the Turks valuable time and manpower to take. He was wrong.

93. *Feldzüge*, ii. Ur. pp. 232-3, 239-41.

94. KA FA 1690-7-4, 4a.

95. MS 54, ff. 481-3.

96. KA FA 1690-7-4, ff. 75, 79, *cf.* 1690-7-8.

97. MS 54, f. 483.

98. KA FA 1690-7-8. In another version of his report he admits that 'this road is the only thing missing from the completion of the dispositions made by His Excellency' (1690-7-10).

99. KA FA 1690-7-4, 4b, 4c. Earlier in the year, while still in Vienna (A, p. 125), Marsigli had worked on detailed plans for the defences below Orsova (MS 5 and MS 8, n. 6). The former is reproduced in *Memorie* (1930), p. 45, but does not illustrate the actual condition of the site in July 1690.

100. Veterani was also too sanguine in his report of 25 July. KA FA 1690-7-ad25.

101. *Feldzüge*, ii. 129; Veterani, *op. cit.*, pp. 95, 100.

102. *Feldzüge*, ii. Ur. pp. 248, 260; MS 55, nos. 1, 17.

103. Veterani, pp. 100-9.

104. A, p. 125f.; *Feldzüge*, ii. Ur. pp. 287-8, 321.

105. Ibid., pp. 308-24.

106. Ibid., pp. 319, 332. Marsigli refers to

'la strada del Cik e Giartz', viz. the route through Csikszerda and Gheorghini, across the watershed between the rivers Maros and Olt. A, p. 125. *Cf.* G. J. Kemény, *Deutsche Fundgruben der Geschichte Siebenbürgens* (Cluj, 1839, 1840), ii. 261.

07. A, p. 126; *Feldzüge*, ii. Ur. p. 325. Marsigli failed to reach Braşov.

08. MS 54, f. 535 (29 October).

09. A, p. 120.

10. MS 54, ff. 598–640 etc. For an account of Marsigli's papers referring to this area, A. Gianola, 'LFM e la Transilvania', *Memorie* (1930), pp. 233–55.

11. Hurmuzaki, *Documente*, v (1885), pp. 368–70.

12. Radonich, *Histoire des Serbes*, pp. 68–70. There had been a similar meeting in Belgrade a few months earlier, after which the bishop of Boros Jenö (Ineu) went to Vienna to negotiate. Leopold issued a new 'privilegium' for the Orthodox church dated 21 August.

13. KA FA 1699–13–22: the modern copy of an unsigned, undated document which from its content I attribute to Carafa. It seems impossible to relate this piece to the year 1699.

14. HHSA. Rom. Varia., xi. 306–18.

15. In 1697 and 1698 Leopold issued the diplomas conferring on the Odescalchi a title and territory in Syrmia. See G. Avanci, *Chorografia Istorica del ducato, e provincia del Sirmio* (Rome, 1700); Hofkammerarchiv, Vienna: MS Ungarn und Nebenländer 502, 'Haupt-Relation, ff. 36–7 and Karten A. 110–1, 2.

16. S. Bischoffshausen, *Papst Alexander VIII und der Wiener Hof* (Stuttgart, 1890), pp. 153–4. According to other accounts the lengthy process of canonisation was completed in 1724.

CHAPTER FOUR

1. The Levant Company's instructions to Hussey, 17 July 1690, assume that he will take the usual route by sea. SP 105/145, ff. 179–83. He left England in October.

2. SP 80/17, ff. 126, 131, 194.

3. 'I am very sorry to hear of the Emperor's ill success in Transilvania, and I am afraid it will occasion his I.M.'s drawing away many of his Troops from the Rhyne the next year.' Carmarthen (Secretary of State) to Paget, 1 October (OS) 1690. Paget Papers, 24. These MSS have been deposited by the Marquess of Anglesea at the School of Oriental and African Studies, London.

4. HHSA. T 157 (July–August 1690), ff. 154–67.

5. For this and the following exchanges, SP 80/17, ff. 126–81; T 159 (March 1691), ff. 194–9; T 158 (January–February 1691, ff. 124–5.

6. T 157 (September–December 1690), ff. 74–6. For the arrival in Vienna of Hussey's Turkish passport on 30 December (OS) 1690, SP 80/155–9.

7. T 158 (January–February 1691), ff. 159–67, (January–March), ff. 67–70, 102–4, (March–June), ff. 132–71; T159 (March), ff. 105–10, 167–79; MS 55, ff. 530–43.

8. T 158 (March) f. 103 and (March–June), ff. 137–8.

9. T 159 (April–June), f. 31 (in Paget's hand, dated 31 March 1691); T 161 (Varia), f. 18 gives Kinsky's notes of a conference with the two English ambassadors on 31 March: item 7 is headed 'De Marsigli'. Marsigli evidently visited Paget with a letter of introduction from Kinsky (T 161 (fz. Kinsky), f. 35). On 6 April Paget wrote accepting the nomination of Marsigli as Hussey's secretary (T 159 (April–June), f. 31).

10. A, p. 131; T 159 (April–June), f. 30 confirms at least one of the 'molte conferenze ne' piu rimoti giardini della città' of Marsigli's account.

11. T 159 (April–June), ff. 17–24, 60–8, 109–13. It is clear from these letters to Kinsky that Marsigli has assimilated perfectly the minister's mistrust of the mediators.

12. A paper of 12 April read and approved by Leopold does not discuss

the retaking of Belgrade, while stating that every effort should be made
to recover Titel – overlooking the
entry of the Tisza into the Danube –
so that *uti possidetis* will allow the
Emperor to keep it in the event of a
treaty. T 159 (April–June), f. 85.

13. Ibid., f. 134.

14. SP 80/199; BL Additional MS 8880,
f. 55; T 161 (Kinsky), ff. 7, 70–1.
Paget, before writing his letter of introduction, had been hoping to accompany Hussey for the first few
days of the journey (BL Additional
MS 34,095, f. 319) but evidently did
not do so.

15. SP 97/20, ff. 176–8. Baedeker's *Austria*, ed. 1896, exactly mirrors
Hussey: 'Scenery monotonous,
banks thinly peopled, towns insig-
nificant' for the stretch below Buda.

16. MS 55 ff. 120–36.

17. T 159 (April–June), ff. 130–1.

18. A, pp. 134–6. Apart from Marsigli's
imperfect Turkish, he had asked two
months earlier that instructions
should be sent to him in Latin rather
than German: because he was not
'egualmente fondato' in this language. T 159 (April–June), f. 67. As
to the Cairo Janissaries, he greatly
admired the accuracy of their shoot-
ing. MS 111, f. 105.

19. SP 97/20; Hussey's despatch of 29
July (ff. 190–3).

20. MS 55, f. 586.

21. SP 97/20, f. 180: an account of the
conference in Italian, signed by
Hussey, Coke, Marsigli and Peroni,
1/11 June; and similar material in T
159 (April–June) ff. 161–72.

22. This opening ploy of asking the
grand vezir for a concession, which
he could credit himself with refusing,
had been prescribed by the ministers
in Vienna. T 159 (April–June), f. 85.

23. Passport for Marsigli, signed by
Hussey, 3/13 June. MS 55, f. 256.

24. Conference of 30 June, and instructions for Lewis of Baden, in T 159
(April–June), ff. 227–60.

25. T 161 (Varia), ff. 81–98. Among his
comments on Ottoman forces he
gives usefully detailed estimates of

the Turkish naval flotilla on the
Danube in 1691. *Cf.* S. Stelling-
Michaud, *Les aventures de M. de
Saint-Saphorin sur le Danube* (Paris,
1935), p. 41.

26. SP 8/9, no. 125 (10/20 July). As he
passed through the Habsburg camp
at Vukovar, Marsigli let it be known
that in Vienna there were strong
hopes of peace before the end of the
campaign. Barfuss to Elector of
Brandenburg, 12/22 July, KA FA
1691-7-7.

27. A, p. 146.

28. Royal Society. Early Letters A, no.
40. For Ashe and his Irish colleagues,
K. T. Hoppen, *The Common Scientist
in the seventeenth century . . . 1683–
1708* (London, 1970). J. W. Konvitz,
*Cartography in France 1660–1848.
Science, engineering and statecraft*
(Chicago, 1987), pp. 1–5, describes
the fresh start made in European
mapwork at this period.

29. J. Keuning, 'Nicolas Witsen as a cartographer', *Imago Mundi*, xi (1954),
pp. 95–110.

30. *Charta Invitatoria, quaestionibus, quae
Historiam Helvetiae Naturalem
concernunt, praefixa. . . .* For the collaboration of Scheuchzer and
Marsigli, see chapters viii and ix
above.

31. RS Journal Book, viii (1690–6), p. 6.

32. RS Early Letters, A, no. 41; Journal
Book, viii. 74; Council Minutes, ii
(1682–1727), p. 112. Shortly before
leaving Vienna, Hussey asked Kinsky
to help him in finding maps of eastern Europe (from the Iron Gates to
the Adriatic) more accurate than any
of those he had been able to buy.
Kinsky replied that Marsigli would
be able to remedy the defects of
Hussey's maps. T 161 (fz. Kinsky),
ff. 118, 119.

33. RS Early Letters, M. ii. no. 1.

34. Already on 9 August Paget suspected
something was amiss. T 161 (Varia),
f. 192. He gave three accounts of the
affair, to Leopold on 21 August
(T 159 (July–August), ff. 187–8);
to Hussey on 15 October, (Paget
Papers, 4, ff. 3–4); and to (?)

Borgomanero on 2 April 1692 (T 162 (April–May), ff. 1, 2). Marsigli's report of 26 July from Belgrade, intended for Kinsky, had been addressed to Paget. T 159 (July–August), ff. 141–7.

35. SP 97/20. ff. 194, 246; ibid., f. 216 (Trumbull).
36. Ibid., ff. 200–4 ('Relatione della Conferenza'); HMC Downshire MSS, I (i). 316–7; the Hague: AR Staten-Generaal, no. 7086 (Colyer's report, 19 August).
37. A, p. 148; SP 97/20, ff. 205–6; T 159 (July–August), ff. 222–5.
38. SP 97/20, ff. 207–8; T 160 (September–October), ff 19–20, 86.
39. A, p. 150–1; T 160 (July–December), ff. 69–70.
40. T 160 (August–September), f. 5.
41. A. p. 160; T 160 (September–October), f. 16.
42. Copies and drafts of 'Punti dati al Sig. Conte Marsigli per sollievo della sua memoria, altresi informatissimo', T 160 (September–October), ff. 54–60. See also T 161 (November–December), f. 162.
43. T 160 (September–October), ff. 48–9; Marsigli's narrative and map, ff. 60–74.
44. A. p. 155.
45. T 161 (Varia), ff. 78–9, 165–84 (this long epistle – with map and post-script – was evidently written in stages, but completed at Braşov by 10 November); cf. T 161 (Varia), ff. 144–5, from Bucharest on 20 November.
46. Corrispondenza, p. 212 (1 July), but by 4 November Leopold feared that the chance of peace was receding (p. 223); SP/9, nos. 125, 134, 153; BL Additional MS 36,662, ff. 35, 125, 131.
47. HMC Downshire MSS I (i), 376, 382, 394.
48. AR Staten-Generaal, Secrete Brieven, no. 85 (Turkije), 3 October 1691.
49. SP 97/20, ff. 246–7.
50. T 160 (November–December), f. 194.
51. A, pp. 159–60.

52. T 162 (April–May), ff. 53–8; T 162 (June–August), ff. 55–8.
53. T 162 ('Informatio pro Legato Anglico Dmo Harbord ...', 31 May), ff. 166–9.
54. T 162 (June–August), ff. 53–4.
55. MS 110 ff. 37–52.
56. Ibid., ff. 319–26. A shorter list has German, Latin, Turkish and Italian names for fish. An English letter from Istanbul has a wonderfully comical account of Marsigli's tantrums on arrival at Istanbul, after which he spent 'almost the whole time in composing a book entitled 'A Description of the Fish in the Bosphorus'. HMC Downshire MSS I (i), p. 399.
57. MS 110 ff. 5–24.
58. Ibid., ff. 284–318, 326–30, 335.
59. A. pp. 159–60; L. F. Marsili, 'Prefazione al catalogo manoscritto orientale', Scritti inediti, pp. 182–3; F. Babinger, Gesammelte Aufsätze, ii. 170–9.
60. Stato militare, ii. 169. He was scandalised to see so many craftsmen 'di tutte le Nazioni Cristiane' engaged on naval construction at Istanbul.

CHAPTER FIVE

1. KA Bestallungsregister: Marsigli 15 February 1693; A. Wrede, Geschichte der K. und K. Wehrmacht, i (1898), p. 529; KA. HKR. Exp. 391, f. 91 (247 Feb. 1693).
2. Marsigli refers to a 'strepito indicibile' at the news of these appointments. A, pp. 167–9.
3. KA FA 1693–13–3. For Leopold's hesitation, Schulte, op. cit., p. 111.
4. A. Arneth, Starhemberg (Vienna, 1853), p. 149; Redlich, Weltmacht des Barock, p. 458.
5. A, pp. 169–70.
6. Marsigli refers to 'questa fondamentale comunicazione', p. 171.
7. Learning of the Habsburg move on Belgrade, the grand vezir in fact changed his plan and marched westwards. He reached Belgrade on 17

September, a week after the Habsburg withdrawal. Hammer, xii. 343–4.

8. KA FA 1693–8–6.

9. Arneth, *op. cit.*, p. 161 and A, p. 177.

10. Contemporary maps of Petrovaradin are in A, p. 176 and Stelling-Michaud, *Saint-Saphorin*, p. 80, with the location of the Marsigli regiment marked H; Fantuzzi, *Caprara*, p. 7; for Marsigli's work on the fortifications in November 1693, MS 56, f. 14.

11. Hammer, xii. 356 and A, p. 178.

12. MS 29 (iv), ff. 2–16, 60.

13. MS 57, ff. 363–4 gives several sets of figures for these items.

14. OD i. 87 (tab. 45).

15. Ibid. vi. 23–9. These investigations on the river Tisza certainly belong to the years 1695–6. The date of his inquiries at Petrovaradin is less certain, but probable.

16. OD vi. tab. 25. Marsigli was using the colour checks and other tests familiar to those who investigated the qualities of mineral springs during the previous century and a half. Both Paracelsus and Boyle refer to the use of oak galls. A.G. Debus, *Chemistry, Alchemy and the new Philosophy 1550–1700* (London, 1987), n. 8.

17. A, pp. 169, 176, 179.

18. Malpighi, *Correspondence*, no. 995.

19. OD iii, 73.

20. MS 29 (ii), ff. 1–28.

21. Ibid., f. 11.

22. f. 15.

23. ff. 17–25.

24. The name appears variously as Breitenburger, Breitenburcher, Praitenbucher in MS 2013 (i), fz. ID ff. 70, 326; MS 56, ff. 122–3; KA HKR. Reg. Exp. 393 (1694) *passim*.

25. KA HKR. Reg. Exp. 391, ff. 70, 326; Exp. 393, ff. 46, 116, 157, 550, 586.

26. MS 57, ff. 375, 382–3.

27. A, p. 179; MS 56, ff. 84–5.

28. A. Schulte, *Markgraf Ludwig Wilhelm von Baden . . . 1693–1697* (Karlsruhe, 1892), i. 254; P. Haake, 'Die Türkenfeldzüge Augustus des Starken, 1695 und 1696', *Neues Archiv für sächsische Geschichte und Altertumskunde*, 24 (1903), pp. 135–54.

29. MS 56, ff. 73–81, 131–3; KA HKR. Reg. Exp. 395 (June 1695), ff. 262, 263, 265.

30. MS 56, ff. 80, 86–90, 106.

31. Ibid., ff. 172–5, 187, 207–9.

32. A, p. 183; MS 56, ff. 108–24, 177–90.

33. On 29 August Marsigli assured the Elector, Heisler and Caprara that his preparations for carrying the army across the Tisza, and the neighbouring marshes and channels en route for Timisoara, were complete. MS 56, f. 124.

34. Haake, *op. cit.*, p. 138; Hammer, xii. 383; A, pp. 184–5.

35. A, p. 185; KA HKR. Reg. Exp. 395, f. 485 (n. 210, Dec. 1695), an entry which describes Marsigli as being 'arrestirt'; Stelling-Michaud, *op. cit.*, p. 95.

36. Starhemberg and Caprara were respectively president and vice-president of the War Council. For these tortuous bickerings I have used HKR. Reg. Prot. 397, f. 51 (January 1696, no. 269) and HKR. Reg. Exp. 398, f. 242 (8 June, no. 43).

37. Schulte, *op cit.*, i. 526.

38. A, pp. 188–9.

39. MS 79, no. 8. Cassini begins by explaining that he had received from Marsigli's brother in Bologna the letter addressed to him.

40. G.D. Cassini, *Lettera astronomica . . . sopra l'ombra de pianeti medicei in Giove* (Rome, 1665). Cassini's calculations in *Ephemerides bononienses . . .* (Bologna, 1668), corrected by *Les hypothèses et les tables des satellites de Jupiter* (Paris, 1693) enabled those on land to arrive at tolerably accurate estimates of their longitude. At sea it remained much more difficult to make the observations.

41. MS 79, no. 9, the earliest surviving letter of Einmart to Marsigli is dated 25 May 1696. I gratefully recall the help given me by the late Dr George Bialocoz in unravelling the correspondence of Einmart and Muller. St. George Ashe (above, p. 109) had become acquainted with Einmart al-

ready in 1690. Hoppen, *op. cit.*, p. 169.

42. OD i. 33–4.
43. For Muller, J.G. Doppelmayr, *Historische Nachricht von den Nürnbergischen Mathematicis und Künstlern* (Nuremberg, 1730), p. 138; E. Nischer, *Österreichische Kartographen* (Vienna, 1925), pp. 52–8; C. Wissmüller, *Der Geograph L. F. Graf Marsigli* (diss. Nuremberg, 1900), pp. 67–70, 102. In these pages I anglicise Müller as Muller.
44. OD i. 43.
45. *Prodromus*, p. 58.
46. MS 100, the main source for the details given, is somewhat inadequately entitled 'Observationes Astronomicae Hungariae habitae Comite Lodovico Ferdinando Marsili . . . Anno 1696'. The original of Muller's periodic notes are ff. 8–12. For his finely drawn illustrations of the phases of the moon, see MS 9, ff. 3–5. For the general topic, L. Bartha, 'The determination of early longitudes and base meridians in Hungary', *Progress in Astronomy*, 28 (1985), pp. 41–8. I am very grateful to Lajos Bartha for his help.
47. MS 100, ff. 3, 12. In the later stages of his journey Muller relied on only two of his needles to measure magnetic variation in the readings.
48. Doppelmayr, *op cit.*, p. 138.
49. A, p. 188; MS 56, f. 353 (the word used was 'Sterngucker').
50. Ibid., ff. 404–14. A map of the Tisza region on f. 414 looks as if it had been drawn by Marsigli with the date (29 July) added by Muller.
51. A, pp. 190–2; S. Stelling-Michaud, *op. cit.*, 112 f.
52. MS 100, f. 7.
53. Some of the astronomical readings of Marsigli/Muller in Hungary were published in 1700 in Marsigli's *Prodromus* (see below, chs. vi and viii), which quickly reached London, Paris, Rome etc. L. Bartha suggests that they were already taken into account in Halley's World Chart of 1702. Certainly G. Delisle's map of Hungary of 1703 was 'rectifiée par les

observations du Comte Marsilli'. Muller returned to Hungary after 1706 and his large map of the whole country was published in Vienna in 1709. There was little further cartographic progress in the region until Samuel Mikoviny began mapping the counties of northern Hungary after 1725. His methods are described in a remarkable 'Epistola'. A.A. Deák, *A 'Hungaria Nova' megrajzolója Mikoviny Sámuel* (Budapest, 1987).

54. Haake, *op. cit.*, pp. 145–50; Redlich, *op. cit.*, p. 464.
55. A, p. 193; MS 56, ff. 360, 364, 368, 422–4.
56. MS 56, f. 423 confirms A, p. 193.
57. 'Bericht des Kf. Friedrich August v. Sachsen', ed. A. Arneth, *A.ö.G.*, 12 (1854), pp. 223–4, 230–2.
58. Ibid., p. 232; FE ii. 337.
59. Braubach, *Prinz Eugen*, i. 244.
60. FE ii. 346–52; *cf.* pp. 337–9, 358–60.
61. Ibid., ii. 356; *cf.* HKR. Reg. Prot. 401, ff. 216, 227, 233.
62. A, pp. 196–8. Although Marsigli states that he presented a written report on his survey, I could not find it.
63. A, pp. 189–90, 194.
64. Ibid., p. 195; HKR. Reg. Exp. 398, f. 462 and HKR. Reg. Prot. 397, f. 657 (Dec., no. 126).
65. MS 113, nos. 20–6.
66. Ibid., no. 24; in a letter of 26 April to the HKR, Schlick 'deprecates' or declines the request, refers to the *acta* of the case which he is sending back, and asks for the removal of Salzer from Szeged. HKR. Reg. Exp. 399, f. 331 (May, no. 155).
67. A, p. 196; HKR. Reg. Prot. 401, f. 216. It should be noted that Starhemberg did not object to the employment of Marsigli for this reconnaissance. *Cf.* KA FA 1697–5–31.
68. HKR. Reg. Prot. 401, f. 174.
69. A, pp. 198, 200f.; MS 113, nos. 5–9.
70. MS 113, no. 5.
71. HKR. Reg. Exp. 399–400, ff. 407, 442, 483; Reg. Prot. 401, ff. 302, 383.
72. MS 113, no. 6; A, pp. 198–9.
73. Eugene refers to Marsigli's order to

'fare mettere ai Ferri uno de' medesimi' officers. Marsigli's barely legible draft of an appeal to Leopold mentions his suspension of the lieu-tenant-colonel. MS 57, f. 59.

74. FE. ii (Military Corr. pp. 53–4), and ii. 150.

75. HKR. Reg. Prot. ff. 302, 383 (4 Sep. 1697).

76. MS 113 no. 7 (8 Sep.). On 25 Sep. and 2 Oct. Eugene wrote again. Aware of the interim judgment against Marsigli he was now counsel-ling a show of patience, prudence and 'soave difesa'. Ibid., nos. 8, 9.

77. MS 57, f. 59; A, p. 199.

78. HKR. Reg. Exp. 400, f. 700 (November, no. 97).

79. HKR. Reg. Exp. 402, f. 342. The phrase 'auss unvermelten Ursachen', associated with Leopold's interven-tions, occurs from time to time in these registers.

CHAPTER SIX

1. MS 79, n. 9 (21 December 1696, 1 February and 3 May 1697).

2. Acta Eruditorum. Supplementa, i (Leipzig, 1692), pp. 207–12.

3. MS 79, n. 7 (from F.B. Carpzov, November 1697–April 1698). Cf. J. Kirchner, 'Zur Entstehungs – und Redaktionsgeschichte der Acta Eruditorum', Archiv für Buchgewerbe und Gebrauchsgraphik, 65 (1928), pp. 75–88.

4. Acta Eruditorum anno 1697 publicata, pp. 404–9, with folding plate, and ibid., 1698, pp. 148–9; Philosophical Transactions, 20 (1699), p. 306; Marsigli, Dissertazione epistolare del fosforo minerale o sia della pietra illumininabile Bolognese . . . a Lipsia anno 1698. For the earlier version of this piece, addressed to Boyle, see Bruzzo, op. cit. pp. 51–60.

5. OD vi. 87–99.

6. OD i. pt. 2, pp. 47–8; OD vi. tab. 34 and pp. 101–10.

7. BUB MS 152, ff. 178–93: 'Sommario delle principali vendite. . . .'

8. MS 113, n. 16.

9. For letters from Doglioli, Trionfetti and Guglielmini in the first six months of 1697, MS 79, nos. 2, 3 and 6. For Guglielmini, W.H. Graf, Hydraulics of Sediment Transport (Littleton, Colorado, ed. 1984), p. 13.

10. P. Boccone, Museo di piante rare. . . . (Venice, 1697), pp. 146, 167.

11. Museo di fisica e di esperienze variato (Venice, 1697) and Curiose Anmer-kungen über Ein und ander naturliche Ding (Frankfurt and Leipzig, 1697, in addition to the Museo di piante rare.

12. MS 12.

13. MS 29 pt.iv: 'Breve abozzo degli articoli p. comporre un Formulario necessario a metter in ordine l'Opera del Danubio'.

14. Ibid., a draft title page containing the words 'Regius Pannonico Mysicus Danubius . . . Opus in quattuor Tomos . . .'

15. MS 79 n. 3.

16. Biblia Sacra / Biblia ectipa, ed. C. Weigel (Augsburg/Nuremberg, 1695–); Abbildung der gemein-nützlichen Haupt-Stände von denen Regenten . . . biss auf alle Künstler und Handwerker (1698); S. Pufendorf, De Rebus a Carolo Gustavo Sueciae Rege gestis . . . libri septem elegantis-simis tabulis aeneis exornati (Nurem-berg, 1696).

17. MS 79 n. 9.

18. The Danubialis operis Prodromus (Nu-remberg, 1700) gives the list and or-der of contents for the six volumes, on which Marsigli had finally settled by 16 August 1698 when the censor in Vienna passed the work for publi-cation. This date, appearing in the Prodromus after the title page, shows that by then Marsigli had assembled nearly all his material. His thinking earlier has been inferred here from his manuscripts, viz. MSS 29 (fz. iv and v), 6, 45, 57, etc.

19. The first series, starting at the Kahlenburg, are MS 45, nos. 3, 5, 6, 11, 14, 16, 18–9, 22, 24–6, 28; the

second series, with the first map missing, are MS 45, nos. 4, 9, 7, 10, 12, 13, 15, 17, 20–2, 29; n. 2 looks like an earlier version of n. 3. In the second series the maps are apparently being redrawn to fit a smaller page. For a synopsis of Marsigli's Danubian and other maps, M. Longhena, *L'opera cartografica di Luigi Ferdinando Marsili* (Rome, 1933).

20. *Cf.* MSS 48 and 50. In the latter, a third out of some sixty maps are Marsigli's work (mostly 1688–92), a third are Muller's (mostly 1696–1700), while the remainder are by others, or are of doubtful authorship, or are simply scraps.

21. There are many examples of this practice in MS 50: nos. 4, 13, 24, 26–7, 34 et seq.

22. Modern Hungarian usage is the converse of this: 'across the Danube' – Dunántúl – is the region on the right bank.

23. Trans-Danubian maps predominate in MS 48, Cis-Danubian in MS 50, but there is also an important group for the Danube itself (and for the Tisza) in the former.

24. The process can be followed in MS 6, which contains early drawings of antiquities by Marsigli (ff. 4–41); Muller reduced them in size and grouped them together to form separate pages of illustrations, ready for engraving (ff. 42–50).

25. For what follows, *Prodromus*, pp. 27–39.

26. To be fair to Marsigli, there are also blank forms in MS 29 v., ff. 62–6 for similar enquiries planned elsewhere on the Danube, and on the Drava and Sava. At an earlier stage he had allotted this topic together with the other descriptions of the river bed to volume I. See also his, and Muller's, drawings in MS 29 v., ff. 2, 16, 21, 44, etc.

27. *Prodromus*, p. 39. It was a commonly held idea, in the seventeenth century and earlier, that base metals left in the earth were gradually transformed into the more precious metals.

28. MS 104: the inventory of ff. 165–78, 182–8.

29. MS 113, n. 27. This correspondent was Ludwig Albert von Thavonat, 'Oberstkammergraf' at Kremnica. (H. Srbik, *Der staatliche Exporthandel Österreichs . . .* (Vienna, 1907), pp. 121–2. Later Marsigli appears to have helped him over the quartering of soldiers in his territory: Marsigli evidently differed from the 'canaglia e di gente' (Thavonat's phrase) who have 'a natural aversion' to mining. MS 79 n. 10 (14 March 1699).

30. MS 11. The engravings here, by Mathaeus Ethesius, mainly have the date 1688. It is not possible to say when Marsigli acquired them.

31. MS 22 contains originals for nearly all the plates of Volume IV; *Prodromus*, pp. 40–9; *cf.* Malpighi to Marsigli on this topic, MS 79 n. 1.

32. Francis Willughby, *De Historia Piscium libri quatuor* (Oxford, 1686).

33. *Prodromus*, p. 49.

34. MS 20 ff. 1, 25, 34, 86, etc.

35. F. Willughby, *Ornithologiae libri tres* (London, 1676).

36. *Prodromus*, pp. 58–9.

37. MS 79 n. 2, (Trionfetti's letters, February–May 1697).

38. *Autobiografia di Luigi Ferdinando Marsili*, ed. Emilio Lovarini (1930) [= A].

39. Pre-eminently from what is now contained in MSS 51, 52, and 55.

40. A, p. 21.

41. Ibid., pp. 119, 122.

42. Ibid., p. 201.

43. Malpighi, *Correspondence*, n. 561; A, pp. 159–60.

44. MS 111.

45. These, already mentioned in chaps. I and IV, were the core of Marsigli's account of the Ottoman forces in all his accounts of the subject from the 1680s until the 1720s. They were authentic in origin, but in various aspects obsolete by 1700.

46. MS 111, f. 82. Marsigli's exposition of Ottoman decline begins on f. 88.

47. *Scritti inediti*, p. 180.

48. For the *Stato militare dell'Imperio ottomano, incremento e decremento del*

medesimo (the Hague and Amsterdam, 1732) see also below, pp. 302–3. The basis of the work is MS 112, a finely written volume which is not easy to date. Probably begun before 1702 with Muller's assistance (the tabulation on f. 104 is in his hand), it was later revised again. Parts of MS 96, which are very early papers, were also used later.

49. MS 108.
50. Ibid. ff. 8, 35, 57–87, 126–8. *Cf.* MS 15, 'La populazione di Transilvania composte di varie nationi . . .', in *Memorie*, pp. 242–53. Sheremetev passed through Vienna early in 1698 on his way to Rome.
51. MS 28.
52. F. Oldenbourg, *Die Endter* (Munich, 1911), pp. 26, 95, and the end-paper of the *Prodromus*. The types used passed into Marsigli's general collections.

CHAPTER SEVEN

1. Hammer, xii. 424 ff.; *Encyclopaedia of Islam*, iv (1976), *sub* 'Karlovci'; arts. by R. A. Abou-el-Haj in *J. of the American Oriental Society*, 87 (1967) and 89 (1969); H. Inalcik's preface to *Dmitrie Cantemir, Historian of Southeast European and Oriental Civilisations* (Bucharest, 1975); H. Uebersberger, *Russlands Orientpolitik in den letzten zwei Jahrhunderten* (Vienna, 1913), pp. 54–60.
2. Additional MS 8080, f. 89 (Pera, 5 Dec. 1697); SP 97/20 ff. 393, 394 (29 Dec.); Paget Papers, 24 (to Kinsky, 29 Dec.): Paget had written to Kinsky both before and after the battle of Senta, emphasising the change of sentiment at the Porte. The two were sedulous in maintaining their correspondence; in Paget's papers are many copies and drafts of 'my letters to Kinsky'.
3. T 165, ff. 1, 18 (to Kinsky, 22, 23 Jan. 1698); Paget Papers, 5 (to William III, 25 Jan.); an elaborate account of conflicting opinions in the Ottoman

court is given by C. Contarini, *Istoria della guerra di Leopoldo primo . . .* , ii. 661–2. For Mavrocordato as dragoman and minister, N. Camariano, *Alexandre Mavrocordato, le grand Drogoman, son activité diplomatique* (Thessalonika, 1970).

4. SP 103/72 ff. 238–9, 246–7; Additional MS 28,942, ff. 76–7.
5. SP 97/21 ff. 16–20 (9 May).
6. J. H. Hora Siccama, 'De vrede van Carlowitz et was darauf voorafging', *Byd. v. vaderlandsche Geschiedenis en Oudheidkunde*, 4 ser. 8 (1910), pp. 43–115.
7. MS 58, ff. 11–34.
8. Ibid., ff. 157–8 (3 May) contains his suggestions for closing the Danube below Orsova.
9. The Una was discussed in greater detail in his 'informazione' of 30 April (MS 58, ff. 71–3).
10. Ibid., ff. 28–9, 32.
11. Ibid., 78, 80. These were certainly Muller's work; presumably fair copies of the text and drawings were made for Leopold.
12. For Habsburg and Ottoman military preparations, FE. ii. 269 ff. and also Contarini, *Istoria*, ii. 609, 697.
13. Additional MS 8080, f. 93; T 165, ff. 56, 124, 126.
14. Rami Mehmed had been chief of the secretaries of the grand vezir's chancery, and would himself become grand vezir beween January and August 1703, when a palace revolution replaced him by Mustafa Daltaban, leader of the old guard unreconciled to the peace of 1699. Mavrocordato was lucky to escape on this occasion but soon recovered power.
15. R. Wittram, *Peter I. Czar und Kaiser* (Göttingen, 1964) i. 164–5. Partly in consequence, the Poles, who were even more reluctant to accept a discussion of peace terms on the basis of *uti possidetis*, agreed to send their envoy Malachowski to Slankamen.
16. T 166 (fz. 2), f. 51; A, pp. 201–3.
17. Ibid., ff. 71, 159–65, 209–10; MS 58, ff. 116, 140–7.
18. T 166, ff. 45, 73.
19. HHSA. Dispacci di Germania 179,

ff. 282, 334, 408–9.

20. FE. ii. Supp., pp. 102–4; MIÖG 46 (1932), pp. 465–76; TE. xv. 381–4; Redlich, *op. cit.*, p. 444.

21. T 166, ff. 256–71.

22. E. G. Rinck, *Leopolds des Grossen, . . . Leben und Thaten* (Vienna, 1709), pp. 1200–1; *Theatrum Europaeum.* xv. 384.

23. FE. ii. 491–6.

24. The Latin formulas employed were: fundamentum pacis possidatio uti possidetis; possessiones certae; possessiones dubiae.

25. T 166 (fz. 2), 81 et seq.

26. Copies of Paget's letters to Kinsky, 14 Aug. 22 Sep. (OS) 1698, in Paget Papers, 24, ff. 54–70; Hora Siccama, *art. cit.*, p. 146.

27. TE. xv. 387; E. Schmourlo, *Sbornik . . . receuil de documents relatifs au règne de l'Empereur Pierre le Grand* (Dorpat, 1903), i. 539–41.

28. V. O. Ludwig, ed. 'Memoiren eines Vergessenen (1691–1716)', *Jb. des Stiftes Klosterneuburg*, vii (1915), p. 34.

29. Paget to Kinsky, 5/15 Sep., pp. 24, f. 64.

30. 'Martik' in *Theatrum Europaeum.* xv. 386.

31. 'Memoiren, pp. 35–6; Contarini, *Istoria*, ii. 722; Schmourlo, p. 541; Rinck, *Leopold*, pp. 1209–12; A, p. 199; MS 58, 303–9.

32. *Fontes Rerum Austriacarum*, 27 (1867), pp. 352–3.

33. Schmourlo, p. 546; A, p. 204.

34. Three contemporary, or nearly contemporary, illustrations of the arrangements at Carlowitz can be compared: *Österreich und die Osmanen*, pl. 30, the endpaper of *Fontes Rerum Austriacarum*, 1867, and Rinck, p. 1210.

35. T 173 (fz. 2 Varia), ff. 93–4.

36. T 167, f. 44.

37. Ibid., ff. 96–9; MS 58, ff. 306, 309; T 168 (fz. 1), ff. 240–54 and (fz. 2), ff. 104–13.

38. T 167, ff. 256–71 and T 170 (Protocollum).

39. T 168 (fz. 2), ff. 47–50.

40. Ibid., ff. 48–9.

41. T 170, f. 10.

42. Ibid., f. 47.

43. A, p. 204.

44. Paget to secretary of state, 16/26 Jan. 1699 (SP 97/21); T 171, *passim*.

45. Ibid., f. 171 (8 Jan.).

46. Dumont, *Traités*, viii (2), 448–51.

47. Marsigli asserts that the Habsburg negotiators balanced their sacrifice here against the advantage gained at what they considered a more important point, the confluence of the Tisza and Danube. *Relazioni*, pp. 44, 49.

48. Clause xviii.

49. MS 58, f. 335 (28 Nov.).

50. T 171 (fz. 2), ff. 248–50 (31 Jan.).

51. Ibid., f. 215.

52. A, p. 208–9.

53. KA Kanzlei vii/159 ff. 1, 8; KA FA 1699–13–4.

54. Ibid., f. 16; instructions of 20 March to the authorities at Graz similarly tell them to collaborate with Marsigli in Croatia, and to have an 'accurate map' made. *Spomenici hvratski krajine*, ed. R. Lopasić (Zagreb, 1889), p. 149.

55. This, and Marsigli's following reports as a boundary commissioner, may now be consulted *in extenso* in the recent magnificent publication, L. F. Marsili, *Relazioni dei Confini della Croazia e della Transilvania a sua maesta caesarea*, ed. Rafaella Gherardi (Modena, 1986) [= R]. Dr Gherardi's *Potere e costituzione a Vienna fra Sei e Settecento. Il 'buon ordine' di L. F. Marsili* (1980) likewise gives a useful account of him at this period – 1698–1701 – but with greater emphasis than my own on Marsigli's involvement with an Austrian 'Merkantilpartei'.

56. Paget to Schreyer, 23 March, (OS) 1700, Paget Papers, 24, f. 18.

57. Nehem to Paget, 5 April, ibid., f. 77.

58. R. pp. 41 7. 57, 61 ('un puro figmento').

59. See above, note 55. MSS 59, 60, printed by Gherardi, are the copies kept by Marsigli; those received by Leopold (which I have not seen) will be found in the Kaunitz collections

formerly at Austerlitz and now in the State Archives at Brno. *Cf. Archivalien zur neueren Geschichte Österreichs*, i (1913), p. 530. Gherardi (R. i. 34–6) lists other relevant papers in the Marsigli collections at Bologna.

60. MS 60.

61. MS 21: Ichnographia Fortalitiorum Limitaneorum, quae, vigore Pacis Carlovitzensis, plurimam partem sunt destructa aut evacuata; uti quidem Relationes huc spectantes clarius docent (in Muller's hand).

62. These are mostly in MS 49.

63. R. pp. 50–2, 58, 72–4; 'Articuli Preliminares', 23 April 1699, MS 16, fz 1, 'Articuli Preliminares', 23 April 1699.

64. R. pp. 44, 49, 63.

65. MS 49, f. 2.

66. R. pp. 68–9, 74; MS 66, ff. 1–19.

67. This is reproduced in R. p. 219, in which the boundary agreed by the commissioners appears with sufficient distinctness. In the original (MS 49, f. 3) another line drawn directly from Slankamen to Morović is also visible.

68. R. pp. 59, 69–70, 85–6, 102–3.

69. Ibid., pp. 68–9, 74–5; MS 49, f. 3.

70. *Cf.* the maps in A. Beyer, *Die Regulirung des Savaflusses* (Zagreb, 1876).

71. MS 66, ff. 26–30, 41–4, 51–4; R. p. 103.

72. Ibid., pp. 78, 104–5.

73. Ibid., pp. 68, 82, 106. In the three sketches of Jasenovac in MS 21 (ff. 9, 10, 11), the island is shown in two but becomes part of the mainland in the third. The amount of flooding along the Sava in the early summer of 1699 must be borne in mind.

74. R. pp. 81-107.

75. 'Mappa Geographica Liniae Limitaneae . . . reservata tamen clausula Insulae Brodensis . . . Testor Luigi. Ferd. Marsigli', KA Kartensammlung B ix c 830. Working copies of this, in two sections, are MS 49, ff. 4, 5. A label states that count Simonetti took the map to Vienna from Novi, 12 June 1699. *Cf.* R. p. 123 for

Simonetti's return. Smaller maps mentioned in Marsigli's despatch also show landing stages and fortified points on the Habsburg shore of the Sava. *Cf.* MS 21.

76. R. pp. 101–2.

77. Ibid., pp. 95–9, 110.

78. KA Kartensammlung B ix c 829 3, which bears Marsigli's seal and signature; MS 66, f. 69, 85.

79. R. pp. 83, 95; MS 49, f. 6; KA FA 1699–13–7a, 8. In Muller's 'general map of the kingdom of Croatia' (MS 49, n. 21) an area between Novi and Sisak is shown as 'terra deserta olim: nunc a Valachis habitata.

80. R. pp. 83–4; the annotation on Muller's map of the region begins: 'Tractus Unna fl. cujus pars Decisa, pars Controversa adhuc est.

81. R. pp. 109, 134–5; MS 66, ff. 89–109.

82. R. pp. 109–14; MS 66, ff. 89–109; MS 49, f. 7.

83. R. pp. 115–20, 134–7, 140–2; MS 49, ff. 7, 8.

84. R. pp. 142–3.

85. Ibid., pp. 158, 178–82; Contarini, Istoria, pp. 733–4; MS 49, f. 15.

86. It should be noted that instructions of 20 March to the Inner Austrian commissioners required the frontier to be sited beyond the valley referred to by Marsigli, giving Leopold a place named Strumica. This maximum objective was therefore not secured. *Spom. Hvrat. Kraj.* iii. no. 75.

87. R. pp. 143–51, 162–4.

88. Above, pp. 30–1. One cannot be certain how far south Marsigli went on this occasion, but a drawing of Muller's shows the course of the river Rama and its junction with the Neretva. MS 66, f. 161 and *cf.* R. p. 226.

89. R. pp. 151, 159–61; MS 49, ff. 11, 13.

90. Ibid., pp. 152–3, 165, 168, 170–1.

91. Ibid., pp. 167, 200–2.

92. Ibid., pp. 203–5.

93. Ibid., p. 213.

94. Ibid., pp. 169, 218; MS 49 f. 13.

95. OD ii, pl. 18, 38, 39; MS 29, i. f. 29.

96. Ibid., pl. 18–9, 39–42; MS 101 A2; MS 6, ff. 51–3.

97. Ibid., pl. 20.

98. Ibid., pl. 20, 32, 44; MS 66, ff. 248–9; MS 101 A1; MS 103, ff. 196–9; MS 7, f. 43.
99. MS 103, ff. 27–34.
100. MS 79, nos. 5, 19.
101. MS 103 f. 277 et seq.; Marsigli, *Scritti inediti*, p. 185; P. Ritter, *Croatia Rediviva regnante Leopoldo Magno Cesare . . .* (Zagreb, 1700) which is dedicated to Marsigli. For Vitezović and his concept of 'Croatia', *Barocco in Italia e nei Paesi Slavi del Sud* (Fondazione G. Cini, 1983), art N. Klaić. pp. 86–9.
102. *Prodromus*, p. 12; OD ii. 34; M. G. Bigourdan, *Annales célestes de 17me siècle* (Paris, 1901), p. 376.
103. MS 66, f. 260.
104. Marsigli, *Dissertatio de generatione fungorum*, Introduction, v, vi, xliii; cf. G. C. Ainsworth, *Introduction to the history of mycology* (Cambridge, 1976).
105. Fantuzzi, Lettere ix.
106. MS 7, ff. 1–3.
107. Ibid., ff. 4–5, a synopsis reproduced in *Memorie* pp. 293–4. Cf. A. Baldacci, 'I fondamenti botanici nell'opera di. L. F. Marsili', ibid., pp. 277–319, which is discursive but useful.
108. MS 7, ff. 8–15, 35–43, 49.
109. Ibid., ff. 61–8.
110. MS 47, n. 4 (73 cm × 38 cm).
111. MS 79, n. 13.
112. Ibid., nos. 4, 23.
113. R. p. 122.
114. Ibid., pp. 167, 185–200. Cf. Gherardi, *Potere e costituzione*, pp. 358–70.
115. KA Kartensammlung B102; MS 49, n. 16. It will be recalled (p. 189 above) that Marsigli had already ordered Hollstein to study the communications of Lika and Crbava, and prepare a map. Hollstein did so, and took one or more maps with him to Vienna from Novi on 28 October. MS 49, n. 19.
116. The map is entitled 'Mappa Geographica facta in usum Commerciorum a Buda et Baja . . .'. However Marsigli expresses a preference for Baja as a trading centre. R.

p. 188.
117. A word missing from the Italian text in R. p. 199 is 'inglesi': the German version in the Hofkammer refers (f. 654) to 'gewisse ziemlich guetten Engländer Tuchen' which, as Marsigli recalled from his stay in Istanbul in 1691, the Levant Company merchants were distressed to find reaching Turkey via Poland and the Principalities.
118. The argument wobbles between a favourable and an unfavourable view of a Habsburg Levant trade, R. pp. 191–9.
119. Ibid., pp. 196, 200.
120. Ibid., pp. 230, 243, 249–65.
121. Ibid., pp. 251, 253, 264.
122. MS 49, n. 18. Also sent were copies of MS 49, n. 21 and MS 21, nos. 14, 23, and a 'tabula' listing the country's ecclesiastical and political subdivisions (MS 49, n. 20).
123. R. p. 262.
124. R. pp. 258–64, 269–70.
125. For Marsigli, the Vlachs are immigrant 'Bosnians, or Turkish Croats'. He gives no hint of their non-Slav or Illyrian origin, as in more modern accounts.
126. R. pp. 291–7; MS 49, n. 24.
127. Marsigli refers to this again in connection with plans for a postal system in Croatia: a bridge at Zagreb, a flying bridge at Sisak, and many smaller bridges would be needed for the postal routes, which were in fact the same as the numbered routes he used in his essay on trade. R. pp. 329–33.
128. Ibid., pp. 297, 302, 315.
129. Ibid., pp. 278, 305.
130. Ibid., pp. 311, 317–20; MS 49, n. 25.
131. Ibid., p. 383.
132. Ibid., pp. 305–6, 311.
133. Ibid., pp. 321–4.
134. Ibid., pp. 344–7, 365.
135. Ibid., pp. 353f.
136. T 174 (fz. 3), 1–6 (18–20 July).
137. KA Kartensammlung B ix c 829 1; MS 49, f. 30; R. pp. 360, 374, 381.
138. Ibid., pp. 359, 365–7, 375–6; *Spom. Hvrat. Kraj.* iii. 177.
139. R. p. 374; MS 66, ff. 284–93.

140. R. pp. 376–90.
141. Ibid., pp. 361, 379, 386.
142. It appears that substantial reforms in property and tax affairs were carried out in Timisoara in 1703. Hammer, xiii. 97.
143. MS 47, *passim*.
144. R. pp. 395–7. At Arad there was a settlement on the south bank of the Maros, and the Pasha held that the defences in question belonged to it: therefore these should be treated like those of the other places in the territory of Timisoara which Habsburg garrisons were due to leave.
145. Kreutel, *Leben und Abenteuer des Dolmetschers Osman Aga*, p. 7; *Reiseführer durch Rumänien* ed. Ghidul României, (Bucharest, 1932), p. 239.
146. R. pp. 395–410.
147. Ibid., pp. 400, 402–3.
148. Ibid., p. 408.
149. Ibid., pp. 4–6; MS 47, n. 3.
150. In 1699.
151. R. pp. 408–13.
152. One of the Visconti maps is reproduced in R. p. 397. *Cf.* Muller's annotation, MS 49, f. 38 (like Marsigli's report, dated 9 October), and his own drawings, ff. 34–9.
153. In older maps (e.g. the Times Atlas, 1920) the watershed on the route between Caransebeş and Mehadia is sometimes entitled *porta orientalis*.
154. From this 'Protestatio' most of the above has to be deduced. R. pp. 420–1, 410.
155. MS 66, ff. 310–20.
156. R. pp. 420–1.
157. Ibid., pp. 420–1, 428f.
158. More specifically this was 'Oltenia', the region with its principal centre at Kraiova on the river Olt. The Prince of Wallachia's title to it was sometimes contested. The Habsburgs held Oltenia between 1718 and 1739.
159. R. pp. 435, 444–5.
160. Ibid., p. 442.
161. Ibid., pp. 445–8.
162. Ibid., p. 426f.
163. Ibid., p. 444; KA Kartensammlung B ix c 743 and MS 49 f. 20 (a copy dated 23 December at the Bistra camp).
164. R. pp. 429–31.
165. Ibid., pp. 445–9.
166. Ibid., pp. 436–8.
167. Ibid., pp. 450, 460, 478.
168. Ibid., pp. 448, 472, 481.
169. Ibid., pp. 453–5, 464–5.
170. Ibid., pp. 427, 466, 484.
171. Ibid. pp. 467, 475.
172. MS 21, ff. 52–65; R. pp. 466–7, 475–7, 509–11.
173. Ibid., pp. 456, 467–8, 477, 480.
174. OD ii. pl. 56; MS 29 i. f. 47.
175. OD ii. pl. 23, 24 and MS 6, ff. 56–7, 85–6.
176. OD ii. pl. 24, 55–9; MS 29 i. ff. 47–8; MS 6, ff. 58, 79–80, 86. Muller's map (MS 47, f. 4) demonstrates that he reached this part of Transylvania.
177. *Corpus Inscriptionum Latinorum*, iii, pt. 2, nos. 1431–1532 *passim*. It would be agreeable to fill up an account of Marsigli's leisure during this winter with some notice of the 'Lexikon Marsilianum' (MS 116), a glossary of approximately 2400 entries, trilingual in Latin, Magyar and Romanian. On linguistic grounds – there is no other evidence – it is believed to have originated in the north-east corner of the Banat, and to be the work of a Transylvanian Saxon. It testifies to Marsigli's interest in material of this kind: but there can only be a presumption that he acquired it in 1700–1 while in the region. I think that he himself never refers to it. C. Tagliavini, *Il 'Lexikon Marsilianum'* (Bucharest, 1930), pp. 179–85.
178. R. pp. 430, 482f.
179. Ibid., pp. 515–6; MS 16, fz. ii.
180. KA Kartensammlung D ix c 632.
181. *Der Neu-eröffneten Ottomanischen Pforten Fortsetzung oder Continuirter Historischer Bericht . . .* (Augsburg, 1700 and 1701). The dedication, with a fine portrait, is to Georg Ludwig, Elector of Hanover, later King George I. According to the *Oxford English Dictionary* 'Porte', denoting the Ottoman government, was first used in English in 1609.
182. Gherardi, *Potere e costituzione*, pp.

111–27, demonstrates the general similarity of Marsigli's thinking on several topics with those of the reform-minded in Vienna.

CHAPTER EIGHT

1. Starhemberg died on 6 June 1701, Mansfeld was appointed on 28 June, but Starhemberg's activity in office had apparently terminated in January. A, p. 212; Fellner–Kretschmayr, *Die öst. Zentralverwaltung*, i. 288.
2. The search for qualified personnel is noted in KA HKR. Reg. Exp. 408 9, ff. 95, 153, 240, 409; Exp. 411, ff. 352–3, 370, 394–5, 402, 407. In February 1701 Salzer himself requested that the tribunal should assemble as soon as Marsigli returned to Vienna (ibid.), f. 144.
3. For Marsigli's version of these proceedings, A, pp. 213–4, but also KA Bestallungen 3147 (27 September 1701); MS 81, f. 1; HKR. Reg. Prot. 413, f. 458 (no. 177, 22 September).
4. It is also probable that Salzer finally paid a much higher proportion of the legal costs than Marsigli. HKR. Reg. Prot. 413, f. 465.
5. He had been detained there since May 1701. J. A. Schenckel, *Vollständiges Lebensdiarium des . . . Kaysers Leopoldi I* (Vienna, 1702), p. 101.
6. FE iv. 175–9, 198, 206. Salzer returned later to Hungary and Transylvania.
7. MS 115: letters from Kaunitz, 8 January, 16 March 1701.
8. A, p. 215.
9. Ibid., p. 216.
10. BL Additional MS 9721, ff. 19, 34; *Feldzüge*, i. 49–51.
11. Additional MS 9721, ff. 39, 79–83. Writing to Lewis of Baden Mansfeld gives a preview of the policy associated with Habsburg rule in the next two centuries: the 'Rasciens' and 'Valaques' will be settled along the new frontier 'de sorte que ces susdites deux Nations maintiendront leur animosite contre cette derniere [the Magyars] et hayront les hongrois du moins autant que les Alemans sont hays des hongrois'.
12. SP 80/18, f. 12.
13. Ibid., ff. 4–5, 24, 27, 31, 90, 94.
14. Stepney added: 'We have had a hard struggle to bring this matter about, and I look upon it as a *coup de partie*, for now we have a powerful sollicitor who will take care that nothing shall be wanting on the Rhine . . .' Additional MS 28,910, f. 318.
15. *Feldzüge*, i. 59, 65–6.
16. A, pp. 214–5; HKR. Reg. Exp. 411, f. 652; MS 115, letter from Salvignoni, 29 November 1701.
17. HKR. Reg. Exp. 414, ff. 1, 41.
18. Marsigli notes that he did not take the highest offer (8000 fl.) for the lieutenant-colonelcy, but promoted the most senior sergeant major of another regiment. *Cf.* HKR. Reg. Prot. 416, f. 73.
19. HKR. Reg. Exp. 414 ff. 56, 237.
20. Ibid., ff. 293, 324.
21. F. Walter, *Wien*, ii. 337; T. Zacharias, *Johann Emmanuel Fischer von Erlach* (Vienna, 1960), p. 117.
22. A, pp. 216–20; HKR. Reg. Prot. 416, f. 339 (8 June 1701).
23. SP 80/18, ff. 295, 348, 358; Additional MS 28, 911, ff. 126, 165, 188, 233.
24. Spindler, *op. cit.*, ii. 444f.
25. SP 80/18, f. 341. He had already secured this permission for the mounted troops (f. 311). *Cf.* H. Hantsch, *Schönborn* (Augsburg, 1929), p. 375.
26. A, pp. 220–1.
27. MS 79 xiii (Trionfetti); G. G. Bianconi (ed.), *Alcune lettere inedite del generale L. F. Marsigli . . .* (1849): my paraphrase of the lengthy letter.
28. MS 79 vii (Manfredi). Manfredi gained celebrity as a poet, astronomer and hydraulics expert. He was the youthful instigator of the Inquieti in 1691. Their assemblies took place c. 1694–1704 in the house of Giacomo Sandri, a physician with firmly progressive views. Cavazza, *op. cit.*, 57–8. At this stage of his

29. MS 104 ff. 26–7. Giambologna's notable small bronze of Neptune, now in the Bologna Museo Civico Medievale, appears in this list.

30. MSS 79 xii and 80 A *passim*. It will be recalled that Filippo was Marsigli's younger brother; he continued to reside in Bologna after the elder brother's departure to Perugia.

31. For comment on the more ambitious proposals for Marsigli's observatory, F. Barbieri and M. Zuccoli, 'Nove lettere di Geminiano Rondelli al conte L.F.M.', *Nuncius*, vi (1991). Rondelli had previously arranged for the dedication to Marsigli of a volume of Ephemerides due to be published in Bologna in 1701.

32. Fantuzzi, Lettere n. 14.

33. MS 89 A (14 February).

34. *Cf.* MS 104 f. 3 and Manfredi's letters.

35. MS 79 xviii and MS 80 A n. 10. No less than 8 copies of the *Prodromus* reached the Royal Society. RS Journal Book 1702, pp. 290, 295.

36. I have compared the *Prodromus*, OD III and MS 34: this last contains revisions made in 1724–5, but the presence of Muller's handwriting makes it possible to infer with fair confidence what alterations were planned after the *Prodromus* appeared and before Muller left Marsigli. The six manuscript volumes of the OD in Bologna are nos. 31, 33–37.

37. Muller's new drawings, after he had seen the sites and objects for himself, appear to have been the originals for OD II pl. 18–20, 23–5, 42, 44.

38. MS 4 n. 6 and MS 35 f. 53.

39. Manzini's offering to Emperor Leopold was a painting of birds. For this artist and Marsigli, Zanotti, *Storia dell'Accademia Clementina*, ii. 93–4.

40. Muller's double-page entry at the start of MS 36 is reproduced in OD v.

41. Ms 37, ff. 93, 94.

42. MS 80A n. 11 (Doglioli, 18 March).

43. MS 79 n. 9 (12 December 1701).

44. MS 35 f. 53, and MS 37 f. 97.

45. This 'contract' is described in MS 82 B, n. 46 (2 February 1703).

46. These letters are in MS 82 B. Finally, 18 'sectiones' of the Danube emerged. Cf. p. 152 above.

47. MS 82 B, nos. 82, 91.

48. Ibid., 71, 74.

49. Ibid., 93.

50. It is less easy to dismiss Marsigli's account because his figures are so close to those of more official records. FE. iv. 476 states that on 7 September 'a new battery of 42 guns and 21 mortars' enlarged the main breach in the town's defences, while Marsigli refers to 42 guns and 22 mortars in a letter of 26 September. Quincy, *op. cit.* iv. 167.

51. FE. iv. 452, 470 2. Of the engineers Marsigli also refers to Fontana of Lucca.

52. MS 83 B, ff. 79, 83, which are in Marsigli's own hand.

53. FE iv. 493 and Lamberty, *Mémoires militaires*, ii. 428.

54. Ibid., 416.

55. A, p. 227. The Kinzig, flowing generally north-west, enters the Rhine at Kehl, facing Strasbourg; the valley offered one of the better routes through the Black Forest, via Villingen, into Swabia. The Ilz, flowing south-west in its upper course before bending north, gave access to the Kinzigtal from Freiburg.

56. OD vi. 3–6.

57. A draft or copy, written 'al Ilz fiume', MS 83, ff. 48, 53. For Menegatti, A, p. 227.

58. MS 128, n. 1. This is the original, signed by Lewis. It was printed by Marsigli in 1705.

59. For Breisach in the years 1697–1704, G. Haselier, *Geschichte der Stadt Breisach am Rhein* (Breisach, 1971), ii. 1–12, and A. Iber, *Die Feste Breisach in der neueren Kriegsgeschichte am Oberrhein* (Freiburg, 1936), 49f. Although firmly based on the original sources in Vienna the latter work leans heavily in favour of Lewis of Baden on every disputable point.

60. Iber, *op. cit.*, p. 47 and *Feldzüge, Urkunden*, nos. 66, 71.
61. Marsigli's principal account of his time in Breisach is the *Exposé de ce qui est arrivé ... au sujet de la reddition de Brisac (Zug*, 1705). *Cf.* Quincy, *op. cit.*, iv. 175–84 and Iber, p. 49.
62. *Kriegs- und Staatsschriften des Markgrafen Ludwig Wilhelm von Baden ueber den spanischen Erbfolgekrieg*, ed. P. Röder von Diersburg (Karlsruhe, 1850), ii. 142, 210 and FE. v. 289, 351. For a contemporary warning on the unreliability of the 'Tabelle' of regimental strengths in the Habsburg army, FE. v. 666.
63. MS 128, nos. 7, 9. 11, 22.
64. Ibid., n. 17.
65. FE. v. 341; MS 128, nos. 8, 9; ZB Zurich: Z. xviii. 502. 8e, 8f ('Marsigliana').
66. FE. v. 349.
67. Ms 80 B and MS 82 contain the relevant letters from Einmart and Muller.
68. *Le Neptune françois* appeared in Paris in 1693, and a pirated edition at Amsterdam in the same year.
69. MS 82, n. 19.
70. MS 80 b, nos. 53, 62, 67.
71. Ibid., n. 63.
72. HKR. Reg. Exp. 418, f. 597, and Prot. 420, f. 474.
73. MS 2013 (2): 'Briefe nach Nürnberg ... 20 Julii 1703'. Marsigli also complimented Eschenbach on his translation of the essay on the Thracian Bosphorus. According to the *Universal Lexikon*, viii (1737), p. 1862, he likewise translated *De Phosphoro minerali* into German.
74. MS 82, nos. 16, 42, 54.
75. Ibid., nos. 14, 20, 44, 65, 76.
76. FE. v. 107; HKR. Reg. Exp. 414, f. 730.
77. MS 82, nos. 92, 112; MS 80 B, nos. 79, 84, 92.
78. MS 82, n. 83; MS 80 A, n. 22. It is tantalising not to be able to say more about the origins or publication of Talmann's substantial catalogue of Marsigli's collections. He was able to

tell Marsigli that the Emperor had spent several hours studying the printed sheets which were passed on to him.
79. MS 82, nos. 86, 8, 38, 68; Fantuzzi, Lettere, nos. 15, 22.
80. MS 2013 (2), vii. Marsigli to (?) Schoder 20 July, 1703.
81. Quincy, iv. 185.
82. Fantuzzi, Lettere, n. 22.
83. Ibid., n. 23.
84. Marsigli, *Dissertatio* (1714), Introduction, para. ix, and pp. 24–5.
85. ZB Scheuchzer MS H150a: notes of letters from Scheuchzer to Marsigli, 13 April, 18 May 1703; see F. X. Hoeherl, *Johann Jacob Scheuchzer: der Begründer der physischen Geographie des Hochgebirges* (Munich, 1901).
86. Scheuchzer MS 311: 'Lettres des Italiens', ff. 51–5.
87. *Helveticus sive itineris Alpini descriptio physico-medica* (Zurich, 1702).
88. *Specimen Geographiae Physicae* (Zurich, 1701).
89. Scheuchzer MS H294 (Woodward to Scheuchzer); for the Englishman's record as a controversialist, J. Levine, *Dr. Woodward's Shield: history, science and satire in Augustan England* (Berkeley, 1977).
90. MS 311, ff. 61–3.
91. Iber, p. 57; Exposé, p. 6.
92. Ibid., p. 5; Répliques, n. 5; MS 128, n. 59.
93. MS 128, n. 32.
94. Ibid., n. 61. This was the so-called 'Josef' or 'Vermandois' Bastion; there were 7 others, of which the one furthest north, at the other end of the town, was the 'Leopold', or 'Bastion Royal'.
95. Iber, *op. cit.*, p. 56 and Répliques, n. 4. Unlike the order to fight to the last man published earlier to the garrison, Arco had no authority to release the contents of Lewis's letter of 30 June. Nor is it easy to accept his (and Marsigli's) reading of its meaning. Vauban already had wind of an intention to surrender during the night of 5 September, i.e. before Arco's council of officers finally met. G. Michel,

Histoire de Vauban, pp. 345–51.

96. *Kriegs- und Staatsschriften* (note 62 above), i. 23, 202, 210–11, 225.
97. Ibid., ii, 198–200; Documenta D, Répliques, n. 5.
98. Ibid., ii. 218–20; ZB 'Marsigliana', *passim*.
99. ZB MS H311, ff. 65–79.
100. ZB MS H298 ff. 73–6.
101. Muller's original drawings, subsequently engraved for OD vi, are in MS 37. Marsigli names Einmart as the engraver of the illustrations appearing in his *De Generatione Fungorum* (1715). It is also difficult to account for Muller's lists and notes in MS 104 – a collection of inventories, some of which reached Bologna via Nuremberg – unless he (or possibly a later messenger) took them with him from Dogern.
102. ZB MS H311, ff. 73–9; MS H344, ff. 17, 19.
103. This artist was Daniel Meyer, whom Marsigli commissioned to make an illustration for his new appendix on the source of the Danube (ZB MS H311, ff. 98–9).
104. E.g. the letters of 2 and 15 January 1704, addressed to Scheuchzer (MS H311).
105. FE. v. 122, 136–7, 158.
106. Saint-Simon, *Mémoires* (ed. Boislisle), xi. 299–300.
107. On the other hand Lewis of Baden noted that he could not put all the officers involved under arrest: if he did so, the regiments would lose their 'commando'. *Kriegs- und Staatsschriften*, ii. 22–3.
108. 'Arco' in *Allgemeine Deutsche Biographie* and *Neue Deutsche Biographie*; for Marsigli and the duke of Burgundy, Iber, p. 71.
109. ZB 'Marsigliana', Z xviii. 502, 8d.
110. MS 128, nos. 36, 37; MS 83, ff. 54–8, 72–5; MS 126, ff. 53–7 (all dated 15 November 1703).
111. R. Huch, *Die Neutralität der Eidgenossenschaft* (Zurich, 1892), pp. 78–83, 90, 103–4; S. Stelling-Michaud, *Saint-Saphorin et la politique de la Suisse* (Villette-les-Cully, 1935), p. 117.

112. Iber, *op. cit.*, p. 76. Marsigli's 'peroration' and submissions on 29 December, MS 134, no. 3.
113. FE. v. Supplement, p. 170.
114. J. F. Maldoner, *Synopsis Militaris, oder Kurtzer Begriff über die Kayserliche Kriegs-Articul* (Freiburg, 1702), pp. 62–4, 555–7. Maldoner was no stranger to Marsigli: they were joint signatories of a 'sententia' of 14 July 1703 on a convicted soldier. MS 2013 (4).
115. MS 128, nos. 42, 46, 47: 'Exhibitio interrogatorium' etc.
116. Ibid., no. 59 is Marsigli's authenticated copy of this letter, dated 24 January 1704.
117. FE. v. 342.
118. Iber, p. 80.
119. FE. v. 710–12; *Ausführliches End-Urthel des Grafen von Arco und übriger Officieren . . . Alt-Breysach (1704).*
120. HKR. Reg. Prot. 426, f. 90 (n. 33, 2 February 1704).
121. LWB, ii. 13–14; HKR. Reg. Exp. n. 558 (April 1704). I owe this last text to the kindness of Professor J. P. Spielman. In one account Thüngen says that two days after he sent his report to Lewis he received from Vienna the authority to proceed. The other states that the order reached Thüngen on 14 February, and that the officer sent with Thüngen's report to Lewis returned to Bregenz at almost the same time.
122. *Ausführliche Relation der zu Bregenz . . . 18 Febr. A. 1704, an . . . Philipp von Arco . . . Execution.*
123. According to another account Marsigli was 'indutus sola toga nocturnali, vulgo Nacht-oder Schlafrock', *Freiburger Diöcesan-Archiv*, 10 (1876), p. 360.
124. HKR. Reg. Exp. (April 1704), no 558; *Declaration so Ich Ludwig Ferdinand Marsigli hiemit ablegen.*
125. Thüngen's reports: Iber, p. 83; *Memorie*, art. Reggiani, p. 82; HKR. Reg. Exp. 428, f. 419 (April 1704), n. 500.
126. LWB, ii. 14; *Memorie*, p. 90; Wrede, *op. cit.*, i. 409; HKR. Reg. Prot. 426,

f. 351 (7 April, 1704), no. 82.

127. MS 126, ff. 29, 31: a draft dated 21 February 1704.

128. *Declaration* (Milan, 1705). *Cf.* p. 261 above.

129. MS 134, no. 20.

130. ZB MS H311, ff. 109–10.

131. BUB Codex 152, n. 10.

132. BL Additional MS 28, 915, f. 249. Stepney to Ellis, 15 March 1704.

133. A, p. 228.

134. ZB MS H311, ff. 116–8.

135. MS 126, ff. 39–40; *Weensche Gezantschapsberichten*, ii. 295.

136. MS 126, f. 102; *cf. Declaration*, 1705.

137. He refers to this on 16 April. MS H311, ff. 116–8.

138. ZB MS H344, n. 14 (f. 293). Vienna, 26 July.

CHAPTER NINE

1. ZB MS H344, nos. 14, 15 (19 and 27 August 1704).

2. MS 136: 'Primi matrici del manifesto . . .'

3. BUB MS152, n. 10.

4. A, pp. 225, 228.

5. All Marsigli's biographers, starting with Quincy (iii. 103, 106), assume that he returned to Bologna in 1704. I could find no convincing evidence that he did.

6. For Rinaldo, L. A. Muratori, *Scritti Autobiografici*, ed. T. Sorbelli (Vignola, 1950), pp. 113–27, 'Rainuldus Este Dux Mutinae'.

7. *Annali d'Italia*, xi (ed. Naples, 1773), p. 380.

8. Momigliano's biography of Bacchini in DBI gives much information. *Cf.* S. Bertelli, *Erudizione e storia in L. A. Muratori* (Naples, 1960) and A. Andreoli, *Nel mondo di L. A. Muratori* (Bologna, 1972), pp. 176–80.

9. Muratori's own account of the effects of the war on his literary activity, *Scritti autobiografici*, p. 48.

10. *Opere*, ed. Falco and Forti, i. 176f,

202–12. Bacchini's 'Riflessioni', *Benedictina* 6 (1952), p. 96. *Cf.* Muratori, *Epistolario*, n. 675.

11. G. G. Orsi, *Considerazioni sopra un famoso Libro Franzese* (Bologna, 1703); L. A. Muratori, *Della perfetta poesia italiana* (Venice, 1706); for a survey of the Arcadian movement, E. Sala Di Fenice, *L'età di Arcadia* (Palermo, 1978).

12. Manfredi secured a new post at the Collegio Montalto in 1704. For the Inquieti in 1704–5, Cavazza, *op. cit.*, pp. 63–4.

13. A, p. 228; ZB MS H344, 22 December 1704, MS H311, 31 December (ff. 183–4), and MS H313, 11 January 1705.

14. Collections more or less complete of the 'Manifesto': BL ref. 1054–1–25 (Répliques de L. F. Marsigli); Zurich ZB refs. xviii 302 and xviii 502; BUB Marsigli MS 2013 (2).

15. ZB MS H313, 20 January.

16. ZB MS H344, 13 February; A, p. 229.

17. MS 125 contains 'Lettere de personaggi che mi anno risposti su'l mio Manifesto'. The text of Fontenelle's reply on behalf of the Académie des Sciences is printed in *Memorie*, p. 447, although 'Lug' has been misread by Fontenelle or by the editor for 'Zug'.

18. ZB MS H313, 14, 16 and 21 May.

19. *Vermeinte Unschuld / Innocence Imaginaire. . . . Antwortliche Postillen / Répliques de Louis Ferdinand Cte Marsigli . . .* (1705).

20. On this point Quincy's material is again difficult to assess. He quotes Marsigli's retrospective views on the merits of Zurich's government and of its arsenal. He gives the text (iii. 129–40) of a long letter to Trionfetti dated from Zurich on 4 June 1705. But the sequence of Marsigli's letters to Scheuchzer from Zug is continuous at this period (H313, ff. 117–175) and without any reference to a meeting between the two. He could well have written to Trionfetti from Zug.

21. Berne Transcripts [=BT]: Avvisi di Lucerna, 4 April 1705. (See W.

Meyrat, *Die Abschriftensammlung des Bundesarchivs*, 1977, pp. 50, 80, 232, 236.) I am grateful to my sister Enid Stoye for copies of the material in Berne on Marsigli.

22. *Memorie*, pp. 258–262 (art. M. Gortani). In Switzerland he was also much impressed by the amount and variety of the timber. He collected samples in order to compare their resins and knot formations, at the same time wishing that he had given more attention to the subject while in eastern Europe. Quincy, iii. 137.

23. Avisi, 4 April; ZB MS H313, 4 May and MS H311, 16 May.

24. ZB MS H313, 23 June.

25. ZB MS H311, 21 May; MS H344, 10 July.

26. ZB MS H344, 2 July; MS H313, 4 July.

27. ZB MS H313, 19 July, and for other details on Marsigli's stay in Milan, A, p. 231; BT Avvisi, 8 August; *Declaration so Ich Ludwig Ferdinand Marsigli hiemit ablege über die Ungültigkeit dess Eyds so Ich auf die zu Bregenz ergangene Urthel hin gezwungen worden bin zu leisten* (15 August 1705, Milan), printed in Zug.

28. KA HKR. Reg. Exp. 431, f. 1196 refers to a copy of Marsigli's Manifesto, but not specifically to the 'Declaration'.

29. *Mémoires du prince François ii Rákóczi*, ed. B. Köpeczi (Budapest, 1978), pp. 97–8.

30. *Zeitschrift für schweizerische Archäeologie und Kunstgeschichte*, xi (1950) and xiii (1952) contains articles by A. Reinle on the whole topic, including two lengthy letters of Marsigli's (xi. 243–7).

31. ZB MS H313, 1 September.

32. BT Paris (Aff. Et): Beretti to Puysieulx, 11 Sep and 23 Oct; P to B, 20 Sep and 29 Oct.

33. Avvisi, 19 September and 3 October; ZB MS 313, 13 September.

34. BT Paris: Torcy to Puysieulx, 30 October.

35. ZB MS H311, 9, 10, and 18 October, 12 December; MS H344, 6 and 13 October.

36. Reinli, *art. cit.*, *passim*.

37. Beretti to Puysieulx, 29 October. Quincy fills the gap by assuming another journey to Bologna at this point. But the text of a letter to Stancari which he gives (Milan, 15 November) would hardly been written if Marsigli had just been in Bologna. It gives instructions about three boxes – containing birds' eggs, samples of wood, and snails – which will arrive there from Zurich and elsewhere. It says nothing about Marsigli's activities in Milan. Quincy, iii. 148–54.

38. ZB MS H311, 29 November, 5 December.

39. Ibid., 30 January, 1706 (ff. 175–80); Quincy, pp. 190–4 (18 January); BT Paris: Marsigli to Puysieulx 10(?) January.

40. Bruno Neveu kindly informs me that the 'tribunal des maréchaux' claimed competence to adjudicate on the point of honour for 'tous les gentilhommes, même étrangers'. *Cf.* Saint-Simon, *Mémoires*, vi, 367.

41. Marsigli refers to 'Monsieur Sallor', who must be the comte des Alleurs, Louis XIV's envoy to Rákóczi.

42. Quincy, p. 194.

43. *Cf. New Cambridge Modern History*, vi. 780–2.

44. L. Frati, 'L. F. Marsigli in Parigi', *Memorie*, pp. 473–7.

45. BT Paris, Marsigli to Puysieulx, 10 January, on his winter crossing of the Jura.

46. L. Dulieu, 'Le mouvement scientifique montpelliérain au 18e siècle', and 'La contribution montp. aux receuils de l'Académie Royale des Sciences', *Revue d'histoire des sciences*, xi (1958), pp. 227–62; D. Roche, *Le siècle des lumières en province . . . 1680–1789* (Paris, 1978). 1, 30, 34, 137; *Histoire de la Société Royale des Sciences établie à Montpellier, i* (1766), pp. 6–9.

47. Ibid., i. 27.

48. Fantuzzi, p. 215 and Lettere, n. 24.

49. ZB MS H311, ff. 190–6.
50. I am deeply grateful to Dr Anita McConnell for her help with this phase of Marsigli's activity. *Cf.* A. McConnell, 'The flowers of coral some unpublished conflicts from Paris and Montpellier during the early eighteenth century', *Hist. Phil. Life Sci.*, 12 (1990), 51, 66; J. Carpine Lancre and A. McConnell, 'Le comte L. F. Marsigli et la Société Royale de Montpellier' (Montpellier, 1985). For a fine study of the coastal region of Languedoc, C. Lenthéric, *Les villes mortes du golfe de Lion* (Paris, 1876).
51. *Histoire de la Société Royale . . . à Montpellier*, i. 66.
52. Marsigli took with him a letter of recommendation (28 May) saying that he desired to see Cassis 'et equelques pesches qui se font en ce quartier', L. L. A. Thibaux, 'Le fleuve souterrain sous-marin de Port Miou', *Revue municipale*, Marseille, October 1956, p. 25.
53. *Histoire physique de la mer*, App. vii (1).
54. *Histoire de la Soc. Roy . . . à Montpellier*, pp. 65–72, 138, and the *Mémoires* in the same volume, pp. 20–2.
55. *Histoire physique*, App. vii (2).
56. Ibid., p. 170.
57. McConnell, *art. cit.*, p. 57.
58. *Histoire Physique*, author's preface and pp. 1–8; Fontenelle's *éloge* for de Chazelles, *Histoire de l'Académic Royale des Sciences* (Paris, 1712), p. 143f.
59. *Histoire physique*, pp. 1–17, and the maps and tables 1, 3, 4; For an appreciation of Marsigli's work as 'the first scientific account' of the Golfe du Lion, F. de Dainville, *Cartes anciennes du Languedoc xvie–xviiie s.* (Montpellier, 1961), pp. 99–101.
60. Ibid., table 10.
61. *Journal des Sçavans, avec les suppléments* (Amsterdam, 1707–8), 35, pp. 346–59 and 36, pp. 302–10.
62. Thibaut, *art. cit.*, 22–3.
63. *Histoire physique*, tables 7 (i), 9, p. 17.
64. ZB MS H311, 19 June 1708 and

Quincy, ii. 38–48.
65. *Memorie*, p. 103.
66. Quincy, pp. 60–2.
67. Fantuzzi, p. 223.
68. L. Simeoni, 'Il Generale Marsili e la difesa dello stato pontificio nel 1708–9', *Memorie*, pp. 91–144, with a comment in Bertelli, *op. cit.*, p. 110.
69. Torcy, writing to the French envoy in Venice, commented: 'J'espère que s'il peut arriver à temps il n'oubliera rien pour faire connaître l'injustice de la cour de Vienna à son égard'. BL. Additional MS 15, 283, f. 114.
70. *Memorie*, pp. 103–4 and MS 78 f. 127 (15 June, 1708).
71. H. Kramer, *Habsburg und Rom in den Jahren 1708–1709* (Innsbruck, 1936), pp. 47–8.
72. H. Kramer, 'Der Werbungsversuch der Kurie in der Schweiz im Jahre 1708', *Zt. f. schweizerische Geschichte*, 14 (1934), pp. 30–37; F. Pometti, 'Studi sul pontificato di Clemente XI 1700–1721', *Arch. d. Soc. Romana di St. Pat.*, 21 (1898), pp. 400–4.
73. *Memorie*, pp. 141–4.
74. Ibid., p. 109.
75. Lamberty, *Mémoires Militaires*, v. 243–5; *Mémoires et lettres du maréchal de Tessé* (Paris, 1806), ii. 276–86; *Instructions Données*, xix (1912), pp. 68–73, and xvii (1911), pp. 367–417.
76. A. Frizzi, *Memorie per la storia di Ferrara* (ed. 1848), v. 168–70; BL Additional MS 20, 284, ff. 82–6 (Rasponi to Gualtieri), Additional MS 20, 264, ff. 104, 145 (Casoni to Gualtieri).
77. BL 1896. d. 9 (a collection of Pope Clement XI's printed edicts).
78. *Memorie*, pp. 118–20.
79. BL Additional MS 20, 451, ff. 133–5.
80. Ibid., ff. 137, 141.
81. H. Benedikt, *Der Pascha Graf Alexander von Bonneval 1675–1747* (Graz, 1959), p. 19; FE. x. 201f.
82. Kramer, 85ff.
83. BL Additional MS 20, 264, ff. 89–91.
84. Kramer, p. 71; F. M. Ottieri, *Istoria della guerra . . . 1696–1725* (Rome, 1728), v. 120f.
85. FE. x. 219–20.

CHAPTER TEN

Several developments in Italy described in this chapter deserve more attention than they are given, but I did not wish to lose sight completely of Marsigli's earlier involvement in eastern Europe.

1. *Memorie*, p. 139; BVB MS Ghiselli 73, ff. 659–62, 736–42, 977–80; 74, ff. 52–4, 661–2.
2. *Memorie*, p. 423 gives Marsigli's recollection after 1720; the other view is taken from BUB MS 152.
3. Stancari died on 17 March 1709, and testimonies to his activity in 1706 and again in 1708 are in Fantuzzi, *Notizie*, viii. 45 and Fantuzzi, *Lettere* 26. At this period Manfredi, as we have seen, played a lesser role in the palazzo Marsigli.
4. E. Costa, 'La fondazione dell'Istituto delle Scienze ed una riforma dello Studio Bolognese proposta da Luigi Ferdinando Marsili', *Studi e Memorie per la storia dell'Università di Bologna*, v (1920), pp. 47–66.
5. *Memorie*, pp. 406–19: 'Parallelo dello stato moderno della Università di Bologna con l'altre di la de' Monti'.
6. Costa, pp. 56–7.
7. G. P. Zanotti, *Storia dell'Accademia Clementina aggregata all'Instituto delle scienze e dell'arti* (1739), i. 15 ff. For the diplomacy between Senate and Pope at this point, *Burlington Magazine*, 112 (1970), art. D. C. Miller, pp. 373–8.
8. BUB MS Montefani, 57, f. 207 and MS Ghiselli, 76, ff. 126–9.
9. *Memorie*, p. 422, *cf.* BUB MS 152, f. 185.
10. *Memorie*, p. 423.
11. BUB MS Ghiselli, 75, ff. 30, 38.
12. G. G. Bolletti, *Dell'origine e de' progressi dell'Istituto delle Scienze di Bologna* (Bologna, 1769, 1780). G. Zanotti, *Le pitture di Pellegrino Tibaldi e di Niccolo Abbati . . . descritte'* (Venice, 1756) is a singularly beautiful account of the sixteenth-century decorations of this building.
13. A, pp. 233–43.

14. An Englishman writing from Rome in November 1711 says that this artist was given a commission for work in St Peter's through the influence of 'Marsigli the Pope's general who has got no credit in recommending a man who is only fit to paint scenes'. However, Clement XI certainly admired Franceschini. D. C. Miller, 'Franceschini's decorations for the Cappella del Coro . . . Bolognese and Roman classicism', *Burlington Magazine*, 124 (1982), pp. 487–92.
15. MS 319, ff. 86–91 (19 September 1714) expresses Marsigli's hostility to Aldrovandi.
16. [Marsigli], *Atti Legali* (Bologna, 1728: BL 716 k. 9), the document entitled 'Instrumentum Donationis'; *Memorie*, pp. 423–435.
17. *Instrumentum donationis . . . Aloysii Ferdinandi di Marsiliis* (?1712: BL 716. k. 10).
18. 'Relazione dell'Assedio di Vienna fedelmente dall'Idioma turco tradotta', ed. A. Sorbelli; *Scritti inediti*, pp. 129–45. For the authorship of this account of the siege, *Bibliotheca Orientalis*, 30 (1973), art. H. Wurm, p. 493. Marsigli probably acquired his original in Istanbul in 1691. For another MS from Marsigli's Turkish collections, F. Babinger, 'Seyid Nuh and his Turkish sailing handbook', *Imago Mundi*, 12 (1955), pp. 180–2.
19. *Memorie*, pp. 415–6.
20. *Instrumentum Donationis* (1712), p. 104; Fantuzzi, *Lettere*, n. 9.
21. *Memorie*, pp. 479–80.
22. MS 319, f. 137 (30 May 1713). He suggested stamping each plate on the back with a small seal; the negotiations for printing the work on the Danube were said to be 'advancing'.
23. MS 319, ff. 1–3 (n. d.).
24. *Osservazioni naturali intorno al Mare, ed alla grana detta Kermes* (Venice, 1711), in the form of two letters, one addressed to Cristino Martinelli of Venice, the other to Antonio Vallisneri.
25. Ibid., p. 43.
26. Ibid., pp. 22–5, 51.

27. *La schiavitù del Generale Marsigli*, pp. 23–9, 38–43, 172.

28. Ibid., 47 ff. and 'Conventiones inter [Marsigli] . . . et homines archiconfraternitatis Sanctae Mariae de Nive', *Atti legali*, pp. iii–xxiv.

29. A, pp. 237–8; MS 137, ff. 3–50, 64–5.

30. MS 137, f. 72.

31. *Ludovico Ferdinando Marsilii . . . Dissertatio de generatione fungorum ad Joannem Mariam Lancisi . . . cui accidit ejus responsio, una cum dissertation de Plininianae Villae ruderibus*, etc. (Rome, 1714); *Giornale de' Letterati d'Italia*, 21 (Venice, 1715), 260 ff.

32. G. C. Ainsworth, *Introduction to the history of mycology* (Cambridge, 1976), pp. 84–5.

33. 'Lettera intorno al ponte fatto sul Danubio . . .', 27 April 1715, *Giornale de' Letterati*, 22 (1715); MS 101, ff. 116–29.

34. Quincy, iv. 84–9; P. Ducati, 'Le anticaglie di L. F. Marsigli', *Memories*, pp. 334–5; A. Neviana, 'Recupero di uno sperduto documento riguardante una verifica nel 1714 al Museo del Marsili in Bologna', *Acta Pont. Acad. Scientiarum Novi Lyncaei*, 87 (1934–5), p. 150; F. Haskell and N. Penny, *Taste and the Antique* (Yale, 1982), p. 116. In June and July 1714 Marsigli refers to the despatch to Bologna of (1) a collection of casts from classical statuary and architecture in Rome, (2) a collection of engravings showing the best work of past masters of the various schools of painting, and (3) a certain amount of literary material illustrating Bologna's previous artistic splendour, e.g. some Carracci letters. R. Buscaroli, 'Lettere artistiche inedite del Generale Marsili', *Atti e memorie della reale Accademia Clementina*, ii (1937), pp. 48–55. It is more difficult to identify the original works of art which passed through his hands.

35. Quincy, iv. 123. Already in March 1708 he wrote expressing an interest in ancient Egypt. Scheuchzer MS H311.

36. Quincy, ii. 116–7, 123, iv. 84–8. Hébert de Quincy is himself an elusive figure: independent sources describe him as an Hieronomite, a reader of Bologna University between 1731 and 1751, and an honorary member of the Académie des Sciences at Lyon.

37. For field surveys in the Appenines carried out by Vallisneri (from 1704), Marsigli and others, F. Rodolico, *L'esplorazione naturalistica dell' Appennina* (Florence, 1963), pp. 54–6, 104–5, 327–8; and for Scheuchzer's tours in the Alps of the same period, above pp. 237, 260. Marsigli sent Vallisneri sketches of Alpine rock strata which duly feature in one of the professor's lectures. Frank D. Adams, *Birth and development of the Geological Sciences* (ed. New York, 1954), pp. 453–4.

38. Morgagni, *Autobiografia*, p. 109.

39. *Memorie*, 424.

40. G. Zanotti, *Storia dell'Accademia Clementina*, i. 49–58; G. G. Bolletti, *op. cit.*, chapters 6, 7. It was obviously not easy to decide precisely what subjects should be studied in the new foundation, and there are several changes of mind noticeable in the sequence of documents: *Memorie*, p. 426, Costa, *art. cit.* pp. 49–50; L. Simeoni, *Storia della Università di Bologna*, ii (1947), pp. 126–7.

41. *Instrumentum Donationis*, p. 106; the biographical/academic details are taken from Fantuzzi, *Notizie, passim*. For Marsigli and Manfredi, *Memorie*, pp. 442, 452–8.

42. Beccari and his colleagues in the Institute certainly carried further forward research in one of Marsigli's favourite topics: luminescence. *Cf.* E. Harvey Newton, *op. cit.*, pp. 157–8.

43. S. Leydi, 'La Stanza dell' Architettura Militare', *I luoghi del conoscere. I laboratori e i musei dell' Università di Bologna*, 1988, pp. 65–71; *Memorie*, p. 442. Marsigli also wanted – in the 'Stanza' for Physics – wooden models, with water flowing through, to demonstrate the hydrology of the Po and Reno valleys, the

Val di Chiana, etc. Nothing came of
this. Cavazza, *op. cit.*, p. 222.

44. *Cf.* 'Motivi delle Doglianze di L. F.
M', *Memorie*, pp. 447–58.

45. A clue to Monti's activity at the
Institute is the title of his work.
Exoticorum simplicium medicamentorum varii indices ad usum exercitationum quae in Bononiensi Scientiarum et Artium Instituto singulis hebdomadis habentur (1724).

46. His letters from Rome addressed
to his 'co-academicians' of the
Clementina have very much the tone
of a commander trouncing his men
(and the Bolognesi in general) for
slackness. Let them try harder and
do better! Buscaroli, *art. cit.*

47. G. Bruzzo, 'L'opera militare e
scientifica di L. F. Marsili nella
difesa della costa ponteficia
dell'Adriatico', *Memorie*, pp. 159–67.

48. 'Storia naturale de' Gessi e
Solfi . . . nella Romagna', *Scritti inediti*, pp. 188–211; M. Longhena,
'L. F. Marsigli sull'Appenino
Modenese e sul Monte Cimone',
L'Archiginnasio 24 (1929), pp. 75–103; *Memorie*, p. 306; Quincy, iv. 58–80; Bruzzo, *Nuovi studi*, pp. 112–6;
Longhena, *Marsili*, pp. 223–35.

49. A. Sorbelli, 'La Stamperia di L. F.
Marsili', *Memorie*, pp. 479–502.

50. ZB MS H310, ff. 89–94 (9 November
1720). In this letter Marsigli refers to
the imminent 'lunga navigazione' of
the next paragraph.

51. 'Lettera di Prefazione . . .', *Scritti inediti*, pp. 173–85; V. Rosen,
'Remarques sur les manuscrits
orientaux de la Collection Marsigli à
Bologne', *Atti d. R. Accademia dei Lincei*, Ser. iii. 12 (1884), pp. 163–294; *cf.* above, p. 197. Assemani himself had recently (in 1717) returned
from travels in the Near East bringing with him a rich harvest of oriental
MSS.

52. *Scritti inediti*, p. 173; *Atti legali*,
'Donatio' to the Dominicans of Bologna of 20 July 1724, confirming another of 7 May 1721. This agreement
stresses Marsigli's desire to facilitate
printing in oriental languages. In

view of the publishing and typographical developments in Bologna
shortly afterwards, one must regret
that he did not persevere with the
idea of publishing his own works
there. A. Sorbelli, *Storia della stampa in Bologna* (1929), pp. 163–92.

53. For Marsigli's voyages and other
travels in 1721–2 I am deeply indebted to Dr Anita McConnell's article, 'L. F. Marsigli's voyage to London and Holland, 1721–1722', *Notes Rec. R. Soc. Lond.* 41 (1986), pp. 39–76, and also for her copies of MSS in
Bologna dealing with this period.
The article contains an English
translation of Marsigli's account, in
this case a Latin text compiled from
his own earlier notes.

54. *Memorie*, p. 446.

55. In November 1721 Marsigli outlined
to Sherard his earlier plans for the
journey. R. S. Sherard letters, n. 681.
Cf. MS 57, f. 39.

56. McConnell, *art. cit.*, p. 47.

57. Ibid., p. 51.

58. R. S. Journal Book 1720–1726, p. 175.

59. Quincy, ii. 168–74.

60. Zanotti, *Storia dell'Accademia Clementina*, p. 128.

61. R. S. Journal Book 1720–1726, pp.
218–9.

62. MS 90 A 17, f. 16 (communicated by
Dr McConnell).

63. Ibid., ff. 5–15.

64. Ibid., ff. 12, 13 and MS 87 F, f. 33.

65. Scheuchzer MS H293 (6 March
1721–2).

66. MS 87 F, ff. 33–5; he had also asked
for Sherard's help in compiling such
a list (R. S. Sherard letters, n. 653).

67. McConnell, *art. cit.*, 51, 58.

68. R. S. Sherard letters, n. 654: Marsigli
relates a year later how he now feels
tired in Holland but has learnt a
great deal.

69. G. A. Lindeboom, *Herman Boerhaave* (London, 1968); Boerhaave,
Correspondence (ed. Lindeboom),
n. 49.

70. R. S. Sherard Letters, n. 757.

71. Ibid., n. 709; MS 37 F, f. 38.

72. Ibid. and McConnell, *art. cit.* pp.
46–7.

73. Boerhaave, *Correspondence*, n. 77.

74. A. McConnell, 'A profitable visit: L. F. Marsili . . . in Holland, 1722–23,' *Italian scientists in the Low Countries* . . . ed. Maffioli and Palm (1989), p. 197.

75. Sherard Letters, n. 654.

76. MSS 90 A 17, and 87 F ff. 33–5.

77. Amsterdam: Gemeentearchief, notarieelarchief, n. 5830, 16 March 1723: there are 3 notarial documents under this date. One of the partners, François Changuyon, was born in Halle of Huguenot parents. Two of the others, Herman Uytwerff of Amsterdam and R. A. Albers of the Hague were half-brothers. Peter Gosse of the Hague was a Catholic. (For many further details, I. H. van Eeghen, *De Amsterdamse Boekhandel* (Amsterdam, 1960–7.) Already in June 1723 the same publishers and a colleague in Rotterdam joined forces again to invite subscriptions for printing another massive work, Bruzen de la Martiniere's *Le grand dictionnaire géographique et critique*. The first volume appeared in 1726. The author expressed gratitude in his preface to Marsigli, 'who was then in these provinces', for help in securing information on Italian towns. Under 'Bologna' in the second volume the account of the Institute of Arts and Sciences is extraordinarily full and glowing.

78. Clause 15: but the wording of the clause is sufficiently vague to allow the Company a right to reprint.

79. H. P. Limiers, *Histoire de l'Académie appelée Institut des Sciences et des Arts établi à Boulogne en 1712* (*Amsterdam*, 1723). There followed in 1724 his *Annales de la monarchie françoise*, and a translation of P. de Stosch, *Gemmae antiquae caelate*. . . .

80. Archiginnasio, Bologna: MS B161 f. 85 (24 August 1723); Boerhaave, *Correspondence*, n. 62.

81. MS B161 f. 102 (19 February, 1724).

82. *Conditions de la Souscription*: BL B 670 (12) and 572 c. 40. A coincidence is worth notice here. In 1723, in Nuremberg another *Prodromus* by another author had appeared: M. Bel, *Hungariae antiquae et novae Prodromus* . . . Mathias Bel of Bratislava – lingua Slavus, natione Hungaricus, eruditione Germanus, as he described himself – undertook to compose a major work on ancient and modern Hungary. It was to be historical and geographical, with attention paid to the Scythians rather than to Romans, but giving placenames, latitudes, longitudes, boundaries, and describing rivers, springs, baths, mines, vineyards, plants and fish. Bel promised a full treatment county by county, which Marsigli had never visualised, but his prospectus certainly owed a good deal to the model first offered in 1700. The younger author, with a more comprehensive knowledge of part of the Danubian scene, was resuming the task which Marsigli had begun. In 1723–4, however, Marsigli's work was close to publication, a decade before Bel's *Notitia Hungariae Novae historico-geographica* (Vienna, 4 vols, 1735–42). Bel had his Muller in Samuel Mikoviny, whose maps figure prominently in the *Notitia*.

83. Van Eeghen, *op. cit.*, iii. 66. While Marsigli was in Holland a much more celebrated author arrived there to arrange a publication by subscription: Voltaire, with his *Henriade*. This fell through. J. Pommeau, *D'Arouet à Voltaire* (Oxford, 1985), p. 155.

84. Marsigli refers to the library of a certain cardinal 'del Basco' (*Memorie*, p. 464). For del Basco, read del Bosco; for 'del Bosco' read Dubois: the late Robert Shackleton, Bodley's Librarian, happily solved this conundrum for me. For Bignon's collections, van Eeghen, *op. cit.*, i. 63–4.

85. I cannot say whether the Company acquired the items it wanted for Marsigli before or during the auction. In one BL copy of the sale catalogue (*Bibliotheca Duboisiana*: 124 b. 9–12) nearly all the prices are recorded. Nor have I explored whether

the Dubois volumes (or contemporary lists of these) are now in Bologna.
86. Boerhaave, *Correspondence*, n. 58.
87. Quincy, ii. 187, who is followed by Fantuzzi.
88. Archiginnasio, MS B161, f. 85; Newton, *Correspondence*, n. 1424 (11 March 1724).
89. OD i, Preface.
90. For Rossi, *Storia dell'Accademia Clementina*, i. 89 and ii. 302–6.
91. However, in Muller's original (MS 31) for the 'Mappa generalis' of the Danube, a compass rose contains the words: 'Declin. Magnet. xi½ in occidentem Viennae Austriae AD MDCXCVI Mense Octobri'. In the published work this becomes simply 'Declin. Magnet. xi cum dimidio in occidentem'. Did Marsigli ask for, or overlook, this omission?
92. OD ii, tab. 27.
93. OD vi. tab. 18, 19.
94. For an account of the Italian and Latin versions of the 'letter to Boerhaave', as also for an English translation, see A. McConnell, 'L. F. Marsigli's voyage to London and Holland, 1721–1722' (*Notes Rec. R, Soc. Lond.* 41 (1986), pp. 39–76). Marsigli states that he finished this letter and sent it to Holland, before starting research on Lake Garda (*Scritti inediti*, p. 11) which makes it all the more difficult to explain why the letter was not printed with (or after) the *Histoire Physique*. The delay until 1732 in publishing the work on the Turks, also asserted to be 'terminato' by 1725, is equally mysterious at present.
95. MS B161, ff. 87, 92, 102; *cf.* A. Sambuca, *Memorie* (1750), n. 80.
96. 'Il Lago di Garda', *Scritti inediti*, pp. 11–123. A useful version of the greater part of this essay can be found in *Scienzati del Settecento* (La letteratura italiana, vol. 45, 1983), pp. 337–415. He also surveyed the hills east of the lake: the fossils he found in a cave on Mt Baldo greatly excited him. Vallisneri, *Opera fisico-mediche* (Venice, 1733), ii. 359–63.
97. R. S. Early Letters M. ii. 2; Archiginnasio: MS B161, f. 108.
98. Ibid., f. 102. He naturally never refers to another minor but interesting point. According to Quincy, a French secretary in Provence was responsible for correcting Marsigli's French while writing the *History of the Sea*, and Quincy himself polished the dedication to the Académie des Sciences. The Latinity of the *Opus Danubiale* was due mainly to Muller and then to Girolamo Melani of Siena, another secretary, who also refined the Latin version of the letter to Boerhaave. Quincy, ii. 257, 267. On the other hand, from the first drafts to the finished version Marsigli's work on the Turks was written in Italian. The publishers added the parallel French translation.
99. Ibid., ii. 189; MS B161, f. 84.
100. Newton, *Correspondence*, n. 1440 and n. 1424 (11 March 1724).
101. Quincy, ii. 220–2; *Memorie*, art. Bortolotti, pp. 435–71, and the reference to Bianconi on p. 450. One may doubt whether the latter would have been an apt choice as a librarian: see L. Frati, *Giambattista Bianconi* (Bologna, 1858).
102. *Memorie*, pp. 447–8; but *cf.* McConnell, 'A profitable visit', pp. 201–2.
103. *Cf.* F. M. Zanotti, *De Bononiense Scientiarum et Artium Instituto ... Commentarii*, vol i (1734). Contrary to Marsigli's strictures, this volume gives a favourable account of the Institute's progress in the 1720s.
104. Interesting details on Manfredi's part in the actual construction of the new observatory appear in Quincy, iii. 110–12 and C. Malagola, *Lettere inedite di uomini illustri bolognesi* (Bologna, 1878), pp. 144–9.
105. This is the view expressed by P. Casini, 'Les débuts du Newtonianisme en Italie, 1700–1740, *Dix-huitième Siècle*, 10 (1978), p. 95.
106. *Memorie*, p. 464.
107. The documents summarised are taken from Marsigli's collection, *Atti legali per la fondazione dell'Instituto*

delle Scienze, ed Arti liberali per memoria degli ordini ecclesiastici e secolari chi compongono la città di Bologna . . . Nihil   Mihi . . . nella stamperia   di   San   Tommaso d'Aquino . . . 1728. A fuller, presumably official, version of the 'second Donation' had already appeared in 1727.

108. *Memorie,* pp. 467–8.

109. Both cardinal Albani and Marsigli were collectors on the grand scale, and it is likely that there was an exchange of valuables between them. The latter's gift to the Dominicans satisfied a wish of long standing (n. 52 above).

110. *Atti legali:* the valediction introduces the sequence of documents illustrating Marsigli's bequests to the city, the Dominicans, etc. The assertion that his original wish was to found a military academy in Bologna had not (I think) been made before 1726.

111. Quincy, ii. 244.

112. Aquino in the kingdom of Naples was close to the birthplace of St Thomas Aquinas; the emblem of the sun and the motto 'nihil mihi' were associated by Marsigli with St Thomas and the Dominicans. *Cf. Atti legali* (12 July, 1724), clause 7.

113. Ibid., ii. 261–2.

114. M. Talmann's catalogue of Marsigli's oriental manuscripts. (pp. 235–6 above) already refers to this item in 1702 (*Elenchus librorum,* pt. vi. 29). The Janissaries' insignia are reproduced in the *Stato militare,* pl. xx–xxii.

Index

Authors
whose works appear in the Notes

Main Index